AN INTRODUCTION TO
INFORMATION
SYSTEMS

DAVID WHITELEY

palgrave
macmillan

First published 2013 by
PALGRAVE MACMILLAN

Palgrave Macmillan in the UK is an imprint of Macmillan Publishers Limited, registered in England, company number 785998, of Houndmills, Basingstoke, Hampshire RG21 6XS.

Palgrave Macmillan in the US is a division of St Martin's Press LLC, 175 Fifth Avenue, New York, NY 10010.

Palgrave Macmillan is the global academic imprint of the above companies and has companies and representatives throughout the world.

Palgrave® and Macmillan® are registered trademarks in the United States, the United Kingdom, Europe and other countries

ISBN: 978-0-230-37050-0

This book is printed on paper suitable for recycling and made from fully managed and sustained forest sources. Logging, pulping and manufacturing processes are expected to conform to the environmental regulations of the country of origin.

A catalogue record for this book is available from the British Library.

A catalog record for this book is available from the Library of Congress.

10 9   8   7   6   5   4   3   2   1
22 21 20 19 18 17 16 15 14 13

Brief Contents

Detailed Contents

LIST OF FIGURES

LIST OF CASE STUDIES

AUTHOR'S ACKNOWLEDGEMENTS

Firstly my thanks to the project team at Palgrave Macmillan. The book was initiated from Palgrave by Ursula Gavin. Assisting Ursula have been Joanna McGarry, Leo Goretti and Nikini Jayatunga – my thanks to them all and particularly Leo, who did a lot of detailed work on the text and organized the accompanying videos. I hope I was not too big a headache to any of them. My gratitude also goes to Peter Linecar, South Bank University, who commented on an earlier version of the manuscript; and to the reviewers, who contributed comments on the text and provided excellent feedback:

- Alistair Beere, Liverpool John Moores University, UK
- Yogesh Dwivedi, Swansea University, UK
- Matt Glowatz, University College Dublin, Ireland
- Pericles Loucopoulos, Loughborough University, UK
- Carl Marnewick, University of Johannesburg, South Africa
- Phil Molyneux, Kingston University, UK
- Mike O'Dea, York St John University, UK
- Jan Recker, Queensland University of Technology, Brisbane, Australia
- Marie Louise van der Klooster, Deakin University, Australia

Other colleagues who have helped, reviewed and encouraged are Keith Miller, Darren Dancy, Stephen Gordon, Pamela Quick, Janet Rothwell, Martin Stanton and Nick Whittaker – my thanks to them as well. As all authors say (and it is true), the design errors and the bugs that have got through the testing stages are the responsibility of the author, not the reviewers.

Finally a mention for my family. My partner Lena Dominelli and our son Nic. Lena is an inspirational academic, a prolific author and an example to me. Nic has wisely left home to study Chemistry in Scotland.

Dave Whiteley

PUBLISHER'S ACKNOWLEDGEMENTS

The author and publishers are grateful to Matt Ballantine (Microsoft), Jos Creese (Hampshire County Council), Stephen Devlin (Macmillan), Richard Hall (CloudOrigin) and Richard Piercy (EMI), who kindly agreed to feature in the Managing Information Systems in the 21st Century video interviews included in this book.

The author and publishers are grateful to the following for permission to reproduce figures, tables and extracts of text:

● Dell Inc, for permission to reproduce Figure 13.1, 'Computer Equipment Lifecycle'. © 2012 Dell Inc. All Rights Reserved.

For permission to use photographs, the publishers would like to thank:

● a_korn, Brand X Pictures, Corbis, Design Pics, Eisenhans, Eimantas Buzas, Elenathewise, Fotolia, Getty, Grafvision, graja, Image 100, Image Source, jamdesign, JohanSwanepoel, PeterFactors, Photoalto, PhotoDisc, Photo_Ma, Punchstock, Sashkin, Stockbyte, Superstock, Tom Kelley Archive.

PREFACE

It has almost become a cliché, nowadays, to say that Information Technology (IT) and Information Systems (IS) are all-pervasive throughout society – but it is actually true. In fact, virtually all businesses use IT and IS in their administration systems and IT is an integral part of the production equipment on the factory floor. Many people have computer equipment at home, carry personal IT equipment when they go out (for example, a smartphone) and IT is built into many consumer durables. The interface between the public and organizations is also mediated by the use of IT: indirectly through call centres, or directly by networked systems. Additionally, IT is an essential component of many of the services we use – for example, the electronic tills in shops, the information displays at the railway station and the electronics built into the aeroplanes we fly in.

IT, and the IS it supports, do not exist in isolation but are linked using Communications Technologies – together we refer to this as Information and Communications Technologies (ICTs). These technologies allow business organizations to work together more effectively: the use of networked IT integrates the business systems of organizations with those of their supplier and customer organizations. The use of the Internet is part of this and it also allows more and more people, with their home computers and their smart phones, to communicate with one another and with organizations across the globe. Facebook is, in effect, one of the busiest social spaces of the early 21st century – it is founded on an impressive IS and IT infrastructure (see the *Facebook case study* on page xxi).

For people everywhere, the ability to access and use IT is a part of their job and their everyday life. The need to use IT systems should be accompanied by an understanding of the technologies involved and the uses to which they are put. Governments throughout the world have recognized these imperatives and have promoted IT awareness in schools, in further and higher education and through adult, lifelong learning schemes.

This book examines IS and IT from a business perspective. Staff, at all levels in organizations, need to understand IT and the IS it supports. The efficient use of IS is essential to the everyday operations of an organization. The innovative application of IS and IT can be key to the achievement of competitive advantage.

The subject area of Information Systems, for business and computing students, includes a study and understanding of:

- Business/organizations – their aims, management, structures and methods of working
- Information Systems and their use within organizations

- The Information Technology used in Information Systems
- The process and techniques of analysing and designing an Information System
- The professional, legal, social and ethical issues involved in the application of Information Systems and Information Technology.

Contents

The book starts, in *Part 1,* by explaining the fundamental importance of IS to businesses and organizations. There is a danger that our notion of IS and IT is limited by our experience of the ubiquitous PC. Corporate IS is much more than that – this is illustrated, in *Chapter 1,* by an extensive case study of the use of IS in the supermarket business.

The use of IS in supermarkets affects all areas of the business: the everyday operation of the shop floor, support functions and management; and it also extends outside the organization down the supply chain and out to the customers who use the e-Shop. In *Chapter 2,* we look at the use of IS in terms of business models and we develop the IS Business Model that we will use throughout this book.

The final chapter in Part 1 examines IS management. For many organizations IS and IT are the responsibility of the IS department – we examine the roles and responsibilities of that department in *Chapter 3.* Alternatives to (or variants of) the central IS department are to decentralize, outsource or offshore IS and IT functions – these business aspects of IS management are also examined.

In *Part 2* we examine some commonly used Information Systems. Corporate Systems exampled in **Chapter 4** are payroll and order processing. e-Business systems are discussed in **Chapter 5** – this includes the examination of the three e-Commerce technologies: electronic data interchange (EDI), e-Shop and e-Markets. These examples of IS are used to emphasize how complex corporate IS is and to examine issues such as usability, security and competitive advantage. As established in the IS Business Model, these systems impact all levels of the organization and its exchanges with customers and partner organizations.

Information Systems process business transactions using Information Technology – the nature and application of IT is the topic of *Part 3.* Computers and IT are the topic of *Chapter 6.*

The Information Systems, which run on the IT, take input data, compute and then output information. In *Chapter 7* we examine the design of the data capture and the requirements for information output (as business transactions and management information). The processing part of the IS involves the use and updating of stored data – *Chapter 8* looks at files and databases with an emphasis on the design of the underlying data structures.

Networking is a vital part of IS provision – it enables the systems to be used from the desktop and/or a remote location. It also provides interfaces between systems, organizations and the general public. Networks are the topic of *Chapter 9.*

The IS provision of an organization is vulnerable. As the IS has become both more dispersed and increasingly vital to the effective functioning of the organization, the topics of privacy and security and resilience have become ever more pressing. Computer security is also examined in Chapter 9.

Central to the IS function is the analysis and design of Information Systems; this is the topic of *Part 4.* There are a number of tasks involved in creating an IS – these can be organized and understood using a system development lifecycle (SDLC). The SDLC is one element of an IS development methodology. These issues are examined in *Chapter 10.*

The design of an Information System is heavily reliant on graphical techniques. In *Chapter 11* we will study use case, data flow, entity relation, sequence and class diagrams. This gives students a good toolbox of IS diagrams (and hopefully it creates a literacy in diagramming techniques which should be useful across all areas of business studies).

Finally we take a brief look at the remaining stages in the SDLC. In *Chapter 12* we sketch an overview of what happens in the programming, testing, implementation and maintenance.

In *Part 5,* the last section of the book, we examine the role of IS in society. Computing only dates back to the Second World War and the internet opened for commercial use in the mid 1990s. The extensive application of IT has created challenges in areas such as privacy, computer misuse and the environment; these are examined in *Chapter 13.* The all pervasive application of IS and IT, including mobile technology, has brought about radical social and business changes, that are summed up in the expression the Information Society – the object of *Chapter 14.* This chapter also discusses careers in IS possibly this can help you when planning your future career.

Supporting teaching and learning resources

This book includes a range of pedagogical features that are intended as a means to support students and lecturers.

At the start of each chapter: Each chapter opens with a short summary outlining the chapter contents. These summaries are also accompanied by a *Learning outcomes* section, setting out the key learning goals for students, and by a list of the *Key terms* introduced in the chapter.

Throughout the book: Extensive use is made of *Case studies* to illustrate the business, IS and IT topics being discussed. The *Facebook case study* on p. xxi introduces a number of topics that are analysed in the book. The extended *Supermarket case study* in Chapter 1 outlines the way in which IS function in an organization and is referenced throughout the book. The chapter on the system analysis and design toolbox includes further case studies to illustrate the techniques being taught and for use in exercises and assignments.

A number of *Themes* are highlighted that are particularly relevant to the business use of IS. These themes are: usability, security, outsourcing and competitive advantage. A further theme is the IS Business Model developed in Chapter 2 – this serves to remind us that the benefits of IS must be applied to all areas of the organization as well as in its business interchanges with other organizations and members of the public.

Moreover, a few specific topics that might be of interest but are not essential to the understanding of the subject are examined in separate *Explanation boxes*.

Finally, some chapters include *Managing Information Systems in the 21st Century* boxes, linking to video interviews with IS practitioners especially recorded for this book (see p. xxii).

At the end of each chapter: Each chapter includes a *Further reading* section, which can be a starting point for further research. A *Comprehension test* will help students check to what extent they have absorbed the chapter contents. A number of *Exercises* are also designed to aid the understanding of the material presented in each chapter. These exercises can be used for self-study, while selected discussion questions can be used for tutorial discussion.

At the end of the book: A comprehensive *Glossary* defines all the key and technical terms in the book, and an *Index* helps students and lecturers looking for specific topics.

Online resources

A number of additional online resources are available to lecturers and students using this book. Students have free access to:

● The **Managing Information Systems in the 21st Century** videos
● Extra **MCQs** for self-test
● An **Additional topics** section including updates from the author
● **Online glossary.**

Lecturers have access to a password-protected section of the website, including:

● A comprehensive **Test-bank** of questions for use in exams, tests and quizzes
● **PowerPoint lecture slides** for each chapter, which lecturers can edit for their own use
● An **Instructor manual** providing guideline answers to the exercise questions in the book.

These resources can be found at: **www.palgrave.com/business/whiteley/.**

 ONLINE RESOURCES AVAILABLE

Case Study Facebook

The social networking site, Facebook, was launched in 2004 and by 2012 had in excess of 900 million users.

For the user, Facebook is a website. Users put up a personal profile and link with other users as friends. It is common practice to have a personal photo gallery and many users will update theirs on a regular basis. Users can check out what their friends are doing and exchange messages (with other individual users or selected lists of friends). Special interest groups can also be set up; sometimes they are used for campaigning purposes. Facebook is accessed from a PC or a smartphone (and there is, of course, a Facebook app). Social networking sites are a significant component of the Information Society, see *Chapter 14.*

For Facebook the content is provided by the users, not by the site owners who simply supply the platform. It is an example of the participatory web – see *Chapter 5* for a discussion of Web 2.0.

An issue for Facebook users is privacy (although not all Facebook users are necessarily that bothered). The personal profile users set up on Facebook is shared with friends. Users can use privacy settings to govern what is shared with whom, but this can be complicated and Facebook seems to keep changing the policy. For Facebook the information set up by users has commercial value: it can be analysed, sold to third parties and it is used to target advertising. Information can also end up being shared with governmental authorities – the US authorities are users of Facebook data – see *Chapter 14* for a discussion of civil liberties in the Information Society.

The Information System and Information Technology behind Facebook are impressive, although the company is not keen to publish much detail. The development team consists of several hundred engineers (developers) using a very agile approach – see *Chapter 10.* Apparently an engineer will volunteer to take responsibility for a project and see it through from start to implementation, in a short space of time. There is a high performance culture and engineers who don't deliver will be eased-out. On the IT side, the system uses a massive number of servers, reportedly 60,000 in 2011. Facebook has two massive server farms in the US with a new one planned for Luleå, Sweden, to take advantage of the cool temperature and renewable energy – see *Chapter 13* for a discussion of green computing.

The idea of Facebook was dreamed up by Mark Zuckerberg with some of his fellow students at Harvard in 2003. The initial incarnation was limited to Harvard students, and was called Facemash – Zuckerberg then went on to develop the early version of Facebook in 2004. Some of Zuckerberg's collaborators on Facemash believed their ideas had been ripped off and the issue has been the subject of legal proceedings – see *Chapter 13* for a discussion of intellectual property rights.

Facebook is now a massive undertaking but the problem (for Facebook Inc.) is how to make money out of the traffic. The general idea is that advertisers on Facebook should be able to target relevant demographics (using the information users have put online) but this does not seem to be working. Click-through rates are, for example, a fraction of those achieved by Google adverts. In 2012 General Motors pulled out from paid adverts on Facebook. One of Facebook's problems is that it does not make any money out of mobile users, and many of its users are moving to their smartphones for access.

Over the years, Facebook has had a number of private investors. In 2012 Facebook sold a proportion of its shares as an initial public offering; the price for the shares that were sold implied an overall company valuation of $104 billion (although the share price fell back after the sale was completed).

Sources include: Filloux (2012), Gersmann (2011), Rushe (2012) and yeeguy (2011).

MANAGING INFORMATION SYSTEMS IN THE 21ST CENTURY VIDEOS

In exploring the subject of Information Systems, it is important to bear in mind that IT and IS are not just about technologies and systems, but also the people who design and implement them. This is why this book includes video interviews with IS/IT professionals who talk about their experience of *Managing Information Systems in the 21st Century*. The interviewees are managers and practitioners working for private companies: EMI, Macmillan and Microsoft, in a public sector organization: Hampshire County Council and a manager who runs his own business: CloudOrigin. Each interview opens with a discussion of the educational and professional background of the interviewee, followed by a few questions on some of the key topics of this book and some advice to students who wish to pursue a career in IS.

The video interviews are fully integrated with the chapter contents. Each interview is presented with a box in the relevant chapter of the book, including a few discussion questions for students. There are five of these interviews in the book:

Chapter 2: Interview with Stephen Devlin, Chief Technology Officer for Macmillan Publishers, who talks about the new challenges that the rise of digital contents (for example, e-Books) poses to publishing companies.

Chapter 5: Interview with Richard Piercy, Executive Vice President, Transformation & Digital Supply Chain at EMI Music, who talks about the challenges and opportunities that the transition to digital has offered to the music business.

Chapter 6: Interview with Richard Hall, Founder and Chief Executive of CloudOrigin, who explains what cloud computing is and how it can add value to the activities of business organizations.

Chapter 14: Interview with Matt Ballantine, Principal Evangelist at Microsoft, who explains how an IT company such as Microsoft can make a difference and bring value not just to other business organizations, but society as a whole.

Chapter 14: Interview with Jos Creese, Chief Information Officer for Hampshire County Council, who talks about the way in which e-Government is bringing about a change in the interactions between local authorities and citizens.

The videos, as well as the transcripts of the interviews can be accessed online in the companion website for this book: **www.palgrave.com/business/whiteley/.**

ONLINE RESOURCES AVAILABLE

TOUR OF THE BOOK

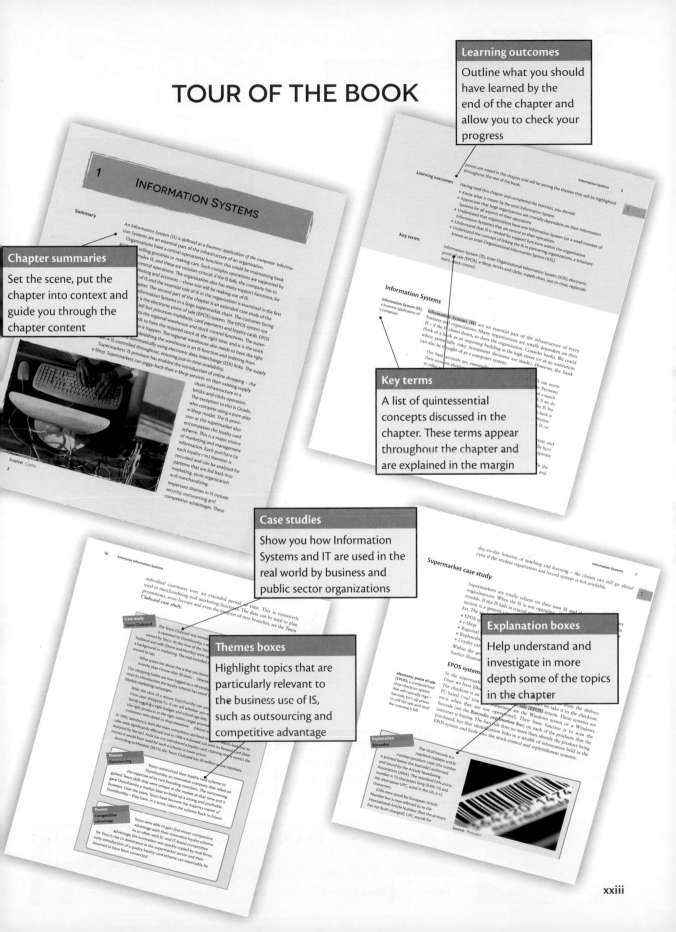

Learning outcomes

Outline what you should have learned by the end of the chapter and allow you to check your progress

Chapter summaries

Set the scene, put the chapter into context and guide you through the chapter content

Key terms

A list of quintessential concepts discussed in the chapter. These terms appear throughout the chapter and are explained in the margin

Case studies

Show you how Information Systems and IT are used in the real world by business and public sector organizations

Themes boxes

Highlight topics that are particularly relevant to the business use of IS, such as outsourcing and competitive advantage

Explanation boxes

Help understand and investigate in more depth some of the topics in the chapter

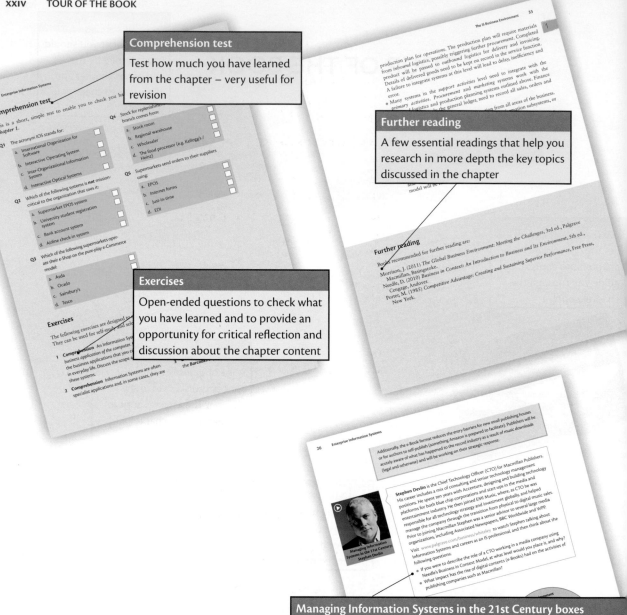

Comprehension test

Test how much you have learned from the chapter – very useful for revision

Further reading

A few essential readings that help you research in more depth the key topics discussed in the chapter

Exercises

Open-ended questions to check what you have learned and to provide an opportunity for critical reflection and discussion about the chapter content

Managing Information Systems in the 21st Century boxes

Video interviews with IS professionals talking about their careers and their jobs – watch them online

Companion website

Visit our companion website at www.palgrave.com/business/whiteley to find a lot of extra materials, exercises and the MIS in the 21st Century videos

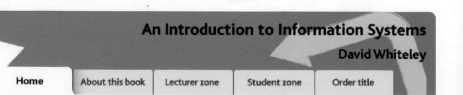

An Introduction to Information Systems

David Whiteley

Home   About this book   Lecturer zone   Student zone   Order title

PART 1 ENTERPRISE INFORMATION SYSTEMS

All modern enterprises are dependent on their Information Systems. The staff communicate by e-Mail. Reports are produced on word processors with copies of spreadsheets in the appendices. Marketing may well be online and involve the use of social media. Additionally, in any medium or large enterprise, the major administrative and financial processes (for example order processing and stock control) will be implemented as Information Systems. The modern enterprise is dependent on its Information Systems for its operations, management processes and interfaces with trading partners.

To start, in *Chapter 1* we define the term Information System (IS) and we outline the topics that are included in the study of IS. The complexity of the Information Systems provision in a large organization is illustrated by an extensive case study of the use of IS and IT in a large supermarket chain. This case study is used in later sections of the book to illustrate further aspects of the study of Information Systems.

In *Chapter 2* Information Systems are examined in the context of the business structure and the environment in which the business/organization operates. We examine Porter's Generic Value Chain and Needle's Business in Context Model and develop our own IS Business Model. The model divides the functions of the organization into operations, support functions and management – the whole operating within a social and economic environment. IS/IT is an essential tool within and across all these organizational levels. The IS Business Model is used to illustrate the application of Information Systems in organizations throughout the book.

Finally, in *Chapter 3* we examine the IS function within the organization. Most organizations have an IS department but some will outsource some, or possibly all, IS/IT functions – we examine both options. The creation of new IS functions involves the setting up of a project team – we look at the structure of an IS project team and the role of the project manager.

1 INFORMATION SYSTEMS

Summary

An Information System (IS) is defined as a *business application of the computer*. Information Systems are an essential part of the infrastructure of an organization.

Organizations have a central operational function: this could be maintaining bank accounts, selling groceries or making cars. Such complex operations are supported by equally complex IS, and these are mission-critical: if the IS fails, the company has to suspend its central operations. The organization also has many support functions, for example marketing and accounts – these too will be making use of IS.

The nature of IS and the essential role of IS in the organization is examined in the first part of this chapter. The second part of the chapter is an extended case study of the application of Information Systems in a large supermarket chain. The customer-facing end of the setup is the electronic point of sale (EPOS) system. The EPOS system not only adds up the bill but processes multibuys, card payments and loyalty cards. EPOS data then feeds into the regional warehouse and stock control functions. The supermarket branch needs to have the required stock at the right time, and it is the stock control IS that makes it happen. The regional warehouse also needs to have the right amount of stock. Replenishing the warehouse is an IS function and ordering from suppliers is done automatically using electronic data interchange (EDI) links. The supply chain is IS-controlled throughout, ensuring just-in-time availability.

Supermarkets' IS provision has enabled the introduction of online shopping – the e-Shop. Supermarkets can piggy-back their e-Shop services on their existing supply chain infrastructure in a bricks-and-clicks operation. The exception to this is Ocado, who compete using a pure-play e-Shop model. The IS provision at the supermarket also encompasses the loyalty card scheme. This is a major source of marketing and management information. Each purchase by each loyalty card member is recorded and can be analysed for patterns that are fed back into marketing, store organization and merchandizing.

Important themes in IS include security, outsourcing and competitive advantages. These

Source: Corbis

| Learning outcomes | Having read this chapter and completed the exercises, you should: |

- Know what is meant by the term Information System
- Appreciate that large organizations are crucially dependent on their Information Systems for all aspects of their operations
- Understand that organizations have one Information System (or a small number of Information Systems) that are central to their operations
- Understand that IS is needed for support functions within the organization
- Understand the concept of linking the IS in partnering organizations, a structure known as an Inter-Organizational Information System (IOS).

| Key terms | Information System (IS), Inter-Organizational Information System (IOS), electronic point of sale (EPOS), e-Shop, bricks-and-clicks, supply chain, just-in-time, replenishment, stock control. |

Information Systems

Information System (IS): a business application of a computer.

Information Systems (IS) are an essential part of the infrastructure of every business and organization. Many organizations are totally dependent on their IS – if the IS closes down, so does the organization. Consider banks. We could think of a bank as an imposing building in the high street (or as an institution where potentially risky investment decisions are made). However, the bank can also be thought of as a computer system:

> Our bank accounts are, essentially, simply entries in an IS. We can access these accounts electronically via the web or using a cash machine. Payments to other accounts are simply debits from one electronic record and a matching credit to a second electronic record in the same, or another, IS. If we do venture into a branch then any transaction still works through the IS but with the bank clerk operating the system. The investment arm of the bank is similarly dependent on IS, since records of stocks and shares and the transactions concerning those financial instruments are equally entries in an IS (or series of networked IS).

The bank system outlined above is complex and very expensive to create and maintain. It is essential to the operation of the business and if it fails the business (and other businesses that are linked to its systems) ceases to operate until the system is back in operation.

These massive IS in large organizations are one end of a spectrum. In the middle of the spectrum are the main systems of smaller organizations and secondary systems and departmental systems in large organizations. At the far end of the spectrum are PC systems, possibly using packages such as Microsoft Office, that can also be classified as IS.

Many of these systems are networked. They may well have links to other systems and/or with customers and suppliers. The electronic integration of operations across organizations creates an **Inter-Organizational Information System (IOS).** Electronic access for customers is provided by e-Commerce systems. Electronic integration along the supply chain from, for example, suppliers, to manufacturers, retailers and ultimately to the customer, is an example of networking and an IOS.

Inter-Organizational Information System (IOS): Information System in separate organizations that are closely coupled and effectively work as a single IS.

Computer networks have merged with mobile networks and customers' access to e-Commerce systems anytime and anywhere. The smartphone is, in effect, a mobile computer and is also used to access e-Mail, the web and social networking applications.

As academics and students, we are likely to have experience of smartphone apps, small PC systems and the user interface of online systems. The study of IS includes such small systems, but it is also essential that we understand and appreciate:

- The nature and architecture of corporate IS
- How a corporate IS is essential to the operations of the organization
- The security and resilience requirements of the IS infrastructure
- How IS is designed and developed
- The impact of IS on society.

All (except the fourth) of these points are illustrated in the extended case study of supermarket IS at the end of this chapter.

Information Systems and organizations

An Information System is a broad categorization. The term does not mean quite what it would seem to imply. The definition we gave above was:

> An Information System is *a business application of the computer*.

An Information System, or a Management Information System (MIS) which is the North American term, is not just about providing information but also about processing business transactions. The IS has a business transaction processing (TP) function as well as being a source of management information. The anatomy of the Information System includes:

- Data capture: The first task is to get data into the IS efficiently and accurately. Data can be sourced from within the organization, from trading partners or members of the public (often using the internet to facilitate direct data input).
- Processing: The computer programs that together make up the system. It is the job of the IS specialist to define and design the processing requirement.
- Data storage: The IS has to *remember*; and its memory is its files and database. Stored data can be conceptualized as standing data, such as a file of customers, and transaction data, such as the customer orders that are passed through the system.

© jamdesign/Fotolia

- Transaction output: Business documents that are output by the system, such as an invoice.
- Management information: Analysis of the business transacted and its financial implications; used to empower management in decision-making and strategy formulation.
- Information Technology (IT): The computers and servers used to run the IS and host the database, the networks that link the system to the users and the desktop, laptop or mobile devices employed by those users.
- People: The IS/IT specialists who design, create and maintain the system and all the other stakeholders who interact with that IS.

The dual role of transaction processing and management information, and the elements that make up the IS, are brought out in the following examples of commonly used IS:

- Payroll: This system starts with details of employees and their rates of pay and processes these transactions, together with the employee's payroll history, to produce bank transfers, payslips and so on. The system also provides management information on, for example, the payroll cost of staff in the various departments within the organization (see *Chapter 4* for an extended study of a payroll system).
- Order processing: The main input is the customer order, which is processed, using customer and product data, to produce delivery note and invoice transactions. In addition to processing the business transactions the system can produce a wealth of management information on what is selling, who is buying and the overall sales totals for each month and year (see *Chapter 4* for an extended study of an order processing system).

Most organizations have one IS (or a small number of IS) that are central to their operations. Examples of such organizations are:

- An insurance company with its policy records, renewals and claims processing system
- A manufacturing company with materials requirement planning (MRP) and production control systems
- A college or university with its student registration and records system.

In addition to these central systems, on which the operations of the organization depend, there are a number of further systems for functions such as marketing, accounts and the customer complaints department.

The central business systems of the organization are supported by an extensive IT infrastructure. Many organizations are totally dependent on their IS and IT infrastructure – the banks, airlines, insurance companies and large multiple retailers are good examples of such dependence. The central systems of these organizations are *mission-critical*, and in these organizations most or all employees will be interfacing with the core Information System. In the supermarket for example:

> EPOS reads the barcodes, looks up the prices of the merchandise and calculates the customer bill. As each item is checked through the EPOS system, the sales are totalled and that total is then taken from the store's stock total to calculate the replenishment requirement for each product sold. The stock replenishment system then comes into operation to order a delivery from the regional warehouse to the store and, after further calculation, electronic orders are sent to the suppliers for stock to be delivered to the warehouse. Details of all transactions are stored and analysed to derive accounts, marketing and management information.

A large supermarket chain concerned with ensuring good stock availability with minimum stock holding requires a very large and sophisticated IS. The system consists of EPOS terminals and back office servers in the stores, warehouse systems in the regional warehouses and, in all probability, a large data centre at a head office site. The supermarket's IS will be linked to its suppliers' order processing IS, thus creating an IOS. The overall system is illustrated in *Figure 1.1*. It costs a large sum of money, and many years of effort will have gone into building and fine-tuning it. The supermarket cannot operate without the system: if, for example, the EPOS infrastructure breaks down, the store has to close its doors (and that occasionally does happen, despite the efforts of the organization to make their systems resilient). There is an extended case study of IS in supermarkets in the second part of this chapter.

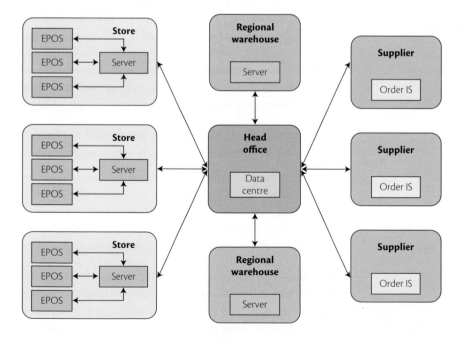

Figure 1.1 Supermarket chain – IT infrastructure.

Not all systems are large and a system's operation is not necessarily critical to the organization. For example, colleges and universities have their own Information Systems, but these do not, in general, greatly impinge on the day-to-day function of teaching and learning – the classes can still go ahead even if the student registration and record system is not available.

Supermarket case study

Supermarkets are totally reliant on their own IS and those of their partner organizations. When the IS is not operating effectively the supermarket is in trouble. If the IS fails in crucial areas, the supermarket has to close down. This section is a generic case study of the IS/IT infrastructure of a (any) supermarket. The study contains the following subsections:

- EPOS systems
- e-Shop
- Regional warehouse
- Replenishment
- Loyalty card.

Within the generic case study there are a number of *real* case studies that further illustrate the overall use of IS in the supermarkets.

EPOS systems

electronic point of sale (EPOS): a computerized shop checkout system that will typically read a barcode, look up prices, record the sale and total the customer's bill.

In the supermarket we are left to select our own goods from the shelves. Once we have filled up our basket, trolley or cart we take it to the checkout. The checkout is an electronic point of sale (EPOS) system. These systems are PC-based (and you can sometimes see the Windows screen or a Windows error when they are not operational). Their basic function is to scan the barcode (see the *Barcodes explanation box*) on each of the products that the customer is buying. The barcode does no more than identify the product being purchased, but that identification links to a wealth of information held in the EPOS system and feeds into the stock control and replenishment systems.

Explanation Barcodes

The retail barcode is a machine readable article number/product code (the number is printed below the barcode) authorized and issued by the Article Numbering Association (ANA). The standard EAN article number is 13 characters long (EAN-13) and the alternative UPC, used in the US, is 12 characters.

EAN once stood for European Article Number but is now referred to as the International Article Number (but the acronym has not been changed). UPC stands for

Source: Photoalto

Universal Product Code (but only has a one digit country code and hence has limited applicability). The format of the EAN-13 is:

- Country code (2 characters), e.g. 50 for the UK
- Manufacturer code (5 characters)
- Product code (5 characters)
- Check digit.

A company needing to barcode its products will apply for its own manufacturer code (within the country code it will be using). Once that is obtained it can then allocate each product its own article number. The check digit is a 10s complement and is used to check that the barcode has been correctly read (the EPOS system bleeps to warn of a misread or invalid barcode).

For the 10s complement check digit, each digit in the article number is multiplied by, alternatively 1 and 3 (the rightmost digit is always multiplied by 3) and the resultant products are added up. So, for the EAN product code (from a book of first-class stamps):

$$50 \mid 14721 \mid 11228 \mid 2$$

We get:

$$5\times1+0\times3+1\times1+4\times3+7\times1+2\times3+1\times1+1\times3+1\times1+2\times3+2\times1+8\times3=68.$$

68 modulo 10 is 8. The check digit is $10-8=2$.

The barcode is calculated when the number is allocated and then checked each time the barcode is swiped.

There are other variants of the product barcode, such as the UPC-12 and the EAN-8. The ISBN book identification number is also represented as an EAN-13 barcode on a book. The article number system is an example of the way trade sectors have to cooperate to enable inter-organizational IS to operate effectively.

Barcodes are used for a number of purposes other than product identification. Delivery services use barcodes to track packets, and your student card may well have a barcode representing your student number. The use of the barcode for data capture is further examined in **Chapter 7**.

There are also a number of 2D (two dimensional) barcode systems. The 2D barcode is standard on airline boarding cards. Many smartphones can read 2D barcodes encoded to the quick response (QR) code standard. One use of these barcodes is to include them on adverts to provide a hyperlink to the company's website.

The EPOS system holds a detailed list of information about each product. When the product is scanned the system uses this list to ensure that:

- The product name and price is displayed and printed on the receipt
- Any special offers (e.g. two for the price of one) can be calculated
- The customer's total bill is calculated.

The EPOS system works well for standardized, pre-packaged items. The barcode is printed on the packaging when the product is made and there is no significant extra cost involved. The system is less convenient for loose items, which either have to be weighed and barcoded by staff at (say) the deli counter or have to be weighed at the checkout.

The EPOS system also keeps the till total and processes card details:

- The cash taken is recorded, totalled and can be reconciled with the cash in the till at the end of a shift

- Card payments are processed. Card details are passed through the supermarket's network to its banking partner for authorization (which is another complex IOS)
- Loyalty cards are processed – we will look at loyalty cards in more detail later in the case study.

Finally, the EPOS system records all the products that have been sold. This data is used to calculate replenishment (restocking) requirements. The general principle is that there is a stock total for each product stocked in the branch. For each sale that is recorded through the EPOS system one item can be deducted from that stock total. When the stock total gets down to the reorder level, more stock can be ordered from the regional warehouse. We will look at restocking later in the case study.

The reliable operation of the EPOS system is crucial to the operations of the supermarket. If the EPOS system is not working the supermarket cannot open its doors. If the sales data is lost the stock control system will be put out of kilter, which will take days to correct. If the payments systems fail, people will not be able to pay without cash (and the majority of payments are made with credit or debit cards). So the EPOS system needs to be resilient (see the *EPOS resilience explanation box*).

**Explanation
EPOS resilience**

The EPOS system consists of a number of EPOS terminals and a backoffice server.

The first vulnerability is improper use of the system. Staff have to log in to the system at the beginning of each session on the checkout. This should ensure that only authorized staff use the checkout and that any improper practices can be traced back to the member of staff involved.

The EPOS system is also vulnerable to a system failure. The failure of one or more EPOS terminals is not necessarily an issue since a typical supermarket has a number of terminals installed. The failure of the server would cause problems – this can be tackled by having a backup server with duplex data and automatic switchover to the backup server should the primary server fail. Some EPOS terminals can also work in *terminal offline* mode using a terminal-based product file and log sales within their own memory (this would not cover card-based transactions that need to be checked over the network).

The EPOS system also needs to be secure against data loss. This is addressed by transaction logging in the terminal system and the holding of all data on the duplex servers (where installed). Providing a duplex copy of the product data on the terminal also reduces network traffic.

The EPOS terminal processes card payment, and customer card data can be vulnerable whilst in the system. Visa (the credit/debit card issuer) identifies the following as the top three security risks (Visa, 2006):

- Many EPOS systems include remote access for system maintenance and troubleshooting. These can be exploited to gain unauthorized access to the EPOS system. The provision of a secure password (not the default) and appropriate encryption of transmissions within and to/from the system are examples of protection measures.
- Most EPOS systems consolidate payment data into a central repository that provides authorization functionality, data backup and management functionality for the system user (in our case the supermarket). Some EPOS systems keep a full copy of the card magnetic stripe (and sometimes pin/chip) data, which is unnecessary and adds to the vulnerability. An attack on the host can give access to payment-sensitive data and allow the data to be destroyed. To minimize risk the retained data must be restricted to the minimum

required for payment processing and the host must be compliant with strict security standards (which are much greater than those applying to the stock control and management information parts of the supermarket's system).

- The third risk is network security (with wireless networks being a particular area of vulnerability). Data needs to be encrypted, activity-logged and secure passwords must be used on all access points.

Themes
Security

The supermarket's IT infrastructure must be secure. In this context security covers:

- Resilience: vital subsystems need (virtually) 100 per cent availability. This includes the EPOS server which can be duplexed with a provision for automatic failover. It is also vital that no EPOS data is lost; this data can also be duplexed within the system.

- Privacy: the supermarket handles customer information, including financial data. This needs to be secured from unauthorized access (for reasons of privacy and to prevent fraudulent use).
- Financial control: the supermarket handles a lot of money, which has to be accounted for. The EPOS logon and till procedures provide an audit trail for till receipts.

An alternative to the standard, staff-operated EPOS system is the self-service checkout. The basic principles are the same but it can save staff resources and customer queuing. An interesting feature of the self-service EPOS is that the bagging area weighs the products and cross-checks that with the weight recorded in the product database.

The product data on the EPOS system is downloaded from the systems at the supermarket's data centre – this allows all products, prices and offers to be kept up to date in all the company's stores. The sales data is uploaded to systems at the data centre and used for replenishment and management information. The network to the data centre will also be used to transfer payment and loyalty card data. Through these links the EPOS system becomes an integrated part of the supermarket's IS/IT infrastructure. A supermarket EPOS network is shown diagrammatically in *Figure 1.2*.

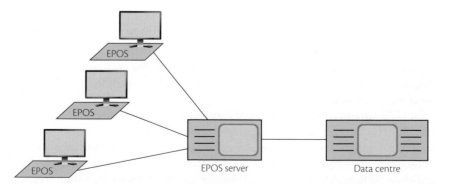

Figure 1.2 Supermarket EPOS network.

e-Shop

e-Shop: an online shop – the website of an internet e-Commerce business.

bricks-and-clicks: a retail organization that sells through a conventional store (bricks) and an e-Shop (clicks).

An alternative to shopping at the supermarket is to buy groceries through the e-Shop online. Most UK supermarkets have added e-Commerce to their conventional retail operations by adopting the bricks-and-clicks model. Tesco is the market leader, with the neat catch phrase *You shop, we drop*. Also in the market are Sainsbury's, Asda and Waitrose, with Morrisons predicted to join soon – out of *the big six*, that would leave just The Co-operative without an e-Shop, and since The Co-operative mainly operates in the convenience market sector, that may be the right choice for them. The other online supermarket is Ocado, which is *pure-play* – they operate from a purpose-built warehouse without any conventional retail operations: see the *Ocado/Tesco case study*.

Case study Ocado/Tesco

Ocado e-Shop. Ocado was founded in 2000 and made its first commercial deliveries in January 2002. The Ocado Group website (Ocado, 2011) states: *Ocado is the only dedicated online supermarket in the UK and the largest dedicated online supermarket by turnover in the world*. Ocado offers delivery of grocery products to customers centrally picked from a single, state-of-the-art, highly automated warehouse (the customer fulfilment centre or CFC). Ocado sells more than 21,000 different products, the majority of which are sourced through Waitrose, the leading quality UK supermarket.

The CFC is located in Hatfield. The single CFC is the hub of a hub-and-spoke network – there are currently some seven spokes. All orders are picked at the hub and then bulk delivered to the spoke depots – the home delivery vans are based in the spoke depots. The model is distinct from Ocado's bricks-and-clicks competitors, which use branches for their fulfilment. The CFC is, in many ways, equivalent to the conventional supermarket's regional warehouse, where goods-in are direct from the suppliers but goods-out are the customer order as opposed to replenishment of a retail branch, hence cutting out one step in the supply chain. The concentration of all e-fulfilment in one dedicated warehouse allows the extensive use of IT and automation (which would not be possible in a retail branch – Ocado claim that the setup is unique and the development of the facility requires a large, in-house IT team). A second CFC was opened in Tamworth at the end of 2012 (Wood, 2010) – the location is close to Hatfield, which probably reflects Ocado's (and Waitrose's, its main supplier) concentration in the southern half of the UK.

Ocado started life as a private company but was floated in 2010. Since its floatation the share price has had a bumpy ride as investors evaluate its ability to compete with its larger bricks-and-clicks competitors. Concerns have included discounting from Tesco and increased online competition from Waitrose (Ocado's primary supplier). Ocado made its first quarterly profit (a very small profit) in 2011, but has yet to achieve a profit over a full 12-month period.

Tesco e-Shop. Tesco dates itself back to 1919 when Jack Cohen first opened his market stall in the East End of London. Tesco first used the self-service model in 1956 and the label *superstore* in 1968 (Tesco, 2011). Tesco is the largest supermarket in the UK by some margin – its market share is just over 30% against just over 16% taken by Asda and Sainsbury's (2011 figures).

The grocery e-Shop tesco.com was launched in 2000 and Tesco Direct, selling a very large range of non-grocery goods, was launched in 2006 (Tesco, 2011). For Tesco (and the other bricks-and-clicks operators) fulfilment has been from selected local stores. This means that paid pickers (shoppers) are collecting the orders of online customers from the same shelves as the ordinary Tesco customers – there is no suggestion that this is a problem but it does mean that Tesco cannot install the automation that Ocado uses. As volumes increase there has been a gradual move away from using branches to having dedicated facilities for the fulfilment of online orders – Tesco have three such facilities in south-east England and further depots are planned (Davis, 2011).

Tesco report a profit on their internet grocery business, but, when the online and conventional retail business are so intertwined, separating out the costs attributable to each mode of selling may be somewhat arbitrary.

Online grocery market. Tesco are market leaders online, with 32% of the market, but their lead is narrow with Asda on 30% and Sainsbury's on 25% (Sayid, 2010). The online grocery market accounted for 3.2% of total grocery spend in 2010 (Telegraph, 2011). There are predictions that this market will grow (as in the *Telegraph's* article) but there are also reports of customers finding the service unsatisfactory and switching back to conventional shopping (see Sayid, 2010). Online shopping is no longer just e-Commerce: all the major players provide for m-Commerce, which includes the provision of i-Phone and smartphone apps.

The *bricks-and-clicks* model allowed supermarkets to set up their e-Shop operations very quickly – they simply use their large retail supermarkets as the e-fulfilment depots for their e-Commerce operations. This model was first adopted by Tesco, which got a head start on their rivals (Sainsbury's started with a programme of purpose-built e-fulfilment depots, but quickly adopted the Tesco model). The dual use of the retail outlet as both the e-Shop and conventional retail may not be ideal. The shop is laid out for retail customers whereas a warehouse layout/infrastructure is more appropriate for e-fulfilment. On the other hand, since the local supermarket is an existing asset it makes sense to use it. The alternative model, of a purpose-built, high-tech distribution depot is used by Ocado. This is no doubt more efficient, but Ocado have only one central depot, so they have the disadvantages of longer mileages on the retail end of the distribution chain.

The model that will win out is probably dependent on how many customers switch to online grocery shopping in the long term. Running a retail supermarket where up to (say) 10 per cent of sales are e-Commerce is workable (and current figures show a lot less than 10 per cent). Should the proportion of the market taken by online sales grow dramatically, the supermarkets would need to take a fresh look at their operations – a supermarket where the car park is empty and most of the *customers* are supermarket staff picking e-Shop orders would not be good economics.

In terms of IS, the e-Shop operations can be a bolt-on to the existing infrastructure. The IS to order the stock is already in place. All that is needed is the e-Shop – a website and the associated backoffice software. Nonetheless, the supermarkets' e-Shops are complex systems. The e-Shop, as a minimum, needs:

● A system to register and log in the customers (normally integrated with the supermarket's loyalty card system)

1

- A database of all products to be sold online (this has much in common with the conventional product database but needs to be enhanced with product pictures and online search capabilities)
- A system to maintain and amend a shopping cart as customers do their online shop (there is also, normally, a provision for stored customer shopping lists)
- Provision for secure online payment
- Facilities for the customer to book a delivery slot (for when the supermarket has available resources and when the customer expects to be at home).

All the above have to be linked to a backoffice system that:

- Produces picking lists (that are sequenced for the layout of the store). The Waitrose system loads the picking lists onto a hand-held computer that is mounted on the trolley being used by the member of staff picking the order.
- Prints delivery notes and schedules the delivery vehicles.
- Integrates with the supermarkets stock control systems (the stock replenishment calculation must take account of conventional sales recorded by the EPOS system as well as sales at the branch via the e-Shop).

A complex e-Shop system, such as a site used by a major supermarket, will cost several millions to set up and maintain.

Regional warehouse

supply chain: the network of organizations that supply merchandise to a retailer. Each first- and second-tier supplier will have their own suppliers, together making up the total supply chain.

Supermarkets have put a lot of effort into developing efficient supply chain logistics. The customer expects to find product on the shelves (and if the product they want, however obscure, is out of stock they will be less than pleased). The supermarket needs to meet this expectation without carrying an excess amount of stock (that will take up space, cost money and, in the case of perishables, go out of date). Thus the supermarket needs a just-in-time supply chain – for retail we normally use the phrase *quick response* – whereby as a product is sold the replenishment infrastructure responds quickly to ensure that the shelves are restocked.

just-in-time: a strategy that seeks to reduce inventory – merchandise is delivered at the time it is needed in the distribution centre or on the shelves of the retail operations.

The physical infrastructure adopted by supermarkets (and other multiple retailers) is a network of regional warehouses or distribution depots. A large supermarket will have, say, 25 regional warehouses located across the country and each supermarket branch will be allocated to the nearest (most convenient) regional warehouse.

The aim is that the supermarket holds just enough stock to keep its shelves stocked. There is no warehouse at the back of the store – just a *goods-in* area where deliveries are held before they are stacked on the shelves.

Deliveries are made to each branch from the regional warehouse on a daily basis and sometimes more frequently. Delivery to the branches is carefully organized: the computer systems calculate the loading of the lorries and the routes they will take (and the progress of the lorries is checked by means of satellite location systems).

The regional warehouse stock is also kept to a minimum – the term distribution depot could be a more accurate description of their function. Stock and stock replenishment at the regional warehouse is controlled in much the same way as stock in each branch. Replenishment systems are discussed in more detail below.

Delivery to the regional warehouse is by the manufacturers (food processors/ importers). The suppliers are expected to respond to orders on a just-in-time basis, with delivery typically scheduled on day of order or day following order. The supplier will be given a slot time for their delivery and will be expected to meet that slot.

In addition to food, many supermarkets are now stocking non-food items (e.g. kitchen ware, electrical goods, clothes). These goods have different logistics requirements and the supermarket may supply them from a smaller network of distribution depots.

Replenishment

replenishment: the process of ordering new (replacement) stock (replenishment works in conjunction with stock control).

stock control: the process of keeping a record of stock quantities and ensuring that an appropriate quantity of product is available.

The **replenishment** system links the branch to the regional warehouse and the regional warehouse to the supplier. The replenishment system's task is **stock control.** The science (or art) of stock control is to have enough of every product line for likely demand without building up any surpluses. Predicting demand is difficult and especially so in food retailing, which is complicated by the short shelf life of some products. Demand depends on the day of the week, the time of the year, the weather and other factors such as the ingredients used the night before delivery on a TV cookery programme. The replenishment system needs data on sales and stock in all stages of the supermarket supply chain. The system also needs to be able to respond quickly should any shortages occur (the customer does not expect to go to the supermarket and see half-empty shelves and to find the ingredients they wanted are unavailable – a dissatisfied customer is easily lost to a rival supermarket).

The first component of the replenishment system is the EPOS system, which has been outlined above. Within the replenishment system the function of the EPOS system is to collect sales data. The EPOS sales data is then sent to the replenishment system at the data centre (which may be a central IT system or a distributed system at, say, each of the regional warehouses).

The replenishment system needs to know what has been sold before it can calculate what new stock needs to be sent to the branch. In a simple case, the branch may have sold 60 cans of a specific brand and size of baked beans – the requirement is to send 60 more (although the system needs to check that some are not already in transit). It could be appropriate to send more to cover sales that are expected in the immediate future or fewer because sales volumes are expected to fall back.

Replenishment of the branches takes place from the regional warehouse. The system has calculated what new product is required (and that will be several hundred different products each day for each store). It produces picking lists for the warehouse staff to select that product, move it to the loading bay, pack it up (in crates, on trolleys or on pallets) and load it onto the lorry. The degree of automation varies, but the IT is used to optimize the picking and the transport process.

As product is allocated to each store from the regional warehouse, the stock at the regional warehouse needs to be replaced (and of course both the stores and the regional warehouse are working on a just-in-time basis). The stock control calculation at the regional warehouse is based on the total stock in that warehouse but also needs to take account of any stock allocated to the stores, predicted demand at those stores, any stock that is in the supply chain from the suppliers and the likely lead time for fresh supplies to arrive. Orders are sent to the suppliers electronically using electronic data interchange (EDI, discussed in *Chapter 5*) and a quick response will be expected. See *Figure 1.3* for a summary diagram.

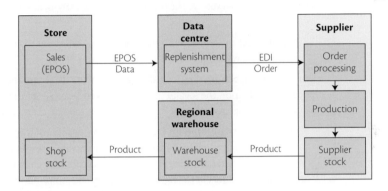

Figure 1.3
Replenishment – data and product flows

Loyalty cards

Several of the large supermarkets run a loyalty card scheme: examples are Tesco's Clubcard and Sainsbury's Nectar (also used by other retailers). The idea of a loyalty card is to tie you, the customer, into one retailer – in practice many people simply have a collection of loyalty cards, bulking up their wallets.

The loyalty card is enabled by the IS/IT infrastructure of the retailer (previous attempts in this field, prior to an IT solution, involved the collection of stamps that were handed out at the checkout). All members of the loyalty card scheme are recorded on a database. At the checkout the customer swipes (or has swiped) their loyalty card, which connects the current checkout session with their details on the database. In turn, this:

- Records the details of the purchases being made by that customer
- Calculates the points accrued by the customer.

The customer can then use their points to help pay for their groceries or to purchase special *gifts* such as electrical goods or holiday travel – an incentive that some customers take very seriously. Customers are also able to access their loyalty card accounts online; the website is designed in such a way as to further encourage customer use of the supermarket's facilities.

The loyalty card is also of benefit to the supermarket. The details of every purchase made by each loyalty card customer is recorded on the data warehouse (a system that enables rapid searches of vast amounts of data: see *Chapter 8*). The EPOS data is essentially only sales data – the loyalty card data enables the supermarket to examine the shopping patterns of individual customers over an extended period of time. This is extensively used in merchandizing and marketing functions. The data can be used to plan promotions, store layouts and even the location of new branches, see the *Tesco Clubcard case study*.

The Tesco Clubcard was introduced in 1995 (Tesco, 2011). The Clubcard is operated by Dunnhumby, a separate company which is now majority-owned by Tesco. At the time of the Tesco Clubcard trial in 1994 Dunnhumby was a husband and wife (Dunn and Humby) start-up company run by two mathematicians with a background in marketing. The trial included data analysis, and the then chairman was moved to say:

> What scares me about this is that you know more about my customers after three months than I know after 30 years.   (Marston, 2011)

Our shopping habits are now logged on a 40-terabyte database, and it is estimated that since its introduction the loyalty scheme has saved Tesco £350m a year on expensive blanket marketing campaigns:

> With the click of a mouse Dunnhumby can profile you faster than the FBI can. From your shopping list it can tell whether you are a single, fast-food junkie or a family juggling a tight budget and school-age kids. The clues enabled Tesco to put the right products in the right stores, target promotions accurately, and lure back customers who dared to shop elsewhere.   (Wood and Lyons, 2010)

In 1995, Sainsbury's, then the main competitor, declined to follow Tesco's lead, but its sales were significantly affected and in 1996 it followed suit with its Reward Card (later replaced by Nectar). Asda has not introduced a loyalty card, claiming that it invests the money it would have used for such a scheme in lower prices.

According to Marston (2011), the Tesco Clubcard has 20 million active members.

**Themes
Outsourcing**

Tesco outsourced their loyalty card scheme to Dunnhumby, an innovative company that relied on the expertise of its two founding members. The outsourcing gained Tesco skills that were unique in the market at that time and it gave Dunnhumby a market base to build up a strong and profitable business. Over the years, Tesco have become the majority owner of Dunnhumby – they have, in a sense, taken the scheme back in-house.

**Themes
Competitive
advantage**

Tesco were able to gain *first-mover* competitive advantage with their innovative loyalty scheme. As so often with IS- and IT-based competitive advantage, the innovation was quickly copied by rival firms. Yet Tesco's rise to dominance in the supermarket sector and their early introduction of a quality loyalty card scheme can reasonably be assumed to have been connected.

The supermarket IS/IT infrastructure

This *Supermarket case study* has provided an outline of the use of IS/IT in a large supermarket chain (and other multiple retailers will have a similar infrastructure). The overall IS/IT infrastructure is complex, vital and expensive – it is as essential to the supermarket as the supermarket's physical infrastructure and the staff (at head office, in the supply chain and in the stores). Any case study of such a complex system (or series of interconnecting systems) can do no more than give an overview of the system. The components of the system, as outlined in this case study are summarized in *Figure 1.4* (see also *Figure 1.1*).

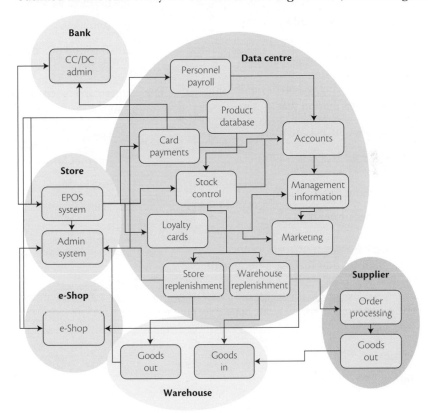

Figure 1.4 Supermarket IS/IT infrastructure (summary).

Supermarkets are constantly developing their IS to increase efficiency and enhance customer service. Developments include:

- The development of the much smaller local/metro outlets in addition to large, out-of-town mega branches
- Self-service checkout. Supermarkets are also exploring scan-as-you-shop systems
- The use of mobile and social networking technologies (even though one can wonder whether we really need a social network just to buy a pint of milk!).

All these developments require development of the supermarket's IS/IT infrastructure. The e-Shop is possibly the most significant recent development – it may yet change the face of food retailing (there is an exercise at the end of the chapter for you to critically assess the advantages and disadvantages of ordering your groceries online and waiting for them to be delivered to your home).

Comprehension test

This is a short, simple test to enable you to check you have absorbed the material presented in *Chapter 1.*

Q1   The acronym IOS stands for:

a.   International Organization for Software ☐

b.   Interactive Operating System ☐

c.   Inter-Organizational Information System ☐

d.   Interactive Optical Systems ☐

Q2   Which of the following systems is *not* mission-critical to the organization that uses it:

a.   Supermarket EPOS system ☐

b.   University student registration system ☐

c.   Bank account system ☐

d.   Airline check-in system ☐

Q3   Which of the following supermarkets operate their e-Shop on the *pure-play* e-Commerce model:

a.   Asda ☐

b.   Ocado ☐

c.   Sainsbury's ☐

d.   Tesco ☐

Q4   Stock for replenishment of the supermarket branch comes from:

a.   Stock room ☐

b.   Regional warehouse ☐

c.   Wholesaler ☐

d.   The food processor (e.g. Kellogg's / Heinz) ☐

Q5   Supermarkets send orders to their suppliers using:

a.   EPOS ☐

b.   Internet forms ☐

c.   Just-in-time ☐

d.   EDI ☐

Exercises

The following exercises are designed to aid your understanding of the material presented in this chapter. They can be used for self-study and selected exercises can be used for tutorial discussion.

1   **Comprehension** An Information System is *a business application of the computer*. List some of the business applications that you come across in everyday life. Discuss the scope and impact of these systems.

2   **Comprehension** Information Systems are often specialist applications and, in some cases, they are very large systems. Desktop packages such as word processors and spreadsheets are also used for business applications (in effect individual Information Systems). List some business applications of desktop applications.

3   **Comprehension** Starting with the detail given in the *Barcodes explanation box* you can investigate

barcodes in more depth. Look in your food cupboard – articles from the same manufacturer will probably have the same country and manufacturer but different product codes. If you have a smartphone that will read barcodes then see what additional information you can obtain (you might need an app like Google Shopper).

4 **Discussion** Retail e-Commerce has taken a considerable market share in areas such as books and music but its inroad into the grocery market has been much less dramatic. Assess the advantages and disadvantages of online shopping for groceries. Are there consumer categories where e-Grocery shopping is more / less advantageous / convenient? If you were the manager of a supermarket chain that did not have an e-Shop, how would you develop an e-Commerce strategy in the current competitive environment?

5 **Assignment** The use of computers and telecommunications can enable work to be done at a location remote from an organization's office; a development known as teleworking (or telecommuting in North America). Discuss the nature of teleworking, its impact on the individual, the organizations for which the teleworkers work and its likely future development.

Your discussion is to be presented as an academic essay of about 2000 words. Reference all the material taken directly from the sources and include a full bibliography.

6 **Assignment** Computers are extensively used in schools and colleges but normally only for the study of IT topics or as an adjunct to more traditional teaching practices. Some educationalists suggest the much wider use of computers in education with information and communications technologies (ICTs) largely replacing face-to-face contact in the classroom. Research and explain possible future uses of ICTs in education and assess their likely impact on the various institutions and different client groups that may be affected.

Your research is to be presented as an academic essay of about 2000 words. Reference all the material taken directly from the sources and include a full bibliography.

2   THE IS BUSINESS ENVIRONMENT

Summary

Information Systems (IS) are an essential part of the infrastructure of businesses/ organizations. IS are used at all levels within the organization:

- At the operations level for the organization's business process – be that manufacture, sales (wholesale/retail), transport or service
- At the operations level for support functions such as marketing, human resources, finance and innovation
- At the management level for management information and decision support
- In the organization's (external) environment for electronic communications with suppliers, customers, government and other stakeholders.

Many Information Systems serve requirements at more than one level. They also need seamless interfaces with other systems if the organization is to operate efficiently.

    These levels are represented in the IS Business Model. The model has four concentric levels: operations, support functions, management and the environment, and IS/IT, which cuts across all levels. This model is used throughout the rest of the book.

Learning outcomes

Having read this chapter and completed the exercises, you should:

- Have an understanding of Porter's Generic Value Chain and/or Needle's Business in Context Model. For copyright reasons the detail given in this chapter is limited, but these models can be accessed in the original texts (see ***Further reading*** *and online*)
- Understand the concept of a supply chain and be able to map out a supply chain model for any given organization or case study
- Know the detail of the IS Business Model. Appreciate what is meant by the operations of an organization and understand the role of support functions and management. Understand that organizations function within, and interact with, the business environment at a local, national and global level

Source: Getty

● Appreciate the role of IS/IT in the operations and support functions of an organization. Additionally recognize that the IS/IT systems are used by management and interface with other organizations in the environment.

Key terms   Operations, support functions, Porter's Generic Value Chain, supply chain, Needle's Business in Context Model, management, strategy, environment (business environment), Information System (IS), Information Technology (IT).

Business functions

operations: the basic function of an organization – what it does, its productive function.

support functions: the additional activities of an organization that facilitate its operations.

Porter's Generic Value Chain: a model that shows all activities that a business has to undertake. The model divides activities between primary (productive) and secondary (overhead) activities. The difference between the cost of the activities and value of the output is the *margin* (profit).

Businesses/organizations all have a basic function which, in business terms, we call their **operations**. Thus a motor manufacturer makes cars, a bank looks after its customers' money, a supermarket retails groceries and a university educates students (well, we try). The operations of an organization, particularly those trading in tangible goods, also require:

● Inbound logistics: Obtaining supplies of components or merchandise
● Outbound logistics: Despatching finished/sold products
● Service: Dealing with any after-sales issues

and all organizations have to market their services.

In addition to an organization's operations there are a number of **support functions** that all organizations must have. These include:

● Strategic management and planning
● Finance and accounting
● Human resources
● Innovation: Planning (inventing) future products and services.

These functions (or a similar list of functions) are nicely illustrated by **Porter's Generic Value Chain**, see the *Porter's Value Chain explanation box*.

Explanation
Porter's Value Chain

Porter introduced his model, the Generic Value Chain, in his book *Competitive Advantage: Creating and Sustaining Superior Performance* (Porter, 1985). This follows on from his more famous Model of Competitive Forces (The Five Forces Model). The Value Chain Model claims to show the activities that all businesses must undertake – although the way

they are organized and the emphasis on each activity will differ between industry sectors and, to a lesser extent, between businesses within a sector.

The model divides activities into primary (productive) activities and secondary (overhead) activities. Primary activities are:

● Inbound logistics
● Operations

- Outbound logistics
- Marketing and sales
- Service.

The secondary activities shown in the model are:

- Firm's infrastructure
- Human resources
- Technology development
- Procurement.

Porter suggests that each business needs to model its specific value chain. Having identified the component activities and linkages each element can then be analysed in terms of cost and value-added so that the overall efficiency of the value chain can be established. The difference between the cost of the business's activities and the value of the business's output is the *margin* – the aim of the analysis is to maximize the margin.

Porter's model also illustrates that an organization (firm) does not exist in isolation but is connected to other organizations (firms) in its value system. Porter's version of the firm's value chain shows:

- The supplier's value chains feeding into the firm's inbound logistics
- The firm's outbound logistics feeding into the value chains of the channels (wholesalers/distributors)
- The channels in turn feeding into the value chains of the buyers.

The importance and complexity of the value chain depend on the nature of the operations and the organization.

*Students are recommended to examine this model in further detail (for their general business studies): see Porter (1985) in **Further reading**.*

supply chain: the network of organizations that supply components to a manufacturer or merchandise to a retailer.

The value system is an important aspect of Porter's model and it is perhaps more simply explained as a **supply chain** – this is particularly significant for organizations that deal in tangible goods, that is, manufacture, wholesale and retail. Each organization will have its own supply chain, but we can represent a generalized example, *Figure 2.1*.

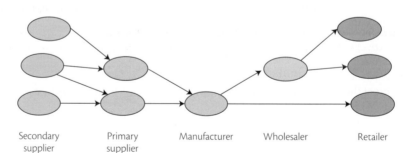

Figure 2.1 Supply chain model.

| Secondary supplier | Primary supplier | Manufacturer | Wholesaler | Retailer |

To explain the supply chain, let us take as an example a manufacturer of PCs. The manufacturer will buy components from its primary suppliers, the chip from Intel or AMC and the hard disk from (say) Hitachi. The primary suppliers in turn have their suppliers, our secondary suppliers (and there may well be a number of further levels behind the secondary suppliers). Once made, the PCs have to be sold. They may be sold through an agent (wholesaler – Porter's *channel*) or they may be sold direct to a large retail chain. Some PC manufacturers also sell direct to the end user – this is not shown on this general diagram.

Supermarkets are another example of an organization with an extensive supply chain – in this case we will place the supermarket (retailer) in the middle or the diagram. In addition to its external suppliers and customers the supermarket can be seen as having an internal supply chain between the regional warehouse and the supermarket branch (with the e-Shop also being part of the internal logistics structure). The general supply chain model in *Figure 2.1* is adapted to the particular circumstances of the supermarket in *Figure 2.2*.

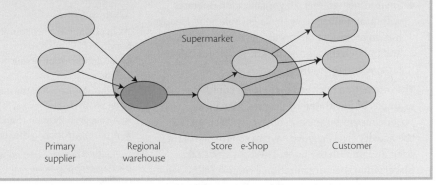

Figure 2.2 Supermarket supply chain.

Needle's Business in Context Model: a model that represents business/organization in four layers: activity, strategy, organization and environment. Needle makes the point that an organization does not function in isolation but in an external social and economic context.

Needle, in his book *Business in Context: An Introduction to Business and Its Environment* (Needle, 2010), underlines the complexity of business activities (a list of functions similar to those shown on Porter's Generic Value Chain). He also contends that it is only possible to fully understand these activities in the context of the business's:

- Structure: The ethos and strategy of the organization
- Organization: How the organization is structured and how it operates
- Environment: The economy and society in which the business operates.

The activities of the business and its context are shown in **Needle's Business in Context Model**: see the *Needle's Business in Context Model explanation box*.

Needle explains his Business in Context Model in his book *Business in Context: An Introduction to Business and Its Environment* (Needle, 2010), The model shows the business/organization operating at four levels:

- activity level
- structural level
- organizational level
- environmental level.

Each level, from the activity level in the centre, operates within the context of the outer levels with the environment level providing the context for all the business's operations and functions. Each level is summarized by a number of activities. In brief these are:

- Activity level: Operations. This is what the organization does – it could be manufacture, sales (retail/wholesale), transport or some sort of service industry [1]
- Activity level: Support functions. The activity level also includes a number of functions the organization needs to run the firm's infrastructure. Needle lists the functions as: innovation, marketing, human resources, and finance and accounting

- Structural level: The management of the organization needs to shape the ethos and long-term future of the organization. Needle lists the functions as: business strategy and management decision-making
- Organizational level: This includes: structure, ownership, size, organizational culture and goals, and organizational politics
- Environmental level: The organization operates within, and interacts with, its environment. Needle lists environment factors as: the economy, the state and politics, the labour market, social and cultural factors, and technology.

The interaction between these levels could, for example, be illustrated by Palgrave Macmillan producing this business/IS university textbook. At the activity level Palgrave have to commission, edit, print and publish the book. These activities take place within their organizational context (although many of the production tasks, such as printing, will be outsourced). The whole business of publishing textbooks is also affected by the environment, where both higher education and technology are changing – are students still buying and reading textbooks? Would an e-Book sell better or do students expect to simply access free (and somewhat random) material on the internet?

---

[1]Wild (1985) identified four basic types of production activity:

- A transformation of raw materials into manufactured articles
- A transformation in the nature of ownership (selling: retail/wholesale)
- A change in location (transport)
- A transformation in the state of the customer (services).

Students are recommended to examine this model in further detail (for their general business studies): see Needle (2010) in **Further reading***.*

These business models are perhaps most easily illustrated by examples of manufacture – and we have already instanced the example of a PC manufacturer and its supply chain above. That PC manufacturer would, of course, also have support functions: human resources, technology development (innovation) marketing, and so on.

The business models can also be applied to service sector industries (although the supply chain aspects of the model will be less significant). To illustrate this we will look at a book publisher. Their operations have two aspects:

- The physical aspect is the printing and distributing of the book (to the retailers). The physical printing will normally be outsourced. The physical book is under threat from the move to the electronic book, the e-Book.
- The *intellectual* aspect is the commissioning, editing and marketing of the book. The author is not a member of the publisher's staff and often the (electronic) typesetting will also be outsourced. The editorial and marketing functions are, however, core functions of the publisher.

The operations of the publisher are supported by (are in the context of) the support functions, the strategy of the publisher and the business environment in which the sector operates. Electronic publishing must be seen as a significant business environment issue – publishers have the example of what has happened to the record industry and they are working on how they can survive, or prosper, in the changed technological environment. These points are illustrated in the ***Macmillan case study*** (Macmillan is the publisher of this book).

1

Macmillan Publishers Ltd is one of the largest publishing groups in the world. The company was originally founded in 1843 by two brothers, Daniel and Alexander Macmillan. Today, Macmillan is owned by the Georg von Holtzbrinck GmbH group and employs 7000 people working in more than 80 countries.

© Eisenhans/Fotolia

The function (operations in terms of the business models) of Macmillan is publishing. Macmillan publishes in a variety of areas, ranging from academic textbooks and scholarly journals to novels. As a result, Macmillan has a number of divisions, including the Nature Publishing Group (NPG), Macmillan Education, Pan Macmillan, Picador and Palgrave Macmillan. Each division employs a series of editorial teams for each of its subject areas/genres. Their role is to identify market opportunities; to commission authors; and then to manage the process of writing, editing and print formatting the content – the latter is generally in the form of a book, a journal or online content.

On completion of the editorial function the content has to be published (in hard copy and/or electronic form) and distributed to wholesalers and retailers (physical and online bookshops) or sold through a company-owned e-Shop. The physical printing of the book is from electronic copy and is outsourced (publishers do not actually *print* books). One could argue, in terms of the business models, that the physical publishing is a support function, but we will classify it as part of operations and distribution as outbound logistics. Distribution is from a state-of-the-art warehouse facility in South Wales.

Macmillan has all the normal support functions one would associate with a large organization. Important support functions include:

- Marketing: The content they publish, however well written, will sell only if brought to the attention of the reading public – for example, teachers and students for academic books.
- Information Systems: Macmillan, like any other major organization, is reliant on its IS/IT infrastructure – and has an IS department to support this (see the ***Managing Information Systems in the 21st Century*** box below).
- Human resources: A knowledge company such as Macmillan is highly dependent on the quality of its staff – HR must cooperate with the editorial departments to ensure that quality talent is recruited and retained.

Publishers operate in *interesting times* – the phrase *may you live in interesting times* is variously seen as a blessing or a curse. The (business) environment for publishing is changing rapidly. Publishers have seen the end of the Net Book Agreement (where publishers set fixed prices for their publications), the development of large bookshop chains and of the online book retailers – all of these developments have exerted price pressures on publishers (books are sold to retailers at a discount from the cover price – large retailers will seek to negotiate higher discounts). Publishers are now faced with a switch from hard copy to electronic books: sales of e-Books are rising fast and how far the change will go and which market segments will be most affected is, as yet, unclear. The move to electronic formats reduces production and distribution costs but not editorial costs. The e-Book format could increase the market but also reduces the amount the customer expects to pay.

Additionally, the e-Book format reduces the entry barriers for new small publishing houses or for authors to self-publish (something Amazon is prepared to facilitate). Publishers will be acutely aware of what has happened to the record industry as a result of music downloads (legal and otherwise) and will be working on their strategic response.

Managing Information Systems in the 21st Century: Stephen Devlin

Stephen Devlin is the Chief Technology Officer (CTO) for Macmillan Publishers. His career includes a mix of consulting and senior technology management positions. He spent ten years with Accenture, designing and building technology platforms for both blue chip corporations and start-ups in the media and entertainment industry. He then joined EMI Music, where, as CTO he was responsible for all technology strategy and investment globally, and helped manage the company through the transition from physical to digital music sales. Prior to joining Macmillan Stephen was a senior advisor to several large media organizations, including Associated Newspapers, BBC Worldwide and WPP.

Visit www.palgrave.com/business/whiteley to watch Stephen talking about Information Systems and careers as an IS professional, and then think about the following questions:

- If you were to describe the role of a CTO working in a media company using Needle's Business in Context Model, at what level would you place it, and why?
- What impact has the rise of digital contents (e-Books) had on the activities of publishing companies such as Macmillan?

The IS Business Model

Both Porter and Needle make the case that an organization must involve a number of functions in addition to its essential business operations (be that manufacture, selling, transport or service). Taking these models together we will create our own four-level model. The layers, starting in the centre with operations, are:

- Operations
- Support functions
- Management
- Environment.

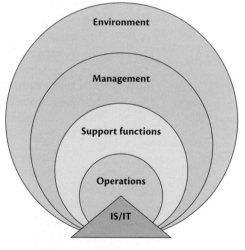

Figure 2.3 The IS Business Model.

All these make use of, and are coordinated by, IS/IT – so the final element of the model is:

- Information Systems and Information Technology (IS/IT).

This gives us our IS Business Model: see *Figure 2.3*.

Let us examine each of these levels, and the use of IS/IT, in more detail.

Operations

The nature of the operations of an organization, and the IS/IT it utilizes, is dependent on what that organization is doing. In *Chapter 1* we examined supermarkets. By the nature of their business they will have an extensive branch network (excepting Ocado as a pure-play e-Tailer) and an emphasis on the efficiency of their supply chain. The extensive use of IS/IT is a necessity for effective operations and competition in the industry. Further examples are:

- Banks: The standard function of a bank is to take in money from savers and lend it to people or organizations that need additional funds – the profit is made by charging more to borrowers than is paid to savers. Although there is a cash handling function, money is mainly electronic. The essential system in a bank is the computer system, which records transactions on the accounts of savers and borrowers. Stated in this way the system sounds very simple but it is, of course, much more complex. The system also has to be secure, resilient and available to bank staff and customers (through the internet and ATM machines). Note, this description does not include any investment banking operations, which will need their own set of systems.

- Manufacture: There are a range of IS/IT tools available for manufacture. The design office can use computer-aided design (CAD) systems to produce engineering drawings. Production can use materials and requirements planning (MRP) systems to make sure the necessary material is available. The production process itself may use machinery that is electronically controlled, generically referred to as computer-aided manufacture (CAM) – the CAM systems can be fed from the CAD systems. Component assembly manufacture, such as vehicle assembly, will use just-in-time techniques where the whole supply chain is controlled by an extensive IS infrastructure (see EDI systems in *Chapter 5*).

- University: The university has a dual role of educating students and of conducting research. Teaching is supported by administration – the central administration system is the student registration and records system. The university needs to know who its students are, what they are studying and how they are progressing. It also needs to know if the students have paid.

The operations of an organization are its raison d'être, and so organizations need to run their operations efficiently and competitively. Most organizations will use IS/IT in their operations function. Large organizations have extensive IT systems and are totally dependent on them to operate. A supermarket, bank or car manufacturer cannot operate without their IS/IT – the exception to this in the above list is the university, where the day-to-day operations are not dependent on the IS (although unreliable electronic teaching aids can still be problematic).

Support functions

Any organization needs an infrastructure in order to carry out its operations. Typically, the organization will need office and (for manufacturer) factory premises – it will also need staff and equipment. In addition to the physical infrastructure there will be a number of support functions. These include:

- Human resources (HR): Responsible for ensuring the organization recruits and retains the staff it needs for its operations and support functions. HR is also responsible for disciplinary procedures and redundancies. IS provision can include an HR package and will include the payroll (see *Chapter 4*).

- Finance and accounting: The organization needs to keep account of its money. Customers need to be billed, supplier invoices settled, staff paid, and profits and losses calculated. Finance will normally use an accounting IS package to record all financial transactions.

- Procurement: All organizations need to buy stuff. Manufacturing and retail businesses have vast numbers of transactions as they buy the primary supplies for their operations. Additionally, all organizations purchase material for use internally, for example stationery and IT equipment; these are known as secondary supplies. It is the responsibility of Procurement to contract supplies at the right price and quality. Procurement can use a procurement IS. Procurement systems will interface with finance and, where appropriate, MRP, stock control and replenishment systems.

- Marketing: The organization will only continue to exist if it can sell its goods or services. Marketing's job is to make sure that the organization reaches new customers and that existing customers come back for more. The most obvious manifestation of marketing is advertising. Marketing may use a customer relationship management (CRM) package. The organization will typically also need a public website and an internal intranet. Note that organizations such as central and local government departments do not, in general, need a marketing function, but they still need to manage their public relations.

- Innovation: The world keeps moving on and organizations need to update and adapt. A retailer will look for new products to sell or new ways to market itself (links with social media and smartphone apps seem to be the current trends). A manufacturer will be seeking to invent new product, update its existing product to add extra features, use new materials or just to look new and cool. Innovation depends largely on people (clever people) but software such as CAD can also play a role.

- Information Systems: The use of IS/IT in the organization needs management and support. The use of specific business IS has already been indicated. There will also need to be a general IT infrastructure to support the business IS, desktop systems (e.g. word processing and spreadsheets) and communications (e-Mail). Large organizations will have a dedicated IS/IT department. The IT function may also have its own IS, such as a help desk system.

Support functions are an overhead – they add cost but not value to a product. They are necessary but need to be efficient and cost-effective. For a small business many of these functions will be carried out by the owner (often in the evening and at weekends); larger organizations will have dedicated departments assisted by appropriate IS.

Themes
Centralization /
Decentralization /
Outsourcing

IS/IT can be a problematic area within organizations. Management know it is essential to their organization but they do not fully understand it and they are often dissatisfied with the provision. The basic model is a central IS department, but this will often attract criticism from other business functions who do not feel they are getting the service they require or value for their money. An alternative model is to decentralize IS to divisions/departments, but this is likely to be detrimental to the provision of coherent strategic Information Systems.

An alternative approach is for the organization to outsource all or part of the IS/IT function. An attraction of this approach is that the outsourcing company is expert in its field and the management of the organization can concentrate on its core operations. That said, IS/IT is not a commodity function and outsourcing can complicate the process of developing the IS/IT to meet changing business needs. Some organizations outsource only the commodity aspects of their IS/IT provision, such as desktop support and payroll (see **Chapter 4**).

The structure of IS/IT provision, within the organization, is further discussed in **Chapter 3**.

Management

management: the act of organizing people and resources to achieve desired goals – normally a function of staff appointed to a managerial role.

strategy: the long-term plan, or direction, of the organization.

All organizations, whether we like it or not, need to be managed. Management are responsible for the general oversight of the business's operations and support functions. Specific functions of management include:

● Strategic planning: Organizations should have some idea where they are headed – what they hope to look like in, say, five or ten years' time. Strategy is simply defined by Johnson, Whittington and Scholes (2010) as:

> Strategy is the long-term direction of the organization.

It is management's responsibility to develop corporate strategy. A formal strategy process would normally:

■ Assess the market for opportunities: This assessment needs to take account of the various factors in the business environment and pick opportunities that are relevant to the organization's area of expertise.

■ Assess the internal strengths and weaknesses of the organization. Moving forward with a new strategy may well involve some risks, so the organization needs to be realistic about what its capabilities are.

■ Perform a gap analysis: The organization must assess its current state (asking, *where are we?*) and how it intends to move forward (*where do we want to be?*).

Examples of strategy formulation could be: an engineering company thinking of a major shift into green technology but worried about the government's commitment to supporting green energy; a university contemplating franchising courses to the Middle East but concerned about the implications for academic quality. Morrison (2011) discusses strategy in a globalized world (see **Further reading**).

The development of a strategy gives a context in which management can plan and gives the staff an idea of where their organization is headed. That said, strategies do not always work out as intended. Johnson, Whittington and Scholes (2010) give Nokia as an example of strategy formulation – only for that company to then fall seriously behind its competitors in the smartphone market.

In addition to corporate strategy an organization may well develop an IS/IT strategy. This could include decisions on: centralization, decentralizing and/or outsourcing IT; standardizing the desktop and adopting a preferred supplier for corporate IS (assuming appropriate systems can be bought in).

- Business structure: Management will also take responsibility for the organization's structure and reporting procedures. A medium to large organization might, for example, adopt a divisional structure. Each division is then given budgetary responsibly for its own activities; this focuses divisional management on generating business and operating efficiently. An example of a divisional structure is a university: faculties and schools/departments are typically required to balance their costs with income from student fees and research funding. A university department is also an example of a functional specialism, with all the experts in a particular field of study being members of the relevant department.

  Management will from time to time restructure their organizations. The plan will be to gain greater customer focus, internal efficiency, or some such aim. Such reorganizations might cause considerable internal upheaval and often there is no noticeable advantage.

- Corporate culture: Organizations have their own ethos. An organization may be very formal, with rigid hierarchies and strong management direction – not necessarily the best approach to foster creativity and initiative amongst staff. Alternatively, an organization might take a more informal approach, but, if this is the case, it still needs to ensure that all staff members are pulling their weight.

  Management will have an idea of the corporate culture it wants to create. Corporate culture is not something that can be created by order – it has to be fostered and nurtured (and management have to lead by example). The culture (or intended culture) of an organization can be summed up in its mission statement. An example of a mission statement that was both short and blunt is *Kill Kodak*, attributed to Fujifilm.

Management requires people – it is not an IT function. Nevertheless, management can be greatly helped by appropriate and reliable information from inside and outside the organization.

In the UK business computer applications are called *Information Systems*, while in America they are called *Management Information Systems*. One of the functions of these systems is to provide management, at all levels, with information to aid the decision-making process (the main functions of most of these systems is to process business transactions – a function that is not properly reflected in the name). A simple example of management information is the payroll which will, as a by-product of its main function, report payroll costs at an organizational and divisional level. Management will be particularly interested in key business measures, such as sales totals for a retailer and student recruitment totals for a university – these should be available from the organization's IS. Outputs from the finance system will also be closely scrutinized by management.

Some organizations will have a specific Management Information System (MIS) using a database fed from other operations and support function systems. Other terms used for Management Information Systems are Executive Information System (EIS) and Decision Support System (DSS). The topic of management information is further explored in *Chapter 7*.

Environment

environment (business environment): the economic, political, social and technological context in which the organization operates.

All organizations are influenced by their environment (the business environment). Factors in the environment, listed by Needle (2010) are:

- The economy
- The state and politics
- The labour market
- Social and cultural factors
- Technology.

Businesses are concerned with the state of the economy. If the economy is doing well, it is easier for a business to prosper, and if the economy is doing badly, the reverse is true. The state can try to create a framework for a prosperous economy but, ultimately, the economy is the sum total of businesses. In order to prosper an organization also needs a labour force with the necessary skills, using appropriate technology and fairly remunerated (and *fairly* can be seen from various perspectives). The organization is also affected by cultural and institutional frameworks – which may, or may not, foster enterprise.

All factors in the environment have to be seen in the context of globalization. National economies are part of a global economy, and the free movement of goods and capital mean that many organizations can outsource internationally or relocate to countries with cheap labour or other advantageous cultural and institutional frameworks. The process of globalization is facilitated by IS/IT where information, orders and payments can be transferred virtually instantaneously. Large organizations may well have facilities in a number of countries – the multinational corporation – and their IT infrastructure will need to reflect this. Furthermore, outside the organization, in the environment, are other entities with which the organization has defined relationships. These entities include:

- Trading partners – buy-side: The companies the organization gets its primary and secondary supplies from. These relationships are particularly significant for manufacturer and retailer which, as already outlined, will execute many purchase transactions.
- Trading partners – sell-side: The companies the organization sells to. For business-to-business this can be components sold to manufacturers or merchandise sold to retailers. The sell-side can also be business-to-consumer, that is, retail.

● Outsourced facilities: A wide variety of functions may be outsourced, from staff catering to running the payroll or the whole IS/IT function. Some companies outsource virtually everything, creating what we call a *virtual organization*.

● Governmental organizations: There are extensive interchanges between businesses/organizations and the authorities – paying the Inland Revenue company and payroll taxes is one obvious example. The organization will also have links to other institutions such as banks and external accountants.

Exchanges with business partners and government organizations may well be electronic, particularly for high volume exchanges in the supply chain (see *Chapter 5* for a discussion of electronic data interchange (EDI), e-Shop systems and electronic markets).

IS/IT infrastructure

Information System (IS): a business application of a computer.

Information Technology (IT): computing equipment (hardware) – the term is now normally understood to also encompass communications technology.

From the above discussion, it should be apparent that IS plays a vital role at all levels of the organization and in the organization's outside links. Information System (IS) and Information Technology (IT) have a central role in the modern organization; this is illustrated by the reconfiguration of the IS Business Model in *Figure 2.4* – the arrows indicate that all levels of the organization, and partner organizations in the environment, are involved with, and dependent on, the IS/IT infrastructure.

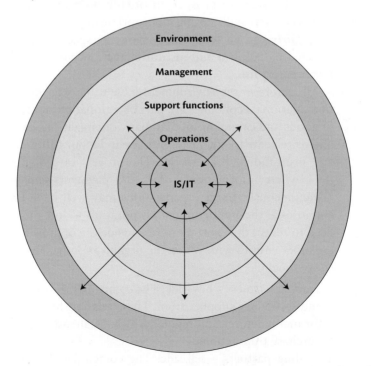

Figure 2.4 IS/IT at the heart of the organization.

To be truly effective, the IS within the organization needs to be integrated:

● At the operations level the various systems should work seamlessly together. Following the rather abstract representation of an organization provided by Porter's Value Chain, orders from *marketing and sales* will determine the production plan for *operations*. The production plan will require materials from *inbound logistics*, possibly triggering further *procurement*. Completed product will be passed to *outbound logistics* for delivery and invoicing. Details of delivered goods need to be kept on record in the *service* function. A failure to integrate systems at this level will lead to delay, inefficiency and error.

- Many systems in the *support activities* level need to integrate with the *primary activities*. *Procurement* and *marketing* systems work with the *inbound logistics* and production planning systems outlined above. Finance systems, particularly the general ledger, need to record all sales, orders and stock movements.
- Management require appropriate information from all areas of the business. The separate IS can have their own management information subsystems, or data can be selectively abstracted and loaded onto an EIS.
- Information and data exchanges with partner organizations (and individuals) in the environment level need to be efficient and effective. e-Commerce technologies can and should be used to automate and integrate these transactions.

The IS Business Model is central to the understanding of the use of IS, IT and digital technology by management and throughout the organization. The model will be referenced throughout this book.

Further reading

Books recommended for further reading are:

Morrison, J. (2011) *The Global Business Environment: Meeting the Challenges*, 3rd ed., Palgrave Macmillan, Basingstoke.

Needle, D. (2010) *Business in Context: An Introduction to Business and Its Environment*, 5th ed., Cengage, Andover.

Porter, M. (1985) *Competitive Advantage: Creating and Sustaining Superior Performance*, Free Press, New York.

Comprehension test

This is a short, simple test to enable you to check you have absorbed the material presented in *Chapter 2.*

Q1 Porter's Generic Value Chain divides activities into primary activities and support activities. Which one of the following is classified by Porter as a support activity?

- a. Procurement ☐
- b. Operations ☐
- c. Outbound logistics ☐
- d. Service ☐

Q2 Needle's Business in Context Model includes finance and accounting as a function. To which level of the model is finance and accounting allocated?

- a. Environmental ☐
- b. Organizational ☐
- c. Structural ☐
- d. Activity ☐

Q3 A medium to large engineering business will have a portfolio of IS. Which of the following systems belongs to a support function (as opposed to the operations level)?

- a. CAD ☐
- b. CAM ☐
- c. CRM ☐
- d. MRP ☐

Q4 Information is important to management and an important source of that information is the organization's IS. Which of the following is *not* a management level IS?

- a. DSS ☐
- b. EDI ☐
- c. EIS ☐
- d. MIS ☐

Q5 e-Commerce can be used for exchanges with trading partners. Trading partners are located at which level of the IS Business Model:

- a. Environment ☐
- b. Management ☐
- c. Support functions ☐
- d. Operations ☐

Exercises

The following exercises are designed to aid your understanding of the material presented in this chapter. They can be used for self-study or selected exercises can be used for tutorial discussion.

1 **Comprehension** Make a list of ten organizations you have come into contact with today (or over the last couple of days). Note whether your interaction with those organizations was facilitated by IS/IT. Outline the nature of the IS used in each case.

2 **Comprehension** Using the *Macmillan case study* (and your general knowledge of book retailing) – map out a supply chain diagram for the company's trade in physical books. Is the supply chain different (and how does it differ) for e-Books?

3 **Comprehension** Outback PCs Ltd produce computing equipment for rugged environments: see the company structure chart below. Examine the IS/IT requirements of Outback PCs and mark the systems they could/should use in each department on the chart – also note any interfaces between systems.

4 **Discussion** For your college or university, teaching students and the associated administration is an operational level activity. From your experience as a student, what IS is used to facilitate this activity? Outline the nature of the IS used and see whether you can identify any linkages. This exercise could be a group discussion and you may wish to quiz your tutor as well. Note that your application to the institution was facilitated by IS/IT – this should be included in your answer.

5 **Discussion** Look up the mission statement of your college or university (there probably is one but it may be somewhat *neglected*). Assess how well your experience of the institution's culture ties up with the mission statement. Discuss and compare your findings with those of your colleagues.

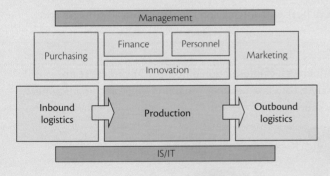

3   IS ORGANIZATION AND MANAGEMENT

Summary

Information Systems (IS) are an essential part of the infrastructure of businesses/ organizations – they are a support function that affects and enables all levels of their activities. The organization and management of the IS function must be a priority for the business. In this chapter we examine:

- The IS function within the organization
- The nature and structure of the IS department
- The use of projects and project teams for the delivery of new IS
- Project management
- Outsourcing of IS and IT provision and its implications for the IS function and the organization.

Learning outcomes

Having read this chapter and completed the exercises, you should:

- Understand the function of IS and the IS department within the organization
- Understand the role of a project, the project manager and the composition of an IS project team
- Understand the concept of IS/IT outsourcing and the associated advantages and pitfalls.

Key terms

Information Systems department, chief information officer (CIO), project team, project manager, system analyst, database designer, programmer, project management, outsourcing, off-shoring, in-sourcing.

Source: Photodisc

The IS function within an organization

The IS function within an organization exists as the interface between the business on one hand and the IT infrastructure on the other. This is shown diagrammatically in *Figure 3.1*.

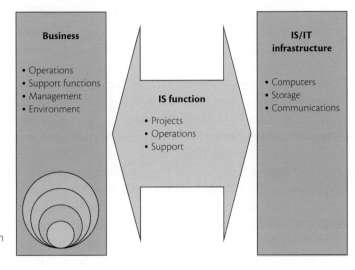

Figure 3.1 The IS function in an organization.

The business (organization) needs IS/IT to effectively and efficiently perform its operations, support functions and to provide information for management (see the IS Business Model in *Chapter 2*). Most or all functions in the organization can be controlled or assisted by the application of IS/IT. It may well be that people within the organization will have the knowledge and expertise to use IT equipment and Information Systems; however, for large complex requirements that interface with other departments and (possibly) other organizations, they are likely to require the assistance of IS specialists.

IT equipment will be dispersed throughout the organization, with many/most employees having a PC or specialist terminal on their desk or at their workstation. All this equipment has to be set up and maintained. The desktop/workstation IT equipment is networked to server and/or central mainframe facilities, and these also need to be operated and maintained. The systems are used to run business IS and desktop software, all of which has to be supported.

The IS function operates the IT infrastructure. It provides support for end users of the system and it runs projects to develop new/enhanced Information Systems.

The IS department

Information Systems department: The department in an organization that is responsible for the provision and maintenance of IS and IT.

chief information officer (CIO): a senior management role; an officer responsible for all IS and IT in an organization.

Organizations, large and small, need effective IS/IT provision. This provision has to be managed and staffed with the appropriate expertise. The obvious way of making and managing the IS/IT provision is to have an **Information Systems department**.

Starting at the top, the IS department will have a manager, a head of department. Both the department and the manager can run under various titles – one such management title is the **chief information officer (CIO)**. The IS manager/CIO can be (and arguably should be) a senior person in the organization. IS/IT involves major investment decisions and makes a significant contribution to the competitive advantage of the organization. This point is illustrated, for example, by the *Supermarket case study* in *Chapter 1* – the use of IS/IT is central to the efficient operation of the supermarket and, over the years, many of the changes in how supermarkets do their business have been as a result of the innovative use of IT. Most (non-IS) managers will have a background in either finance or the main business (operations) of the organization. Having a CIO to represent the IS/IT contribution at the top table is important if the potential of IS is to be fully realized.

The CIO must look outwards, from the IS department, to the management/strategy of the organization. The CIO also looks inwards to the management of the IS department. Sections/functions in the IS department might include:

- Business analysis: A small group of IS specialists who look at the strategic development of IS/IT within the organization
- Operations: The staff responsible for operating and maintaining the IT infrastructure, such as mainframes, servers, network and desktop (PCs)
- Help desk (user support): Support for end users with desktop queries and issues with the use of the business IS
- Projects: Teams set up to write new IS, install bought-in IS and/or make major enhancements to existing IS.

A possible organizational structure of an IS department is shown in *Figure 3.2*.

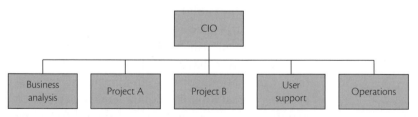

Figure 3.2 An IS department.

While *Figure 3.2* gives a possible organizational structure, the size and shape of the IS function vary from organization to organization. For a small organization the function may be covered by a single person, whereas in large organizations the IS function can employ several hundred people. A university is an example of an organization that will have an IS department. The university's reliance on business (administrative) Information Systems is normally less marked than other organizations of a comparable size, but a university does need to cater for the diverse IT requirements of academics and large numbers of students (see the *MMU IS Department case study*).

Manchester Metropolitan University (MMU) is one of the largest UK universities, with a student population in excess of 30,000 and an intake of about 10,000 new students each year.

Source: Design Pics

MMU has a head of IT reporting to the secretariat and the vice-chancellor, but the IS/IT function is decentralized, with each facility (and central administration) having its own IT Services department. The head of IT is not formally responsible for the separate IT departments but has the role of setting policy and standards for IS/IT throughout the university.

The core function of administration is to keep student records. This starts with the admissions process and tracks students through offer, acceptance, registration, module choice, exam board results to graduation. Student records are kept by using bought-in IS packages (separate systems from different suppliers for student records and exam board records). These systems need to interface with and be used by administrators and academics throughout the university. The process is not always a happy one – whether this is a deficiency of the software or a lack of user training is unclear.

A further administrative process (support function) is accounts. The accounts function uses an ERP[1] system bought from an external company, SAP (SAP is a, or the, premier supplier of ERP systems and not the cheapest option – the purchase of SAP software might reflect the powerful position of the accounts function within a university). The accounts function seems satisfied with their SAP software but the faculties can find the requirement on them to supply data complex and burdensome.

The accounts function is also responsible for the payroll. The payroll system has for a number of years been outsourced to an agency specializing in payroll services. A recent decision replaced the outsourcing agreement with the use of SAP payroll software to be operated in-house (the jargon is that the payroll is being *in-sourced*). The use of SAP for both payroll and accounts should ensure an efficient interface between the two systems. Other central systems include personnel records, library and the university website.

Provision of IT facilities for academics and students is the responsibility of the Faculty IS teams. The university currently has a Microsoft policy and the Faculty IS team is responsible for implementing the MMU standard desktop and software provision. The Faculty IS team also provide help desk support to staff and students. Exceptions to the standard desktop are made where there is an academic need for alternative facilities. For example, the School of Computing, Mathematics and Digital Technology has Linux, Apple and *supercomputer* facilities, in addition to the standard MMU Microsoft provision; it also has its own IT technicians and budget for dedicated computing provision.

Academic and student use of IT is somewhat unpredictable: the IT requirements for study and research activities tend to be quite diverse, as opposed to the rather more predictable use of IS in most businesses. All staff and students have a university e-Mail account. There is also an emphasis on e-Learning using a Moodle Virtual Learning Environment (VLE) – support for the VLE is outsourced to another university. For students, the University has an *Acceptable Use Policy* which allows students to use IT for whatever they choose provided it is not illegal (e.g. pirate downloads) or offensive (e.g. pornography).

A special problem in university IT provision is the churn of user accounts. Each September there are 10,000 new student accounts (including e-Mail and VLE) to be set up – a process that is now automated with a link from the student records system. Student accounts are server-based, so the student can access their data from any university computer, from their halls or anywhere else via the internet.

MMU is connected across its sites and to other educational establishments in the north-west of England via Net North West (a private high-speed metropolitan area network). Net North West is in turn connected to JANET (a private government-funded high-speed network linking all UK HE institutions) and to the wider internet.

---

[1] ERP stands for enterprise resource planning system. These are bought-in application systems generally appropriate to large organizations. They cover areas such as manufacturing, stock control, finance and personnel. The systems provide integrated solutions and claim to incorporate state-of-the-art business models.

The IS function requires expertise that may not be readily available in the organization and can make extensive use of consultants (outside experts bought in on short-term contracts). Organizations may also outsource some or all of their IS/IT requirements – this is looked at in more detail later in this chapter.

New IS facilities can be a major (and risky) undertaking – the normal approach is to set up a project structure; this is looked at in the next section.

Projects

project team: a group of IS/IT specialists, led by a project manager, that is set up to develop and implement a new Information System.

The standard way of developing a new Information System is to designate it as a project and to set up a **project team**. The project team may be formed within the in-house IS department or the development may instead be outsourced (with the contracting organization setting up the project team).

A project team is a group of people, with the required (specialist) expertise, brought together to create an artefact. Projects and project teams are set up to, for instance, build a bridge or develop a new car – in our case, the project team's task is to create a new IS.

The purpose of a project is that it provides focus. The project is transitory: it is allocated resources for the task in hand and at the end of the project these resources are dispersed. The project's objective is to deliver; the requirement is that the new IS application is completed on time, on budget and to an acceptable quality. The project team is led by a project manager and it is his/her responsibility to ensure this delivery. The project manager needs to be focused (and ruthless) – non-delivery is the failure of the project manager and the consequence of that failure can well be his or her dismissal.

The main resource requirement of the project team is people. The project manager will want experienced staff with the appropriate expertise. The structure of a (generalized) IS project is shown in *Figure 3.3*.

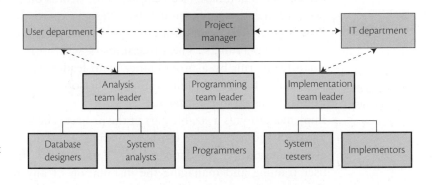

Figure 3.3 An IS project team.

The project team has important interfaces with the users and the IS/IT department.

Vital to the project team and the project manager are good relationships with the user department. It is the user department who have sponsored the project – possibly they are funding it. Moreover, it is the user department that understands the requirements of the project; in the IS team it is the job of the system analysts to discover these requirements and work out how they are effectively systematized and computerized. The relationship with the user department is a tough one. The user department will always want more or want something a bit different – but too much change will jeopardize the timescale and the budget of the project.

The project also needs to interface with the rest of the IS/IT department. The project might be using the existing IT infrastructure or may need new kit – all this needs to be worked out (in fact an extensive change to the IT infrastructure can be a project in itself). The project will probably have interfaces with other IS – possibly older IS using different technologies. These interfaces need to be designed and the responsibility for them needs to be accepted. Project team members may well have (vital) expertise in existing live systems, but the project manager needs to protect the resource of his/her project (if team members are diverted to maintaining existing systems the project schedule will be jeopardized). The relation of the project manager to the rest of the IT department is, again, a tough one.

The functions included in the project team, and shown in *Figure 3.3*, are:

project manager: the manager of a project team. The role of the project manager is to plan the project, run the project team and ensure effective delivery.

- **Project manager**: responsible for the delivery of the project. Needs to liaise with stakeholders in the user and IS/IT departments. Responsible for agreeing the overall design and ensuring the quality of the system. Project management involves the monitoring of progress against timescale and budget (see section on Project Management).

system analyst: a member of the IS team who investigates the user requirements for a new system and then designs how those requirements will be realized as an IS using IT.

database designer: an IS specialist with expertise in data analysis and the design of databases.

programmer: an IT specialist who writes and tests computer programs.

- **System analyst**: The role is to talk to users, determine user requirements and convert those requirements into the design for the IS. The process of system analysis and design is described in *Chapter 10* and the techniques that are used are taught in *Chapter 11*.
- **Database designer**: The database is a crucial part of the system design. Large systems with a significant number of users can be made (or broken) by the design of the database (see *Chapter 8* for details on databases). The project needs to include significant database design expertise.
- **Programmer**: The design from the system analyst is implemented as software by the programmers. The programmers will normally be organized into small teams run by a programmer team leader. The programmers are also responsible for initial (unit) testing of the software. The programming function is discussed in *Chapter 12*.
- Implementation is a sizable part of the project. The software must be tested – a system and acceptance test is a common approach in this area. There are also requirements for data capture, data cutover (from existing systems), user training and managing the installation of any new IT infrastructure. Testing is discussed in *Chapter 12*. Once the software has been tested and the other preparations have been made, the system can go live – and hopefully it works well once it is live. Implementation does not have specific job roles in the way that other parts of the project have – one approach is for selected members of the system team to move over to these roles once their analysis and design tasks are finished.

The structure and size of the project team is obviously dependent on the nature of the requirement and the technology being used. Many IS projects are for the installation of bought-in application packages (for example the SAP ERP systems in the *MMU IS Department case study*). This will cut down the requirement for analysis and might remove any requirement for programming. The installation of a significant package in a medium/large organization can still be a significant project with much of the emphasis being on the implementation functions.

Project management

project management: management of the project team to ensure that the project is delivered on time and on budget.

Projects, particularly large projects, need careful planning. Planning is a function of **project management** and would normally be the responsibility of the project manager. It is the project manager's job to draw up the plan and then to deliver on time, to budget and in accordance with the plan.

To plan a project the overall task needs to be broken down into manageable sized chunks. The breakdown is needed for:

- Estimating: The normal procedure for arriving at an overall time and resource estimate is to first estimate for each component of the project separately and to then add up all the component totals to form an overall estimate. Estimates are normally made in terms of man-hours (a term that might sound rather sexist but person-hours does not quite sound right). Estimates for computer projects are notoriously inaccurate but a bottom-up approach gives more chance of arriving at a plausible figure.

- Planning: Once estimates have been derived for each component of the project the components/tasks can be scheduled to produce a plan. The plan needs to take account of the so-called task dependencies (that is, tasks that cannot be started until one or more other tasks have been finished) and it should try to even out the workload within the project team. The PERT technique can be used to evaluate task dependencies and derive the critical path to project completion (see *Chapter 12*).
- Work allocation: The components used for estimating and planning are the units of work allocated to a team member (or a small sub-team). Each component has an expected effort and duration so that team members know what is expected of them. Team members should be allocated one task, or a limited number of tasks, at any one time – this assists in monitoring progress. The Gantt chart can be used to show task allocations to team members (see *Chapter 12*).
- Progress monitoring: Monitoring needs to take place on a regular basis – weekly would seem to be a logical choice. Progress monitoring should check the time spent on each activity and progress towards completion. This can then be checked against the planned effort and deadlines to see if the task is on schedule or if there are any problems. Delays need to be detected early so that corrective action can be taken, if possible, before any problems build up. Progress can be recorded on the Gantt chart.

For a computing project, a high-level breakdown of a project is provided by adopting a system development lifecycle (SDLC). The SDLC sets out the major stages involved in developing a computer system. For instance, the waterfall lifecycle divides a project into five stages:

- Feasibility study
- System analysis and design
- Program and unit test
- System and acceptance test
- Operations – implementing and then maintaining the system.

These major stages provide a framework for the project plan. Lifecycles, including alternatives to the classic waterfall lifecycle, are further discussed in *Chapter 10*. Note: some authors give a different number of stages in the waterfall lifecycle, but the underlying principle is unaltered.

Outsourcing

outsourcing: obtaining goods or services, in this case IS and IT services, from an outside supplier in place of an internal source.

Outsourcing can be defined as:

> Obtaining goods or services from an outside supplier in place of an internal source.

This is a rather broad definition. In practice, outsourcing is seen as using an external supplier for goods or services that might normally or reasonably be sourced internally. In terms of computing provision it would not be normal or reasonable to build one's own computers – but it is reasonable to provide the organization's IS requirements using an internal IS department. Functions of the internal IS department that might be outsourced include:

- Desktop (PC) maintenance and support
- Software development (of bespoke applications)
- Hosting (using servers operated by an outside supplier).

Some organizations have outsourced all their IS/IT provision. Outsourcing should be seen as a strategic decision. There is a distinction to be made between outsourcing commodity IS/IT functions (e.g. desktop support or the payroll) and strategic systems that may well be a significant part of the organization's competitive advantage. Organizations that have created new business models based on the innovative use of IS and IT will, almost without exception, have developed their applications in-house – Amazon and Facebook are both examples of this.

The organization needs to retain some in-house capability so that it can monitor the progress of the outsourcing agreement, measure contract compliance and prepare for contract extension/renewal. The outsourcing of the payroll function is discussed in *Chapter 4* and the use of external cloud computing services in *Chapter 6*.

The advantages of outsourcing all or part of the IS/IT provision are seen as:

- Cost: Outsourcing can be (or can be seen as) a cheaper alternative to running the service in-house.
- Expertise: The outsourcing company specializes in IS/IT services; it has the expert staff and the experience.
- Economies of scale: The outsourcing company can spread the cost of the IT infrastructure over all its clients.
- Focus on core business: In-house management can concentrate on the organization's main business (where they have expertise) without diverting resource to manage support functions, in this case IS/IT.
- Performance criteria: An outsourcing contract can set service levels that must be met; compensation has to be paid if service levels are missed.
- Capital vs. revenue: An outsourcing agreement can be contracted at a standard monthly charge; any capital expenditure on new IT would then be the responsibility of the outsourcing provider.

The outsourcing has to be wrapped up in an agreement – a contract that is probably going to run for a number of years. Getting the contract right can be problematic. Willcocks et al. (2011) report a study of 182 outsourcing agreements where 20 per cent of the agreements were prematurely terminated. Dealing with unpredicted requirements not covered by the contract tends to be expensive. Getting a realistic view of how well the outsourcing of IS/IT works is difficult. The managers who outsourced the work are not very likely to raise questions about their decisions and the outsourcing agency will of course maintain that it is providing a good service. Over the years the organization gets locked into the outsourcing arrangement – and it no longer has the resources to do the work in-house. The outsourcing agency is aware of the situation and it is not unusual to bid low for the initial contract in the expectation that extra work will come along for which the customer can be charged at inflated prices.

offshoring: outsourcing to an overseas supplier of IS/IT services.

A practice related to outsourcing is **offshoring** – the practice of sending work overseas, particularly to countries where labour is cheaper. The main destination for IS/IT offshoring is India: Infosys and Tata Consultancy Services are major players and Bangalore is the main centre. A large organization might offshore its software development or, if projects are outsourced, the outsourcing agencies might offshore some of their workload. Some companies offshore some of their customer IT support – Dell is one example of this.

in-sourcing: taking work back in-house after ending an outsourcing arrangement.

Sometimes IS/IT work that has been outsourced can be taken back in-house – a practice known as **in-sourcing**. This may take place at the end of an outsourcing contract, because an outsourcing contract has proved unsatisfactory or because technological change has made an in-house operation more practical or economical than it once was. As has already been explained, ending an outsourcing arrangement is difficult since much of the knowledge and expertise about the function has, effectively, been transferred to the outsourcing supplier.

Themes
Security

Outsourcing IS/IT means handing access to and/or control of the organization's processing and data to a third party. Any outsourcing agreement needs to include provision for confidentiality and security. Issues that need to be covered include:

- Data security: Proper provision needs to be made by the outsourcing agency for data protection and data backup.
- Data privacy: The organization's data needs to be protected against disclosure to competitors and into the public domain.
- Process privacy: The organization's proprietary software embodies processes that can be significant to its competitive advantage; these need to be protected from disclosure.

- Contract termination: The organization needs to have guarantees that it will have access to its data and proprietary software at the end (planned or premature) of the outsourcing contract.

It may be that a professional outsourcing agency has better privacy and security provisions than the organization that is doing the outsourcing. Nonetheless, security risks need to be covered in the contract. The outsourcing agency might also be under contract to competitors, which raises intellectual property issues.

The UK Government is an extensive user of IT outsourcing – this includes sensitive data such as personal tax data (see the **HMRC IS/IT Outsourcing case study**). Provision must be made for the privacy of this data.

Some of the most dramatic outsourcing agreements have been with the UK Government (see the **HMRC IS/IT Outsourcing case study**). Most or all UK Government departments have outsourced all their IS/IT provision. Outsourcing has been put out to competitive tender, with cost being the main criteria for acceptance of the tender. The tender has included the transfer of all computing equipment and IT staff to the outsourcing agency – the contractor pays an initial lump sum to the government for the facilities that have been transferred. Outsourcing can be an issue for the staff that are transferred to the outsourcing agency, but their conditions of employment are protected by the Transfer of Undertakings (Protection of Employment) Regulations. Transferred IS/IT staff can also find they have new improved career opportunities in the outsourcing agency. The outsourcing contracts are for a fixed term and are re-tendered at the end of the period. It is true that the existing contractor has the advantage of expertise in the user's requirements; nonetheless, some of the contracts have been successfully switched to other suppliers.

> **Case study**
> **HMRC IS/IT outsourcing**
>
> Her Majesty's Revenue and Customs is a merger of the Inland Revenue and Customs and Excise Departments – as with any merger, each component has a separate IS/IT infrastructure and there is frequently a case for rationalization.
>
> In 2003 Capgemini signed a contract for the so-called Aspire outsourcing contract. The Aspire project was designed to modernize and rationalize IT services and to save money. The contract replaced previous outsourcing agencies including EDS and Accenture.
>
> One part of the project was the introduction of the new PAYE tax system (NPS). The system is employee-based as opposed to the old system where the data model focused on the employer and the data was spread across 12 separate databases (Ritter, 2010). This gives the tax inspector a single view of all an individual's various employments – an approach that is more appropriate to modern-day working practices, where people often change jobs and/or have more than one job. The new system, as is often the case, created a number of anomalies and provoked quite a lot of public criticism (Computing, 2011)
>
> The Aspire contract has been extended and modified over time – it now runs to 2017. It has included extra work but has also made cost savings. HMRC has also taken over responsibility for Aspire subcontractors from Capgemini with the intention of introducing more competition. Spending on Aspire in 2010/11 was £765m (Hitchcock, 2012).

Further reading

Books and papers recommended for further reading are:

Boddy, D., Boonstra, A. and Kennedy, G. (2009) *Managing Information Systems: Strategy and Organization*, 3rd. ed., Prentice Hall, Harlow.

Beynon-Davies, P. (2009) *Child Support Agency and the CS2 Information System* (case 25), Palgrave Macmillan, http://www.palgrave.com/business/beynon-daviesbis/students/casestudies.html.

Willcocks, L. P., Cullen, S. and Craig, A. (2011) *The Outsourcing Enterprise: From Cost Management to Collaborative Innovation*, Palgrave Macmillan, Basingstoke (e-Book).

Comprehension test

This is a short, simple test to enable you to check you have absorbed the material presented in *Chapter 3*.

Q1 Which of the following acronyms is used for the head of the IS department (and while you are sorting this out, check what the letters stand for)?

a. CEO ☐

b. CIO ☐

c. PA ☐

d. VC ☐

Q2 The (main) role of the business analyst in the IS department is to:

a. Analyse competitors to establish benchmarks and 'best of breed' comparators ☐

b. Examine the strategic development of IS/IT within the organization ☐

c. Research suppliers of outsourced IT services ☐

d. Examine the cash flow of the organization ☐

Q3 Projects teams are set up to:

a. Develop new Information Systems ☐

b. Operate and maintain the organization's servers and mainframes ☐

c. Provide support for users of IS and IT services ☐

d. Design the organization's databases ☐

Q4 The project team must talk to the users and determine the user requirements – this task is the responsibility of:

a. The database designers ☐

b. The system analysts ☐

c. The programmers ☐

d. The system testers ☐

Q5 Outsourcing to an overseas supplier is called:

a. Overseas outsourcing ☐

b. Off-shoring ☐

c. Exsourcing ☐

d. Oversourcing ☐

Exercises

The following exercises are designed to aid your understanding of the material presented in this chapter. They can be used for self-study or selected exercises can be used for tutorial discussion.

1 **Comprehension** Check out the IS/IT department in your university or college (the university website will contain helpful information). Draw a structure chart for the university IS/IT department.

2 **Discussion** In a group, look up on the web for a company that has outsourced (or off-shored) its IS/IT department. See if you can add to or qualify the advantages and disadvantages of outsourcing listed in this chapter. Discuss with other groups in your class the similarities and differences between IS/IT outsourcing in different countries.

3 **Discussion** The default model is for an organization to have a central IS/IT department. An alternative approach is to decentralize responsibility to the departments/divisions of the organization (as is the case in the *MMU case study*). Assess and discuss the advantages and disadvantages of decentralized, as opposed to centralized, IS/IT provision.

4 **Assignment** Prepare a (draft) business case for outsourcing the technical and user support for your university student computer labs. The case should be concise (a single sheet of paper – but it should look business-like, so fill up that sheet). If the support is already outsourced then make the case to in-source it (and don't be too critical of your existing technicians – remember, they could well have complaints about their users).

PART 2 INFORMATION SYSTEMS IN BUSINESS

This section looks at the business use of Information Systems. The application of IS and IT in organizations is both widespread and diverse and it would not be sensible or realistic to attempt to catalogue all their uses. The aim is therefore to give a number of examples that will help the reader acquire an overall impression of the scope, nature and importance of IS and IT. There is a bias in the examples towards large organizations; the reader is less likely to be familiar with these applications of IS than with the use of PC desktop packages.

Two applications that have longstanding and widespread use in business are payroll and order processing. These business systems consist of a number of subsystems and the system designer needs to tailor the system design to meet the circumstances and requirements of each organization. Payroll and order processing are examined in *Chapter 4*.

A more recent development in IS is the use of the internet to extend access to stakeholders out in the business environment. Many of these internet-enabled applications can be classified as e-Commerce. We examine the three e-Commerce technologies: electronic data interchange (EDI), e-Shop systems and e-Markets. e-Commerce systems and e-Commerce technologies are the subject of *Chapter 5*.

4   CORPORATE SYSTEMS

Summary

The main Information Systems used by medium and large organizations are an essential part of their business processes. They may be developed *in-house*, bought in as a package system, or the processing can be outsourced to a third party. To illustrate the nature of such systems this chapter looks at two widely used systems types:

- Payroll: All organizations have to pay their staff, but many outsource the function to a specialist bureau. The organization has to update the standing data for the payroll system: details of the staff, rates of pay and any variances that apply that week or month. Once all the data is updated the payroll can be run, producing the payment and payslip for the staff while also calculating pensions, tax and national insurance. To pay a large number of staff, reliably and on time, requires a well-designed and efficiently run system.

- Order processing: Many organizations have significant order processing functions. At the retail end of the supply chain the business has to order in stock to put into its shop. Further down the supply chain, organizations both take in orders from their customers and send out replenishment orders to their suppliers. The order processing system has to hold data on the products and normally on customers and suppliers. The system processes incoming orders to produce picking lists, delivery notes and invoices. On the replenishment side, it issues replenishment orders and then processes goods-in and invoices.

Payroll and order processing are just two of the systems that an organization might use – they have been selected to illustrate the nature of Information Systems, their complexity and some of the issues that arise when such systems are designed.

Learning outcomes

Having read this chapter and completed the exercises, you should:

- Appreciate the complexity of Corporate Information Systems and the divisions of those systems into subsystems
- Understand the interaction of staff with the Information Systems and that the system must be designed to produce an effective business process
- Appreciate the way systems analysts have to think about the stakeholder requirements when designing a system.

The chapter is based on two examples: a payroll and an order processing system. Students need to understand the workings of these systems and how they can be applied in different business contexts.

© graja/Fotolia

Key terms	Payroll, order processing, standing data, transactions, electronic funds transfer (EFT), stock control, replenishment, enterprise resource planning (ERP) system.

Corporate systems

The extensive use of Information Systems by organizations was discussed in *Part 1*. In particular, the ***Supermarket case study*** illustrated the extensive investment made in IS and IT by large organizations and how the use of computer systems affected the organization at all levels. This chapter follows on from that to look at some of those business systems in more detail. The systems chosen are **payroll** and **order processing**.

payroll: an Information System that calculates and pays the wages/salaries of the staff of the organization.

order processing: an Information System that processes customer orders, allocates stock and arranges delivery, invoicing and payment.

The systems are illustrated by using a dataflow diagram (DFD) and, for order processing, an entity relationship diagram (ERD) – two of the diagrams used in systems analysis and design. Note that in the DFD:

- The ellipses are externals – usually someone who interacts with the system, such as the personnel office staff.
- The boxes are processes – where the tasks are performed, for instance to maintain the salary file with details of any pay increases.
- The open ended boxes are datastores – we can see them as files in the context of the use of DFDs in this chapter, such as the salary file.

See the example in *Figure 4.1*; these techniques are discussed in more detail in *Part 4*.

Figure 4.1 Sample DFD.

There are several intentions in describing these systems. These include:

- Demonstrating the complexity of the overall Information System and the subsystems that are used within that system
- Showing the way that IT systems and human systems interact and work together
- Illustrating the way that systems analysts have to think about user requirements when designing a system.

The reader is asked to bear these points in mind when reading the case study and to use their imagination to fill out the picture that the author is attempting to create. Note that these systems are large and complex; to develop any of these systems, for a large organization, would be a multi-million investment.

Payroll

All organizations have to pay their staff and the norm is to use a computerized payroll system. The running of the payroll does not *add value* – it is just a function that has to be fulfilled. Organizations can buy in payroll software or outsource the job to a specialist bureau.

Themes
Outsourcing

The running of the payroll is a necessary function, but it is not a strategic system – there is no competitive advantage to be gained by running the payroll in-house. To use business jargon, it is mission-critical but not a core competency.

Outsourcing the payroll removes the need to employ specialist staff and to keep up to date with changing regulations and tax requirements – it is the job of the payroll provider to look after all these aspects, and, if necessary, to spread the costs over a number of customers. Outsourced payroll services will:

- Accept data input in a form that suits the customer
- Deliver sealed payslips to the customer's premises
- Manage payments via the BACS electronic payments system (the electronic payments are sent to BACS, which then makes the transfer to each employee's personal bank account)

- Manage end-of-year tax returns with electronic submission to HMRC
- Provide management information to the customer's HR and accounts functions.

Many organizations outsource their payrolls. Outsourcing providers tailor their services to meet the needs of small, medium and large organizations. Options range from outsourcing the whole payroll function to having in-house online control of the outsourced payroll system. One of the big suppliers of outsourced payroll services claims to produce over one million payslips a month.

An alternative to outsourcing the payroll is to buy ready written payroll software from a supplier that will, as part of the software maintenance agreement, update the software in line with any legal and taxation changes. Some organizations that have outsourced their payroll are now choosing this route and in-sourcing the function.

---

standing data: data held in an Information System that is relatively constant over time and is used as reference data during the processing of transactions.

transactions: a business document (possibly electronic) that is input to an Information System and processed to produce a business result.

The main processes involved in running the payroll are shown in *Figure 4.2*. The processes can be grouped into those processing **standing data** (processes 1–3) and those processing the payroll **transactions**, the payroll calculation (process 4) and payment and reporting (processes 5–8). The processes and their implications are described in more detail below.

Payroll standing data

The first three processes (Process 01, 02 and 03) are concerned with maintaining the data on the people to be paid and the rates they are to be paid. This information has to be supplied by the personnel department. It is updated during the period (week or month) before the payroll is run. It is useful if the personnel department has terminal access to the system; this makes it possible to implement last-minute changes should this prove to be necessary. For example, if a new member of staff joins part way through the month it is helpful if they can be entered onto the system in time for the payroll so that they get paid for the work that they have done. The three main standing data functions are:

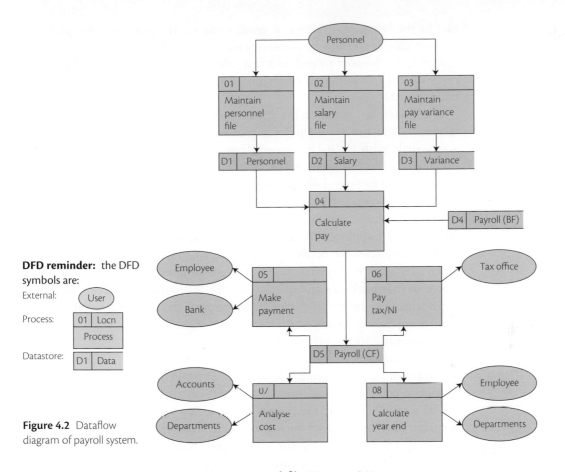

2

DFD reminder: the DFD symbols are:

External:　User

Process:　01 | Locn
Process

Datastore:　D1 | Data

Figure 4.2 Dataflow diagram of payroll system.

- Maintain personnel file (Process 01):

  The payroll needs a data file of all the people who are to be paid; we will call it Personnel (D1). For each person the file has to contain:

  - The payroll number, NI (national insurance) number, name, office location and address
  - The salary grade code (see salary file) and tax code (supplied by HMRC)
  - Details of any other deductions, such as for a pension scheme, charitable donations and court orders.

  The personnel data can be added (for a new employee), updated (where the details of an existing employee change) or logically deleted (when a person leaves – the personnel record will be marked as deleted but retained on file to calculate the last period's pay, the P45 tax details and deal with any queries that subsequently arise). The data must be as accurate and up to date as possible – the system can help with this by including comprehensive validation to make sure that no invalid data is entered into the system (the system cannot stop incorrect data but it can prevent invalid data being accepted).

- Maintain salary file (Process 02):

  Some organizations pay each employee an individually agreed salary; some allocate each member of staff to a grade and then pay them in accordance with the salary scale for that grade. For the former requirement, the individual's salary is included on the personnel file and there is no need for a salary file. In the latter case there is a grade code on the personnel file and that corresponds to an entry on the salary file – where there are large numbers of staff it is much easier to update a few salary scales than the individual wage rates for each of hundreds of members of staff. The salary file is shown as datastore D2.

The salary file contains the grade code – for example, lecturer, senior lecturer – and the rate of pay for that grade code. For some jobs there is a pay scale with annual increments for the grade, and where that applies the pay scale has to be stored. Accessing the pay scale needs to be thought about – if the personnel file contains the grade and point on the scale then it will have to be updated each year; if it contains the grade plus the date and point at which the person joined the pay scale then the system can calculate which point is applicable when the payroll is run.

The salary scale file needs to be updated to contain the latest salary scale when new rates of pay are agreed. It needs also to contain previous salary scales so that back-pay and queries can be dealt with. The salary scales for a grade need to be set up with a start date and the system calculates which scale is applicable for any particular run.

- Maintain variance data (Process 03):

The final element of standing data is the variance data – datastore D3. Variances are one-off changes to be applied to the current payroll run (and as such, it could be argued, are not properly classified as standing data).

The sort of things that variances are used for is overtime, sick leave and bonuses. This data is input during the current period and then applied at the end of that period's payroll run – there will be a fresh set of variances for the next period. Some organizations will have a lot of variances, for instance where there is a lot of overtime or salespeople are paid a commission. Other organizations, such as universities, would have not very many transactions on the variance file.

Payroll calculation

At a given time, as near to the end of the period as possible (but leaving some time for recovery if anything goes wrong) the payroll calculation is run. The payroll staff have been busy updating personnel details, variances and, if necessary, the salary scales – that is, in many ways, the end of their task. Once the payroll commences there is no more intervention required – the system takes over.

The payroll calculation is Process 04 on the diagram. It can be seen as having two parts:

- Calculate gross pay: To calculate an employee's gross pay we need to get that person's details from the personnel file (D1); look up the pay scale that corresponds to their grade code on the salary file (D2) and find any variances that apply to the individual on the pay variance file (D3). The gross pay is then the required proportion of the salary (one week's or one month's) plus or minus any variances. This is simple in principle but more complex when all the exceptions and variations are taken into account.

● Calculate net pay: Following on from the gross pay calculation, taxes and national insurance are deducted to calculate the net pay – the money the employee is actually going to get. Taxes have to be calculated using the individual's tax code. The first calculation is tax for the financial year to date. The tax payable this month is the tax for the financial year to date minus the tax already paid up to the end of the previous month (a bit complex, but it works). To achieve this we have to read in last month's payroll details (datastore D4 on the diagram) and find the brought forward (BF) payroll details for the person we are looking at.

After the pay calculation we format a new payroll record and write it to a carry forward (CF) payroll file (datastore D5 on the diagram). The carry forward payroll details are used for payment and reporting in the next stage of the processing and are also the input to the net pay calculation in the payroll run for the next period.

To achieve this matching of one person's details from several different files we must pay attention to the file structures. If, for example, we have the personnel (D1), variance (D3) and payroll (D4/5) files in the same order (presumably the payroll number order) then the details for the next employee will normally be the next record on each of these files. The pay calculation is *controlled* by the personnel file – we start with the first person on that file and then just process each person until we reach the end of that file.

Payment and reporting

Having calculated the payroll we now must pay the staff. Payment can be made by cash, cheque or electronically, direct into the employee's bank account – the last of these three is now the normal option. To make the payment we must read the payroll CF file (D5) and format an electronic cheque. The details of each employee's bank are on the personnel file and, in our example, have been replicated on the payroll file. In the UK, the electronic cheques are made out for each employee and sent to BACS, an electronic funds transfer (EFT) system that transfers the money to the appropriate bank account for each employee (other countries have similar EFT systems).

electronic funds transfer (EFT): networked systems that transfer funds between bank accounts (typically in separate banks), for example BACS, SWIFT and CHAPS.

As well as paying employees, each person receives a payslip detailing the gross pay, deductions and net pay for the period (see *Figure 4.3*).

Payslip		This month	Year to date
John Doe Date: 31/05/2013 NI: AB 12 34 56 C	Gross pay	3,891.33	7,602.96
	Pension	249.04	486.49
	AVCs	0.00	0.00
	Taxable pay	3,642.29	7,116.47
	Tax	751.07	1,434.53
	NI	313.27	622.94
	SSP	0.00	0.00
Office code: Man634C	Total deductions	1,313.38	
	Net pay	2,577.95	

Figure 4.3 Sample payslip.

This detail can again be taken from the payroll CF file (D5). Some care is needed in designing the system for such a print run. The issues include:

- Confidentiality: The payslip is confidential and has to be packaged in an envelope. For a large payroll the process for stuffing the envelopes will need to be mechanized. Alternatives are special stationery that will fold up into an envelope or that is chemically treated, or three-part paper where the confidential details appear only on the second of the three sheets.
- Print crashes: Printers are not the most reliable pieces of kit and they can be even more problematic when continuous pre-printed or multipart stationery is used. For a large payroll it is advisable to have a re-start mechanism programmed in so the print run can be restarted from the last good payslip produced (as opposed to having to restart the print run from the beginning). Where pre-printed stationery is used there will also have to be test prints to ensure that the print is correctly lined up in the right place on the form.

A recent innovation is to make the payslip electronic so that employees can access their own payslips online. This bypasses any printing issues, but means that appropriate privacy controls would need to be set up.

Themes
Usability

The payslips have to be despatched to the various offices within the organization and distributed to the staff. If they are printed in pay number order they will have to be hand sorted which takes time. It is much more efficient and user friendly to sort the payroll file by office location before the payslips are printed.

The making of payment and the printing of the payslips are shown as Process 05. Further tasks that need to be performed using the brought forward payroll file include:

- Paying tax and NI (Process 06): The organization is responsible for the deduction of tax and national insurance from the pay of its permanent employees. In the UK, these deductions then have to be paid and accounted for to HMRC, the government's tax collection department (from large organizations the HMRC takes electronic payments and an electronic exchange of information).
- Cost analysis (Process 07): The organization will require management and financial information from the payroll. The information required will depend on the organization – an obvious requirement is the staff costing per division or department so that this can be fed into the analysis of that department's financial performance. Further reports will be required, perhaps particularly at the end of the year or when there is a wages negotiation taking place. Often it is useful to sort the data file for reports – if the requirement is for departmental totals then we can sort the file into department code order and then analyse the pay for each department in turn.
- Calculate year end (Process 08): At the end of the financial year every employee (UK employees) has to get a P60 form specifying pay and tax totals for the year (year-end data is submitted to the HMRC on a P11D

form – the submission can be electronic). The system will also perform some sort of archive of this year's final payroll file before the system starts again with zero year-to-date pay figures for the new financial year. There are also likely to be further year-end management information reporting requirements (both for the financial year and possibly for the company's own end of year).

The system described here is just an outline of what a payroll system needs to do. Each organization that runs a payroll will have a system configured for its own needs, but the general principles of the system will be similar to those described above.

The payroll is unusual, for a business IS, in the way it has to run. The focus of the system is on a single run at the end of the week or month. Prior to the run the standing data is updated by the personnel/payroll department, but the actual payroll run and subsequent prints are just a big batch job requiring no user intervention. The data structures have to facilitate both online access (to update the standing data) and efficient batch running – not an easy trick to pull off. This is further discussed in *Part 3*.

2

Order processing

stock control: an Information System that ensures that an appropriate quantity of product is available where required, e.g. in the warehouse.

replenishment: an Information System for ordering new (replacement) stock. The system produces a replenishment order and also processes goods-in and payments.

Wherever goods are traded the organization involved needs an order processing and stock control system. Once the order arrives at the supplier the organization has to process that order and then, in turn, replenish its stock by making more product or ordering in fresh supplies (see also Porter's Value Chain discussed in *Chapter 2*).

Order processing systems are used by retailers, wholesalers, manufacturers and other organizations for purchasing secondary supplies. The order processing system may be integrated into the whole IS infrastructure of the organization or it may be a more modest, freestanding system. For medium and large organizations the system is computerized – for a small shop it may be entirely manual, almost intuitive, although the principles are the same.

The order processing system can be split into three major subsystems (see *Figure 4.4*):

- Process customer order
- Process replenishment order
- Maintain standing data.

The process customer order subsystem corresponds to the outbound logistics activity in Porter's Value Chain and the process replenishment order to Porter's inbound logistics. The *Supermarket case study* in *Chapter 1* includes the requirement for a replenishment system as the supermarket orders new supplies for its regional warehouses. The retail side of the supermarket is not an order processing system – except for the e-Shop where the customer's order is taken online.

The standing data is applicable to both the customer order and the replenishment order subsystems, and that is where we will start.

DFD reminder: the DFD symbols are:

External:

Process:

Datastore:

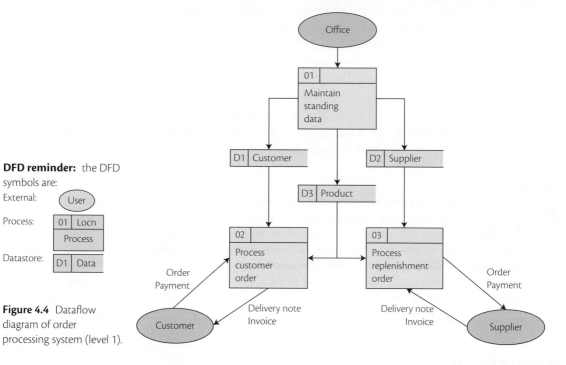

Figure 4.4 Dataflow diagram of order processing system (level 1).

Order processing – standing data

To use an order processing IS we must have a file of product/stock data. In addition, in order to process customer orders we may well need a customer file and for replenishment orders we will require a computerized list of suppliers. There is a second level, more detailed, dataflow diagram for this subsystem, shown at *Figure 4.5*.

For each product that is made, bought or sold we need product/stock data. On a computer system we require a unique code for every record, and for the product that will be some sort of product code. For grocery and general merchandise there is the EAN/UPC code (also used as the barcode: see *Chapter 1*) – for other products the firm may have to invent its own product codes.

In addition to the product code there will be:

- Product description and possibly other product data
- Price information
- Stock totals
- Warehouse information.

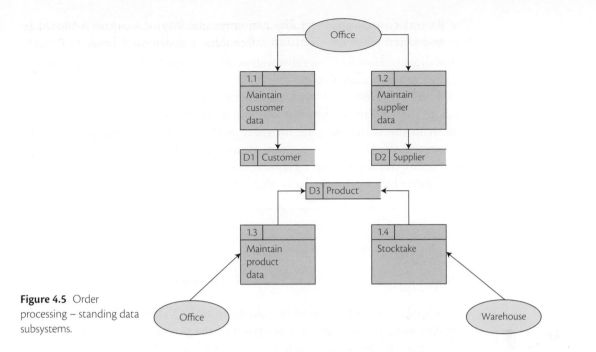

Figure 4.5 Order processing – standing data subsystems.

For a small order processing system the information may be fairly minimal, but for more complex systems there may be many data items for each product. Examples of some of the complexities involved are:

- The basic price data are the purchase price and the selling price. Prices may, however, vary with the quantity supplied and according to specific customers or classes of customers (the variations may be special prices or percentage discounts). Additionally, prices will change over time and the invoicing and accounting systems need records of past prices. All this information can add up to a complex structure which has to be maintained – organizations need to balance the enthusiasm of their sales staff for special deals against the effort of keeping a complex price structure in good working order.
- Stock totals, on the face of it, seem quite simple – if we have 200 cans of beans and we expect to sell 400 in the next period we had better order some more. In reality it is (or can be) more complex. Stock totals that we may wish to maintain for each stock item include:
  - Free stock: The stock that is available for allocation to any new orders
  - Allocated stock: Stock that has been allocated to orders but is still on the shelves, or in the bin, awaiting picking and despatch
  - Backorder stock: When stock runs out we may *backorder*, that is, place orders that are saved up until fresh stock arrives. The backorder stock total is in effect negative free stock – it is the stock we need to fulfil outstanding orders
  - On-order stock: The quantity of replenishment stock that has been ordered but not yet delivered
  - Re-order stock level: The stock level at which new stock must be re-ordered (if it takes one week for fresh stock to arrive then the re-order level should/could be the maximum normal weekly demand)

■ Re-order stock quantity: The minimum quantity of stock that should be re-ordered when the free stock falls to the re-order stock level.

If the organization has several warehouses there must be several stock totals for each of those warehouses.

The art (or science) of stock management/stock control is to have enough stock to meet all the orders that come in without having large quantities that just sit in the warehouse, tie up space and capital and possibly, eventually, get written off. Using the above stock quantities we can calculate replenishment needs (see for example *Figure 4.6* – not the most sophisticated of stock calculations but it gives the basic idea).

<table>
<tr><td>if</td><td>re-order-stock-level > free-stock – backorder-stock + on-order-stock</td></tr>
<tr><td>then</td><td>re-order-quantity = re-order-stock-quantity + re-order-stock-level –
(free-stock – backorder-stock + on-order-stock)</td></tr>
<tr><td>else</td><td>no action.</td></tr>
</table>

Figure 4.6 Order processing – replenishment calculation.

● e-Shop data: If goods are to be sold in an e-Shop there will also have to be one or more pictures and a description of the product. Extensive additional data may also be needed, such as customer reviews. Note: for a large e-Shop the product data will be held on file (a database) and the webpages are generated *on-the-fly* as they are requested.

The product file is shown on *Figure 4.5* as datastore D3.

Where orders are taken from trade customers and payment is on invoice or statement we would need a customer file. Each customer is allocated a customer number and there will also be details such as name, address, credit limit and contact details held for each customer. Having a customer file reduces the amount of data that has to be handled each time an order is placed – typing in the customer number accesses all the other customer detail. Arguably more significant is the fact that a customer file allows a check to be kept on customer credit – customers may be accepted onto the books only after their credit record has been checked; they will be supplied with goods only if they are reasonably reliable with their payments.

For a large system, customer details will be complex. Among the additional data that may be held are:

● Delivery information: Some customers will have a number of sites and will wish to specify the address where the goods are to be delivered. Each site can be a separate delivery point with its own delivery point code and address.

● Billing information: Some customers will want goods delivered to one address but the invoice sent to the head office – or possibly one of several different offices where the various accounts are administered. Each office can be a separate invoice point with its own invoice point code and address.

In addition to customer files held for business-to-business systems, customer details may also be held for retail customers, particularly by online or catalogue operators. Where the goods are paid for prior to despatch there is no need to check on the customer's credit status, but the details may still be used for despatch and for promotional purposes. The customer file is shown as datastore D1.

The third major category of standing data is supplier data. If the order processing system includes replenishment, then the system needs to know the supplier for each product, the contact details for that supplier and possibly further details as well. The supplier file is shown as datastore D2.

Each of these three categories of standing data has to be maintained. New products, customers and suppliers have to be put up, existing details have to be updated and redundant records are marked as out of use (we cannot normally delete the details as they are required for orders still in the system and for accountancy and audit purposes).

A final area of maintenance is the stocktake. If everyone uses the computer system properly the stock figures should remain accurate (if you have an order processing/stock control system and bypass it for certain transactions you end up in a real mess). However, over time, discrepancies can develop between theoretical stock (the count on the system) and actual stock (the stock in the bin or on the shelves), and these discrepancies need rectifying. To make sure that the stock totals are accurate it is normal to do a stocktake – once a year, once a quarter or some other continuous system (because the business cannot afford to stop operating while the stocktake is done). Stocktake requires that the actual stock is manually counted and then the stocktake count is reconciled with the theoretical stock totals held on the system. Any discrepancies have to be investigated, accounted for and the theoretical stock totals updated to the actual stock totals.

Themes
Competitive advantage

For most suppliers, competitive advantage is (conceptually) simple – it is just about providing excellent service (at the right price), and the order processing system has a vital part to play in that.

Crucial to service quality is stock availability. The warehouse must have enough stock for orders that might come in without there being excess stock taking up space and costing money. The system needs to work on a just-in-time/quick-response basis, for which the stock replenishment calculations are crucial.

Supply is also dependent on the rest of the supply chain, and organizations must be constantly vigilant to ensure that their suppliers have the same standard of performance as they seek to offer to their customers.

Process customer order

Process customer order breaks down into five major steps (some of which may not be used in a direct selling retail system). The steps are:

- Enter and allocate order
- Print picking list
- Confirm pick and despatch
- Invoice
- Receive payment.

See *Figure 4.7.* We will consider these in more detail below:

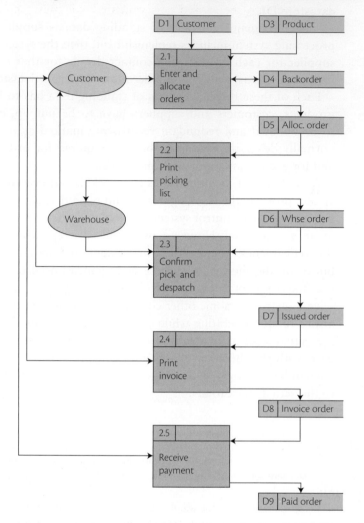

Figure 4.7 Order processing – process customer order.

The first step is to enter and allocate orders (Process 2.1). If the orders come in on paper we will need order entry clerks to type the orders into a form on the screen – a simple enough task but one that takes time and adds to costs. We also need procedures to follow if there are any errors on the order form or the goods are not available in stock. Alternative ways of receiving orders are:

- Telephone orders: The customer rings in and the order is typed in while the customer is on the phone. With the customer on the phone we can sort out any misunderstandings, and any problems with stock availability can be discussed – the customer may accept an alternative product (for example, printer ink cartridges from an alternative supplier if the ones from the printer manufacturer are out of stock).
- e-Orders: Orders from an e-Shop or the customer's replenishment system (see *e-Order processing* below).

As the order is entered into the system it is allocated a unique, computer-generated order code (it may be that the customer also had an order number but that could duplicate with codes from other customers). As the order is entered into the system it is validated – it must be in the correct format (primary validation) and it must cross-check with the standing data on the system. These cross-checks (secondary validation) include:

- Customer: The system reads the customer data and checks that the customer code is valid, that it exists on the system and that the customer is still one the firm wishes to do business with.
- Product: For each product (order line) on the order we must read the product data and check that it is a valid product code and one we are still selling. If the customer is on the phone we can read back the product name, which gives a further check against any mistakes.

Having read the product data for each product we can proceed to allocate stock. If there is sufficient stock available we subtract the order quantity from the free stock total and add the quantity to the allocated stock total. If there is not sufficient stock we can backorder the product – this means holding the order until there is stock available (see datastore D4) and adding the order quantity to the backorder total. A complication arises if an order has some order lines that can be fulfilled and some which have to be backordered – in which case, do we backorder the whole order or split the order with some of it being backordered and some being fulfilled in the normal timeframe? (The same sort of issue will also arise if we have some stock but not the full order line amount.)

Some time after the order is entered and allocated the picking process begins (Process 2.2). For the warehouse to pick the goods the system needs to add the warehouse location information to the order line data and produce a picking list (the basic picking list is a piece of paper that lists the product code, quantity and warehouse location – it is the document that the warehouse worker uses). At its simplest, there is a picking list for each order and the warehouse staff wander around the warehouse, find the goods, pack them in a box and label it for despatch. That said, warehouses are often large and the products can be of disparate size and weight. Warehouse systems are often complex in order to cope with these parameters and to achieve efficiency – some warehouses are largely automated. Warehouses adopt a variety of solutions; some of the requirements and variations are explored below:

- Organizing the warehouse

  The warehouse needs to be carefully organized to promote efficiency, to minimize the time and effort that it takes to add new stock into the shelves, racks or bins and to balance that with the efficiency of picking the products from their location for despatch. It may be that the products are heavy and/or bulky – this will require goods handling equipment (some form of forklift truck) and probably pallets. Some organizations have a mixture of large, bulky items and small items and may need to segment the warehouse so that each classification of goods can be appropriately racked and handled. Some organizations take in bulk supplies and break packs down into small quantities for despatch. This may require a bulk storage area and a separate picking area that is kept supplied from the bulk storage area. Most organizations will have a fixed location for each product, but in some the storage space will be allocated dynamically by the system when fresh supplies are delivered to the warehouse.

- Printing the picking list

  The picking list is traditionally just what it says it is – a simple list of products, quantities and warehouse locations – the information that the warehouse operative needs to do the job. For some warehouses the picking list is printed as a series of sticky labels that can be attached to the product as it is picked – the label could include a barcode for automated sorting of the product in goods-out. In some cases the picking requirement will be displayed on a small screen on the forklift truck, in a picking bay or on a hand-held device. The *full monty* is an automated picking system with no need for a picker or a picking list – but obviously the robot picking equipment needs the same sort of picking data.

- Consolidating the pick

  Picking each order individually is not necessarily the most efficient way to proceed – particularly if the warehouse is large and it takes several minutes to move from one location to the next. This problem can be eased by sorting the pick lists so that staff can move around the warehouse in the most efficient sequence. It may be more efficient to split the orders by warehouse area and to consolidate a number of picking lists together (e.g. the picker walks round once with a list of 100 products for 20 orders as opposed to 20 times with individual orders). The downside is then sorting the product out into the individual orders (but automation may take care of that).

- Despatch

  Once the goods are picked they have to be packed and despatched. At its simplest the warehouse worker carries a cardboard box and packs the goods as they are picked – possibly the system can calculate the size of box that is needed for the order and print labels for the box at the same time as the picking list is produced. Some warehouses have standard size containers for picking; these are placed onto a moving belt system that can sort the boxes for the appropriate goods-out bay – some shops use this sort of system in their regional depots. Other warehouses may need to do the packing after the picking – this can range from wrapping up a couple of books to shrink wrapping pallets of bulk groceries or machine parts.

Picking and despatch are ideally one step. On occasion there will be a problem with the pick – the stock that the system thought was available cannot be found or is damaged, and then the system needs to be updated to show what has actually been despatched rather than what the system thought should have been despatched. Thus it is arguably necessary to have an additional step that confirms that the pick is completed and the actual quantities sent. The procedures to be adopted need to be as quick as possible – unless problems occur the confirmation step is a waste of time. The process of confirming the pick (Process 2.3) could just consist of typing in the identity number of the picking list with additional procedures if exceptions have occurred. Where the picking details are displayed on a hand-held device then confirmation/exceptions can be dealt with as the picking takes place.

As well as picking documentation we will need a despatch note – a form sent out with the goods to tell the customer what is in the consignment. This could be printed with the picking list (the one document could serve both purposes). It would seem to be better to print it out after the pick has been confirmed and any amendments have been made. The problem with printing the despatch note separately is that it then has to be married up with the consignment – a tad messy, and more decisions for the system designers.

Once the goods have been sent we can invoice the customer (Process 2.4). Invoicing practice tends to be dependent on the traditions of the business sector. The invoice may be sent with the goods, despatched by post or be sent at the end of the month (for all orders from that customer in the month). Some trade sectors send an invoice for each order and then a statement at the end of each month – the invoice is ignored and payment is made in respect of the statement. Whichever procedure is adopted the system has to have a process for printing the invoices. It is a fairly simple batch process but needs to include procedures for reminder invoices that are sent to late payers.

The final step on the customer orders side is to process payments (Process 2.5). As payments arrive we have to identify which invoices the payment is for and mark those invoices as paid (this is not as easy as it sounds if the customer is paying for part of the invoice and disputing the remainder – or simply misquotes the invoice/statement reference). Once the invoice is paid, that is the end of the story; but we keep the data available for management information and accounting (see Order processing management information subsection below). If payment is not received within reasonable time we have to send a reminder invoice or, if payment is still not forthcoming, stop further orders for that customer.

This outline of processing customer orders covers the basic processing and some of the possible complications. To keep the complexity in bounds we have omitted mention of process re-engineering developments such as e-Commerce and self-invoicing – some of these developments are outlined in the e-Order processing subsection below.

Process replenishment order

Processing replenishment orders is very much the mirror image of processing customer orders. The customer orders outlined above, very probably, came from the buyer's replenishment system. Equally, the organization that processes customer orders can have its own replenishment system for buying in new stock to replace the goods that have been sent out to customers – see, for example, the supply chain models in *Chapter 2*. The data flow diagram for the replenishment subsystem is shown at *Figure 4.8*. The steps are:

- Calculate replenishment requirements
- Print replenishment order
- Receive goods
- Match invoice
- Make payment.

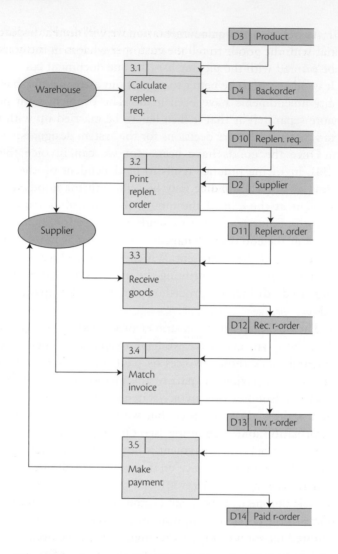

Figure 4.8 Order processing – process replenishment order.

The steps in more detail (but less detail than for order processing) are as follows:

The first step is to decide what to buy (Process 3.1). This may be done in a periodic run, say once a week, where all stock totals on the product file are reviewed and the replenishment decisions are made. Where stock totals are to be kept low and replenishment is fast, the replenishment calculation may be made daily or even as part of the customer order processing as stock is allocated to orders. The frequency of the replenishment decision is a matter of balancing the stock held against the size and frequency of the replenishment order and any discounts that may be available for volume. An example replenishment calculation is shown at *Figure 4.6*.

Once we have decided what we need, we can send out the replenishment orders (Process 3.2). The product data includes the supplier code, so we can access the relevant supplier data – we may well sort the replenishment requirements into a supplier code order so that we can include all the requirements from each supplier on a single order. Replenishment orders can then be printed and sent out or they may be faxed or sent electronically (see the subsection on e-Order Processing).

Once the replenishment order is sent we have to wait for the goods and their delivery documentation to arrive. When the goods do arrive they have to be put into the rack, bin or on the shelf. The physical process of goods-in is accompanied by the administrative process of matching the delivery note to the replenishment order held on the system (Process 3.3) – we need to know what replenishment orders have been received so that we can update free stock, allocate any outstanding backorders, calculate future stock requirements and authorize payment when invoices come in. The process of matching the delivery note will also indicate where the goods are to be stored – particularly if the system works on dynamic allocation of storage space. If the goods are required for immediate despatch, then the merchandise is sent straight from goods-in to goods-out – a procedure known as *cross-docking*.

Some time after the goods arrive there will be an invoice. As with goods-in this is a matching process (Process 3.4). This time we are checking the invoice against the replenishment order and the delivery note. If the goods haven't arrived or were not satisfactory we will not pay. If the goods have arrived we need to mark the order to be paid. Where the supplier issues both invoices and statements, we probably ignore one of these documents (rather a waste of time, but that's business) – arguably we don't need an invoice at all but we will come to self-invoicing later on.

The final step is payment (Process 3.5). It could be that we pay the invoices as they are processed, but, more than likely, we save them up for a weekly or monthly payment run (and then possibly delay them a bit longer so that the money stays in our bank account rather than being with the supplier) – not friendly, particularly for small businesses, but that is the way in which much of business operates.

Two of the processes in this side of the system are matching processes (plus the invoice matching on the customer order side). These are not the most computer-friendly procedures but they are jobs that have to be done – electronic data interchange (EDI) can help a lot with these (see *e-Order Processing* below).

e-Order processing

Most orders printed out from one computer system are typed into another, and the same is true of most of the other documents involved in trade exchanges. Typing in the details from these documents takes time, causes delay, introduces errors – all of which costs money. Using paper to transmit data from one computer system to another does not make a lot of sense – it should be more accurate and efficient to communicate electronically in a business-to-business, e-Commerce transaction using EDI (see *Chapter 5*).

As well as orders generated by a customer order processing system there are orders for secondary supplies, orders from small businesses and orders from retail customers. Many of these orders can now come in from the web and, again, this is part of e-Commerce using an e-Shop type system.

The basic e-Commerce transactions between, on the one hand, the customer's replenishment system (using EDI) and, on the other hand, the e-Shop with the supplier's order processing system are shown in *Figure 4.9*.

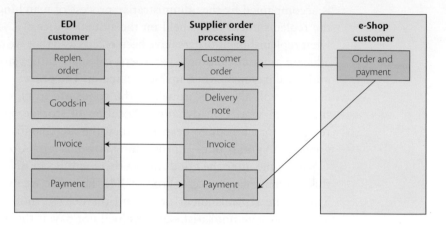

Figure 4.9 e-Order processing – electronic exchanges.

Some of the advantages of e-Order processing are:

- The e-Shop gives the organization a retail outlet with much reduced staff and premises costs. Orders from the e-Shop go straight to the order processing system with no need for data entry.
- Electronic orders from the customer's replenishment system can be processed as quickly as the trading partners want them to be. There are no postal delays, no data entry costs and no transcription errors.
- Electronic delivery notes can be used, which automate the process of matching the delivery to the replenishment order. Yet these do not prove that the physical delivery has taken place – they can be used in conjunction with a barcode labelling system on the delivery cartons.
- Electronic invoices neatly automate the process of matching to the order and the delivery note – the only disadvantage is that you can no longer argue that the invoice must have been lost in the post!
- Electronic payments cut out the chore of writing or printing the cheques. They are the norm for payroll and they are becoming the norm for trade transactions.

A further change that is being introduced in order processing, often in conjunction with EDI, is self-invoicing. The procedure is that the customer pays for what is delivered and the invoice step is abandoned. Ford UK successfully introduced this change for transactions with its component suppliers and reduced the staff involved in supplier payments by over 90 per cent.

The technologies of e-Commerce and its application in e-Business are discussed in more detail in *Chapter 5*. The use of an order processing system in an e-Shop is illustrated in the *Amazon case study*.

Case study
Amazon

Amazon UK runs their fulfilment operations from a gigantic warehouse called Marston Gate near Milton Keynes (with several more warehouses opened, or about to open, in the UK).

The Marston Gate warehouse covers 500,000 sq ft and has three miles of conveyor belts. The warehouse employs about 600 full-time staff and augments that number with temporary staff at peak periods – the numbers can go up to about 2000 during the Christmas period.

Amazon stocks a vast range of diverse products, which makes automation difficult. New stock from goods-in is *shelved* by hand, and the picking is also done by hand. The conveyor system takes product from goods-in to where it is to be stored and also takes items from packing to goods-out for despatch. The IS/IT systems backs up the manual operations – including hand-held computers used by the pickers.

Source: Getty

Stock is stored in seemingly random locations with product categories mixed together – this cuts down on picking mistakes and spreads things out to avoid congestion. For most products there are no more than six items at any one location (and there can be multiple locations for any product).

Pickers use hand-held computers that tell them what to pick and guide them along the shortest route to the nearest storage location for the product they require. Pickers pass items to the packers where the goods are parcelled up and labelled with a barcode.

For despatch, a machine adds the address label, the packet is weighed (for the IS to check that the correct items have been included) and the parcel is sorted into the appropriate postal bin for its final destination. All these despatch processes are automated and controlled by the IS using the barcode data.

Sources include Burkham (2011) and Wallop (2009).

Order processing – management information

A computerized order processing system means that we have a full detailed history of all the products we have bought and sold, back to when the system started. Having all this data means that we can have virtually any management information we want (although it may take a little time to programme the request). Some examples of the management information we may ask for are:

● Sales reports: What has been sold when and to whom. Numerous combinations can be derived. One report could be sales values by month and region for the year to date. A simplified version of such a report can be seen in *Figure 4.10* – the report shows a problem with March sales in the eastern region, something the management would want to follow up.

Dave's data processing supplies
Sales report by region   March 2013

	January	February	March
South	67, 000	68, 000	70, 000
East	246, 000	244, 000	168, 000
North	56, 000	54, 000	58, 000
West	96, 000	103, 000	104, 000
Total	465, 000	469, 000	400, 000

Figure 4.10 Management information – sales report by region.

- Invoicing reports: What invoices are outstanding and for how long; if the total customer debt is increasing or decreasing; if there are any bad debtors that need following up.
- Stock reports: What is the stock turn (how many times do we turn over the stock in a year?) and what is stock availability (how many times do we backorder because we are out of stock?).

These are just a few examples of the sorts of management information we can ask for. The accountants will also be looking for financial information and will use the system to drive the general ledger and other finance systems. Management information is further discussed in *Chapter 7*.

Themes
Security

Management information from the order processing system is dependent on the order data that is accumulated over the months and years – the data needs to be kept secure, with regular backups, so this source of information is not lost.

Data security is important for management information but it is vital for the operational part of the system. The order/replenishment order transactions will be active for a number of weeks from when they are raised until they are paid. The security of that data is vital to the business process. Data backups are the standard way of securing the data – an order processing system would probably require daily backups.

A special data security issue is online data entry, such as telephone orders. Data backup would not secure these as a whole day's worth of orders could be lost before the backup is taken. The system needs a system of data logging and applying the data log to roll forward the database should the system fail – this can be part of the transaction processing (TP monitor) and database (DBMS) software, but it still needs to be properly incorporated in the system design.

Large organizations that take many orders might run duplex systems with *hot standby* (should the operational system fail the second system switches in automatically – all data is duplexed, in real time, on both systems). The large online retailers, for example, cannot afford to have a message on their e-Shop saying 'Sorry, system bust, please try later' – well, not very often.

Order processing – data structures

The data requirements for a system can be shown on an entity relationship diagram (ERD) – this representation helps the systems analyst design the database. The data requirements for a simple order processing system are shown in *Figure 4.11*.

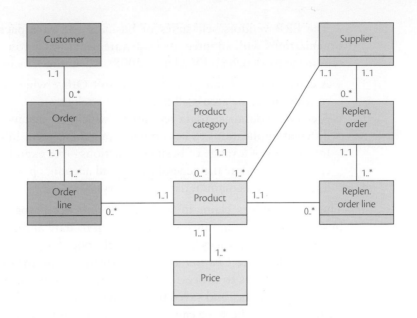

Figure 4.11 Order processing – data structure.

These data requirements can be summarized as follows:

- Each customer will place zero, one or more orders.
- Each order will have one or more order lines (there is an order line for each product ordered).
- Each supplier will receive zero, one or more replenishment orders.
- Each replenishment order will have one or more replenishments order lines (one for each product ordered).
- Each supplier will supply one or more products.
- Each product category will have zero, one or more products.
- Each product will have zero, one or more order lines (on different orders).
- Each product will have one or more prices (keyed on start date).
- Each product will have zero, one or more replenishment order lines (on different replenishment orders).

The order processing system will, in all probability, be implemented using a database management system (see *Chapter 8*) and the structure of the database will be derived from the ERD (see *Chapter 11* for further detail on constructing an ERD).

ERP systems

enterprise resource planning system (ERP): third-party application software that provides organizations with system integration across a range of standard business processes.

An order processing system will not normally be outsourced in the way a payroll might be outsourced (although some organizations might outsource the whole of their warehousing/fulfilment operations, which would include the necessary IS). The appropriate option for this requirement could be to buy in a ready-written order processing software package which would probably be referred to as an **enterprise resource planning system (ERP)** package.

The ERP vendors sell suites of business software packages that provide organizations with an integrated software provision across a range of business requirements (Koch and Wailgum, 2008). Advantages include:

- A consistent *look and feel* (cf. Microsoft Office where the look and feel is roughly the same across all the desktop packages)
- A common database (data repository) which, for instance, allows data from different applications to be combined in management information reports
- Integration of a range of business functions – for example, order processing can readily update the general ledger and accounts payable subsystems (also a function of a common data repository).

The ERP vendors claim to include *best practice* – the ERP firms research business processes and include the most up-to-date and advantageous in their software. ERP packages were particularly popular as a solution to the year 2000 problem (see ***Chapter 10*** for an explanation of the millennium bug) and to update systems to process the Euro currency – the software included solutions to these issues and saved the organization the problem of amending their legacy systems. The same can be true for an organization wishing to introduce e-Commerce since an ERP system should include such facilities (or integrate with additional ERP modules).

All this sounds ideal. However, installing a new IS is rarely easy, and the same applies to ERP. ERP packages are not cheap. Changing business practices to match the ERP way of doing things is not easy either (an alternative can be to adapt the ERP, but this too has its problems). Converting data from legacy systems to the ERP will also be an issue.

The biggest supplier of ERP systems is SAP – their package for order processing is called procurement and logistics execution.

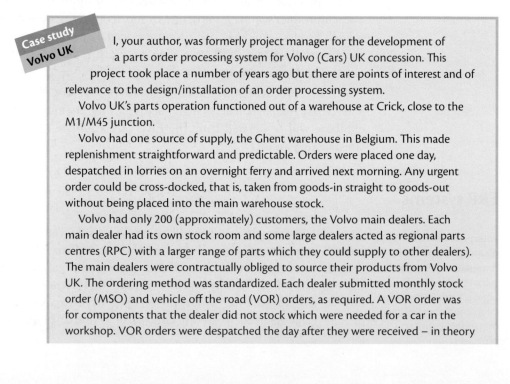

Case study
Volvo UK

I, your author, was formerly project manager for the development of a parts order processing system for Volvo (Cars) UK concession. This project took place a number of years ago but there are points of interest and of relevance to the design/installation of an order processing system.

Volvo UK's parts operation functioned out of a warehouse at Crick, close to the M1/M45 junction.

Volvo had one source of supply, the Ghent warehouse in Belgium. This made replenishment straightforward and predictable. Orders were placed one day, despatched in lorries on an overnight ferry and arrived next morning. Any urgent order could be cross-docked, that is, taken from goods-in straight to goods-out without being placed into the main warehouse stock.

Volvo had only 200 (approximately) customers, the Volvo main dealers. Each main dealer had its own stock room and some large dealers acted as regional parts centres (RPC) with a larger range of parts which they could supply to other dealers). The main dealers were contractually obliged to source their products from Volvo UK. The ordering method was standardized. Each dealer submitted monthly stock order (MSO) and vehicle off the road (VOR) orders, as required. A VOR order was for components that the dealer did not stock which were needed for a car in the workshop. VOR orders were despatched the day after they were received – in theory meaning that no Volvo owner had to wait more than 48 hours for a repair. Parts were priced at retail and then discounted to the dealer – the discount on a stock order was substantially greater than on a VOR order.

The warehouse was large (several acres) and the parts very diverse (from a tiny bolt or washer up to an engine or a whole car body). The picking of orders was broken down by area (some hand-picked – some requiring specialist forklift truck type equipment) and the picking lists sorted to warehouse aisle/bay order. As Volvo had only 200 customers the orders could be reassembled for despatch – there were 200 squares painted on the floor, one for each dealer. Each square had a pallet placed in it, parts were added to it as they were picked and the pallet was shrink-wrapped when deemed full.

The primary business objective of the warehouse was to ensure that Volvo owners got a good service (and that Volvo's reputation for reliability was maintained). Central to this was the VOR order. As already explained, the aim was to provide a next-day service. Generally the part would be supplied from the UK Crick warehouse but if it had to come from Ghent it would still be available overnight. In the unlikely case that Ghent did not have the part it could be flown to Ghent from the Swedish Gothenburg factory and still be on the overnight delivery to Crick.

2

Further reading

Books recommended for further reading are:

Brady, J., Monk, E. and Wagner, B. (2012) *Concepts in Enterprise Resource Planning*, 4th ed., Thompson, Boston, MA.
Magal, S. and Word, J. (2012) *Integrated Business Processes with ERP Systems*, Wiley, Hoboken, NJ.

These books are ostensibly about ERP systems but they give a good coverage of the Information Systems requirements of an organization.

Comprehension test

This is a short, simple test to enable you to check you have absorbed the material presented in *Chapter 4*.

Comprehension test: Payroll

Q1 Computer systems can be used to sort transactions into a convenient order. What sequence is recommended by the author for the payslips print from the payroll?

    a.   Payroll (employee) number ☐
    b.   Office location ☐
    c.   Department ☐
    d.   Salary grade code ☐

Q2 The order processing system can include provision for backorder. Which of the following summarizes a backorder?

    a.   A low priority order for reserve (background) stock ☐
    b.   An order refused as the customer has exceeded their credit limit ☐
    c.   A standing order for regular weekly/ monthly supplies ☐
    d.   An order that is saved as it cannot be fulfilled from current stock ☐

Q3 All data entered into a computer system, e.g. the order entered into an order processing system, must be validated. Secondary validation requires:

a. A check by a second member of staff ☐

b. A cross-check with standing data files ☐

c. Validation by a second computer program ☐

d. A simplified validation regime ☐

Q4 Which of the following standing data is used by both process customer orders and process replenishment orders?

a. Customer ☐

b. Product ☐

c. Supplier ☐

Q5 Product data can include a number of stock totals, one of which is *free stock*. This figure represents:

a. Stock that is available for allocation to customer orders ☐

b. Old stock that will be despatched free of charge ☐

c. Stock that is in goods-in ready to be stored in the warehouse ☐

d. Stock that is surplus to requirements and can be taken by staff ☐

Comprehension test: Order processing

Q6 In the context of an order processing system, a picking list is:

a. A list of products normally selected by a customer ☐

b. A list of products to be despatched from the warehouse ☐

c. A list of customers eligible for a special discount ☐

d. A list of products to be ordered from suppliers ☐

Q7 Customer payments have to be matched to the:

a. Order ☐

b. Picking list ☐

c. Delivery note ☐

d. Invoice ☐

Q8 Electronic data interchange (EDI) is an e-Commerce technology that can be used for:

a. Transactions between the customer's replenishment system and the supplier's order processing system ☐

b. The secondary validation of customer's orders ☐

c. Typing in customer orders ☐

d. Orders from retail customers ☐

Q9 Corporate systems tend to be large and expensive to develop and install. Which of the following strategies might an organization be advised to use to mitigate this issue in the case of an order processing system?

a. Outsource the running of the system to a bureau ☐

b. Write a system incorporating a database ☐

c. Use e-Commerce technologies ☐

d. Install an ERP system ☐

Q10 An ERP is designed to:

a. Plan the deployment of resources (staff, investment, etc.) to the divisions within the organization ☐

b. Integrate software provision across a range of business requirements ☐

c. Assist entrepreneurs in planning investment in new businesses ☐

d. Plan the deployment of IT resources in the organization ☐

Exercises

The following exercises are designed to aid your understanding of the material presented in this chapter. They can be used for self-study or selected exercises can be used for tutorial discussion.

1 **Comprehension** Why might some organizations outsource their payroll operations? Do the reasons for outsourcing payroll also apply to order processing?

2 **Comprehension** Using the formula in *Figure 4.6* and the following stock figures:

- free-stock   60
- backorder stock   0
- on-order stock   50
- re-order-stock level   200
- re-order-stock quantity   50

Calculate the appropriate re-order quantity. Assuming that the on-order stock arrives later today but there are also three more customer orders for 80, 30 and 50, what will the backorder figure be?

3 **Comprehension** The chapter includes an ERD for the order processing system but not the payroll system. Sketch an ERD for a payroll system (as explained in this chapter). Note that a detailed explanation of ERDs can be found in *Chapter 11*.

4 **Discussion** Orders may be sent in on paper and then they have to be keyed into the system – this takes time and can be error-prone. What other media/methods can be used to submit orders? From a business viewpoint, what are the advantages/disadvantages of each approach? Discuss.

5 **Assignment** Some medium and large organizations use ERP to meet their Information Systems requirements. Investigate ERP and write an essay that explains what an ERP system is, the process and pitfalls of switching to ERP, the advantages and disadvantages of using an ERP system. The essay should be about 2000 words long – it must include an introduction, conclusions, full referencing and a full bibliography.

2

5   e–BUSINESS SYSTEMS

Summary

Organizations use IS/IT to execute commercial transactions with customers, suppliers and administrative authorities. The technologies that are used are referred to as e-Commerce and the use of e-Commerce in the organization as e-Business.

    The use of e-Commerce can speed up business processes, save cost and develop new markets. There are three distinct e-Commerce technologies that can be deployed:

- Electronic data interchange (EDI): Used for automated, high volume business-to-business (b2b) transactions. Extensively used by multiple retailers (e.g. Tesco) and component assembly manufactures (e.g. Ford)
- Internet e-Commerce (e-Shop): Used for business-to-consumer (b2c) (retail) sales and for b2b procurement of secondary supplies (e.g. for office supplies). The e-Shop allows the consumer to home shop 24/7 but there is generally a waiting time for goods to be delivered. The e-Shop can also be accessed on the move using a mobile device (m-Commerce)
- Electronic market (e-Market): An intermediary service where suppliers post their offering and buyers can easily select the product that best suits their needs. The best-known example of e-Markets are the airline booking systems.

Trade transactions are executed as a number of stages: order, delivery, invoice and payment are the essential steps – known as the trade cycle. Using e-Commerce for transactions changes the dynamics of each of these stages – sometimes speeding things up and making cost savings and sometimes having an opposite effect. The trade cycle is an essential tool for the analysis of e-Commerce and its effect within the wider concept of e-Business.

© Grafvision/Fotolia

76

Learning outcomes	Having read this chapter and completed the exercises, you should:

- Appreciate that corporate Information Systems are networked to form Inter-organizational Information Systems (IOS)
- Understand electronic data interchange (EDI) as a business-to-business (b2b) technology
- Understand internet e-Commerce (i-Commerce/e-Shop) as a business-to-consumer (b2c) technology
- Understand electronic markets (e-Markets) and the business dynamics that have limited their application
- Be aware of, and be able to evaluate, developments such as mobile e-Commerce (m-Commerce) and Web 2.0
- Appreciate and be able to evaluate e-Commerce technologies and e-Business practices as a tool for competitive advantage.

2

Key terms	Electronic commerce (e-Commerce), internet e-Commerce (i-Commerce), business-to-consumer (b2c), business-to-business (b2b), electronic business (e-Business), electronic data interchange (EDI), electronic market (e-Market), mobile e-Commerce (m-Commerce), Web 2.0, trade cycle, EDI standard, e-Shop, shopbot.

e-Commerce/e-Business

electronic commerce (e-Commerce): commercial transactions formulated at a location remote from a trading partner and executed using Information and Communications Technologies.

internet e-Commerce (i-Commerce): a business operation processed via an e-Shop. The shop front is a website that connects to a backoffice system on a server. Used for both business-to-consumer and business-to-business operations.

Electronic commerce (e-Commerce) is a term popularized by the advent of commercial services on the internet. Amazon opened its virtual doors in July 1995 and internet e-Commerce (i-Commerce) has been growing from that point on.

The growth of i-Commerce has been a part of the internet phenomena. Back in 1995 the internet was a rather obscure facility used by academics for communicating research data and accessing supercomputer centres (the internet was officially opened for commercial use in April 1995). Two decades later it is used for work and play, every day, by many millions of people across the world. The growth of the internet, its applications and its impact on society has been dramatic – it has been called the internet revolution and the term revolution is, in this instance, justified.

Nevertheless, e-Commerce did not start with Amazon's first e-Shop. Predecessor services that date back to the early 1980s included:

- b2c services, using videotex technology, such as France's Minitel and services such as Prodigy in the US
- b2b services using EDI in sectors such as vehicle assembly and the multiple retailers
- e-Markets such as airline booking systems and the financial markets.

business-to-consumer (b2c): transactions between businesses/ organizations and their customers (retail consumers).

business-to-business (b2b): transactions between businesses/ organizations.

The term e-Commerce is closely associated with **business-to-consumer (b2c)**, i-Commerce, but sensibly is also applied to all forms of **business-to-business (b2b)**, inter-organizational electronic transactions and to the technologies used for those transactions. Turban et al. (2008) define e-Commerce as:

> the process of buying, selling, transferring, or exchanging products, services and/or information via computer networks.

And Jelassi and Enders (2008) have a longer description:

> Electronic commerce deals with the facilitation of transactions and selling of products and services online, i.e. via the internet or any other telecommunications network. This involves the electronic trading of physical and digital goods, quite often encompassing all the trading steps such as online marketing, online ordering, e-Payment and, for digital goods, online distribution.

electronic business (e-Business): commercial operations conducted using e-Commerce.

The use of e-Commerce has changed the nature of business – and we use the term **electronic business (e-Business)** when discussing the broader impact of e-Commerce. e-Business, as used in this chapter, is defined as:

> e-Business is commercial operations conducted using e-Commerce.

The advent of e-Business has enabled new businesses – for example, Amazon and eBay as online retailers and Google and Facebook as online services. e-Business has also changed the way that business is done:

- Business has been speeded up. For example, orders that took weeks to process now require next day (or same day) delivery.
- Customers (business or consumer) can go online and do their ordering/shopping, from wherever they are, 24 hours a day and seven days a week (24/7).

The range of goods and services that can be traded online is virtually unlimited. e-Commerce transactions include, for example, holiday bookings, selling books, auctioning bric-a-brac, just-in-time (JIT) delivery of components to a car factory and share dealings by a hedge fund.

e-Commerce technologies

e-Commerce is, in part, a technology-defined concept: it is electronic. There are a range of technologies used in e-Commerce. The principal distinction is between those transactions where the trading partner (customer) is a person using a computer and where it is a computer system that incorporates automated trading processes (see *Figure 5.1*).

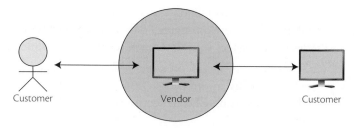

Figure 5.1 e-Commerce trading partners.

Customer   Vendor   Customer

electronic data interchange (EDI): the electronic transfer of commercial transactions between Information Systems.

electronic market (e-Market): an Information System, accessed electronically, that allows sellers to list products or services for sale and buyers to search, compare and purchase those products or services.

mobile e-Commerce (m-Commerce): i-Commerce conducted using a mobile device – a smartphone, laptop or tablet – when away from the home or office.

Web 2.0: i-Commerce (or non-commercial internet) system that utilizes user-provided content. The participatory web.

Where a person (business or consumer) operating the transaction uses a keyboard and a screen, the type of e-Commerce is an e-Shop or i-Commerce. Alternatively, an automated trading process, used by business, will code the transaction as an electronic message that will be automatically sent to the vendor: this type of e-Commerce is **electronic data interchange (EDI)**. There are some additional technologies (variances on technologies) that are also deployed:

- **electronic market (e-Market):** An intermediary system (independent of the vendor) that lists offerings from a number of vendors. An e-Market can be available to business and/or retail customers and would normally be accessed using i-Commerce.
- **mobile e-Commerce (m-Commerce):** i-Commerce conducted using a mobile device when away from the customer's home or place of work, included in the section on i-Commerce.
- **Web 2.0:** i-Commerce systems that utilize user-provided content (a relatively ill-defined concept but eBay and commercial transactions on social networking sites fall within this concept), also included in the section on i-Commerce.

See *Figure 5.2* for a Venn (type) diagram representing all these technologies.

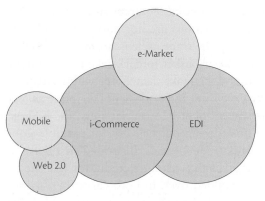

Figure 5.2 e-Commerce technologies.

The trade cycle

trade cycle: the steps/exchanges involved in a commercial transaction, e.g. order, delivery, invoice and payment.

A business transaction involves a number of steps – referred to as the **trade cycle**. The basic steps are best illustrated by looking at a simple, b2b transaction. This involves:

• Search		Finding the trading partner
• Negotiate		Agreeing terms of trade
• Execution	• Order	Specifying the goods (or services) required
	• Delivery	Delivery of the order
• Settlement	• Invoice	The request for payment
	• Payment	Settlement of the invoice
• After-sales		Any follow-up transactions

These steps, for a b2b transaction, are illustrated in *Figure 5.3*.

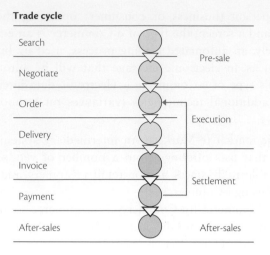

Trade cycle

Search — Pre-sale
Negotiate
Order — Execution
Delivery
Invoice — Settlement
Payment
After-sales — After-sales

Figure 5.3 Trade cycle (b2b).

b2b transactions are normally conducted on credit terms. The goods are ordered and delivered soon afterwards, in the execution phase. Settlement takes place at a later date with an invoice being sent out (say) at the end of the month and payment (say) after an additional month has elapsed. Many b2b transactions are repeated with regular orders for components or stock – this is indicated by the arrow, on *Figure 5.3*, with the loopback from payment to order. This repeat ordering requirement is where EDI is likely to be applicable.

Retail, b2c transactions are not normally conducted on credit terms. When we go into a shop the trade cycle is normally as follows: we pick up the goods and put them in our basket (order), take them to the till for checkout (invoice and payment) and then take them home with us (delivery). For conventional b2c transactions, execution and settlement take place as (essentially) a single step.

As with conventional b2c transactions, the e-Shop transaction is paid for at the time of ordering but delivery (of tangible goods) will take place after settlement. This trade cycle is illustrated in *Figure 5.4*. Note that, while on b2b the seller gives the customer credit, for b2c the customer is paying before the goods are handed over. In both cases there is no simultaneous *exchange of value*, and this has implications for trust in the transaction (a significant issue for b2c i-Commerce). Note also that, for a b2c, i-Commerce transaction, there is unlikely to be any opportunity for negotiation, and this step has been omitted from the diagram.

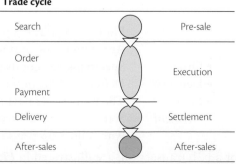

Trade cycle

Search — Pre-sale
Order — Execution
Payment
Delivery — Settlement
After-sales — After-sales

Figure 5.4 Trade cycle (b2c e-Shop).

EDI systems

EDI is used for b2b transactions that occur on a regular basis to a pre-determined format. For the most part it is used for purchase transactions – for instance supermarkets buying supplies of cornflakes or a vehicle assembler purchasing wheels to fit to the cars on the production line.

EDI is most commonly applied in the execution and settlement phases of the trade cycle (see *Figure 5.3*). In the execution of a simple trade cycle, the customer's order can be sent by EDI and the delivery notification from the supplier can also be electronic. For settlement the supplier can use EDI to send the invoice, and the customer can finish the cycle with an electronic funds transfer via the bank and an EDI payment notification to the supplier. This whole cycle may be more complex and other electronic messages can be included. The cycle can be repeated many times, as often as the supermarket wants to buy cornflakes or the vehicle assembler needs new supplies of wheels. For an example of an EDI system, see the *Teleordering case study* at the end of this section.

EDI can also be used for standardized and repeated transactions that do not fall within the usual definition of trade exchanges. One major user of EDI for non-trade messaging is the UK Tax Authorities (HMRC), for example for payroll PAYE data. The HMRC provides a number of ways of making PAYE returns, including EDIFACT EDI (see agreed message standards below). The use of EDI is particularly appropriate for this since most payrolls are processed by a relatively small number of bureaus which generate a large number of transactions and have the technical expertise to implement EDI systems.

EDI definition

EDI is often summed up as *paperless trading*. More formally, EDI is defined, by the International Data Exchange Association (IDEA), as:

> The transfer of structured data, by agreed message standards, from one computer system to another, by electronic means.

This definition of EDI has four elements, each of them essential to an EDI system:

1. Structured data:
   EDI is applicable to documents that conform to a standardized format and are composed of codes, values and (if necessary) short pieces of text; each element has a strictly defined purpose. For example, an order has a standardized layout, usually includes codes for the customer and product, and has values such as quantity ordered.

2. Agreed message standards:
   The EDI transaction has to have a standard format. The standard is not just agreed between the trading partners but is a general standard agreed at trade sector, national or international level. A purchase order will be one of a number of agreed message standards.

3. From one computer system to another:
   The EDI message sent is between two computer applications. There is no requirement for people to read the message or re-key it into a computer system. For example, the message is directly between the customer's purchasing system and the supplier's order processing system.

4. By electronic means:
   In almost all cases this is by data communications; sometimes networks specifically designed for EDI will be used.

Structured data: trade transactions, such as orders and invoices, are examples of *structured data* – for example, an order for office supplies (20 staplers and 40 boxes of staples: see *Figure 5.5*).

ORDER			Office Services Ltd
From:			123 London Road
			Sheffield
			S2 4HT
			Address code: 6464326
To:			
	Sheffield Stationery		
	110 Glossop Road		
	Sheffield		
	S10 2JT		
	Address code: 1149646		Order ref: AC6464
			Order date: 15.03.2013

Qty	Description	Product code
20	Stapler: metal half strip	50023084156932
40	Staples: 5000 26/6	50023084340447
	end of order	

Figure 5.5 Sample (paper) order.

The order is structured, and each data item has a standard place. Another order to the same supplier for other products or to another supplier for different requirements would have the same structure and similar contents.

On the order many of the data items are represented by codes – for example, supplier address code and product code (although, on the paper order, they are also spelt out in words). A number of trade sectors have their own standardized coding system – the most visible is the EAN/UPC, used on groceries and general merchandise as the barcode (see *Chapter 1*).

In many organizations, the order (particularly for primary supplies that are required on a regular basis) will be output from a computer system such as a stock control/material and requirements planning (MRP) system. The order will also, usually, be input into an order processing system when it arrives with the supplier. This application of computer systems makes the use of codes important and also raises the question as to why the order cannot be transferred electronically achieving a saving in time, effort and a reduction in errors – hence the requirement for EDI.

EDI standard: a standard for coding business documents as EDI messages, e.g. EDIFACT or standards defined within XML.

Agreed message standards: At the heart of any EDI application is the use of an *agreed message standard*, which requires an **EDI standard**. The essence of EDI is the coding and structuring of the data into an application and machine-independent format – anything less is simply a system of file-transfers.

Coding and structuring the documents for business transactions is no easy matter. There have been a number of EDI standards developed in various industry sectors or within a specific country and there are complex committee structures and procedures to support them. Examples of these standards are Odette (automotive industry), Tradacom (UK ANA) and ANSI-X12 (US Standard).

Following on from the various sectorial and national EDI standards is the United Nations (UN) EDI Standard: EDIFACT. This is the standard that is used in the example in this chapter and it is the standard that should be adopted for any new EDI application.

The application of the EDIFACT standard can be illustrated using the order shown in *Figure 5.5* – that order coded into EDIFACT is shown in *Figure 5.6*.

```
UNH + 000001 + ORDERS : 2 : 932 : UN'
BGM + 220 + AC6464'
DTM + 4 : 20130315 : 102'
NAD + BY + 6464326 :: 91'
NAD + SU + 1149646 :: 91'
UNS + D'
LIN + 1 ++ 50023084156932 : EN'
QTY + 21 : 20'
LIN + 2 ++ 50023084340447 : EN'
QTY + 21 : 40'
UNT + 11 + 000001'
```

Figure 5.6 Sample EDIFACT interchange.

The interpretation of the EDIFACT order is as follows:

- UNH+000001+ORDERS:2:932:UN'   Message Header
  - Message Number   000001
  - Message Type   ORDERS
  - Version   2
  - Release   932
  - Control Agency   UN

- BGM+220+AC6464'   Beginning of Message
  - Message Name Code   220 i.e. order
  - Document Number   AC6464 i.e. order number

- DTM+4:20130315:102'   Date/Time/Period
  - Qualifier   4 i.e. order date
  - Date   20130313 ~ 15mar2013
  - Format Qualifier   102 i.e. century date

(continued overleaf)

- NAD+BY+6464326::91'   Name and Address
  NAD+SU+1149646::91'
    Party Qualifier   BY i.e. buyer
                                               SU i.e. supplier
    Address Code   6464326 and 1149646
    Code List Agency   91 i.e. user defined

- UNS+D'   Section Control
    Section Identification   D i.e. detail segment

- LIN+1++50023084156932:EN'   Line Item
  LIN+2++50023084340447:EN'
    Line Item Number   1 and 2
    Item Number   50023084156932 and
                                               50023084340447
    Item Number Type   EN = EAN Code

- QTY+21:20'   Quantity
  QTY+21:40'
    Quantity Qualifier   21 i.e. ordered quantity
    Quantity   20 and 40

- UNT+11+000001'   Message Trailer
    Control Count   11 i.e. eleven segments
    Message Number   000001 as in UNH

- Formatting Characters
    Data Element Separator   +
    Component Data Element Separator   :
    (within a composite data element)
    Segment Terminator   '

Decoded, the order is:

The order identification is:
- Order Number   AC6464
- Order Date   15.03.2013

From Office Services Ltd:
- Customer Address Code   6464326

To Sheffield Stationery:
- Supplier Address Code   1149646

For Staplers and (refill) Staples:	Qty	Product
Line 1 Staplers	20	50023084156932
Line 1 Staples	40	50023084340447

The EDIFACT coding of the order provides a machine independent, unambiguous specification of the requirements that can be sent/accepted by any system with the appropriate EDI software.

Each transaction, in this case an order, is a message. Several messages can be sent in an interchange and EDIFACT also specifies the interchange header and trailer.

The full EDIFACT standard is defined on the UN website. It is vast and, to the untrained eye, very complex (which is one of the criticisms made of traditional EDI). That said, once one knows one's way around, it is simple enough and only a small number of segments are likely to be needed for any specific requirement.

A number of organizations are now using XML messaging (see the *XML explanation box*) in place of traditional EDI (e.g. EDIFACT). Users of XML EDI include Walmart and its UK supermarket chain Asda. It is also used by Microsoft in its BizTalk server, Sun for its ebXML and by new internet-enabled markets such as Commerce One (Chaffey, 2007). It is claimed that:

- The standards are simple (you can devise your own).
- XML software is readily available (and some of it is free).
- XML can be transmitted on the internet (but then so can traditional EDI).
- It is new (and by implication, new means better).

The big drawback of XML is that it is a meta-language (that is, a language used to define another language) and hence there are no generally agreed XML EDI message standards for trade transactions within the XML definition. Organizations are defining their own XML EDI messaging standards (there are also attempts by trade standards bodies to bring some order into the scene). Large organizations can define their own messaging standard, and that probably suits them. However, smaller organization could receive differently defined messages from a number of trading partners, each requiring a separate implementation; it takes them back to where they were 30 years ago.

A new technology should be adopted because it provides a new capability or because it improves on an existing facility. It is far from clear what advantage is to be gained from replacing existing EDI applications with XML messaging – but that won't stop it happening.

The order shown in *Figure 5.5* and coded into EDIFACT in *Figure 5.6* could alternatively be coded in XML (see *Figure 5.7* overleaf). The tags have been defined by the author.

One computer system to another: EDI systems are used to communicate business transactions *from one computer system to another*. As we saw above, the EDI message is not designed for ease of reading by the staff of the organization. The intention is that the message will be automatically generated by (say) the stock control/replenishment system of the customer organization and will be read and processed by the order processing system of the supplier organization. The EDI exchanges for the basic trade cycle are shown in *Figure 5.8* overleaf.

EDI messaging between the computer systems of trading partners is part of a system of close cooperation between organizations in the supply chain. Linking of systems in this way integrates the operations of customer and supplier organizations. This (virtual) integration of the IS/IT is then referred to as an Inter-Organizational Information System (IOS).

```
<? Xml version = "1.0 standalone = "yes" ?>
<purchase-order order-no = "AC6464">
 <order-header>
    <reference-no>AC6464</reference-no>
    <date>20130315</date>
 </order-header>
 <company>
    <company-no>6464326</company-no>
 </company>
 <supplier>
    <supplier-no>1149646</supplier-no>
 </supplier>
 <order-item>
    <item-ean>50023084156932</item-ean>
    <quantity>20</quantity>
 </order-item>
 <order-item>
    <item-ean>50023084340447</item-ean>
    <quantity>40</quantity>
 </order-item>
</purchase-order>
```

Figure 5.7 Example of XML EDI interchange.

XML stands for eXtensible Mark-up Language. XML is a mark-up language designed for use on the web. XML is derived from SGML (standard general mark-up language), as is HTML. Data coded in XML looks similar to HTML but with the important difference that the tags are determined by the system designers/system users rather than being predetermined by designers of the language. Hence XML is a meta-language (a language used to define another language).

The format of XML tags is <name> (start tag) and </name> (close tag). There is no pre-set library of names – the user (or application) define their own. The tag will normally be describing the data – thus in *Figure 5.7* the author has, for example, created <purchase-order> and <supplier> tags. Three further rules are:

- Every opening tag must be matched by a closing tag
- Tags can be nested (and any nesting must be a strict tree structure)
- Tags are case sensitive (<item-ean> and </item-EAN> would not match).

The document data is normally included between tags, for example:
    <item-ean>50023084156932</item-ean>

The start tag can also be given parameters, for example:

    <purchase-order order-no="AC6464">

XML documents can be associated with further XML files, for example:

- DTD or schema: This defines the XML structure allowed in a document and can be used to check that the XML is *well formed*
- Style sheet: Uses XSLT to reformat the XML – usually for display or printing.

XML is used for many purposes. It can be used to interchange data between databases, to specify webpages, for communication in web services and it is also being used for *the transfer of structured data, from one computer system to another, by electronic means* (three out of the four elements of our adopted definition of EDI).

XML is a recommendation of the World Wide Web Consortium (W3C). w3schools.com has excellent material on XML. A useful XML book is Goldfarb's XML Handbook (2003).

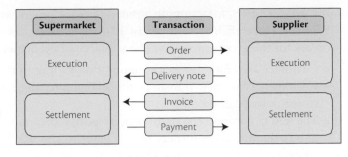

Figure 5.8 EDI exchanges for a stock replenishment system.

Electronic means: the final part of our definition of EDI is *by electronic means*. The normal (or traditional) way of transmitting an EDI message is using a value added data service (VADS) – also known as a value added network (VAN).

The VADS is a *post and forward network*. This network is centred on a computer system with communications facilities. For each user of the system there are two files:

- The postbox – where incoming messages are placed
- The mailbox – where outgoing messages can be picked up.

The use of postboxes and mailboxes provides *time independence* and *protocol independence*, that is:

- The originating organization can send its EDI transmission to the VADS whenever it is ready and using any of the network technology and protocol combinations that the VADS is equipped to receive. The EDI transmission can contain messages for several trading partners.
- The recipient organization can pick up its EDI messages at a time of its choice and, possibly, using a different network and protocol combination from that used to send the message(s) in. The recipient organization may be picking up messages from several trading partners.

The VADS postbox and mailbox arrangement is shown diagrammatically in *Figure 5.9*.

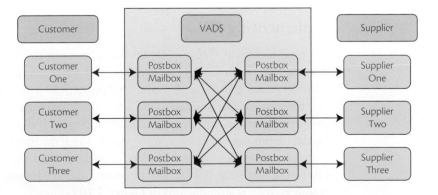

Figure 5.9 VADS – postbox and mailbox files.

If Customer Two, for example, needed to place orders with Supplier One and Supplier Three then it formats an EDI interchange containing a number of orders for those two suppliers. The sequence of events would then be:

- Customer Two establishes a communications link to the VADS system.
- Customer Two then transmits the EDI interchange and it is temporarily stored in its postbox.
- The VADS computer system inspects postboxes, unpacks the interchanges, moves the messages (orders in this case) to the mailboxes of the intended recipients and repackages them as new interchanges. The inspection of postboxes is frequent and, to all intents and purposes, the interchanges are immediately available in the mailbox of the recipient.
- The users of the system establish a communication link to the VADS system at their convenience. Let us assume that Supplier Three comes online.
- Supplier Three inspects its mailboxes for new interchanges. On finding the order from Customer Two (and possibly further messages from other customers) it causes them to be transmitted to its own order processing system.

The EDI interchange is then available for processing in the user's application. A number of organizations have set out to provide VADS. Two such services that are extensively used are the AT&T network and GEIS (General Electric Information Services). The VADS providers emphasize their privacy, security and reliability and offer a number of other services, such as message validation, message logging and consultancy.

The main alternative, and an increasingly popular alternative, to a VADS is the use of the internet for EDI transmission. In particular, the internet is seen as a natural match with the use of XML messaging. The use of the internet for EDI would normally require the use of a protocol such as AS2/AS3 to envelope the EDI message – and possibly a third party to post and forward the messages (this sounds a bit like a VADS!). When using the internet, security and reliability are two of the major concerns; unlike the traditional VADS, the internet does not guarantee the safe delivery of data you send into it. The plus side of using the internet is that it is cheaper than the commercial networks. The cost of EDI VADS services seems to be of particular concern to small organizations that have relatively low usage of EDI.

Implementing EDI

The final technical element of the EDI system is the EDI software. If Office Services Ltd is to send an order from its stock control system to Sheffield Stationery (see the example order in *Figure 5.5*) it needs to code that order into the agreed EDI standard and transmit it into the chosen VADS. To pick up the order at the other end, Sheffield Stationery has a similar need to extract the data from the network and to decode the data from the EDI message into its order processing system. The coding/decoding of the EDI message and the interfacing with the VADS are normally achieved using EDI software. The overall picture is summarized in *Figure 5.10*.

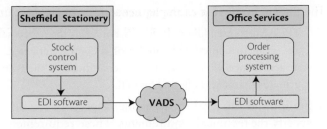

2

Figure 5.10 Sending an order using EDI software.

The EDI software is normally bought in from a specialist supplier. There are a number of software houses that supply EDI solutions; the EDI software can also come from the VADS, a major trading partner or be a facility of an ERP system. The basic functions of the EDI software are the two already outlined, namely:

- Coding business transactions into the chosen EDI standard
- Interfacing with the network/VADS.

Many EDI software packages provide additional functions. These may include:

- A trading partner database integrated into the EDI software. This can be used to determine which standard and which network is to be used for each trading partner
- Support of multiple EDI standards
- Facilities for the formatting of internal application data to and from the EDI standard
- Facilities for transactions to be sent by fax or e-Mail to suppliers that do not use EDI
- Interfacing with a variety of EDI VADS (including the internet)
- The option to encrypt the EDI message
- Facilities for the automatic acknowledgement of the EDI message
- Message tracking and an audit trail of messages sent and received.

On the administrative side, setting up an EDI system requires a lot of discussion with trading partners. Manual systems rely, in part, on the common sense of the people involved; when these interchanges are automated the machines just do what they are told (well, they do on a good day!).

The appropriate way to document the details of a trading arrangement between electronic trading partners is an EDI Interchange Agreement. The agreement makes clear the trading intentions of both parties, the technical framework for the transactions and the procedures to be followed in the event of a dispute. The EDI Agreement is a document signed by both trading partners before electronic trading begins. Guidance that is provided with the European Model Electronic Data Interchange (EDI) Agreement (EU-IA) includes:

> For EDI to be a successful alternative to paper trading, it is essential that messages are accorded a comparable legal value as their paper equivalent when the functions effected in an electronic environment are similar to those effected in a paper environment, and where all appropriate measures have been taken to secure and store the data.

The EU-IA, in the text of the agreement, includes the clause:

> The parties, intending to be legally bound by the Agreement, expressly waive any right to contest the validity of a contract effected by the use of EDI in accordance with the terms and conditions of the Agreement on the sole grounds that it was effected by EDI.

In addition to the legal (or legalistic) aspects of the agreement it is important to specify the technical requirements. These requirements include:

- The coding systems that will be used for identifying entities such as organizations and products, and attributes such as quantities
- The EDI standard that is to be employed and, within that, the messages and data segments that will be used
- The network and, if applicable, the protocol that is to be used.

Model agreements are available from various parties, including trade organizations.

**Themes
Security**

An important aspect of EDI is the privacy and security of the messages and their exchange. The first point is to ensure that interchange of messages is reliable. In the first instance this is a matter of procedures at both ends of the trading agreements. Rigid procedures are required to ensure that all the processes are run and that they reach their successful conclusion – an old-fashioned requirement called *data processing standards*. Further aspects of security are:

- Controls in the EDI standards and the transmission protocol, e.g. the control count of segments in the EDIFACT UNT trailer
- Protection against tampering, e.g. by including a digital signature
- Privacy of message – encryption can be used
- Non-repudiation (where a party denies sending or receiving the message). This can be addressed using a receipt acknowledgement message or a *trusted third party* to audit trail all transactions.

The need for security in an EDI system should be kept in proportion; after all, EDI is very probably replacing a paper-based system where computer output orders, without signatures, were put in the post and eventually manually keyed in by an order entry clerk. Transmission and EDI message controls are automatic. Checks over and above that all come at a cost; encryption and digital signatures both require extra software and procedures; message acknowledgements require additional software to generate the message and to match it to the original transaction on the other side of the trading relationship.

The overall facilities for EDI privacy and security are summed up in *Figure 5.11*.

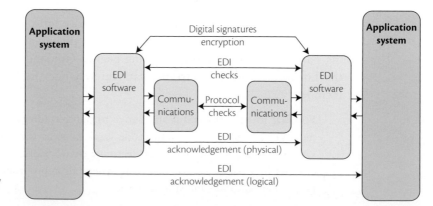

Figure 5.11 EDI privacy and security.

Advantages and disadvantages of EDI

EDI can bring a number of advantages to the organizations that use it. It should save considerable time on the exchange of business transactions and has the potential for considerable savings in costs. The direct advantages of EDI include:

- Shortened ordering time: The EDI message can be in the recipient's system as quickly as required – the same day for overnight processing or within minutes for immediate processing
- Cost cutting: The principal saving from the use of EDI is the potential to save staff costs on data entry and query resolution. Stationery and postage costs are also saved. The cost savings need to be offset against the system development and network costs
- Elimination of errors: No data entry errors
- Accurate invoicing: Electronic invoices should automatically match to the corresponding order and delivery note (not an easy process when performed manually)
- EDI payment: Payment and payment advice can also be made by EDI. An electronic payment advice will be automatically matched against the relevant invoices.

Indirect advantages of the use of EDI can be:

- Reduced stock holding: The ability to order regularly and quickly reduce the amount of goods that need to be kept in a store room or warehouse at the shop or the factory. For many JIT manufacture and quick-response supply systems, stockholding is eliminated altogether, with goods being delivered only as they are needed. Reduced stockholding cuts the cost of warehousing, the double handling goods (into store and then out again into the factory or shop) and the finance required to pay for the goods that are just sitting in store.
- Build to order: The use of EDI (and other technical developments) has reduced the manufacturing cycle time – in the case of car manufacture from about 13 weeks to 2 weeks. This has made it possible for the car manufacturers to build to order. They can take the customer's specification (body colour, trim, accessories, etc.) and build that car. Previous practice was to try to persuade the customer to settle for a car that was already in stock.
- Cash flow: Speeding up the trade cycle by getting invoices out quickly, and directly matched to the corresponding orders and deliveries, can and should speed up payments – and hence improve cash flow.
- Customer lock-in: An established EDI system should be of considerable advantage to both customer and supplier. Switching to a new supplier requires that the electronic trading system and trading relationship be re-developed, a problem to be avoided if a switch of supplier is not essential.

To gain these advantages EDI has to be seen as an investment – there are costs upfront and the payback is longer term. The costs are the setup of the EDI system (hardware, software and network) and the time required to establish agreements with trading partners. The savings only start when there is a significant volume of business transacted using EDI, a point that is called the *critical mass*.

EDI can be simply used to replace paper transactions with electronic transactions – this is the normal route taken in the initial installation of EDI. The full advantage of EDI is only realized when business practices are restructured to make full use of the potential of EDI – when EDI is used as an enabling technology to change the way the business operates: JIT manufacture and quick-response supply

being prime examples of where EDI is used as an enabling technology to gain competitive advantage. Competitive advantage gained by innovative IT applications can be short-lived as competitors install similar systems and the use of the IT system becomes a business norm. Requirements for complex and expensive IT systems do, however, become a barrier to market entry.

Nielsen's Book Data lists bibliographical details of all English language books published worldwide (previously this service was known as Whitaker's Books in Print). Nielsen also provides a registration service that allocates codes, including ISBNs,[1] for organizations involved in the book trade. The Nielsen database, at the time of writing, contains 7.4 million unique ISBNs published or distributed in the UK and Ireland and 16.2 million unique ISBNs in total. Book Data is available to the trade in a variety of formats and forms the basis of the catalogues of most online book retailers.

Built on the Book Data database is Nielsen's Book Net/Teleordering service. This is an EDI system that allows bookshops to place orders with over 60,000 publishers, distributors and wholesalers – users of the service do not need to identify the supplier, the system does that for them. For book trade customers the service can be installed on a simple PC (in a small bookshop), integrated with an EPOS system, and large bookstore chains can build it into their own internal systems. Suppliers (publishers and distributors) will receive their EDI orders directly into their internal Information Systems – small operators can avoid the complications (and benefits) of EDI and opt to receive an e-Mail notification and then access their order as a webpage. The system allows the use of Tradacoms, EDIFACT or ANSI-X12 EDI standards.

Sources include Nielsen (2012). Note there are other providers of EDI services to the book trade.

[1] ISBN is the International Standard Book Number, it is a 13-digit code used to uniquely identify every book that is printed (the same book in different formats, e.g. hard/paperback will have separate ISBNs). The ISBN conforms to EAN standards and can be used as a barcode (see **Chapter 1**).

i-Commerce (e-Shop)

At the heart of most that is good about the internet lies the simple, seductive offering – what you want, when you want it. You want to buy an obscure book or track down a cheap holiday? Get online. Do it. Now!

(adapted from Waldman, 1999)

Internet e-Commerce (i-Commerce, the **e-Shop**), is used for b2c transactions. Well-known examples are amazon.com and tesco.com, but there are many thousands of other e-Shops and just about anything can be bought online.

The basic model is the e-Shop – and the two instanced above are for tangible goods. i-Commerce, however, has a much wider scope – it can be used for:

e-Shop: the website of an internet e-Commerce business.

- Intangibles such as music downloads, software and tickets
- Account-based services such as a bank account, stocks and share dealing, and gambling
- b2b transactions, typically for secondary supplies, such as office stationery, where EDI would not be appropriate.

i-Commerce can be summed up as:

> A server-based system, for commercial transactions, accessed from outside the organization via the internet and using a web interface.

The essential IT structure is a client-server system (see *Figure 5.12*).

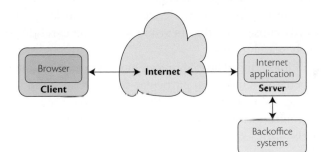

Figure 5.12 e-Shop IT infrastructure.

The concept of setting up a retail operation online sounds simple enough. Possibly the main advantage is that you can have national (or international) coverage without the cost of setting up a chain of retail outlets. But there are real differences that must be addressed:

- Location: You don't pick up customers who just walk past your high street store – customers have to find your electronic location.
- Product: The customer cannot see, smell or touch (or try on) the product – customers can only have words, pictures and possibly sound.
- Payment: This has to be electronic and over a network and this creates security issues.
- Delivery: Customers cannot take tangible products home with them – these will probably take a few days to arrive.
- After-sales: If there is a problem the customer cannot simply take their purchase back to a physical shop.

The e-Shop trade cycle

The importance of these issues depends on what you are selling to whom. These issues arise at different stages of the trade cycle (see *Figure 5.4* for the trade cycle and *Figure 5.13* for e-Shop interchanges). We will examine the implications for an e-Shop system at each stage of the trade cycle.

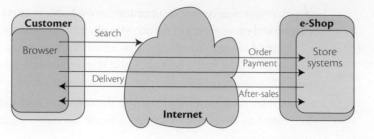

Figure 5.13 e-Shop trade cycle interchanges.

Search: There is no point in setting up a shop unless your target customers can find you. This is true on the high street (or in a shopping mall), where the mantra is *location, location, location*. It is also true on the internet, where the equivalent is getting your site onto the first page of the search engine results.

Search engine optimization (SEO) is big business. There are three basic approaches to getting your site recognized by the search engines:

- Site content: The search engines index sites on their content and their links. The starting point is the content of the <title> and the <meta> tags. The words chosen for the meta tag should be carefully thought out to match likely search terms.
- Paid for listing: The e-Shop can pay the search engine (or search engines) for its site to be linked to particular search terms (and that can be restricted to a geographical area). Again the words chosen must be carefully thought out.
- Optimization: Site owners can get themselves up the listing by playing a few tricks – for example, creating links to their own site or repeatedly accessing the site. That said, the search engines try to detect and then ignore sites that play tricks. There are also consultancies which, for a fee, will optimize your listing position on the search engines.

Note, for example, that in the early days of the internet searches, amazon.co.uk came up with the American term *bookstore* but not the English term *bookshop*.

In addition to the search engine the site can attract traffic by:

- Advertising: Conventional adverts can be placed, for example, in the press, on billboards or on television. These are not cheap options and potential customers still have to get online and find the site – adding a QR barcode that can be scanned to make the link is one way of avoiding this issue.
- Clickthroughs: This is online advertising. The advantage is that the advert leads straight to the e-Shop but, of course, the user has to be on the site with the link in the first place. Clickthroughs are often paid for – this can be per clickthrough or for clickthroughs that lead to a sale. Paid for clickthroughs need software that account for them. A somewhat unusual example of the use of clickthroughs is the *milliondollarhomepage* (see the **case study**).
- Bricks-and-clicks: Many large, conventional shops have set up a parallel e-Shop, creating a bricks-and-clicks operation. Customers who know the conventional store can also be attracted to the e-Shop.
- Social media: Businesses, including e-Shops, are setting up on Facebook and sponsoring celebrities to include mention of them in their tweets. There is a lot of hype about using new media for advertising and it can backfire

if it provokes a negative reaction. Social media sites can also check your personal data and send you adverts they think could be relevant.

- Reputation: There are a few large and well-known e-Shops whose sites people can go to straightaway. Good feedback from satisfied customers can enhance an organization's reputation and the fact that a site is well known enhances the customer's sense of security.

Case study miliondollar-homepage

The milliondollarhomepage was set up by Alex Tew in 2005. Alex was a student trying to finance his way through university. The home page contained a million pixels (in a 1000 x 1000 grid). Pixels were sold in 10 x 10 blocks for a dollar per pixel and the purchasers could choose the design for their square. The idea got a lot of publicity and all the pixels were soon sold – after all, $100 is not a lot of money to chance on what might turn out to be a bit of good marketing. Alex Tew made his million dollars – but did not complete his degree.

The whole site looks like a colourful patchwork quilt. When a visitor runs their mouse over the site the title/slogan of the area pointed to is displayed. If the visitor clicks the area they will be taken on a clickthrough link to the site of the owner of the pixels. The homepage is accessible at: http://www.milliondollarhomepage.com/.

Order: An e-Shop, just like a conventional shop, needs to be well designed and carefully laid out. The customer needs to be able to easily locate what they are looking for and the product needs to be well presented.

In an e-Shop the presentation is limited to description, pictures and (possibly) sound. For many products this is adequate and in some cases could be an advantage – a bookshop can include reviews that would not be readily available in a conventional bookshop. For products like fresh food (where we might like to select our own apples) and clothes (where trying the garment on could be a good idea), the e-Shop has its limitations. Whatever the product the e-Shop must make a good effort to display it – and, for a large e-Shop, this means a significant overhead.

An e-Shop, excepting the very small e-Shop, will have a product database. This allows product data, including prices and stock totals, to be readily updated. The product pages of the e-Shop are then generated *on the fly* from the product database using server side scripts. The requirement for a database also applies to e-Shops selling non-tangible items, such as tickets, where a booking system is required.

Most e-Shops will also include an electronic basket, trolley or cart – an analogy to the supermarket. The basket is an interesting piece of software (we will come to that later). The electronic basket is also superior to its conventional equivalent – you can readily see what is in it, the total spend is displayed and goods can be electronically returned to the virtual shelf (there is also talk of developing a smart trolley for use in a conventional supermarket).

Payment: The payment has to be online, which normally means having to use a credit or debit card. Other options are e-Cash, an account (with PayPal being a hybrid option) or in some cases, and in some countries, paying the postman on delivery. Payment always has security issues and these are magnified in online transactions. An essential difference is that there is no simultaneous exchange of value. In a shop you make a payment and get your goods at the same time – online, you pay first and (you hope) get your goods later (b2b transactions are different: the standard there is to get the goods first, on credit, and pay at a later stage).

Electronic payments are vulnerable. There are three areas of vulnerability:

- Customer: Is the person making the transaction the legitimate user of the payment instrument?
- Transmission: Are the payment details secure as they are sent over the network?
- Supplier: Is the e-Shop what it purports to be (that is, are the employees honest and is the e-Shop secure)?

Much of the emphasis in e-Shop security has been on the transmission aspect of the problem (which was probably never the biggest threat area). This is amenable to a technical fix – the use of encryption (SSL – Secure Socket Layer encryption, using a public and private key system).

At the customer end, the problem is knowing whether the person submitting the payment details is the legitimate owner of the card/account. Payments are made using the *customer not present* protocol and hence there is no signature/pin number check (and the person submitting the payment may not even be in possession of the physical credit/debit card). The problem is exacerbated by the availability of stolen card details from the supplier end or other e-Commerce transactions. There is also a problem with users who make card payments and then deny making the transaction.

Security at the customer end has been enhanced by small changes. Credit/debit cards now have a three-digit security code and some accounts are associated with an additional password check. Customers of online banking can be issued with a calculator like a password generator. None of these measures solves the problem but, to borrow a phrase, *every little helps*.

It is to be noted that, from the customer's point of view, the credit card is much more secure than a debit card. With a credit card the customer is, in effect, buying from the credit card company and the credit card company is making the purchase – hence it is the credit card company that is liable for any loss should things go wrong. This is not the case with a debit card, where one is spending one's own money and also technically liable for any fraud on the account (although banks in the UK have tended to be very helpful – they do not want the security of the system to be questioned). An advantage of an account/e-Cash is that one only puts at risk the amount of money in the account – presumably not a vast sum.

At the supplier end, problems range from hacking attacks that gain customer payment details to phishing (fraudulent) websites. Website designers need to address security issues – for instance, customer payment details must be encrypted and, arguably, they should not be retained at all. A neat way of minimizing security risks you will see on websites is where you are asked only for a random three characters of a password – hence stopping any employee seeing the full password for that customer.

Delivery: In conventional retail the customer takes the goods home with them. In the case of the e-Shop the goods have to be delivered – and that takes time and costs money. It has been said that you could sell anything online – provided it fits through a letter box. Books and CDs fit into this category, and they have the following advantages:

- Postage is fairly cheap.
- They are not too likely to be damaged or stolen.
- It does not matter whether the recipient is at home or not (provided books are not in oversized cardboard packages that do not fit the letterbox!).

These are some of the reasons why Amazon's founder Jeff Bezos chose books for his pioneering e-Shop.

As i-Commerce has developed, the range of goods available has widened and the e-Shops have had to develop a range of solutions to tackle the fulfilment/delivery problem. The range of delivery options is illustrated in the following list:

Delivery mode	Example products	
Electronic	Tickets, music, software	Cheap to operate, immediate, can fail on large files. Potential for fraud/piracy
Postal	Books, CDs	Low cost, relatively fast (good if product fits through letterbox)
Courier service	Electronic equipment	Significant price, secure for valuable items, needs customer to be at home or in the office
Local depot	Supermarket, white/brown goods	Significant price, needs local delivery depot/booked delivery slots
Click-and-collect	Bookshop, catalogue store, supermarket	Order online and customer picks up at the local branch

The e-Shop needs to carefully think out and plan its e-Fulfilment processes delivery issues as they affect supermarkets were discussed in the case study in *Chapter 1*. Warehousing, picking, packing and delivery need to be appropriate, efficient and cost-effective – and it also should consider the customer's needs (picking up goods from the sorting office or arranging a re-delivery is problematic for busy people).

The e-Shop software includes elements of the fulfilment process. This may be a system for the download of electronic products or a system for booking a slot for grocery delivery. An e-Shop for tangible products will also need an efficient order processing, stock replenishment and warehousing system (see *Chapter 4*). A bricks-and-clicks business has the advantage that much of the infrastructure is already in place for its bricks-and-mortar operations. An option for a pure-play (online only) operator is to outsource the fulfilment (warehousing, picking, packing and delivery can be outsourced to a specialist logistics company or, possibly, a wholesaler).

Managing Information Systems in the 21st Century: Richard Piercy

> **Richard Piercy** is an executive vice-president at EMI Music. He works in the technology department and has global responsibility for business transformation; he also runs the global digital supply chain which is responsible for the digital manufacturing and distribution of all EMI Music's creative output. Prior to joining EMI Music, Richard ran the digital division of a pan-Asian sports media business based in Singapore, where he managed the internet properties for key brands such as the Asian PGA Tour, Asian Football Confederation, Asian Basketball Confederation and Korean National Soccer Team. Richard's career started as a consultant with Accenture and Boston Consulting Group.
>
> Visit www.palgrave.com/business/whiteley to watch Richard talking about Information Systems and careers as an IS professional, and then think about the following questions:
>
> ● In what ways has the advent of digital changed the music industry (for example, the ways in which artists create music and how companies sell and distribute it)?
> ● Would you describe music companies as b2b or b2c organizations, and why?

After-sales: The e-Shop offering needs efficient and effective after-sales procedures – an e-Shop that does not plan for this can soon get a poor reputation that is very difficult to shake off. As always, the issues that need to be dealt with depend on the nature of the product – some examples are:

● Clothing retailers must plan for a high rate of returns – and have systems to cope with those returns. Most/all e-Shops take returns – some e-Shops send out a pre-paid delivery label for returns. The danger for the e-Shop is that some customers order goods just to try them on and send back most of what they order.

● Electronic goods that don't work. The solution here can be a good help line where the operator can assess the problem. The laptop being used to write this book did not work when first ordered – when I rang up to report the problem the company asked me to try a couple of things and then told me to repack the laptop – and a courier arrived next morning with a replacement: that was good customer service.

Good after-sales is essential but it comes at a cost and some customers will take advantage of it. A bricks-and-clicks operation means that after-sales can be dealt with at a conventional outlet, which could be the best solution all round.

Shopbots

shopbot: shopping robot used to access other internet e-Commerce businesses with or without the agreement of the third-party site.

A special category of e-Shop is the **shopbot** (or price comparison website). The name comes from shopping robots. The original shopbots used to access other e-Shops by a process known as web-scraping – the shopbot would access the e-Shop, generate an automated transaction and then decode the result from the HTML code of the response. Note that sites that ask you to type in a code that is presented as a distorted picture are doing this to stop access by bots.

Modern price comparison websites work in cooperation with the e-Shops they link to. This is achieved using a web-services interface between the price comparison website and the e-Shops it works with. Using the web-services interface the price comparison site can send a request to the e-Shop (for example for an insurance quote) and the e-Shop will send back its quote. The comparison site will then list the quotes it has obtained – generally these will be in price order and the customer will, very probably, choose the cheapest. The price comparison site is paid for each successful clickthrough sale.

Arguably, however, there is a problem with this process. Easy price comparison pushes down prices. This sounds advantageous for the consumer – but, of course, low prices can mean low quality. For the supplier the marketplace can simply become unprofitable with a downward price spiral where, in the end, everyone loses. To combat these effects certain tricks can be employed. One is to reply with a very cheap deal, such as the basic holiday insurance package, and then, once the customer has clicked through, offer the gold and platinum options at substantially higher prices (a bit like those airfares priced at £1 each way that end up costing £120 for the return flight you eventually book).

m-Commerce

If you can do your shopping at home, why not on the move? (I have even had students using e-Shops in my e-Commerce lectures!)

Initially, m-Commerce was just an e-Shop website displayed on a mobile phone. Issues were the small screen, slow networks and lack of a (good) keyboard. m-Commerce did not take off as the pundits initially predicted (and after all, what is so urgent about doing one's Tesco shopping that it won't wait until one gets home?).

More recently, phones have got smarter and many e-Shops have now issued their own app. We can now have Tesco or Amazon apps on our mobile. In truth, this is not a big change. The presentation in the app can be smarter and there can be more client side tricks, but any transactions still go through to the server for processing – as with the conventional e-Shop. For the e-Shop, the customer who downloads an app seems a bit like a locked-in customer. How much apps progress m-Commerce (and customer loyalty) remains to be seen: the marketers are making a lot of smartphone developments – but then, they always do.

There are some areas where m-Commerce could be a real advantage, though. Doing a supermarket shop or buying a book could wait until you get home – the product will not arrive for a couple of days in any case. Putting in your final bid on an eBay auction is, however, time-critical (even if you are in an e-Commerce lecture). Transactions on a stockbroker or a betting shop site could also be time-critical – m-Commerce could have a real utility for those who indulge in these markets.

Web 2.0

Web 2.0 is a notion. It is the idea that the nature of web usage is changing from being an information source (*read-only*) to a vehicle of participation (*read-write*). The notion of the participatory web is illustrated by facilities such as:

- Wikis and Wikipedia
- Free software and participatory software development.

There is a limit to how much an individual, or an organization, can do. Involving a wider (volunteer) community, or linking together resources, can create an artefact that is better, more relevant and more dynamic than the offering of any single organization or information provider. That is a part of what Web 2.0 is about.

Some of Web 2.0 is community. It is free, like Wikipedia, and as such is not a part of e-Commerce. Where e-Commerce can benefit from Web 2.0 is where user participation and/or user feedback is turned into a commercial asset. A prime example of this is Amazon, where a part of the facility they present to their customers is user feedback in terms of book reviews (Amazon has accumulated much more of that information richness than any of their competitors). A second example could be Tripadvisor which specializes in hotel reviews but also provides clickthroughs to hotel booking sites. Arguably, eBay is also Web 2.0 since its auction content is user-driven.

Another part of Web 2.0 is the social web, with *community* sites such as:

- YouTube: The video upload site
- Instagram and Pinterest: Photo-sharing sites
- Facebook: A social networking site (see the **Facebook case study** at the front of the book)
- Twitter: A place to share one's profound thoughts and comment on the minutia of life.

These are privately (commercially) owned sites, but the content comes from the participants. The commercial side of the site is its ability to display and target advertisements – the value of these sites runs to many millions of dollars (or pounds, however you wish to measure it). The sites that gain this value are the ones that attract the most participants. Once one of these sites gets a clear lead then there is a snowball effect – there is no point in belonging to a social networking site where there is nobody to network with.

So for Web 2.0, is it possible to derive an e-Business model? Web 2.0 is a dynamic, evolving concept and new models can and will evolve (some authors are now suggesting a Web 3.0). Existing examples suggest that it is about gaining user participation and then leveraging user data/user supplied content for commercial gain. The business model is summarized as:

> The Web 2.0 e-Commerce Model: A community site built with user-provided content that can be leveraged for profit by the owner of the infrastructure.

Note that the concept of Web 2.0 is closely associated with O'Reilly and a conference hosted by the publisher of that name in 2004. The paper *What is*

Web 2.0 is (at the time of writing) available online (O'Reilly, 2005). (But note that the O'Reilly paper is somewhat orientated to the technical dimension of Web 2.0 rather than the participatory ethos that the concept has evolved to represent.)

The e-Shop as an IS

The heart of an e-Shop is its Information System. The shop front is the website (or a smartphone app) – the operations are the backoffice system.

The website needs to be good. It needs to be simple to use, to be able to download quickly and look attractive. Much of it will probably be created on the fly by server side scripts from the database (as mentioned above). Sites such as those for a supermarket or a large bookshop will offer thousands of products and hence have to be able to generate thousands of different webpages. The site will use client side scripts for form validation and fancy features like image roll-overs. The site will include forms for the user to input data that is then sent to the server side system.

The e-Shop may well provide for user registration and login. This is a form on the website that links to a customer database on the server side. Customer details, once logged in, can be retained, held in session variables and be used as the customer navigates the site. Customer login can lead to personalization of the website. Requiring customer registration has many advantages for an e-Shop but it can, equally, deter new customers – UK and European customers are wary about handing out their personal details.

Themes
Security

The e-Shop customer database needs to be secure (using encryption and firewalls). Customer data can also be used for marketing purposes (but any use of customer data must conform to the requirements of the relevant Data Protection legislation: see *Chapter 13*).

Database security must also be applied to order data. The order includes electronic payments and the details of the payment card/account must be secured against hacking and also against any dishonest behaviour by e-Shop staff.

The e-Shop may well need a shopping basket. This allows the customer to select a number of items before checkout. A good basket lets the user see what they have selected, how much it will cost and, if required, take items out of their basket. The basket is a temporary data store and is normally implemented using session variables/cookies – using these techniques the basket can belong to the current session but disappear should the session end (without a checkout).

Checkout takes place once the customer has finished shopping. Once the customer and payment details have to be taken (or confirmed if already known to the system) the shopping basket becomes an order that is stored on the e-Shop database. To take payment, the e-Shop will normally connect to its bank/merchant account provider for authorization. All these transactions need to be as secure as possible (as discussed under the Payments subsection). Any failure during the checkout needs to leave the system in a consistent state and preferably with the customer also understanding the situation.

The e-Shop may have other user interchanges for product search, feedback, storing shopping lists, booking delivery slots and so on. There will also be additional information/interest pages included in the e-Shop.

The e-Shop can be used by many users at any time – the volume is unpredictable. Users are connected over a public access network from computers that are unknown to the system (and possibly using different operating systems and browsers). The path each user will take when navigating the e-Shop cannot be predicted. The server side scripting/software environment needs to cope with this complexity and ensure consistent and safe results for all users. The e-Shop database must be protected: if it does not record a completed, paid-for order the details of the session are wiped out.

Once the order is taken it has to be processed. The IS for an order processing system has been outlined in *Chapter 4*. Other types of e-Shops – such as ticket booking and music downloads – will need their own specialized backoffice IS. The e-Shop IS is summarized in *Figure 5.14*.

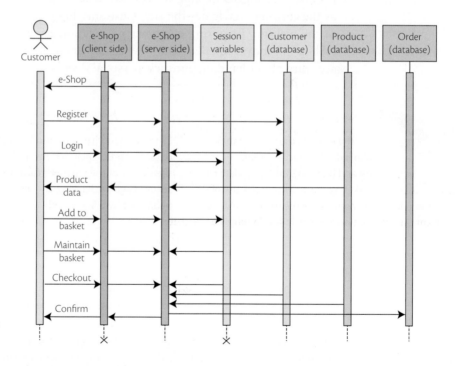

Figure 5.14 e-Shop Information System summary diagram (using UML sequence diagram conventions, see *Chapter 11*).

e-Shop market changes

At one level, the e-Shop is no more than a virtual shop. The shop buys in merchandise and sells it on to its customers. The shop is online and the goods are delivered from a warehouse – it is a virtual equivalent of a traditional shop. It is also similar to the traditional mail-order retail model but with the catalogue replaced by the website.

All of this is normal in the development of new forms of IS. The first systems merely automate and computerize the pre-existing business model. However, IS/IT can open the door to *business process re-engineering* – a phenomenon that is developing in i-Commerce.

An example of an industry that is being reshaped by i-Commerce is the music industry (the record industry). This industry was enabled by technology, first the vinyl record, then the CD. The industry had its own structure, with bands signed-up, records made, and massive promotion and sales. The advent of the MP3 player started changing that pattern – since music could be downloaded the record shops started to close. Downloads from official websites could be replicated by file-sharing and pirate download sites. Downloads, official or pirate, reduced the revenue streams of the record companies, which are now in decline. These changes also reduced the royalties of the bands – particularly the top bands. The technology (recording as well as downloads) could also set the bands free to produce and promote their own music without a record company (but also without a sure way of generating income for themselves). The overall effect of these changes on the music scene has been dramatic, and the change is still to play itself out.

Other industries that have (or are) being reshaped by i-Commerce are:

- The book trade: Online sales have meant that conventional bookshops have struggled and the number of high street bookshops has significantly reduced. The most recent development has been the e-Book and the e-Reader – this will further pressurize conventional bookshops. The e-Book makes it possible for authors to self-publish – a development that may well significantly affect conventional publishers.
- Bric-a-brac (and other second hand goods): These items used to be sold via a small-ad in the local newspaper or at auction, or they may have been thrown out. Now they are sold, in massive quantities, on eBay (with Facebook also getting in on the act).
- Holidays: Most flights and many holidays are now booked online with a consequent reduction in the high street travel agent trade. People are also looking around online for bargains and making up their own holiday packages – again affecting travel companies and their profitability. It could be argued that online bookings have been one of the enablers of the budget airline business model.
- PC manufacturing: Here there has been a move to make PCs to order (as opposed to holding large stock): see the ***Dell case study***.

The effect of e-Commerce varies from sector to sector. Online sales of groceries, for example, still represent well under 10 per cent of the market and nobody can be certain it will grow dramatically (see the ***Supermarket case study*** in ***Chapter 1***). Not everyone wants to order food for a week at a time and wait three days for delivery. Not everyone wants their apples and pork chops selected by someone else.

Case study
Dell

Dell Computers was started by Michael Dell in 1984 and achieved top spot in the worldwide PC market in 1999 (since then it has slipped back a bit but is still one of the market leaders).

Dell developed a unique business model. All sales were direct to the customer (through the website or telephone orders) and all manufacture was *configure to order* (all PCs were built to a

Source: PhotoDisc/Getty

specific order – never to stock). The manufacturing process also employed just-in-time (JIT) techniques, with frequent orders for components and minimum stockholding at the factory.

This JIT and quick-response model means that the customer gets their PC configured to their specification within a few days and Dell is not left with stocks of PCs with less popular (possibly obsolescent) specifications.

On the financial side there is no intermediary (agent or retailer) to take a slice of the price. The JIT approach gives a *negative cash conversion cycle* (the customer pays for the PC before the supplier is paid for the components).

The Dell process is highly integrated and automated. The online order feeds into the manufacturing scheduling system and is then used to control the configuration of components and software throughout the manufacturing process. Shipping is also highly automated, and customers are given facilities to track their order throughout its build and shipping process.

Since 2005, Dell has lost its leading position in the PC market. Dell's competitors have learnt from and emulated their production and sales methods. Also, Dell has started selling through selected retailers (in addition to direct sales). Stories of poor customer support have not helped Dell's market position.

The Dell story was impressive through the 1990s and into the first part of this century. As with all business models it is difficult to keep at the top of the game for ever. The position of all PC manufacturers is affected by the status of the PC that has become a relatively cheap commodity item (with Apple as an exception, thus far).

e-Markets

The third e-Commerce technology is the e-Market (see *Figure 5.2*). The e-Market is the oldest of the e-Commerce technologies and can be dated back to the 1970s, when early computerized airline booking systems were extended to offer flights from more than one airline. e-Markets are also widely used in stock and commodity trading.

The e-Market can be seen as a modern equivalent of the marketplace – free markets that are central to liberal economic (capitalist) theory. The base line model, or analogy, for the market economy is the produce sale in a rural market town. The model is one of supply and demand; let us take as an example the humble potato. If there has been a good potato harvest and supply outstrips demand, then prices will go down until some suppliers withdraw from the market and equilibrium is reached. If there has been a poor harvest and potatoes are in short supply, the price will go up until the number of customers willing to pay the higher price matches the available supply of potatoes.

For a market to work effectively there are three conditions (from McAfee and McMillan, 1997):

- There are as many buyers as sellers and none of these buyers and sellers represents a significant fraction of total demand or supply.
- The goods or service to be transacted is homogeneous or standardized, that is it does not have idiosyncratic or differentiated features across distinct units.
- Buyers and sellers are well informed about the quantity and characteristics of the goods as well as the transaction price.

Whether the market mechanism has ever operated in pure form is a matter of conjecture. The development of the modern industrial, and post-industrial, economy challenges the simple concepts of markets. The market is no longer local, many goods and services have become more complex (and hence less homogeneous), large organizations operate in the market with the power to distort market mechanisms and, as a consequence of all these factors, it becomes harder to be *well informed about the quality and characteristics of the goods as well as the transaction price*.

Electronic markets

An electronic market is an attempt to use Information and Communication Technologies (ICTs) to provide geographically dispersed traders with the information necessary for the fair operation of the market. The electronic market can bring together product, price and service information from many or most suppliers of a particular class of goods or in a specific trade sector. Easy access to information on a range of competing product offerings reduces the search cost of finding the supplier that best meets the purchase requirement. An electronic marketplace can be defined as:

> An inter-organizational information system that allows participating buyers and sellers to exchange information about price and product offerings.
>
> (quoted in Been et al., 1995)

The electronic market is, in effect, a brokering service to bring together suppliers and customers in a specific market segment. The position of the electronic market as an intermediary between suppliers and customers is shown in *Figure 5.15*.

The electronic market uses a computer system with network access to replace the traditional physical market. The sellers post details of their products or services on the computer system. The details are in a standardized

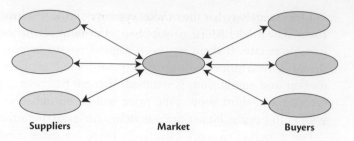

Figure 5.15 Electronic market as an intermediary.

form, set by the electronic market, so that offerings can be readily searched and compared. The buyers then use the electronic market to find an offering that best suits their needs (and often the aim will be to find the cheapest).

The particular strength of an electronic market is that it facilitates the search phase of the trade cycle; it is about finding the best buy (on whatever criteria the customer may wish to apply). Having found an appropriate offering the electronic market will then, normally, include facilities for the execution and settlement of the transaction.

Usage of e-Markets

Electronic markets are exampled by the airline booking systems – first developed in the late 1970s. Currently there are four large airline booking systems that list most scheduled flights available worldwide. These systems are Amadeus, Galileo, Sabre and Worldspan – they are referred to as the global distribution systems (GDS) – see the *Sabre case study*. The use of these systems was until recently via an intermediary; in this case the customer wishing to purchase a ticket does so via a travel agent.

Electronic markets are also used in the financial and commodity markets and, again, the dealing was done via intermediaries; to buy stocks and shares a member of the public uses the services of a stockbroker.

The advent of the web and its use for e-Commerce has changed the way that some long-standing e-Markets are accessed. The public can now have access to the airline ticket and stock market e-Markets via the web (although the human intermediaries would suggest that you might get a better deal if you availed yourself of their expert advice and personal service). Examples of e-Shops that are front ends to e-Markets are Expedia, Opodo (travel/airlines) and the major banks (and others) that provide stockbroker services.

The advent of the web has also facilitated a new generation of e-Markets. These are generally implemented using the services of software companies/ market facilitators such as Ariba. These new generations of e-Markets are variously referred to as:

- Virtual marketplaces
- Internet enabled e-Procurement systems
- Vortals (vertical portal – a portal specializing in a single market segment).

An example of a b2b market is Covisint, which was set up in the automotive sector (General Motors, Ford, DaimlerChrysler plus Renault-Nissan) for the supply of automotive parts.

Organizations that use these systems can have requirements to integrate their use of the e-Market with their internal procurement systems. The use of e-Procurement systems is further discussed in the next section. Business-to-consumer systems that have similarities to e-Markets are online auctions and shopbots: these have already been discussed in this chapter.

e-Procurement systems

Organizations, particularly large organizations, are automating their procurement systems. For the regular repeat procurement of primary supplies an EDI system is likely to be the appropriate solution. For secondary supplies (and possibly the search stage of the trade cycle for primary supplies) an e-Market might be the optimum approach.

One approach to setting up an e-Procurement system has been to invite a range of suppliers to provide their catalogue details in electronic form. These details are then set up on the e-Procurement system and can be searched to find the best (cheapest) offering for any particular requirement. The catalogue details can also be made available on the company intranet so that budget holders can make their own purchase decisions, which are then processed by the e-Procurement system. Such a system allows users to select the best deals, and then the purchases can go through internal control processes. Also, the purchases can be integrated with the company's payment and accounting systems. A diagram of such an e-Procurement system is shown in *Figure 5.16*.

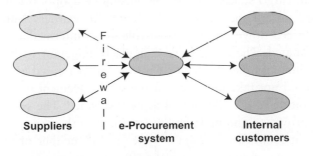

Figure 5.16
e-Procurement.

Advantages and disadvantages of e-Markets

The advantages of an e-Market to the customer are self-evident. An airline booking system, for example, shows a screen with all the flights from (say) New York to Los Angeles. The consumer can make an informed choice without having to spend time and effort finding out which airlines fly that route and then contacting each of the airlines to obtain flight times, price and availability details. Once a flight is selected, the system facilitates the booking of that flight, paying the fare and supplying the e-Ticket.

The use of the electronic market does require that the customer trusts the vendor. This is not an issue in the case of the airline booking (where the risk is arguably no greater than any other sales channel), but it has been an issue when the e-Market mechanism has been tried for natural/perishable products.

A case in point was an attempt to set up an e-Market mechanism by the Dutch flower markets (see Kambil and van Heck, 1998). In this case there was a lot of business logic in using an e-Market. It would have saved shipping the produce from the supplier to the market and then shipping it again to the customer. However, in the end the e-Market arrangement was not successful. One reason put forward for this was that customers did not want to commit to purchase a consignment of flowers/plants unless they had been able to check them for quality and freshness.

For the seller, the advantages of the e-Market are less evident. The most competitive seller may do well; the e-Market makes available information on their product and the advantage of that offering should be apparent. Less competitive suppliers are likely to be forced into price reductions, and the competitive effect may force all suppliers to cut prices, possibly below the level at which it is possible to make a profit (as is the case on some air transport routes). The situation is summed up by Been et al. (1995) as follows:

> The effect of an electronic market in a commodity market is the more efficient distribution of information which decreases the profit possibility for sellers. By the introduction of an electronic market search costs can be lowered. If buyers face lower search costs it will be more difficult for sellers to maintain high price levels.

The paper from which this quote was taken is a case study of Reuters' attempt to set up an electronic market, at Schiphol in the Netherlands, for the sale of air-cargo space. The system encountered opposition from the freight forwarders and the carriers. The freight forwarders feared that prices would be forced down and that their role as an intermediary would be reduced or eliminated. The carriers were similarly reluctant to become involved, arguing, among other points, that the e-Market treated air-cargo as a commodity and did not take into account the service element of business. In the end the operation of the system had to be suspended. The system relied on the carriers providing and updating information on their space availability and on the freight forwarders using the system; since neither of these classes of players was prepared to participate, the system could not function.

Future of e-Markets

Malone, Yates and Benjamin (1987), in their seminal paper *Electronic Markets and Electronic Hierarchies*, predicted a move to electronic markets (from electronic hierarchies, i.e. EDI), a move that has not taken place. The operation of electronic markets is not, in general, to the advantage of the vendors, and it is the vendors who have to provide the information (the computerization of pre-existing financial and commodity markets is a somewhat different case).

The advent of the internet has, however, given the opportunity for a new class of e-Markets in the field of e-Procurement. These new, vortal e-Markets were *hot property* at about the turn of the century (just after the dot.com crash) but the enthusiasm was short lived and probably misplaced; since that time a number of the vortals that were set up have ceased trading.

The (true) e-Market remains a niche application, with most e-Commerce conducted through EDI type systems or using e-Shop (for b2b and b2c) applications.

2

Case study
Sabre

Sabre is an airline booking e-Market, also known as a global distribution system (GDS). Sabre also caters for hotel bookings, car rentals, etc. but its origins are in airline bookings: this is the aspect of the business we will concentrate on.

Sabre started as an American Airlines (AA) system. Back in the 1950s the growth in air travel meant that AA's manual systems could not cope with the volume of business and so AA had to look for a new solution. Sabre arose from a chance meeting between the airline president and an IBM salesman – it was a joint project between the two companies. Sabre went live in 1960 using two IBM mainframes; by 1964 all of AA's booking activity had been migrated to the system. The system was originally only used by AA agents (taking calls from travel agents) but it was expanded to travel agents themselves in 1976.

By the 1980s, the system was carrying flight listings and taking bookings for other airlines. It became apparent that AA was manipulating the listings to give their own flights prominence over the flights of competitor airlines. The practice was investigated by the US Congress in 1983 and in 1984 the practice of *screen bias* was outlawed.

In 1996 Sabre was opened for direct consumer access through the website Travelocity.com; Sabre also owns other online brands including lastminute.com. AA and Sabre separated in 2000.

Sabre is the largest of the four major GDSs. It connects to over 400 airlines (as do the other GDSs) and interfaces to each airline's own airline reservation system. The airlines pay a commission to the GDSs (and to travel agents), so it is advantageous to the airlines if customers book directly with them through the airline's own website (direct bookings also avoid easy price comparisons with the offering of competitors). Budget airlines generally avoid listing their flights on GDSs.

Sources include Sabre (2012).

Further reading

Books recommended for further reading are:

Chaffey, D. (2011) *E-Business and E-Commerce Management*, 5th ed., Prentice Hall, Harlow.
Doganis, R. (2006) *The Airline Business*, 2nd ed., Routledge, Abingdon (Chapter 7: e-commerce@ airline.co).
Spector, R. (2002) *Amazon.com: Get Big Fast*, Harper Business, New York (e-Book edition 2009).
Whiteley, D. (2000) *e-Commerce: Strategy, Technology and Applications*, McGraw-Hill, London.
Whiteley, D. (2002) *The Complete e-Shop*, Spiro, London.

Journal articles recommended for further reading are:

Porter, M. (2001) 'Strategy and the Internet', *Harvard Business Review*, March 2001, pp. 62–78.

Comprehension test

This is a short, simple test to enable you to check you have absorbed the material presented in *Chapter 5*.

Comprehension test: EDI systems

Q1 Which of the following definitions applies to EDI?

    a. A commercial transaction formulated at a location remote from a trading partner and executed using Information and Communications Technologies ☐

    b. The transfer of structured data, by agreed message standards, from one computer system to another, by electronic means ☐

    c. A server-based system, for commercial transactions, accessed from outside the organization via a public access network ☐

    d. An IOS that allows buyers and sellers to exchange information about price and product offerings ☐

Q2 Which of the following is the UN EDI standard?

    a. Odette ☐

    b. Tradacom ☐

    c. ANSI-X12 ☐

    d. EDIFACT ☐

Q3 Which of the following standards can be used as the framework for EDI messaging?

    a. SGML ☐

    b. HTML ☐

    c. XML ☐

    d. XSLT ☐

Q4 The essential facility of a value added data service (VADS) is:

    a. Consultancy services from the VADS supplier ☐

    b. Use of TCP/IP protocol ☐

    c. The ability of anyone to use the service free of charge ☐

    d. Post and forward ☐

Q5 For EDI security a trusted third party can be used to:

    a. Determine the legal jurisdiction used to resolve disputes ☐

    b. Ensure the privacy of the message ☐

    c. Prevent tampering ☐

    d. Ensure the non-repudiation of the message ☐

Comprehension test: i-Commerce

Q6 Which of the following definitions applies to i-Commerce/e-Shop?

a. A commercial transaction formulated at a location remote from a trading partner and executed using Information and Communications Technologies ☐

b. The transfer of structured data, by agreed message standards, from one computer system to another, by electronic means ☐

c. A server-based system, for commercial transactions, accessed from outside the organization via a public access network ☐

d. An IOS that allows buyers and sellers to exchange information about price and product offerings ☐

Q7 The IT structure of an e-Shop is:

a. An app run on a PC or a smartphone ☐

b. An order processing system run on a mainframe ☐

c. A client-server system ☐

d. Peer-to-peer computing ☐

Q8 Which of the following HTML tags is a prime source of keywords for the search engine indexing system?

a. H1 ☐

b. HTML ☐

c. FORM ☐

d. META ☐

Q9 Which encryption scheme is normally used for secure transmission of e-Shop payment data?

a. Pretty good privacy (PGP) ☐

b. Secure socket layer (SSL) ☐

c. Endpoint encryption ☐

d. Point-to-point encryption (P2PE) ☐

Q10 A price comparison site can also be referred to as a:

a. e-Market ☐

b. Shopbot ☐

c. Web service ☐

d. Smartphone app ☐

Comprehension test: e-Markets

Q11 Which of the following definitions applies to an e-Market?

a. A commercial transaction formulated at a location remote from a trading partner and executed using Information and Communications Technologies ☐

b. The transfer of structured data, by agreed message standards, from one computer system to another, by electronic means ☐

c. A server-based system, for commercial transactions, accessed from outside the organization via a public access network ☐

d. An IOS that allows buyers and sellers to exchange information about price and product offerings ☐

Q12 For an e-Market to work effectively the goods offered must be:

a. Tangible ☐

b. Intangible ☐

c. Homogeneous ☐

d. Non-perishable ☐

Q13 The airline booking e-Market systems are collectively known as:

a. e-Travel markets ☐

b. Global Information Systems (GIS) ☐

c. Global airline booking markets (GABM) ☐

d. Global distribution systems (GDS) ☐

Q14 An e-Market acts as a:

a. Regulator ☐
b. Intermediary ☐
c. Network provider ☐
d. After-sales service ☐

Q15 The major disadvantage of an e-Market to suppliers is:

a. That it tends to force prices down ☐
b. Access to markets is limited ☐
c. Requires 24/7 availability ☐
d. Stops them from running their own e-Shop ☐

Exercises

The following exercises are designed to aid your understanding of the material presented in this chapter. They can be used for self-study or selected exercises can be used for tutorial discussion.

1 **Comprehension** List the four main elements of an EDI system.

2 **Comprehension** List transactions that take place between business trading partners that seem suitable for EDI implementation. Suggest some business communications that would not be suitable for this technology.

3 **Comprehension** In the section on advantages and disadvantages of EDI, EDI is compared with paper orders. If the orders were communicated in a phone call, which advantages and disadvantages would still apply?

4 **Comprehension** Use the internet for an online shopping trip and see how easy it is to find what you want, how well the sites work and whether you get good value for money (but stop before the payment stage!). Set yourself an objective before you start. Suitable subjects are:

- A flight to New York. Choose a set of dates, such as the first Friday in February and returning the following Monday. Set out from your home town choosing the most convenient airport but balancing that with getting a good deal (and if you live in North America set the destination as Paris).
- You have come to university/college with your expensive new PC and you are now rather worried about the level of thefts from student accommodation. A large dog is one possibility but seems a bit impracticable: get online and find some insurance for your PC that would suit your circumstances and your budget.

5 **Discussion** Continuing from Question 4. If the question is done as a class exercise, then compare results. Which search engines with what search keys worked best (or did some students find their e-Shop in other ways)? Did the sites found/sites used belong to the service providers or were they the sites of agents/brokers? Were the sites attractive and easy to use? Who got the best deal and how did they find it?

Now put yourself in the position of the manager of a company providing the services you were looking for (flights, insurances, etc.). On the basis of your search, how do you think that the e-Commerce strategy of such a company might be improved? Discuss.

6 **Research** The music (record) industry has been changed by the move to e-Shop music downloads and has been severely undermined by the widespread availability of pirate copies. The advent of the e-Book portends a similar seismic change in the book publishing/book selling sector. Examine these changes and likely developments in this market. Assess their potential effect on authors, publishers and book retailers.

7 **Research** Facebook was floated on the Nasdaq stock exchange in 2012. To justify its valuation, Facebook needs to derive a substantially greater income from its (commercial) activities than was then the case. Discuss how Facebook could/should increase its revenues without alienating its user base. Note there is a *Facebook case study* at the front of the book.

PART **3** COMPUTER SYSTEMS

Chapters

The essential structure of an Information System is that we put data in and get information out. Data has to be processed in order to be converted into information (or another data set); for an IS the processing engine is a computer system. The process may look up data saved from a previous process and may itself save data for use in later processing. These four basic components of an IS are represented below:

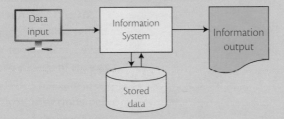

Data in – information out

The business use of computers requires some knowledge of Information Technology – we look at this in *Chapter 6*. The design of each part of the system is an essential part of the IS role. We will look at data capture and management information in *Chapter 7*, followed by data storage in *Chapter 8*. Most IS are networked (and even where an Information System is stand-alone it is likely to be run on a networked computer). Networking may be to provide desktop access to the system or it can be a more complex network linking systems and/or providing internet access. Networks and the security of computer systems and computer networks are looked at in *Chapter 9*.

6 COMPUTERS AND INFORMATION TECHNOLOGY

Summary

Information Systems (IS) are the business applications of the computer – Information Technology (IT) is the computing and communications infrastructure on which the IS run.

Computing can be dated to the 1940s and the commercial use of computing to the following decade. Early computing was restricted to large companies and government departments, which used mainframe computers.

Today computers are ubiquitous. There is a PC on every desk and in every home (well almost) and many of us have a smartphone in our bag or pocket (in effect a portable computer). These computers are networked to servers within the company, at the telecom provider and across the world.

Many IS are shared systems, and that requires the right combination of clients, servers, mainframes, networks and storage to operate effectively. The IS can be configured as client-server systems. Sometimes the provision of IT is outsourced – one approach to achieve flexible and scalable server resources is cloud computing. It is the job of IS professionals to ensure that the necessary IT is in place to run the IS that they are specifying.

At the heart of all this IT provision is digital computing, constructed out of logic circuits. Computers use binary arithmetic, are designed in accordance with Von Neumann architecture and the operation of the computer is dependent on the programs. The technology element of IT is introduced at the end of this chapter.

Source: Getty

Learning outcomes

Having read this chapter and completed the exercises, you should:

- Appreciate the range of computer systems available and how they might be configured to provide the Information Technology infrastructure of an organization
- Understand the concepts of a client-server system and cloud computing
- Have obtained a general understanding of how computers function (binary, logic circuits, Von Neumann architecture and programming languages).

Key terms	Information Technology (IT), system software, application software, first-/second-/ third-generation computer, network, database, personal computer (PC), server, main-frame, supercomputer, secondary storage, operating system (OS), client-server system, web services, cloud computing, Software as a Service (SaaS), binary, logic circuit, Von Neumann architecture, programming language.

Information Technology

Information Technology (IT): computing equipment (hardware) – the term is now normally understood to also encompass communications technology.

system software: generic software that operates and controls the IT and provides an interface for the running of application software.

application software: programs used for a business purpose – an Information System.

Information Technology (IT) is the equipment we use in computing – business, personal and mobile computing. Our usage of the term IT encompasses the use of communications technology – this can be made explicit by specifying Information and Communications Technology (ICT) but, with communications now an integral part of almost all computing, the distinction seems unnecessary.

The operation of IT is, in general, dependent on software. **System software** is necessary for the IT to function – the operating system being the prime example. We will consider the system software as part of the IT domain.

The use of IT often requires application software. This might be a general-purpose package such as a word processor, or something more business specific, such as payroll software. **Application software** is an Information System (IS) (note that some authors see IS as part of IT: this does not seem useful; computing is the appropriate term to encompass the combined field of IT and IS).

3

The development of IT

first-generation computers: early computers dating from the 1950s. They were large machines: the logic functions were implemented using valves, and each valve was a logic gate.

Computing dates back to the 1940s with the development of machines such as Zuse (Germany), Colossus (UK, wartime code-breaking), ENIAC (US) and Baby (Manchester University) – with some argument about which was the first computer, depending on how a *computer* is defined. The first computer to run a routine office job was created in 1951. The computer was the Leo 1, developed by Joe Lyons (a British catering company) in conjunction with Cambridge University. These early computers are labelled **first-generation computers**. They were large machines: the logic functions were implemented using valves (vacuum tubes that looked like small light bulbs) and each valve was a logic gate (see *Technology* below).

Early computers were not the beginning of data processing. Prior to the use of computers, large organizations had made use of punched card systems. This involved recording data by punching holes in standard size cards. The first use of the system was the Hollerith system – developed for processing the 1890 US Census (card systems were also in use for controlling machinery such as the Jacquard weaving loom). Data on the punch cards could be sorted, collated and tabulated using a series of *conventional machines* (as opposed to computers). The machines were programmed using wiring board (there was a wiring board for each application). The tabulator could make calculations and format printed output. Conventional machines could be used for complex and sophisticated data processing tasks. In the 1950 and 1960s first-generation computers (with punch card input and output) were used in conjunction with conventional equipment.

second-generation computers: used commercially from the 1960s; they used transistors, in place of the valves, for their logic circuits.

Second-generation computers came into commercial use in the 1960s; they used transistors, in place of the valves, for their logic circuits. This made the computer smaller and more reliable. The second-generation machines typically had a larger memory and a range of peripherals (card reader, disks, tapes and printers). These machines, and their peripherals, were still large – they would be housed in a sizeable air-conditioned room and some required water cooling. Data entry was via punched cards or punched paper tape. A picture of a second generation mainframe computer is shown at *Figure 6.1*.

Figure 6.1 Mainframe computer. © Tom Kelley Archive/Getty

The next stage in the evolution of the computer was a change in technology from the transistor to the integrated circuit (silicon chip). This technology replaces the transistor (a discrete component) with transistor equivalents *printed* onto a small piece of silicon. A chip can contain several million transistor equivalents. The use of silicon chips in computer design drastically reduces both cost and size. The design of second-generation computers was gradually evolved into

third-generation computers: evolved from second-generation computers with integrated circuits replacing transistor logic circuits and magnetic core memory.

third-generation computers, which incorporated chip technology. Up to this stage, all computers were mainframe computers (although some smaller ones would be referred to as mini computers).

The use of the silicon chip eventually led to the introduction of the microcomputer or PC (personal computer; an Apple falls into this category, even if that might offend Apple enthusiasts). The history of PCs starts in the 1970s. Initially PCs were called microcomputers and had their processors, for the first time, on a single chip – a microprocessor. The PC also required memory chips as opposed to the bulky magnetic core memory that had been used in mainframe (and mini) computers. The PC, as we know it, can be dated to 1977 with the introduction of the Commodore Pet, Apple II and Tandy TRS-80. The introduction of the PC was consolidated in 1981 by the introduction of the IBM PC.

The IBM PC signalled the start of serious business use of the PC. Initially the PC was quite expensive and use was limited. Over the years the PC developed. Changes included:

- Dramatic increases in computing power (much of it soaked up by ever more complex, and processor-hungry, system software)
- The change from a monotone character screen to the graphical screen displays we use today
- The change of operating system from DOS (command line) to an operating system accessed via a graphical user interface (Windows/Apple OS X)
- The inclusion of networking capacity, as a default, in the PC.

The PC is now a commodity item, it is relatively cheap and available from a wide range of suppliers. A PC on the desk or at a workstation is the norm in business (including specialist workstation equipment such as the electronic point of sale (EPOS) terminal which is based on a PC). Many or most homes (in developed countries) will also have a PC and many people will have a laptop, tablet or smartphone that they use on the move.

The PC is only the visible end of a modern IT structure. The PC, whether in business or in private use, is networked to server systems. For private use the network is the internet and the servers belong to the ISPs and to organizations such as Google and Facebook. For business use the connection will be to corporate servers, some of which may be large enterprise servers or mainframe computers. Businesses also make use of IT capacity in server farms, possibly using outsourced cloud computing providers. Scientists, academics and students are connected via extranets/the internet to services run on servers, including supercomputers used for processing large mathematical models.

See *Figure 6.2* for a diagram representing the evolution of computer systems from their start in the 1940s to the present day.

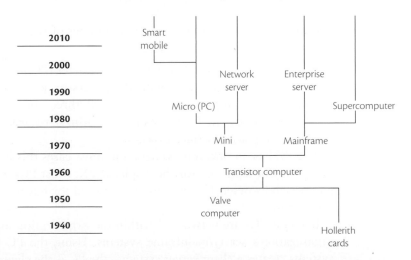

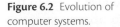

Figure 6.2 Evolution of computer systems.

Two further developments that are of great significance in the IT revolution of the last half-century are:

- The development of networking
- The development of databases.

network: a connection between computer systems allowing the sharing of resources and information.

Networks: The use of computers is now intimately connected with networking and telecommunications. Our PCs are connected to the internet and can access information and facilities held on servers across the globe. PCs at work are connected by local area networks (LAN) for communications and access to enterprise systems. People on the move use smartphones and portable devices as computer terminals – for work and personal transactions. Businesses are in turn connected to other organizations to exchange information and to execute paperless commercial transactions.

Networking started in a simple way in the late 1970s, with local networks connecting *dumb terminals* (a computer-like device that did not provide any local intelligence) to the organization's mainframe. Over the years the terminals became PCs, the networks became faster, the internet was deployed and latterly mobile networks were developed and then interconnected with the internet. Networks are further discussed in *Chapter 9*.

database: a file management system for organizing and cross-referencing data that is held on secondary storage.

Databases: Computer systems hold large stores of data/information. This might be text documents on our PCs and office systems, or standing and transaction data held and used by business systems. This data is held on secondary storage, typically on hard disks, with large organizations needing vast data storage capacity.

The data needs to be organized, updatable and accessible. For most IS the data will be structured using a database management system (DBMS). For large systems, particularly multi-user systems, the design of the database is crucial to achieving an acceptable performance (not a trivial problem). Databases are further discussed in *Chapter 8*.

IT equipment

The above sections have introduced a number of types of IT equipment. Now it is time to explain these in more detail.

personal computer (PC): a small, general-purpose computer, used by one person. The computer can be used stand-alone or to access systems or data over a network.

Personal computer (PC): The personal computer (PC) is a small computer. The PC can be a desktop model with the processor, keyboard and screen linked by wires, or a portable/laptop where all three components are integrated into a single unit. The PC has its own built-in hard disk (some use solid state memories in place of a hard disk).

The PC has an operating system – in most cases this is Microsoft Windows but it may be Linux or, for the Apple, OS X. Most PCs will use office utilities and a web browser. The PC can also be used for business applications and/or for games.

Business PCs are networked within the organization and give access to the organization's server/mainframe systems. Using the PC to access enterprise systems creates a client-server system – the PC is the client.

server: a networked computer that runs applications and/or stores software/data for access by end user computers (clients).

Server: The server is a computer that provides services to other computers. Universities have servers with their student records system on them – the server is then accessible by all staff who have the authority to access/update student records. There will also be servers where students have file space, enabling them to access their work from wherever they may be around the university, or at home.

The uses of servers are many and various – there are servers in the organization (as exampled above) and other servers *out there* on the internet. This includes the servers of organizations such as Google and Facebook – these organizations have vast computing power provided by server farms (that is, large warehouses containing many interconnected computer systems).

A range of computers may be used as servers. The server might be just an ordinary PC (in a rack, without screen and keyboard) or it can be something much more powerful. Operating systems that are used include Microsoft Windows and UNIX.

mainframe: a large powerful computer used for commercial applications – essentially a server but distinguished by its size and resilience.

Mainframe: The mainframe is a very powerful multiprocessor system. A number of processors run the applications (central processors) and further processors are responsible for input/output processing, memory control, etc. The mainframe is designed to provide a very high level of service availability – it has redundancy built in and should switch out any failed units without interrupting processing. Meantime between system failures is measured in years (not something we can claim for our PCs!). The mainframe is used for mission-critical systems connected to large networks and large databases – mainframes are used by businesses such as banks. IBM (2011) claim:

> All of the top 25 world banks run their businesses on mainframes.

In their article *What is a Mainframe* (2011) IBM suggest:

> a mainframe is what businesses use to host the commercial databases, transaction servers, and applications that require a greater degree of security and availability than is commonly found on smaller-scale machines.

In years gone by, the main computer of a large organization would have been a mainframe. Nowadays, that central computing function may well be provisioned by a number of servers, as we have seen. The function of a mainframe is somewhat similar to the servers but there is a qualitative difference. Some large organizations still have a requirement for a mainframe. IBM has been, and still is, the main supplier of mainframes.

supercomputer: a large powerful computer used for scientific applications – optimized for processing large vectors or arrays of floating-point numbers.

Supercomputer: The supercomputer is a fast computer normally dedicated to scientific processing. The types of application that use supercomputers are calculation-intensive, often involving large vectors or arrays of floating-point numbers. The requirement of a supercomputer is to optimize the speed of calculation – as opposed to commercial computing which is normally input/output intensive. The speed advantage of the supercomputer is to quickly execute a mathematical operation on all the values in a vector or array – as opposed to commercial computing which typically operates on one transaction at a time.

Currently, supercomputers use massive parallel processor or computer cluster technology. Thus they consist of a large number of processors and the data in an array can be distributed across those processors for simultaneous processing.

3

Supercomputer clusters are typically constructed from standard computer components. Countries and companies vie for top spot in the international league table of supercomputers. At the time of writing, top spot is taken by an American machine built by IBM: it's called Sequoia and has 1.5 million cores and a top processing speed in excess of 16 petaflops (10^{15}). Note that a processor chip can contain multiple cores – the latest prototype supercomputer chip from Intel has 50 cores. Sequoia has just taken the top spot from the Japanese machine called K – built by Fujitsu and with a top processing speed in excess of 10 petaflops (Fujitsu, 2011). Details of the race to have the top supercomputer are regularly updated on the Top500 website (Top500, 2012).

Weather forecasting is one application of supercomputing. Forecasting models use weather readings from the worldwide network of weather stations, interpolate values for the gaps between weather stations and then roll forward the historical and current weather position to predict what the weather will be. Supercomputers have allowed the granularity of the calculations (using smaller squares on the map and shorter time intervals) to be decreased, bringing about increased accuracy. My own university (Manchester Metropolitan) has its own modest, supercomputer used for computational fluid dynamics research, for example, to model coastal features (estuaries and costal defences) and calculate the dangers of wave overtopping.

secondary storage: any medium to which the computer can write data in machine-readable format. The essential secondary storage device is the hard disk.

Secondary storage: A secondary storage device is a non-volatile medium for storing software and data – in our PCs this is the hard disk. Larger computer systems need larger secondary storage; the simple solution is a larger disk or an array of disks.

The size of the hard disk on a PC is typically in the range of 128 to 1000 gigabytes (gb). Servers may well require more storage and can use disk arrays. This arrangement includes many disks in the system and reduces contention (delays) by providing multi-channel access – a system recently announced by Quantum provides 320 terabytes (tb) of storage (1 tb = 1000 gb). A variant on disk arrays is a RAID, or redundant array of independent disks. The RAID story is rather complex, with a number of levels (specifications), but it is designed to speed up data transfers by using multiple disks and provide fault tolerance by mirroring data.

Other secondary storage devices include diskettes, CDs, DVDs and pen drives. These are essentially PC-level devices (and the solid state pen drive SSD is rendering the other technologies redundant). Secondary storage for backup purposes can also be achieved by copying files onto disk space on a web server or using automated tape libraries. Backup can be onto file space provided by an external cloud computing provider.

Networks: Most computers are networked. Our home computers have a broadband internet connection via an internet service provider (ISP). At work (or the university) computers are networked using a local area network (LAN) to the organization's servers and the server will, in turn, be linked to a wide area network (WAN), very probably the internet.

Networks use a variety of technologies for transmission (wire, fibre, wireless), connecting networks (routers, bridges) and they employ a network protocol to *format* the data (TCP-IP on the internet). This is outlined in more detail in ***Chapter 9***. Many Information Systems are provided across a network (see Client-server system, Web services and Cloud computing sections below).

System software: In order to operate, a computer needs software; crucially it needs an **operating system (OS)**.

operating system (OS): system software that manages the computer hardware and provides an interface to the application software.

The operating system manages the hardware and provides an interface for the application software (Information Systems). The OS is a complex, multi-tasking piece of software. The OS needs to deal with many events that can happen both randomly and rapidly – every data input and file transfer creates an interrupt that must be acknowledged and logged before processing of the current task is resumed. The OS has facilities for accessing and controlling machine resources that applications do not (or should not) have. The OS is responsible for:

- Multiprocessing: Some computer systems will have two or more processors; the OS must support and make optimum use of all the processors
- Multitasking: Many computer systems will run more than one application at a time. The OS must ensure effective time-sharing between all these programs (the basic mechanism is that while one program is suspended, waiting for a data transfer, another program can be making use of processor time)
- Multithreading: This is multitasking within an application: for example, a TP system with many users logged on at any time
- Memory allocation: The OS must allocate main memory to itself and all the programs it is running. The OS will page-out parts of its own code or that of applications to make space for the code that is currently being executed (or seems more likely to be executed – which is why some facilities on your PC run quickly at some times and quite slowly at other times)
- File and network interfaces: The OS is the interface between the computer and the application. The OS knows the physical location of files and allocates space for new files – all file transfers pass through the OS. Similarly the OS must handle messages coming in from and sent out to the network. The OS makes use of additional processing capacity provided by, for example, the graphics and network boards to facilitate these processor-intensive functions.

The OS also needs an operator interface. On the PC this is the keyboard, mouse and screen – with a point-and-click graphical user interface (GUI) that gives the user the facility to run applications as well as checking system status and setting system parameters. A server or mainframe OS will run from a separate control console – typically a PC system that interfaces with the job control language of the main system.

Examples of PC operating systems are Microsoft Windows, Linux and OS X. Servers can run on Microsoft Windows or UNIX; mainframes can use UNIX or their own proprietary operating systems.

The term system software includes other general-purpose software utilities. On the PC most functions are built into the OS whereas on other machines some system software will be implemented as separate utilities. Virus scanning software could be considered to be an example of a system software utility.

client-server system:
a distributed model of
computing – the system
is wholly (or partly)
located on a server and
is accessed by the users
through their client
computers.

Client-server system: This is a distributed model of computing – the system is wholly (or partly) located on the server and it is accessible by users through their client computers, typically a PC. The principle is diagrammatically represented in *Figure 6.3*.

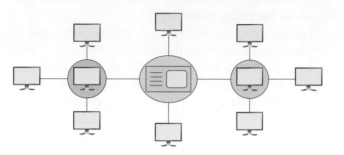

Figure 6.3 Client-server system.

Some client-server systems have a *thick client* where part of the system is run on the client and part of the system on the server. The majority of client-server systems have a *thin client* that amount to little more than a dumb terminal accessing the system on the server. The server system needs to be a shared system, which adds complexity (it can be processing for more than one, and possibly several hundred, users at any given time).

A client-server model that provides for multiple users is a transaction processing (TP) system. A TP system can be built using bought in TP middleware software or it can be written using facilities built into languages such as Java and C++. A complex TP system will need to be able to receive and schedule many requests, arising from multiple user sessions, and access a range of applications. The system needs to retain state (save data) for each user session and associate that data with the incoming message. The system may be multiprogramming, accessing one or more databases, and could possibly be distributing processing across several servers. The system needs to provide for recovery from any system failure and that system recovery must work in tandem with software that recovers the database to a consistent state. CICS is IBM's transaction processing middleware and is used for mission-critical enterprise systems on mainframe computers.

A cheaper way of creating a client-server business system is to use web technology. The client runs a browser that can use server side scripts to access the business system on a server – many software packages are supplied with a web interface. The use of a browser on the client makes that part of the system machine independent (or it should do!) – a disadvantage is that web interfaces are more *clunky* than a well-designed TP interface. Some of the applications you use at university probably use a web interface – for example, the student registration system and the virtual learning environment (VLE). Internet e-Commerce is also an example of this model.

Mainframe and supercomputers are accessed by their users from client systems. It can be argued that the whole internet is a client-server system – the client runs a browser and the webpages are served from the service provider's server. Access to the internet is via an ISP server (or the in-house equivalent in an organization). That said, using the term client-server system to describe the internet is possibly unwise – it would be better to reserve the term for business systems.

web services: a flexible way of deploying and accessing applications across the web.

Web services: Web services, also known as service-oriented architecture (SOA), are a flexible way of deploying applications across the web. Web services are:

> Self-contained, self describing, modular applications that can be published, located and invoked across the Web.   (IBM, quoted by Vasudevan, 2001)

Within web service architecture there are three major roles: service provider, service requestor and service registry. The interactions between these roles are illustrated in *Figure 6.4*.

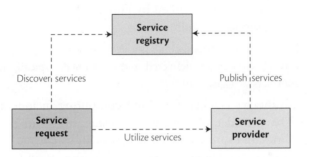

Figure 6.4 Web service roles.

The service provider has the role of implementing the service (the application). The service requestor is any consumer of the web service. The service requestor utilizes a web service by initializing a network connection and sending a request. A logically centralized directory is known as the service registry. The service provider can publish itself and the services it offers in the service registry. The service registry can be interrogated by the service requestor to discover a service provider that offers a required service.

The messages sent between the service requestor, service provider and the service registry are formatted using XML (extensible mark-up language: see *Chapter 5*). XML formats used in the SOA architecture include:

- SOAP (simple object access protocol): Defines a format and rules for describing the content or messages
- WSDL (web service description language): A description of how to access web services and operations that will be performed
- UDDI (universal discovery, description and integration): Maintains the directories of information about web services, keeps track of their capabilities, location and requirements in a universal format.

Web services are used, for example, by price comparison websites to access the e-Shops they make comparison between – the e-Shops provide an XML interface. Web services have also been used by a number of organizations as the architecture for interfacing disparate systems, in particular old (legacy) systems.

The full power of the architecture, with web services publishing themselves across the web and making themselves publically available via an open service registry, does not seem to have happened. SOA is an architecture that could, for example, bypass the GDSs (airline booking e-Markets). One issue with open web services is that anyone can access the services, including users one would not want to do business with.

cloud computing: processing or data storage that is carried out on IT provided by a third party – similar to outsourcing but the relationship with the provider is less formal and the facilities are more generic.

Cloud computing: One way of consuming computer services is to make use of the (or a) cloud. The suggestion is that computing is a utility that should simply be bought – the users need not know how IT services are provided or where they are located – they can just make use of the cloud IT as and when required and pay for the services used. A comparison is made with (say) electricity, which is simply bought from the grid. Very few organizations would construct their own power station, so why, the comparison suggests, construct and manage one's own data centre?

Cloud computing is defined by Fujitsu (2011), a provider of business cloud computing services, as follows:

> In pure business terms, cloud is a flexible, scalable, pay-per-use model for the way IT services are delivered and consumed, typically through short-term contracts. (Fujitsu, 2011)

The advantages claimed for cloud computing include agility, scalability and cost. The provider of the cloud presumably is in possession of extensive IT facilities and spreads the costs across all its clients. The user is then able to access the computing power, or new facilities, as and when required, without the need to engineer its own IT for peak loads or new developments. The cloud provider is also an IT specialist and should be on top of all security and resilience issues.

The comparison of cloud computing to a utility service is most obvious where general-purpose (utility) software services are required. A cloud service familiar to many of us is Google Docs. The Google service provides e-Mail, a diary and online equivalents of word processing, spreadsheets and presentations. An advantage of using the cloud version of these utilities/documents (as opposed to one's own PC) is that they are shareable and available anytime, anywhere; they can be accessed using a PC or a smartphone. The use of these utility cloud services is free (or relatively cheap) as service providers seek to gain market share – at some stage they might become payable services.

The use of the cloud for business (enterprise) software, such as payroll or accounting software, is less obvious. The cloud would need to host the specific application required by the client and deal with issues such as licensing and specialist support. There could be a case for this type of service, but attempts to set up such services before the term cloud was coined were not generally successful – users tended to find pay-for-use, application service providers (ASPs) too expensive. A new incarnation of the ASP model is **Software as a Service (SaaS)** where software and user data are located in the cloud. Access is normally via a web browser from the client's machine; again, this is a pay-for-use service. One might also ask how such a cloud service differs from a traditional outsourcing of the organization's IT.

Software as a Service (SaaS): a pay-for-use service to access an IS. The software and user's data are located in the cloud and the user accesses the service on a pay-for-use basis.

With all this talk about cloud computing, let it be remembered that the user still needs computing and networking equipment. Access to the cloud is via the user's, or the organization's, own PC/mobile device. The cloud provides the server side of the infrastructure. Access from the client is generally via a web browser – and the interface can be more *clunky* than the interface to a utility run on the PC or a TP interface.

Fujitsu (2011), in their cloud computing documentation, claim that pay-for-use cloud computing replaces capital expenditure with operating expenditure and gives flexibility to meet changing business demands.

Themes
Outsourcing

Using an external supplier of cloud computing is a form of outsourcing. Utility cloud computing services provide a means of sharing and archiving desktop utility documents without the need to set up an in-house service. It provides an additional advantage in that the files are available on the move – not necessarily the case with an in-house IT infrastructure. For enterprise computing, cloud computing can be traditional outsourcing by a different name.

The term cloud computing comes from the convention of using a cloud symbol to represent a network (see *Figure 6.5*). We can also say that computing is *out there, in the cloud*, an expression that could sound, and possibly is, a bit vague and uncontrolled.

3

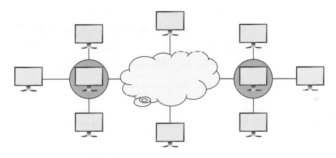

Figure 6.5 Cloud computing.

Managing Information Systems in the 21st century: Richard Hall

Richard Hall founded CloudOrigin in 2009 to focus on the business impact of cloud computing in public and private sectors. He is currently working with blue-chip brands around the world, venture capital, private equity firms and IT suppliers of all sizes.

Richard graduated in Computing and Artificial Intelligence from the University of Sussex in 1989 where he won a BT sponsorship in Expert Systems and wrote for the computing section of the *Guardian* newspaper. Formerly UK Chief Technology Officer and Marketing Director for Avanade, the global Microsoft and Accenture joint venture, he has worked on some of the world's largest application and infrastructure solutions. An Accenture Certified QA Partner, he was trained to review the largest technology and business process outsourcing (BPO) deals.

Richard has been a member of various standards bodies and is co-author of the first FpML specification for Foreign Exchange trading. In 2010 he was elected a Fellow of both BCS (the Chartered Institute of IT) and the Institute of Directors.

Visit www.palgrave.com/business/whiteley to watch Richard talking about Information Systems and careers as an IS professional, and then think about the following questions:

● How has cloud computing changed the value chain of IT?
● Why has cloud computing become even more valuable to business in an age of global economic crisis?

Technology

The modern computer is a complex device (with much of the complexity packaged in the chips). Nevertheless, the essential working of the computer can be appreciated with some understanding of:

● Binary numbers
● Logic circuits
● Von Neumann architecture
● Programming languages.

binary: a number system with the base 2 (as opposed to the decimal system which is base 10).

Binary numbers: The digital computer works in **binary**. In mathematical terms, binary is a *number system*. Our normal number system is decimal: it works to the base 10 and has ten digits: 0, 1, 2, 3, 4, 5, 6, 7, 8, 9. We can specify this by writing 13 as 13_{10}. The binary number system works to the base 2 and has two digits: 0, 1. We can specify the binary equivalent of 13_{10} 1101_2. See *Binary arithmetic explanation box* for a brief introduction.

Explanation
Binary arithmetic

Numbers in digital computers are binary – numbers to the base 2. For binary there are only two digits: 0 and 1.

Arithmetic operations work on the same principles, whatever the base used. Using the base 10 – if we add 9 + 1 we get 0 carry 1, i.e. 10_{10}. Similarly, using the base 2 – if we add 1 + 1 we get 0 carry 1, i.e. 10_2. So to add $13_{10} + 9_{10}$, which in binary is $1101_2 + 1001_2$, we have:

13	1101
+ 9	+ 1001
22	10110

Calculations in your computer are in binary. The computer needs to subtract, multiply, divide and use binary fractions; however, this simple example of addition shows the basic principle.

Decimal numbers can be converted to binary using a number of algorithms. We will use a process that repeatedly divides by two, down to zero, with the remainders at each stage forming the binary number. Hence to convert 22_{10} to binary the process is:

22/2　= 11　r = 0
11/2　= 5　r = 1
5/2　= 2　r = 1
2/2　= 1　r = 0
1/2　= 1　r = 1

The binary equivalent or 22_{10} is then read bottom up, giving 10110_2.

Binary numbers can be converted back to decimal making use of the binary series:

$2^0 = 1, 2^1 = 2, 2^2 = 4, 2^3 = 8, 2^4 = 16, 2^5 = 32$, and so on.

The conversion from binary to decimal is achieved by adding up the binary column headings where a 1 is present. For 10110 we get:

32	16	8	4	2	1
	1	0	1	1	0

Giving 16 + 4 + 2 = 22.

In a digital computer, there are two states: 0 (zero) and 1 (one). These digits can be represented by an electric current and as a magnetic state on, for instance, a disk. Many computers use an eight-bit byte format. Numeric values are recorded as binary numbers – for example, 13 would be 00001101. Characters are represented as binary codes – for example, using the EBCDIC standard, 'A' is 11000001 and 'a' is 10000001.

logic circuit: an arrangement of logic gates to perform a specific logic function.

Logic circuits: The heart of the computer is the central processor. The processor is a complex arrangement of logic gates – on early computers these were valves or transistors but they are now transistor equivalents *printed* on a silicon chip.

A logic gate has a very simple function – it has two (or more) inputs and a single output. The binary value of the output is determined by the binary values presented at the inputs. We can design computer logic using just three logic gates: AND, OR and NOT. For example, a two input AND gate will output a one if both inputs are one, and a zero for all other input combinations.

The individual logic gates form circuits that perform the logical and arithmetic operations of the computer (see *Logic Gates explanation box*).

3

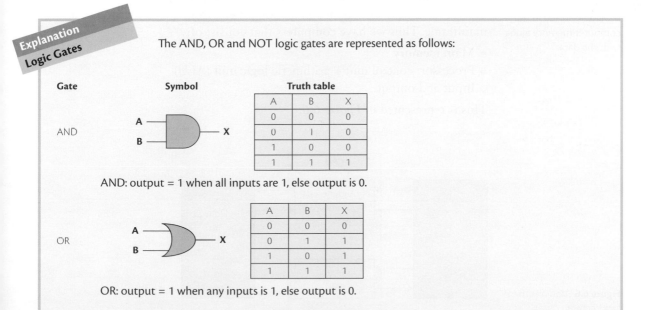

Explanation
Logic Gates

The AND, OR and NOT logic gates are represented as follows:

Gate	Symbol	Truth table

AND

A	B	X
0	0	0
0	1	0
1	0	0
1	1	1

AND: output = 1 when all inputs are 1, else output is 0.

OR

A	B	X
0	0	0
0	1	1
1	0	1
1	1	1

OR: output = 1 when any inputs is 1, else output is 0.

A	X
0	1
1	0

NOT: output = 1 when inputs is 0, else output is 0.

These logic gates are used to design digital logic circuits. A simple example is adding two binary digits to produce a sum (S) and a carry (C), e.g.: 1 + 0 = 1 carry 0; 1 + 1 = 0 carry 1. This function is known as a half adder (a full adder is a more complex circuit that adds the carry back in). This is shown below as a circuit diagram and a truth table:

Symbol

Truth table

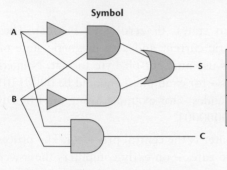

A	B	S	C
0	0	0	0
0	1	1	0
1	0	1	0
1	1	0	1

Note: some text will also represent NAND (not-and), NOR (not-or) and XOR (exclusive-or) – all these logic functions can be constructed using the above logic gates and we need not examine them in this text.

Von Neumann architecture: the computing principle introduced by Von Neumann in 1945 whereby the program should be stored in the computer memory along with the data.

Von Neumann architecture: The architecture outlined by Von Neumann is the basis for the design of all digital computers. The computing principle introduced by Von Neumann in 1945 is that the program should be stored in the computer memory along with the data. This principle, and the model that derives from it, is still applied in all computers, from a small laptop to a large mainframe. Thus we have computers that consist of:

- Main memory
- Processor: control unit + arithmetic logic unit (ALU)
- Input and output.

This is represented in *Figure 6.6*.

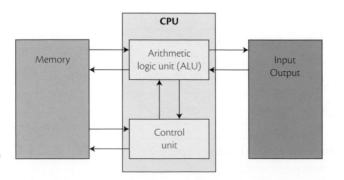

Figure 6.6 Von Neumann architecture.

The operation of a computer, as each instruction is retrieved from memory, is summed up as follows:

1. A *program counter* points to the next program *instruction* in the *memory*.
2. The *instruction* pointed to by the *program counter* is retrieved from the *memory* and placed in a *register* in the *control unit*.
3. The *control unit* analyses the *instruction* and
   ~ Switches in the appropriate function of ALU
   ~ Retrieves data from memory to a register in the ALU.
4. The *instruction* is executed.
5. The *program counter* is incremented (or for a *go to* it is amended).

The operation of the computer is controlled by the *clock* – pulses from the *clock* control each stage of the cycle (the clock speed of the chip is specified as cycles per second when you buy a PC). A register is a small unit of memory in the CPU used to hold the instruction or data that is currently being processed. The data in the memory is electronically processed as indicated above. A (simple) provision of registers in the CPU is shown in *Figure 6.7*.

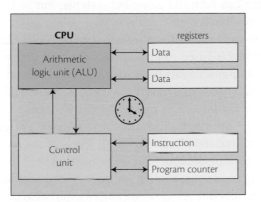

Figure 6.7 CPU and registers

programming language: an artificial language used for communicating instructions to a computer. The language of the computer is its machine code.

Programming languages: The computer operates using a machine code – with a separate instruction for each function of the ALU. Machine codes are specific to the machine/processor chip. Machine code programming is technical and time-consuming, and most programming is done in a high-level language. A simple example of machine code programming could be to add together the numbers located in memory at A and B and put the result into C. In a high-level language, once the variables have been declared, this could be coded as one line in a program:

```
c = a + b;                Java
ADD A TO B GIVING C.      Cobol
=A1+B1                    Excel spreadsheet – in cell C1
```

This high-level language addition operation, which makes good sense to the programmer, has to be converted into machine code. The conversion is carried out by a piece of software called a compiler or an interpreter. The machine code could be something like:

```
LDX   1   A          Load A into register 1
ADX   1   B          Add B to register 1
STO   1   C          Store register 1 into C
```

This is a very simple example but I hope it illustrates the point and ties up with the above description of a computer system.

The IT infrastructure

The IT infrastructure needs to facilitate the IS and IT requirements of all levels of the IS Business Model (see *Figure 2.4*). The organization's IT infrastructure must support:

- Enterprise systems: These systems support the operation level of the organization. They are run on servers/mainframes and accessed from desktop systems throughout the organization.
- Departmental systems (for support functions, e.g. human resources and marketing): The IT required for these systems depends on the number of users – they can be stand-alone PC systems, but in large organizations they will be server-based with client access.
- Office systems (for word processing, spreadsheets, etc.): Typically PC-based but can be server-based to provide security and shared access.
- Internal communications: A lot of communications is by e-Mail, and the IT infrastructure needs to support that requirement. The organization can also have an internal internet, a closed system we term an intranet.
- Management information: Access to company performance and financial data – by management (but also at all levels of the organization).
- External communications: The organization will have formal links with external organizations, trading partners, customers and the like. There will also be informal linkages making use of internet access (some of which may be by the staff using the facilities for personal use).

Providing and maintaining an appropriate IT infrastructure is costly in terms of skills, time and money. However, IS and IT are pre-requisites for doing business.

Further reading

Books recommended for further reading are:

Hennessy, J. and Patterson, D. (2012) *Computer Organization and Design: The Hardware/Software Interface*, 4th ed., Morgan Kaufmann, Waltham, MA.
Petzold, C. (2000) *Code: The Hidden Language of Computer Hardware and Software*, Microsoft Press, Redmond, WA.

Comprehension test

This is a short, simple test to enable you to check you have absorbed the material presented in *Chapter 6*.

Q1 Which of the following is best suited to run an enterprise system where a high degree of service availability is essential?

    a. Personal computer ☐

    b. Server ☐

    c. Mainframe ☐

    d. Supercomputer ☐

Q2 In a client-server system with a thick client:

    a. All processing and data storage takes place on the server ☐

    b. Processing (and possibly data storage) is shared between the client and the server ☐

    c. All processing and data storage takes place on the client ☐

    d. The client uses a browser to access the system on the server ☐

Q3 In binary arithmetic, $1010_2 + 111_2 = :$

    a. 1101_2 ☐

    b. 1111_2 ☐

    c. 10001_2 ☐

    d. 10101_2 ☐

Q4 A logic gate that outputs a 1 if, and only if, all inputs are 1 is an:

    a. AND Gate ☐

    b. OR Gate ☐

    c. NOT Gate ☐

Q5 In a digital computer using Von Neumann architecture, at run time:

    a. The programs are hardwired and data is held in main memory ☐

    b. The program is in main memory and all data is held on disks ☐

    c. The program is held on disk and the data is held in main memory ☐

    d. The program and data are held in main memory ☐

3

Exercises

The following exercises are designed to aid your understanding of the material presented in this chapter. They can be used for self-study or selected exercises can be used for tutorial discussion.

1 Comprehension Convert the following decimal numbers to binary:

    a. $7_{10} =$

    b. $9_{10} =$

    c. $13_{10} =$

    d. $27_{10} =$

2 Comprehension Add the following pairs of binary numbers:

    a. $1000_2 + 111_2 =$

    b. $1001_2 + 111_2 =$

    c. $1111_2 + 111_2 =$

    d. $1010_2 + 10101_2 =$

3 Comprehension Convert the following binary numbers to decimal:

a. $1000_2 =$

b. $1001_2 =$

c. $1111_2 =$

d. $10101_2 =$

4 Research College/university PC labs are normally networked to a server system. What facilities do the servers (as opposed to the PC clients) in your PC labs provide?

5 Discussion Most banks have a branch network but account details are held on a central mainframe system. What are the advantages of having account details and processing centralized in this way? Are there any potential disadvantages? Discuss.

6 Research One application of supercomputing is weather forecasting – use the web to find other areas of study that make use of supercomputer facilities.

7   DATA AND INFORMATION

Summary

To a user, the computer is a black box. Users input data and they, or a co-worker, extract information.

The data input requirement varies according to the application. In the case of a word processor it will be free text; in the case of a payroll system the input is strictly defined. Whatever the data requirement, the data capture method needs to be carefully designed for ease of use and, as far as possible, to ensure the accuracy of the data.

The output from the computer system can be a business transaction or management information. A business transaction could, using the payroll example, be the payslip or the payment into the employee's bank account. Management information might, for example, be an analysis of payroll costs by department. Management information must be accurate, timely and appropriate.

The computer system also holds data on secondary storage – this is examined in *Chapter 8*.

All these elements – input, output (and storage) – are designed in the system analysis and design process by the IS specialist.

Learning outcomes

Having read this chapter and completed the exercises, you should:

Source: Photoalto

- Understand the importance of data capture interface design in Information System design
- Appreciate a range of data capture technologies, their capabilities and their limitations
- Be able to design a data capture interface for an Information System
- Understand the importance of business transaction and management information design in Information System design
- Understand the levels of decision-making and the nature of decision-making within the organization
- Be able to design a management information report for an Information System.

Key terms

Data capture, data capture technology, barcode, chip, radio frequency identification device (RFID), mark sensing, optical character recognition (OCR), speech recognition, interface design, primary validation, secondary validation, human–computer interaction/human–computer interface (HCI), management information, Anthony's triangle, structured decisions, unstructured decisions, analysis report, exception report, key target report, ad hoc report, data warehouse.

Data in and information out

As outlined in the summary of *Part 3*, the essential structure of an Information System is that we put data in, process it with an IS running on a computer system and get information out. The IS may also use secondary storage. These four basic components of an IS are represented in *Figure 7.1*.

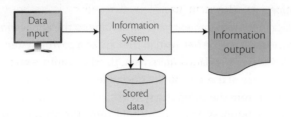

Figure 7.1 Data in – information out.

The design of each part of the system is an essential part of the IS role. In this chapter we will be looking at data capture and management information – the storing of data on files or a database is then addressed in *Chapter 8*.

Data capture

data capture: getting the data from the people who have it and into a form that can be input into a computer system.

The **data capture** requirement is to get the data that is needed, from the people who have it and in a form that can be put into the computer system. Traditionally this is a two-stage process:

- The data, possibly from a customer or a member of the public, is recorded onto a paper form.
- The form is used by a member of the organization as a keying document for the data to be typed into the computer system.

Examples of this could be a HMRC tax return or a student registration document used to enrol on a university course.

Using a paper form can work reasonably well. The person filling in the form may well not be used to the requirement, but they have time to read the instructions, look up the required details and think about the data they are submitting. Yet typing in the data is a slow, expensive (for the organization) and error-prone process. More and more organizations are making data capture a one-stage process:

- The data is typed directly into the system by the end user – possibly a customer or member of the public who is not a habitual or trained user of the system.

Direct-user data entry is now the norm for student registration (with much of the data having been already supplied electronically by the Universities and Colleges Admissions Service (UCAS)) and is an option for people filling in their tax return. Direct data entry may or may not be advantageous to the person supplying the data – it is advantageous to the organization needing the data as it saves the cost of data entry.

Data capture technology

data capture technology: technology used for data capture. This can be a keyboard and screen but the term is more usually applied to automated data capture.

The most common **data capture technology** is the keyboard and the screen – and arguably not too much has changed in the half-century or more that computers have been in use. The data entry is no longer by punched cards but it is still typed on a QWERTY keyboard, and this process is slow, time-consuming and error prone.

The norm for keyboard data entry is to have a form displayed on the screen and the user fills in the boxes on the form – in effect we have taken the paper form and reproduced it on the screen. The design of the form (screen layout) is important – as it is for a paper form. We will come to screen design later.

Given the issues with typing/keyboard data entry it could be helpful to see if the process can be automated in some way. Over the years a number of data capture technologies have been tried, with varying degrees of success. These include:

- Barcodes: Familiar on pre-packed grocery items but used for a wider range of applications
- Magnetic strips: Mainly used on plastic cards we keep in our wallets for various purposes. Possibly now replaced by a microchip
- Chips: Data can be held on a card in a microchip. The chip can hold a lot of data, it can be updated, it is secure (one hopes) and possibly it can send radio signals
- Mark sensing: These have been used in a range of applications but their main current application is the National Lottery
- Optical character recognition (OCR): Using carefully formed characters, magnetic-ink characters or possibly document scanning
- Scanners: Where a document is scanned and kept as an image
- Speech recognition: We can talk to the computer – but, unfortunately, it does not always understand
- Automatic recording devices: Used in applications such as weather recording and in industrial processes
- Hand-held devices: A computer that can be taken out on location (saving writing the data down and then typing it in back in the office)
- Electronic data interchange (EDI): A lot of data is printed out from one computer and typed back into another – transferring data electronically would seem to make sense

That is a wide range of options but they all come with limitations – hence most data is still typed in. Let us examine these data capture technologies in more detail and see what they can do for us.

barcode: used for data capture – to read the pre-printed item/ transaction identity from a packet or form.

Barcodes are a technology we are all familiar with – we looked at barcodes as used in supermarkets in *Chapter 1*. Further applications of barcodes include:

3

- Courier services where the packet is barcoded with an identity that allows the packet to be automatically sorted (for its next destination) and its progress to be tracked
- Cards such as a student card or a loyalty scheme card. This can be scanned to identify the person or an account they own
- Airline tickets (e-Tickets and boarding passes) where the barcode can be checked at each stage of our progress through the airport.

The (traditional) barcode contains very little data – for the EAN-13 (International Article Number) on retail products it is 13 characters. Additionally, the barcode has to be pre-printed on the item or a card. The circumstances where a barcode can be used for data capture are limited (although it is widely used in those limited circumstances). The barcode can be read easily and quickly. The power of the barcoded data is that it links up with the product, transaction, account or personal data held in the computer. This simple data item, perhaps 13 characters, then retrieves information that says, for example, the product is a can of beans, price 75p but 50p since we have bought two. Alternatively, it might say that this packet that has just arrived in Northampton from Manchester should be automatically sorted onto the lorry that is leaving for Liverpool (yes, Manchester and Liverpool are next to one another but the parcel delivery services do things differently).

Two-dimensional barcodes that can contain much more data are now being introduced. A popular application for these barcodes is to include them on adverts or publicity material that people can scan in on their smartphones.

Magnetic strips are mainly used on cards such as staff cards and credit/debit cards; they are also called swipe cards. They have the advantage of being able to store more information than a barcode, typically 60 characters. Their disadvantage is they are insecure – they can be read and reproduced by fraudsters (mainly a problem for applications such as credit and debit cards). For simple applications, such as a loyalty card, a barcode could be sufficient. For applications, such as credit/debit cards, a microchip, embedded into the card, is a more secure option.

chip: used for data capture, the chip can be embedded in a plastic card or a document such as a passport. Contains more data and is more secure than alternatives such as a magnetic strip.

Chips are a recent development. The common usage is to have a computer memory chip embedded in a smart card. The use of the computer chip allows much more data to be stored and increases security but, for applications such as a credit/debit card, the purpose is much the same as the magnetic strip – to identify the card holder.

Smart cards are also used as stored value cards. The card can be updated with an amount of money and that money can be exchanged for a service (with a running total of the remaining value being maintained on the card). Stored value cards are used for transport services – the London Oyster card being one such service. Stored value cards can also be used within organizations for services such as meals (hence cutting out the need for cash handling). One useful aspect of this in schools is that the pupils on free school meals don't have to be identified – they just have the appropriate credit value loaded onto their cards.

The data storage capacity of the embedded chip is more fully exploited in the biometric passport. The chip on these passports includes passport details but also biometric data for facial, fingerprint and iris recognition. The use of a biometric passport allows the border control to record the person's identity while at the same time checking that the passport belongs to the person attempting to cross the border. Biometric passports can be used in electronic, self-service, border control gates where they are installed. Note that non-biometric passports use OCR technology to read the passport details – any biometric checks, other than a manual photograph check, have to be accessed through the border agency/immigration authority's computer system (which will not contain details of all potential travellers).

A recent development in smart card technology is contactless smart cards – the usage is much the same as a standard smart card but the process is speeded up.

Contactless technology is also a feature of the **radio frequency identification device (RFID)**. The RFID is a cheap chip that can be attached to an object. When the object (and hence the chip) comes within range (limited to a few metres) of an interrogator (reader), it is activated and transmits its identification data. RFIDs were designed for tracking goods – affixed to say a pallet, the movement of the consignment can be tracked through the supply chain with (perhaps) greater ease than using a barcode. RFIDs have a range of applications, including the tagging of pets and livestock (where the RFID can be injected into the animal or attached in an eartag).

Mark sensing works by reading marks recorded in pre-set positions on a paper form. Applications have included meter reading and student tests, but the main current application in the UK is the National Lottery. See also *Meter reading data capture case study*.

For the lottery the punter has to choose a set of numbers that they think might get lucky. At the newsagent (or other store) they can pick up a lottery mark sensing card. The card has columns for each number to be chosen in an entry and the player just marks the numbers they think are going to be lucky. They pay, the card is fed into a terminal and the job is done: the bet is recorded in the lottery's central server and the customer gets a receipt (betting slip). The data that is recorded is just the number (and the outlet conducting the transaction). It is the customer's job to work out whether or not they have a winner, and, if they do, to make a claim.

As a data capture method, mark sensing can, in specific circumstances, be very effective, but it does need specially printed forms and machines to read them. An interesting use of the National Lottery system was to sell entry tickets to the Millennium Dome (if you can remember that far back – the Dome is now the O2 Arena). The Dome came in for a lot of criticism, but the ticketing system, piggybacked on an existing infrastructure, was very effective.

Optical character recognition (OCR) in its original form was a way of inputting limited amounts of data. The system worked with pre-formatted forms and the user wrote down the data in stylized form – much like the characters displayed on the petrol pump. In many ways the procedures and applications resembled mark sensing, and it was also used for meter reading.

---

radio frequency identification device (RFID): used for data capture, the RFID is a cheap chip that can be attached to an object. When the object comes within range of an interrogator it is activated and transmits its identification data.

mark sensing: used for data capture, mark sensing works by reading marks recorded in pre-set positions on a paper form. The main current application is for lotteries.

optical character recognition (OCR): electronic reading of characters, scanned from paper documents and converted to machine encoded text.

While the original, stylized, form of OCR seems to be no longer in use there are applications for OCR that read normal type or even handwriting. OCR is used on mail sorting machines to read the postcodes.

Other forms of character recognition data capture include:

- Magnetic ink character recognition (MICR): This is a form of character recognition that is more reliable than traditional OCR, but it does rely on expensive, quality printing. The main application of MICR is cheques. Cheque clearance is a high-speed process using special machines. The machine can read the account numbers while the operator types in the amount – a much quicker and more reliable system than a fully manual process could be. That said, the number of transactions made by cheque are declining and banks would like to phase the cheque out altogether.
- Document scanning: Scanners can include OCR. Some applications will scan documents (such as insurance claim forms) but can recognize key data that can be used in a document management system for indexing purposes. This technology can also be used to digitize documents that only exist in printed form – some old books have been digitized in this way.

Scanners will take a digital image of a document. Some organizations scan incoming documents and then use the scanned document in a document management system (DMS). DMSs are used by some insurance companies to process claims. The DMS controls the progress of the claim as it passes between departments in the insurance company. The staff processing the claim add administrative details as conventional computer data but the claim form is kept as an image, thus saving data entry costs. As noted above, scanners can incorporate character recognition facilities.

speech recognition: recognizing what is being said and recording it as text.

Speech recognition can cut out all the typing that is involved in data entry – a lot of work has been done on speech recognition but its applications are still limited. There is a distinction to be made between voice recognition used for access control and speech recognition used for data capture.

Speech recognition is used by some call centres. It can work well but it is frustrating when it fails to recognize your voice (and shouting at it does not help much). An example of a speech recognition system is the option on the train enquiry service to use a fully automated line where all the details of the required service (day, time departure point, destination) are dealt with by the speech recognition software; but this can be hard work.

Speech recognition software is also available for personal use, typically for input to a word processor. The software has to be trained to recognize the user's voice. Its main application is for people with a disability that makes using a keyboard difficult (or impossible).

Automatic recording devices are used in industrial process control systems. Complex machines will record their operational performance and any exceptional conditions are input into the overall process control systems. Aeroplanes and trains incorporate this technology. Rolls-Royce, for example, receive data in Derby from all their in-service modern jet engines and can liaise with airlines and maintenance engineers on any action that needs to be taken (including safety-critical emergency action).

Another example is unmanned weather stations, where weather data is automatically recorded and fed into the national Meteorological Office and shared through the World Meteorological Organization.

Hand-held devices can be taken out of the office to where the data is available and thus avoid the need to fill in a form for later data entry. Examples of the application of hand-held devices are the gas/electricity meter reading made by a reader who comes to your door, and use in supermarkets for stocktaking.

Laptops, tablets and smartphones can also be seen as hand-held devices. An instance of the use of a laptop as a hand-held device is a gas service engineer who records service details on a laptop and prints out a service record for the customer in their own home.

EDI is electronic data interchange. EDI is used for the electronic transfer of commercial transactions from one computer system to another (see *Chapter 5*). A lot of data printed out from computer systems is typed into another, which takes time and causes errors. Electronic data transfer, be it EDI or just a cut and paste, would seem to make a lot of sense. The problem is that creating an electronic interface can require additional software and the investment is not always worthwhile (and even if it could be worthwhile it might not achieve the priority required for the development to be authorized).

The use of various data capture technologies is nicely illustrated by the application of technology to the business of reading domestic utility meters: see *Meter reading data capture case study*.

Case study — Meter reading data capture

Virtually all houses are connected to the electricity grid; many also have gas and an increasing number are having water meters fitted. All these meters need reading, which normally involves meter readers, often one for each utility, walking round the area and visiting each house. Where access to the meter is achieved the reading has to be recorded (against the relevant customer details) and then that reading needs to be transferred to the billing system back at the organization's office.

Meter reading used to be paper-based. The billing systems of the utility companies would create a list of the meters to be read and the meter reader could then use this documentation to record readings (or the failure to access the meter). This data would then need to be transcribed into the billing system when the meter reader returned to the office.

Paper-based meter reading was enhanced by using mark sensing or optical character recognition. The use of these technologies automated the input of the readings to the billing system but required that each visit be recorded on a separate card – adding to the cost of preparing the *list*. The cards were termed *turnaround documents* – they were printed out by the billing system and then re-input once the meter reading had been recorded. The input process had to read both the printed customer details and the manually recorded meter reading. The use of these technologies has been superseded by the introduction of hand-held devices.

The meter reader turning up with a small hand-held computer is now the norm. The technology has a number of advantages:

- The display on the hand-held device tells the meter reader which are the next premises to be visited (this is also true of a paper list).
- The reading that is typed in can be verified (a credible reading should be a reasonable increment on the previous reading).
- The readings can be downloaded to the billing system as an electronic transfer.

The communications between the billing system and the hand-held device can be over the mobile phone network – possibly particularly relevant where meter reading has been outsourced from the utility company.

Technology used for meter reading is continuing to advance. In some countries and in some areas, meters are being fitted with transmitters and the meter reader, with a hand-held device, just needs to walk or drive by to collect readings (eliminating the problem of not being able to collect readings when people are out). A potential development is for the meter to transmit its reading to the utility – one possibility is for the message to be encoded as a signal through the electricity network. All these developments require investment and can require radio frequency (in competition with other requirements for limited bandwidth).

Another development is the installation of smart meters and a smart grid. Smart meters, as well as transmitting usage data to the utility, keep the customer informed of usage – the customer may then change their pattern of consumption to save money (and, from a green perspective, energy usage). Ambitions for a smart grid include being able to adjust consumption to avoid high usage periods or spikes in consumption – an example could be that the automatic switch on of a fridge is delayed for a few minutes until a spike in electricity consumption passes.

The business of meter reading in the UK was complicated by the deregulation of the market with the (nationalized) monopoly utilities being replaced by competing private companies. These changes mean that several companies are doing the rounds, checking the meters of their customers. Many of the utility companies have outsourced this task to independent meter reading organizations.

Data entry

Where data entry cannot be automated, data has to be typed in using a keyboard. The keyboard is normally used in conjunction with a screen that displays an input form and shows what has been typed. Where automated data entry is used it may have to be supplemented by typed data entry – cheque clearance, for example, uses MICR for the cheque number and account identity but the remaining details have to be typed in.

The data entry may be by the user of the service or it may be by specialist data entry staff – in both cases the data entry interface needs to be carefully designed. In *Chapter 8* we will use an example of a simple order processing system to illustrate how a database functions – an **interface design** to enter details of a new customer is shown in *Figure 7.2*.

interface design: designing the human–computer interface to be easy and efficient to use.

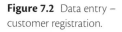

Figure 7.2 Data entry – customer registration.

This process looks simple enough but there are a number of design issues:

- Validation: The system (and the system designer) needs to do all it can to make sure only valid data gets entered into the system – to do this we include primary and secondary validation.

  - **Primary validation** is checking for format. For the form in *Figure 7.2*, the system should check that mandatory fields are filled in, the postcode is a valid format and the credit limit is numeric.
  - **Secondary validation** is checking for consistency with data already on the system. In this case we could try to check if the customer is already registered by looking for duplicate company name and/or postcode (but it is possible matches could be legitimate, as when two companies have the same name).

- Confirmation/transaction: Some functions take two or more screens to complete the transaction. For simple customer registration the new customer needs to be assigned a unique customer number – this could be displayed back on a confirmation screen (but be careful: excessive use of confirmation screens is an annoyance).

The design and implementation of the transaction is, in part at least, dependent on the system infrastructure, and specifically whether the processing takes place on a free-standing PC, the client or the server. Local processing on a PC or a *thick* client can carry out validation as the data is typed in. Remote processing on a server means that the screen has to be submitted before the validation can be done and an error screen is generated if problems are found.

The system could alternatively be web-based, with the form displayed in a browser. This is essentially a client-server system but the webpage can include a client side script which performs the primary validation.

Note that the system would also need facilities to find, display, amend and suspend a customer – we cannot normally delete a standing data record as the data is still needed for transactions already in the system and for management information.

primary validation: the checking of data against pre-set rules (for format, range, etc.) during data capture.

secondary validation: the checking of data against other data already held in the system.

3

Another transaction required in an order processing system is to enter the order. The data required for an order is minimal – all that is needed is:

- Customer number
- Product code } for each product ordered
- Product order quantity

(there can be a lot more details to enter, e.g. a customer order number and order date).

The complications are:

- Customer number: Needs to be validated against the database, to ensure that the number exists and is valid for new orders. The customer might not know their number and so a search on name could be helpful (and difficult since names do not have a strict format). A display of the company name and postcode could be a helpful confirmation.
- Product code and quantity: The code needs to be validated against the database to ensure that the code exists and is valid for new orders. The quantity needs to be validated against free-stock (is the customer informed if the product is unavailable, can the system suggest an alternative or does the system create a backorder?). A display of the product name could be a helpful confirmation.
- Order confirmation: The system could total the full cost of the order and check that against the credit limit (it could also be checked with the customer if they are online or on the telephone). The system could calculate an expected delivery date.

On a stand-alone system all this could be done on one screen (assuming not too many products were required). The system could validate data and display confirmations as the transaction progressed (see *Figure 7.3* for a possible layout).

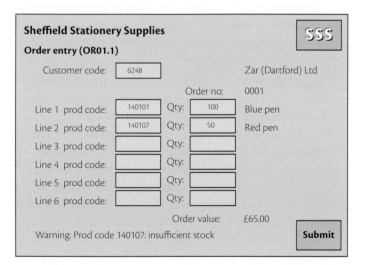

Figure 7.3 Data entry – order entry.

Designing a user interface requires close consultation with users, usability testing and a good dose of common sense. Clifton et al. (2000) say about data entry:

> The main point to bear in mind is that a clear, consistent structure should be designed for the data entry sequence. The system should behave consistently and give feedback so that operators can tell where they are in the sequence and whether anything has gone wrong.

Here are some design guidelines for designing data input screens:

- Screen headings: Include appropriate headings on each screen, including the transaction name and a screen-id. The user (and the help desk, if required) then knows which function is being used.
- Identifying data: If there are several screens in a transaction then include identifying data on the second and subsequent screens. If, in our example, there was a second screen to the order entry process (for more order lines) we could repeat the customer's code and name on that second screen.
- Visual verification: Where it is available, give back a description of an input code. In the example, where the user selects the product code we could come back with the product name and possibly avoid an incorrect selection.
- Cursor position and cursor sequence: The cursor should be in the first field ready to type and the sequence of input boxes (and the cursor sequence) needs to be logical. The sequence should also tie up with any paper documents we intend to transcribe.
- Standard position for data: If the same data is to be output on two or more screens then, if possible, keep it in the same place and format. On-screen error messages should also appear in a standard position.
- Confirmation screen: For something like a 'delete', the system can output details of the record to be deleted and require confirmation. Don't overdo it: for instance, confirming an amend would normally be a waste of time.
- Keep the screen tidy and uncluttered.

Additional features we might incorporate into our screen and transaction design include:

- System menu(s): A list of system facilities allowing users to select the one they want to access
- Dropdown menu: This is where there is a limited number of pre-set options and the user selects just one by clicking on it. A virtue of a dropdown menu is that the user cannot enter invalid data
- Radio buttons: A limited set of pre-set options displayed as buttons and the user selects one of them by clicking on it. An example of the use of radio buttons is for the selection of gender (normally only two mutually exclusive options)
- Objects/icons: Here (possibly instead of a menu entry) we have a small picture (icon) that represents an instruction, selection or data item – the icon should be self-explanatory (an ideal that is not always achieved). These are widely used with PC software but are normally less appropriate for application software and data input.

3

Human–computer interaction (HCI)

human–computer interaction/ human–computer interface (HCI): the science, or art, of designing system interfaces, principally for data capture but also for websites, transaction output and management information.

The science, or art, of designing system interfaces is the subject area of **human–computer interaction** or **human–computer interface** design, both referred to by the acronym **HCI**. The study of HCI involves the disciplines of psychology, sociology, linguistics, graphic design and ergonomics.

Roger Pressman (2009) bases his discussion of HCI on Mandel's three golden rules:

- Place the user in control
- Reduce the user's memory load
- Make the interface consistent.

The first point, place the user in control, is the opposite of the system being in control. Users should be able to use the system in a way they feel comfortable with, that fits in with what they are doing and that is appropriate to their level of experience. The user should be able to interrupt the task that is under way and, if necessary, undo the actions already taken. The technicalities of how the system operates should be hidden from the user.

The more the user is required to remember, the more stressful and error-prone the system becomes. We can reduce the user's memory load by reminding the user of past actions on the current screen – the point has already been made that the screen design should include appropriate heading information and repeat key data that has already been established in the transaction. We can also help user understanding by disclosing (or asking for) information in a logical sequence.

The final point is that the interface should be consistent. A user who has learnt to use one transaction in a system should not have to start the learning process again when he or she takes on further transactions. This is helped by adopting a consistent design style to both the layout of screens and the way the system is operated. If, for example, the system uses control keys then they should have the same, or a consistent, effect wherever they are used.

In designing a user interface we need to cater for all sorts of users. Users might be classified as:

- Novice or expert user of IT
- Casual or regular users of any given transaction or facility.

Two possible user types (derived from the four parameters given above) are:

- Expert regular users who usually just want to get on with the job. They do not need a screen that is cluttered with explanations of what should be done, that contains facilities for looking up simple codes, or navigation paths that require several steps before the next transaction is started. They may, for example, prefer a hot key system (**ctrl+n**) rather than a menu system to select the next, or an additional, function.
- The novice or casual user of the system needs a lot more help. Menu systems, on-screen instructions, code selection and help facilities can all assist the person who is new to the system (or a part of the system).

The novice or casual user will, very probably, soon become something of an expert and the facilities that once were a great help then, if not cleverly designed, become a hindrance. General-purpose software, such as a Microsoft package, can obviously attempt to cater for all levels of user experience. A more modest application, developed for a limited user population, has to balance the cost of facilities and options against their likely use. Nevertheless, the underlying points on levels of experience and on good HCI design are valid and should be borne in mind.

Themes
Usability

The aim of interface design is to make the data capture process as easy to use as possible. A well-designed user interface reduces stress and minimizes errors.

Usability extends beyond the interface to the design of the workstation. Under European Union (EU) Occupational Safety and Health Law, employers are responsible for the design of the workspace and safe working practices of habitual users of visual display units (computers with monitors). Workstations must have adjustable chairs, appropriate lighting and computer displays should be of high quality. Staff must be given regular breaks away from the computer. Concerns include repetitive strain injury (RSI), skeletal deformities and eyesight damage from computer displays.

Management information

management information: information output from an Information System to aid staff in effective decision-making in the management of the organization.

In the introduction to this chapter, and in *Figure 7.1*, we summarized the Information System as data input and **management information** out – this was a simplification. The output from the IS can be:

- Business transactions, such as the payslips from a payroll system
- Management information, such as a payroll cost analysis by department
- Data for processing by another system. A payroll sends electronic money to the BACS system to be cleared from the company's account and to be paid into the accounts of employees (see *Chapter 5* for EDI systems).

An order processing system similarly produces business transactions, management information and possibly EDI interfaces to other organizations in the supply chain. Payroll and order processing systems were examined in *Chapter 4*. A summary diagram of an order processing system is shown in *Figure 7.4*.

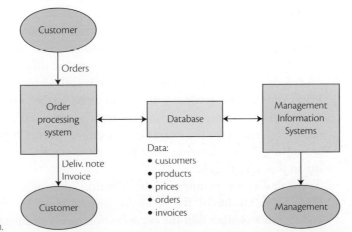

Figure 7.4 Transaction processing and management information.

The relationship of transaction processing to management information is shown in *Figure 7.4*. The business transaction side of the order processing system starts with orders and produces delivery notes and invoices. All the order data is stored on the database along with the customer and product data. The database can then be used by the Management Information System to correlate and summarize the data and hence produce information for management at all levels.

Levels of decision-making

Management information produced from the organization's Information Systems needs to be appropriate for the intended purpose. A very useful model to represent the different levels of decision-making in an organization is **Anthony's triangle** (Anthony, 1965).

Anthony's triangle distinguishes between three different levels in the management structure of an organization, represented as a pyramid:

- The strategic level (at the top of the pyramid)
- The tactical level (in the middle)
- The operational level (at the bottom of the pyramid).

At the top of the organization there is a relatively small population of senior managers. Their role is, or should be, to determine the strategic direction of the company. Their decisions are passed down through the management hierarchy. Below the strategic layer is middle management, whose role is the tactical planning and control of the organization's activities. The third tier is the operational level, the base of our triangle. The operational level is concerned with day-to-day decision-making at the production level. Feedback is passed back up the structure to the tactical and strategic level (who may or may not take any notice!).

Reporting/information requirements differ at each of the levels of the triangle. In general terms, the requirements can be summarized as follows:

- **Strategic:** Strategic level decision-making is, in general, the province of the top tier of managers/the board of directors. The decisions appropriate to this level are major marketing, organizational and investment decisions. Examples are to build a new factory, open new branches or invest in a new product range. To assist in making this level of decision, top managers will need reports on trends from both inside and outside the organization. From the organization's Information Systems they need summary reports on trends in sales and/or the overall financial performance of each division. From outside the company they will need to be informed on the performance of their competitors and on trends in the national and international economy. If we take the example of a sales report, a top manager may want a monthly report showing sales per region and the trends that are developing in the sales figures.
- **Tactical:** Tactical planning is the function of middle managers. The middle manager is aware of the strategic direction set by the board and must endeavour to ensure that the organization meets strategic targets. The middle

Anthony's triangle:
a business model representing the levels of decision-making in an organization. The model is used in the discussion of management information.

manager needs to be aware of what is happening within the department or at the branches and take action to deal with events or take advantage of trends, as they occur. Examples would be a marketing manager who may want to adjust prices, make a marketing push to deal with a problem or take an opportunity shown by an analysis of sales. Most of the information for tactical management comes from within the organization, much of it from the company's Information Systems. Continuing with the example of a sales report, the middle manager would need sales reports for every branch in the area and, at a more detailed level, for each product range within the branches.

- **Operational:** The final level in the triangle is the operations level. This is where the day-to-day activity of the company takes place: stacking the shelves in the supermarket, matching payments to invoices in a finance department or teaching students in a university. The information needed at this level is short term and almost exclusively internal. The information is on specific cases that require action: there are no bananas, Blogs and Co. have not paid the last three invoices or a student has missed three tutorials plus an assignment and needs chasing up.

The reporting requirements for each of the three levels are different. Decisions taken at the strategic level, for example, are generally based on external sources of information, while at the tactical level information sources are mainly internal, and information for operational decisions is usually sourced within the department. Furthermore, strategic decisions are taken less frequently (monthly, or even yearly) and have a long-term and broad impact, while tactical and operational decisions are made more frequently (even on a daily basis, in the case of operational management) and have a more immediate (and limited) effect.

Themes
IS Business Model

Levels of decision-making (in Anthony's triangle) and sources of management information correlate with the IS Business Model (see **Chapter 2**).

Management in the IS Business Model corresponds to the strategic level in Anthony's triangle. Internal sources of information at this level will come from both operations and support function levels – using the Information Systems that cut across all levels of the organization. Strategic management also take market intelligence from the environment level of the IS Business Model.

The operations and support function levels also require management information. This requirement is again supported by IS which should supply information appropriate to Anthony's tactical and operational levels.

Structured and unstructured decisions

structured decisions: decisions that can be made where there are clear rules and the necessary information is available.

As well as requiring different levels and sources of information the nature of decision-making is different at different levels of management:

- **Structured decisions:** At the operational level decisions will tend to be structured. A structured decision is one where:
  - There are clear rules on how the decision is to be taken

- The information on which the decision is to be taken is clear and readily available
- The information requires no interpretation.

If these conditions are met the decision will be repeatable. If the same information is presented several times, or if different people were given the same rules and information, the decision outcome would be the same in each instance. Examples of such decisions are:

- Deciding the amount of income tax to be deducted from a worker's pay
- Sending an invoice reminder where a bill has not been paid.

The information available at an operational level will normally meet the requirements for structured decisions. Many of the decisions that would once have been made by clerical or shop floor workers will be programmed into the relevant IS. In the case of the income tax example, this would be part of the payroll system. Invoice reminders can also be automated, as is the case with red bills from utility companies – other organizations may take a less structured decision where they chase up some customers but act more leniently where they judge that a stiff reminder could jeopardize the business relationship.

unstructured decisions: decisions that have to be made without clear rules and where the necessary information is incomplete or unavailable.

- **Unstructured decisions:** Decisions tend to become less structured as one progresses up the management hierarchy. An unstructured decision is one where:
  - There are no clear or complete rules on how the decision is to be taken
  - The information on which the decision is to be taken is unknown or not readily available
  - Any information that is available requires interpretation.

In these circumstances the decision will not be repeatable. The same person on different occasions, or two different people, may make very different decisions in what might appear to be similar circumstances. Unstructured decisions are greatly affected by *gut feelings* or intuition. Examples of such decisions are:

- Deciding whether and where to build a new supermarket
- Deciding which university to go to and which course to choose.

The risk involved in making an unstructured decision can be reduced by collecting as much information as possible and by consulting appropriate experts, that is, trying to make the decision more structured. Information that could be available will come from both inside and outside the organization and will be uncertain and/or need interpretation. Some internal information will come from the Information Systems but other information will be more informal/anecdotal. External information can include statistics from government and trade associations but it will also come from reading newspapers and from chatting to managers in other organizations – a good excuse for a round of golf?

Not many decisions are totally unstructured (and purely structured decisions may well be automated). Most decisions lie on a spectrum between structured and unstructured and the position on that spectrum has some approximation to levels of management (as illustrated by Anthony's triangle). A third factor is the scope of decisions. Higher managers make broad decisions that affect the future direction of the company whereas, lower down the hierarchy, decisions have a narrower scope. Yet focused decisions can still be very important for the individual concerned. Examples are the decisions a doctor or a bank manager may make on an individual case. These three dimensions of decision-making, hierarchy, structure and scope are put together graphically in *Figure 7.5*.

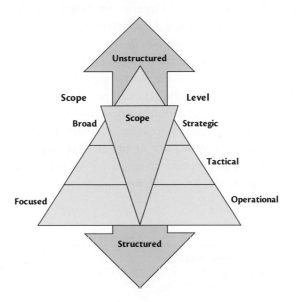

Figure 7.5 Dimensions of decision-making

Management information reports

Next we will look at the way that Information Systems can contribute to the management and decision-making process. To do this we will examine a number of types of management information reports (analysis, exception and key target) and use examples to show how they might be used.

analysis report: a style of management information report where totals are set out in a two-dimensional grid.

Analysis report: The basic type of report is an analysis report that tabulates information on a two-dimensional grid. An analysis report could be a monthly report of top management showing sales, by month and by region. A simple illustration of such a report is shown in *Figure 7.6*.

Sales analysis by region			03 Apr 14 (IR01)
	January	February	March
South East England	157, 000	169, 000	172, 000
South West England	97, 000	103, 000	94, 000
Central England	232, 000	263, 000	187, 000
North England	67, 000	87, 000	91, 000
Scotland	63, 000	72, 000	84, 000
Wales	23, 000	24, 000	23, 000
Total	**639, 000**	**718, 000**	**651, 000**

Figure 7.6 Analysis report – sales by region

The manager, looking at the report in *Figure 7.6*, might start with the *bottom line*. From that bottom line we see a steep rise of sales for February and then a fall back in March – this may seem a bit odd but March sales are still above January so, arguably, that is not so bad. Possibly we would just put the report to one side but make a mental note to check which way things are going in April.

If our manager felt a little less hassled, then she might look more closely. If she did look at the figures by region she might see that the south-east, north and Scotland had maintained a rising trend, the figures for Wales had remained fairly steady, and the dip in sales in March was accounted for by poor figures in the south-west and central regions. Having identified these anomalies, the next step would be to find out why – possibly there would be an abrupt call to the south-west and central regional managers to get to head office early the next day and explain the problem (their problem!).

The south-west regional manager, having received a summons to head office, is going to have a look at his analysis reports (if he has not already done so). One of the reports he has is for sales for each product category for each month in his region: see *Figure 7.7*.

| Sales analysis by product category | | | 03 Apr 14 |
South-West England			(IR02)
	January	February	March
Fresh meat	24, 000	23, 000	9, 000
Fruit & veg	15, 000	17, 000	16, 000
Frozen goods	8, 000	10, 000	12, 000
Dry goods	31, 000	33, 000	35, 000
Other goods	19, 000	20, 000	22, 000
Total	**97, 000**	**103, 000**	**94, 000**

Figure 7.7 Analysis report – sales by product category.

Looking at this report it soon becomes clear where the problem is – meat sales have collapsed. The manager needs to work out why, possibly by looking at some more detailed reports. What was the problem: a problem with getting product from the supplier, special offers from competitors or has everyone in the south-west region turned vegetarian? From the tone of the call from head office it seems that his story had better be a good one!

This illustration shows the use that can be made of analysis reports and the hierarchy of detail that might be used to inform different levels of management. You might also notice that the use of an analysis report requires detailed inspection. There are advantages to that but we could make the manager's job easier by presenting a report with a more immediate impact.

We will explore some alternative ways of presenting information in the next two subsections.

To produce this report the system has to read through all the sales that have been made in the current year, look up the prices and add up the required totals. This is not a difficult task to program but it will take some time to run – presumably there will be a lot of sales on the database that have to be read through (the design of the database can help shorten the run time – this is one of the many performance requirements to be considered when the database is designed). Note that if you have to produce such a report, you should make sure that the totals cross-correlate – observe that the total line in *Figure 7.7* matches the regional total line in *Figure 7.6*.

The reports shown are just two of the analysis reports that might be produced from an order processing system. *Figure 7.8* lists other analysis reports that might be produced, which is not to say that all of them should be produced – there is a problem of having more information than can be usefully used. A similar long list of possible reports could be given for most other categories of IS.

Order processing analysis reports – examples
- Sales by month for current year
- Sales this month by sales area
- Sales this month by product category
- Number of orders by month for current year
- Value of orders by month for current year
- Age of credit (unpaid invoices) analysis
- Credit outstanding per month for current year
- Value of stock by product category
- Stock turn
- Stock availability
- Number of orders on backorder, by month, for current year
- etc.

Figure 7.8 Example analysis report titles for order processing

exception report: a style of management information report where only cases that meet exception criteria are reported.

Exception report: Often in examining management information we are looking for problem areas that require attention. As we have seen above, with an analysis report, we can search through and find exceptions, but it could be more helpful if the system identified the exceptions for us; this is what the exception report is designed to do.

We could have an exception version of the sales analysis report. Such a report would give details of any area where sales have fallen by a given percentage or failed to meet target. This might not be the best approach – it may be better to get information for the whole picture. If, however, we had 500 shops or 2000 sales people, an exception report might be helpful (it could give the top 10, an average figure and those who failed to meet the target; thus putting the exceptions in a general context).

A more common and useful example of an exception report would be that of invoices not paid after a given period. Note that for this (and for many other reports) the order is important. If the report is given in customer number order then the consistent bad payers are highlighted. An example is given at *Figure 7.9* – note that Mike's Meat seems to be problematic whereas, possibly, Fred's Fish just needs a gentle reminder.

Unpaid invoice report				03 Apr 14
(Invoices unpaid after 60 days)				(IR03)
Customer	164923		Mike's Meat Ltd	
			Rem.	Part
Inv No.	Date	Total	No	Paid
6023465	15.10.13	7, 026.00	4	Y
6133492	16.11.13	13, 974.00	3	N
6246555	14.12.13	18, 127.00	2	N
6319845	15.01.14	11, 849.00	1	N
Customer	170029		Fred's Fish	
			Rem.	Part
Inv No.	Date	Total	No	Paid
6137426	19.12.13	7, 623.00	1	N

Figure 7.9 Exception report – unpaid invoices.

To produce an exception report, we must first set parameters to define what an exception is. This can be problematic. There is no point in setting an exception level that reports virtually every case – for example, 60 days would be inappropriate if the average time to pay an invoice is 90 days. It is also necessary to update exceptions periodically: for instance, expecting an increase of sales of 5 per cent when inflation is 2 per cent is very different from the same target with inflation at 7 per cent.

Exception reports are most likely to be applicable at the tactical and operational levels of the hierarchy.

Key target report: Another approach is to set key targets and to then have a brief report that monitors performance against those targets.

key target report: a style of management information report where performance data is calculated and set out against pre-defined targets.

For this approach the key targets should be limited in number, carefully selected and achievable. *Figure 7.10* shows a key target report for a warehouse. The five targets chosen are:

- Stock turn: The number of times that the (average) stock item is sold in the year – the target is 12
- Stock availability: The proportion of orders that have been met using stock that is in the warehouse – the target is 98 per cent
- Orders processed day 1: The proportion of orders that are processed on the day they arrive – the target is 98 per cent
- Backorder time: The time it takes to get stock and process the order where the stock was not initially available – the target is 2 days
- Write-offs: The proportion of stock that gets lost, damaged or too old to sell – the target is 2 per cent.

Key target report – March 2014 south-west warehouse		03 Apr 14 (IR04)
	Target	Actual
Stock turn:	12.00	10.31
Stock availability:	98.00 %	99.25 %
Orders proc day 1:	98.00 %	83.96 %
Backorder time:	2 days	3 days
Write-offs:	2.00 %	3.46 %

Figure 7.10 Key target report.

The report shows a reasonable performance. The stock turn is down but availability is above target, which suggests that stock levels could be slightly reduced – and that might also help on write-offs. The throughput of orders on day one is well below target (but not disastrous). This needs looking at. Is it just a temporary problem caused by high demand or staff absences, or is there a need to strengthen the order processing area?

Target setting has, over recent years, become popular in the public sector – targets are set, for example, for trains leaving and arriving on time, and for students passing exams. All these require a key target report to show performance against the target. In many cases the target is political and unlikely to be met. In some cases, the data to make the measurement is not readily available and resources are diverted from achieving the target to collecting data to monitor the target. (In the case of our order processing example, all the data to monitor the target should be available from the order processing system.)

Key target reports would usually be aimed at the strategic and tactical management levels.

ad hoc report: a style of management information report which is constructed to meet a specific, unplanned, information requirement.

Ad hoc report: As well as formal reports that might be produced on a regular basis there will also be occasions when other information is required. These could be for almost any reason – possibly there is a proposal for a new sales campaign and information is required that is not available from regular analysis.

The problem with ad hoc reports is that they can take a time to prepare, to test and possibly to run (if there is a large database that is not optimized for the intended enquiry). The preparation time can be considerably reduced by the use of a fourth-generation language/report generator (SQL being the obvious example) where the report is specified by parameters rather than being programmed in the traditional way. Some report generators are used by users, thus relieving the IT department of the task. A further problem is testing the ad hoc report to ensure that the results obtained are correct (and there are examples of important management decisions taken on the basis of incorrect information from ad hoc reports). One useful *trick* is to make the ad hoc report produce control totals that cross-check with a tried and tested, regular report.

An example of an ad hoc report I remember being involved in was at Volvo. There had been a hit-and-run accident and the police had found a speck of paint, analysed it and determined it was from a Volvo of a certain model and date range. Our problem was to find the registration numbers and owner details of cars that met that specification. Three of us came in overnight, took over the mainframe when scheduled processing finished, wrote a program and had a list of cars ready for the police before the office opened next morning.

Graphical presentation: Reports from bulk printers may well make use of a true (non-proportional) font, for example courier. This type of report layout might be improved using ink jet or laser printers and a proportional font – the sort of printers that are typically used with PCs but can also be available for bulk printing.

Modern printing facilities can also be used to present reports in a graphical form. The sales analysis report presented in *Figure 7.6* would show the trends more clearly if each region's sales were shown as lines on a graph: see *Figure 7.11* (although there is a limit to the number of regions that can reasonably be presented on one page). The graphical presentation makes it clear that the sales decline in the central region is much more marked than in the southwest region – a point that was perhaps less obvious in the analysis report.

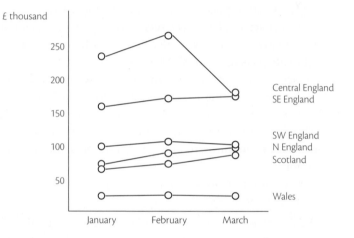

Figure 7.11 Graphical presentation: Analysis report – sales by region.

Management information can also be imported into a Microsoft Excel spreadsheet for further analysis or to use the graphical representation features. The information shown in *Figure 7.11* is re-represented using Excel, as a column-chart in *Figure 7.12*.

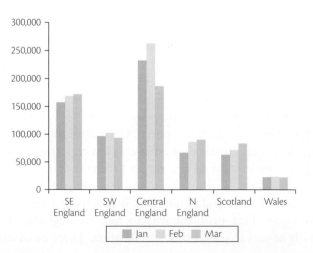

Figure 7.12 Microsoft Excel graphical presentation: Analysis report – sales by region.

One problem with graphs is the temptation to analyse everything, even when it does not provide any useful information. In our example we could have a pie chart showing the proportion of the sales total achieved by each region – this might look pretty but it seems unlikely to inform any management decisions.

Electronic Information Services: The IS can also be used for information displays to employees or to members of the public. Key performance data/business statistics can be extracted from the IS and published on the web – using an intranet for internal distribution and/or the organization's website for public display.

An example of this, at an operational level of detail, is the information displayed on train or aeroplane arrivals on websites, and the information displays at the train station or airport (see *Rail travel information case study*). A similar sort of display is now being made available for motorists with information displays on the motorways, also feeding into radio traffic news and Sat Nav systems. Some of this information is static, but the examples given need to be real time.

Case study
Rail travel information

Travel can be frustrating – and it is particularly frustrating when one does not know what is happening. In times gone by there was sometimes a member of the station staff to keep passengers informed, but now the information is provided electronically.

Before the passenger goes to the station there is extensive information on the web. In the UK, National Rail Enquiries and the train operating companies (TOCs) include information on any planned engineering work and the delays that are likely to be caused. More immediately there is a live departure board that will list the status of all (or selected) arrivals or departures from any given station. This information can also be received on a mobile phone; departure information can be received by SMS and some train companies also have their own smartphone apps. Information is also available through a telephone enquiry service – including an automated service using speech recognition (phone accounts for only 5 per cent of enquiries).

Source: Brand X Pictures

Displays at railway stations come in various shapes and sizes. Taking the electronic displays (and leaving aside poster displays, announcements and asking staff – all of which can be problematic), we have:

- At most city terminal stations a large departure board listing all the trains about to depart. These displays are generally easily visible. They are easiest to follow if your intended destination is the final destination of the train – if you want an intermediate station, and you are unfamiliar with the service pattern, they can be more problematic. The board is frequently updated and these changes often take place while the customer is trying to read the information.

3

- Smaller stations tend to use a video monitor to display a summary of services. Typically, this shows the start and end point of the service. This does not necessarily help a traveller who is looking for an intermediate station and who is not familiar with the service – for example, a display at Sheffield station listing the 07.33 Norwich to Liverpool on platform 2a is only useful to someone going to Manchester if they know that the train passes through Manchester.
- Most stations also have a video monitor or dot-matrix on the platform giving the next train due at that platform. This display gives the destination and all intermediate stations, but you have to find the right platform before you can consult this display.

A new type of display is being installed at some large stations. It lists all available destinations, in alphabetic order, and the time and platform for the next train. There is one of these at Manchester Piccadilly but, as there are too many stations to be listed, it switches between two lists of stations – often before one has found the information one is looking for.

The information for the passengers comes from a system called Darwin, developed by TOCs, Association of Train Operating Companies (ATOC) and Network Rail. Darwin draws information from ITPS (timetables), TRUST (train reporting system) and TDs (signalling system) and makes *intelligent* predictions of service outcomes. Darwin, as the name implies, is expected to evolve (Kessell, 2011).

Passenger information is a demanding environment. There is a lot of information; it has to be displayed so people can view it from a distance; some customers have special needs and each customer requires only a small subset of the information that is available. The train companies have to accommodate all these factors as they design and evolve their systems.

Data enquiries: The final type of report is the data enquiry. All systems need to give the facility to look up each element of standing data and any transaction. For an order processing system, just for the customer order side of the system, we will need enquiries for: customer, product, order and invoice. The enquiries will be by key – order reference, for example – but may also include alternative search keys for cases where the key is not known – all orders for a specified customer. This is very much an operational level enquiry/report. It is simple enough but vital for the everyday operation of the system. The enquiry output is likely to be short and the default option would be to display the results on the user's screen.

MIS, EIS, DSS and data-mining

As already outlined, most of the data for management information is going to come from the organization's transaction processing systems. This data can be analysed as a subsystem of the main transaction processing system or it can be fed across, possibly in a summarized form, into a specialist management reporting system. These specialist systems are variously classified as:

- **Management Information System (MIS):** Originally a specialist system for analysing business data and producing reports for the management of the organization. The plane makers Lockheed were one of the pioneers in this field. Nowadays usage of the term can be much broader and less well defined. In the US the term MIS is generally taken to refer to any business computer application and it will very probably include transaction processing as well as management information facilities.
- **Executive Information System (EIS):** A system designed to provide analysis and reports used by top managers. The system normally has its own database that holds data extracted from the company's business information systems and possibly outside sources (such as stock market data). The system will have ad hoc reporting facilities which allow executives to specify their own analysis using point-and-click technology. The system will also include facilities to produce analysis in graphical format for inclusion in management presentations.
- **Decision Support System (DSS):** Similar to an EIS but designed to support decision-making. The system will have its own database and be able to analyse past and current performance but will also have tools to test out the effect of policy decisions. The sort of question that may be asked is a *what if* question, such as, if we invest in a new factory what will be the effects on sales? what will be the effects on cash flow? This is a more complex tool than the EIS and generally used by the executive's research/support staff rather than the executive in person.

data warehouse: a (large) database designed specifically for analysis and reporting.

An alternative approach to abstracting data to a specialist MIS is to store all available data on a specialist **data warehouse** system. These systems are used by organizations with large volumes of transactions – multiple retailers are a typical user and the *Supermarket case study* in *Chapter 1* included the use of a data warehouse system. Using the data warehouse the retailers are able to record every sales transaction and also to associate those transactions with specific customers, where a store card has been used. The data warehouse can then be used to analyse customer shopping habits and inform the design of the shop layout or a promotional campaign.

The special quality of the data warehouse is the ability to traverse and analyse large volumes of data at high speed – a process known as data-mining. The analysis performed using the data warehouse could take place on the database of the main IS; however, as neither the equipment, nor the data, is optimized for analysis and retrieval, it would take too long (and disrupt the processing of standard business transactions).

Information and operations

Business Information Systems can spawn vast quantities of information, and this information is readily supplemented from sources outside the organization, using both old and new media sources. Frequently there is more information than people can cope with and often it is removed from the context that would make it meaningful. Information is seen as *power* and as a *precious resource*, but, as with anything, we can have too much of a good thing – we use the term *information overload* (but that is only one aspect of the problem).

The emphasis on information and its power to shape and take forward an organization can be overdone. The basic function of any organization is the delivery of the product or service – that is what the customer or sponsor pays for. Appropriate information is vital to the efficiency and appropriateness of the operation of the organization, but it is not an end in itself.

Organizations put a lot of effort into streamlining their operations, but there is an equal need for economy in the use of *information workers* in the management levels and support functions. An often quoted example is the level of measurement, recording and reporting that is expected of school teachers which does nothing to enhance, and can detract from, the education delivered to the pupils. Similar examples exist in many organizations, but they are usually not reported (management jobs are created by the task of assessing and discussing management information – managers are not about to deliberately put themselves out of a job). A recent report on the relative decline of British Airways (BA) (Clark, 2002) reports that:

> BA's reaction to every crisis is to drop a few more planes and routes. But it is a top heavy company with a rather overblown HQ.

It is for these reasons that this book looks at business systems as primarily operational systems and secondly as Management Information Systems.

Themes
Usability

The aim of interface design is to make the management (and other IS output) as usable and informative as possible. The portfolio of management information reports should be kept under review and updated as necessary. It is commonplace to add new reports but avoid cancelling any existing reports (nobody is prepared to take responsibility for saying that the information no longer serves a useful purpose).

Systems and facilities should also be accessible to the disabled – this includes websites. Appropriately designed websites can, for example, be accessed by screen readers (text to speech or text to Braille) and should be usable without a mouse – this is not easy but it can be achieved.

An example of a simple measure to aid access is to include a meaningful text alternative for images (using the *alt* parameter on the *img* tag). W3c (The World Wide Web Consortium) include *Web Content Accessibility Guidelines* in their online documentation (W3c, 2012). Organizations such as the Royal National Institute of Blind People (RNIB) in the UK, offer a testing service to check webpages for accessibility.

Access for disabled people is justified on ethical and, in many cases, commercial grounds. Access is also a requirement of the UK Equality Act and similar legislation in other countries. The full implication of the law, in this respect, is yet to be fully tested in court. See *Out-Law* (2012) for further discussion of this topic.

Further reading

Books recommended for further reading are:

Johnson, J. (2010) *Designing with the Mind in Mind: Simple Guide to Understanding User Interface Design Rules*, Morgan Kaufmann, Burlington, MA.

Pressman R. (2009) *Software Engineering: A Practitioner's Approach*, 7th ed., McGraw-Hill, Maidenhead. (The chapter on user interface design is useful additional reading.)

Comprehension test

This is a short, simple test to enable you to check you have absorbed the material presented in *Chapter 7*

Comprehension test: Data capture

Q1 The 13 digit EAN code is used for data capture in conjunction with:

a. Mark sensing

b. Barcode reading

c. Speech recognition

d. Magnetic ink character recognition

Q2 Documents can be scanned in (as images) and then processed in conjunction with:

a. Order processing system

b. An enterprise resource planning (ERP) system

c. Executive Information System

d. Document Management System

Q3 All data input must be validated. Secondary validation is:

a. Client side validation

b. Parity/checksum checking

c. Checking that the format of the data is valid

d. Checking for consistency with data already held within the system

Q4 Interfaces should be designed in accordance with the principles of HCI. HCI stands for:

a. Human–computer interaction

b. Hardwired computer input

c. Human–computer input

d. Hand–held computer input

Q5 There are three golden rules of HCI (Mandel). Which of the following is not one of the golden rules?

a. Make the interface consistent

b. Validate all data entry

c. Reduce the user memory load

d. Place the user in control

3

Comprehension test: Management information

Q6 Anthony's triangle represents three levels of management. Which of the following is **not** one of these three levels?

- a. Operational ☐
- b. Executive ☐
- c. Strategic ☐
- d. Tactical ☐

Q7 Decisions taken by top managers, using terms used in this chapter, tend to be:

- a. Tactical ☐
- b. Structured ☐
- c. Unstructured ☐
- d. Irrational ☐

Q8 An organization needs, on a monthly basis, to examine the sales performance of all of its regions. Which type of management information report would best meet this requirement:

- a. Exception report ☐
- b. Analysis report ☐
- c. Key target report ☐
- d. Ad hoc report ☐

Q9 An organization needs, on a regular basis, to chase up on customers who have not paid their invoices by the due date. Which type of management information report would best meet this requirement:

- a. Exception report ☐
- b. Analysis report ☐
- c. Key target report ☐
- d. Ad hoc report ☐

Q10 Which of the following system classifications attempt to predict what will happen (as opposed to reporting what has happened):

- a. Decision Support System ☐
- b. Workflow Management System ☐
- c. Executive Information System ☐
- d. Management Information System ☐

Exercises

The following exercises are designed to aid your understanding of the material presented in this chapter. They can be used for self-study or selected exercises can be used for tutorial discussion.

1 **Comprehension** *Question background*: Most university departments monitor the progress of their students so they can provide *encouragement* to any student who seems to be getting into difficulties (not attending or not submitting assignments). Assume that there is to be a Student Progress Monitoring Information System. The system will be set up with a full set of student class lists – attendance at each session (lecture, tutorial, etc.) and marks for each assignment will be recorded as the academic year progresses. Assume that each course has a Year Tutor whose job is to monitor student progress.

Questions:

- Suggest three distinct methods/technologies for collecting attendance data (one of which should be a paper register) and assess the merits and drawbacks of each. Note that class sizes may be large and that students can be tempted to fraudulently claim attendance.

- For the paper register option, design a data capture transaction that could be used to input the attendance data into a Student Progress Monitoring Information System.

- Design a management information report for the Year Tutor. Note which type of report you have used and suggest a frequency for production of the report (i.e., daily, weekly, monthly, end-of-term or end-or-year).

2 **Comprehension** *Question background:* Government are greatly exercised by setting targets, monitoring performance against those targets and then finding excuses when the target is not achieved. Further and higher education is not exempt from this process. Areas where targets have been set include recruitment from less privileged backgrounds (by various ethnic and socio-economic categories) and the dropout rates of students after they start their courses (at each stage of the course). Your college or university wants to monitor the achievement of these targets across all its departments.

Questions:

- Choose one of these target areas and sketch an analysis, key target and exception report for the requirement (make up some target figures if you need to).

- Assess the appropriateness of each report to the management information requirement.

3 **Discussion** *Question:* A case study in this chapter discussed the provision of train departure/arrival information. How could this situation be improved? Are there any alternative technologies that could be utilized to make sure that individual passengers have easy access to the information they need? Would any changes be beneficial from a business perspective, and how?

4 **Discussion** *Question background:* Many readers of this book will have recently joined a college or university. To gain a place you will have filled in an application form that was then assessed by the admissions tutor. Let us assume that we are looking at a course in a prestigious university. It has an equal opportunities admissions policy, we have three candidates and one place to fill. All three candidates have two As and a B in their GCSE A-level exams and good references from their school. Dipesh went to a well-known, fee paying, private school and has been an active participant in the sports, social and community activities offered at that school. Andrew comes from Liverpool and has been at a comprehensive school in a rundown part of the city – he does not include many out-of-school activities in his application. Louise comes from Stratford-upon-Avon, attended the town's grammar school and is just finishing a *year out* on a community project in Mexico.

Questions:

- Is the decision of the admissions tutor structured or unstructured?

- How can he/she fairly decide between these three candidates?

- Should there be some form of rating system and what factors should be included? Discuss with your colleagues.

5 **Assignment** *Question background:* Voting systems in Britain have, traditionally, been simple and manual. For the Houses of Parliament there are *single member constituencies* and a *first past the post system*. Voting requires the citizen to turn up at a polling station, get ticked off the register, and fill in the ballot paper with a cross against the preferred candidate (voters can alternatively register for a postal vote). Counting is also a manual process, with papers being sorted into piles for each candidate, counted into batches (of say 100) and then the batches are counted to determine the result. A ballot paper would be something like this:

Manchester Central			
Bloated	Bob	Free Beer Party	
Cameron	David	Conservative Party	
Cartwright	John	Monster Raving Loony	
Clegg	Nick	Liberal Democratic Party	
Miliband	Ed	Labour Party	

Place an X next to your preferred candidate – only vote for one candidate

This simple manual system is now under review. Drivers for change include:

- The perception that the system could be improved using technology.

- The introduction of proportional representation systems, e.g. for the European Parliament – these systems make counting more complex.

- A steady decline in the proportion of the voters who turn out to vote.

An obvious option is to make use of IT, but the use of technology is not without problems (or potential problems) – security is just one example.

Questions:

- List system requirements (e.g. cost, security, etc.) that could be used to assess and design a possible voting system.

3

- Use your list of requirements to assess the current paper based system (this process could be iterative and you may need to modify your requirement list).

- Identify two distinct technologies that could be used to automate the voting and/or counting process and assess them against your requirements.

- Conclude which of the three technologies comes out top and why. Make your recommendations.

Background notes on voting systems are provided on this book's companion website. You can enhance your answer with further research into the issues involved in this question.

8   FILES AND DATABASES

Summary

To a user, the computer is a black box. Users input data and they, or a co-worker, extract information (see **Chapter 7**).

The computer system also holds data on secondary storage. Stored data can be divided into standing data, such as a list of employees, or transaction data, such as monthly payroll transactions. Stored data needs to be secure and access to that data needs to be efficient (the accuracy of stored data is determined by the data capture process). Data can be stored on separate (conventional) files – for example, program and word processing files. For an Information System, the main data storage will normally use a relational database. Access to the database is through the database management system (DBMS). Examples of DBMSs are Microsoft Access for PC systems and Oracle for large business systems.

File and database design is an essential part of the system analysis and design process; for commercial systems it is the principal determinant of run time and can make the difference between the success and failure of the system. File and database design is the responsibility of the IS specialist.

Learning outcomes

Having read this chapter and completed the exercises, you should:

- Understand the role of secondary storage (typically the hard disk) in the operation of the computer and of Information Systems
- Appreciate the nature of databases and the implications for Information System design
- Understand the use of data structures to facilitate data access in files and databases
- Understand the importance of sizing, particularly in the design of large systems.

Source: Getty

Key terms   Secondary storage, hard disk, database, relational database, third normal form (TNF), primary key, foreign key, structured query language (SQL), SQL restrict, SQL project, SQL join, sizing, serial access, hash random, index access, index sequential, network database.

163

Data storage

All computers, from the largest mainframe to the ubiquitous PC, use *secondary storage* devices. Secondary storage is used to hold software and any data that is retained by Information Systems.

Secondary storage is any medium to which the computer can write data in machine-readable format. The essential secondary storage device is the hard disk. Other secondary storage devices include the solid-state drive (SSD), pen/usb flash drive, optical disk (CD/DVD) and various sizes and shapes of magnetic tapes. Large systems and large organizations will have correspondingly large storage requirements – these can be catered for using disk arrays which contain multiple disk drives (providing for massive storage capacity and increased resilience). Other technologies associated with large-scale storage requirements include RAID, storage virtualization, data warehousing and the facilities available from cloud computing providers.

Secondary storage is distinct from the main memory of the computer. Data is in the main memory when the program is running but that data has to be written to a file, on a secondary storage device, if it is to be retained after the process is completed and the computer is switched off.

This book is being written using Microsoft Word and the text is saved to a file on the hard disk when the author finishes working on it. The file holding this chapter is on a PC and is relatively small. Files used by business Information Systems can be much larger and may be on mainframe or central server systems with vastly more disk space than a PC system. All data retained on a computer system is held on files. That data may be:

- Software: All the software used on a computer will be held in files on secondary storage. This includes the operating system, system software and application programs. The basic format for a PC software file is the executable (.exe) file; there are equivalent forms for other operating system environments. Further files may be used for software, including the program source files (on the machine where the software is developed and maintained).
- Data: Stored data is perhaps typified by the business data used by Information Systems. Examples of such data are:
  - Standing data such as the customer and product files in an order processing system, or the personnel file in a payroll system;
  - Transaction data such as the order file in an order processing system, or the monthly payroll file in the payroll system.

  The concept of data files also extends to documents used with desktop software, such as the document files used by word processors or the HTML files of the World Wide Web.
- System: A third category of files are those used by the system. Complex software, such as the operating system, have their own data files. These files are used for various system parameters and for storing run-time information where it might be required to facilitate system recovery.
- Archive/security: Program or data may be copied from the computer system onto a portable medium (pen drive, optical disk or magnetic tape) for:

- Security in case the working copy on the hard disk is lost or corrupted
- Archive where the data is no longer needed for everyday use but is to be retained, in machine-readable format, in case there is a need to access it at a later date.

Archive/security copies can also be transferred to another computer system – possibly a system that can be used as a standby if the main system fails.

For many Information Systems the data is held on a database. Although the database is a sophisticated way of organizing and accessing data, the data on the database is still held on one or more files. The way data is organized and accessed on a file or database is an important part of system design.

Databases

database: a file management system for organizing and cross-referencing data that is held on secondary storage.

A **database** management system (DBMS), in the context of Information Technology and Information Systems, is:

> A file management system that collects all (or most) of the system's/organization's data within one (conceptual) file and provides sophisticated methods to access that data. (The file management software is the DBMS and the conceptual file is the database).

If we take the order processing system that was outlined in *Chapter 4*, in place of the several datastores (conventional files) shown for customers, products and orders we could have just one (conceptual) file containing all the data that we required.

We can take the concept further and use a single database to serve all the Information System requirements of the organization. The order processing system has a customer dataset: this could also be used for the customer relations management (CRM) and marketing systems. Similarly, a product dataset could be used for any warranty, material requirement planning (MRP) systems and/or the product catalogue on an e-Shop.

There are considerable theoretical benefits in having all the organization's data on one database, a *corporate database*. In practice, such an all-embracing system is complex, costly and unwieldy – hence they are not often implemented. A possible exception to this is the banks, many of which have integrated systems that link the data on different financial products to a single customer database.

The use of the database should make the development of the system easier and the data more readily accessible (particularly where we need to access related data from more than one dataset). That said, the use of the database comes at a price. The price is the additional software that has to be purchased (which can be expensive for large systems) and system performance (if the database is not carefully designed).

The DBMS is primarily a file management software provision that can be incorporated into the user's application program. Most database packages now incorporate their own application generators and whole systems can be (and are) developed using these facilities, with little or no need for additional programming.

Data structure

With a database, we are attempting to build a data structure that represents and makes accessible the data that belongs to, and is needed by, the Information System. These requirements are represented by the entity-relationship diagram (or the object-oriented class diagram) produced during the system analysis and design process: see *Part 4*. An example of such an entity relationship diagram, for an order processing system, was given in *Chapter 4* and is reproduced, with the addition of a simple list of attributes, in *Figure 8.1* (for simplicity's sake the data requirements of the replenishment subsystem have been omitted).

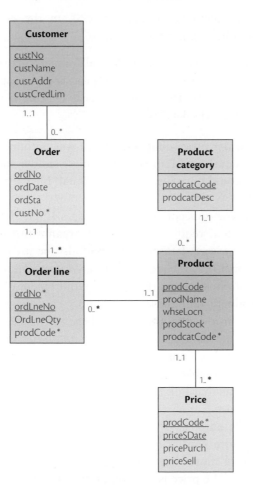

Figure 8.1 Order processing – ER diagram.

This structure shows the need for:

- customer data
- product/price data
- order data (which also covers picking and invoicing requirements).

The structure also shows the relationships between customers and orders, as well as orders and products. The relationships on the ER-diagram are:

- A **customer** *submits* zero, one or many **orders**
- An **order** *contains* one or many **order lines**
- A **product** *is supplied for* zero, one or many **order lines**
- A **product category** *classifies* zero, one or many **products**
- A **product** *is charged at* one or many **prices** (historic prices are retained).

Relational databases

There are a number of database paradigms but the one that is normally adopted is the relational database approach. This is used by the most popular DBMSs currently in the marketplace. Currently available DBMSs include:

- Microsoft Access
- MySQL (an open source/freeware product)
- Microsoft SQL Server
- Oracle
- db2 (IBM's relational DBMS).

The relational approach to database design is credited to Edgar Codd, who worked in the IBM laboratories in the late 1960s. The relational approach is based on the mathematical concepts of relations and sets. Essentially we convert the data to **third normal form (TNF)** and then use the resulting relationships as the basis of the database design. The entities and attributes given for the order processing data requirements are in TNF.

Third normal form (TNF) is an analysis and rationalization of data requirements into entities and attributes that identify the underlying structure of the data requirement. Each entity has a unique key attribute (or a unique compound key formed by more than one attribute). In TNF, no entity includes any attributes that repeat (occur more than once) for any key value and each attribute is identified by the key of its entity. The conversion to TNF can be achieved using a table method (called relational data analysis). This approach to creating TNF is documented in *Part 4*. The ER-diagram shown in *Figure 8.1* is in third normal form.

Using the order processing system data we can now see how a relational database is described, designed and used. Starting with the example of the product entity we have:

Entity	Attributes	
Product	Product code	prodCode
	Product name	prodName
	Warehouse location	whseLocn
	Stock total	prodStock
	Product category code	prodcatCode

To document product entity as a relationship in a relational database we use the following notation:

Product (<u>prodCode</u>, prodName, whseLocn, prodStock, prodcatCode*)

---

relational database: a database organized in accordance with relational principles, that is, based on the mathematical concepts of relations and sets.

third normal form (TNF): an analysis and rationalization of data requirements into entities and attributes that identify the underlying data structure.

3

For this relationship:

- The relationship name is **product,** it comes first and it is normally shown in bold if we are typing the database's schema
- The attributes are listed in brackets
- The **primary key** (product key) of this relationship is <u>prodCode</u>, denoted by the underline.
- This relationship includes a **foreign key**: prodcatCode*, denoted by the asterisk.

See *Key explanation box* for further details.

Using the format described for documenting the product relationship we can now document the complete order processing database, as follows:

Customer (<u>custNo</u>, custName, custAddr, custCredLim)
Product category (<u>prodcatCode</u>, prodcatDesc)
Product (<u>prodCode</u>, prodName, whseLocn, prodStock, prodcatCode*)
Product price (<u>prodCode*</u>, <u>priceSDate</u>, pricePurch, priceSell)
Order (<u>ordNo</u>, ordDate, ordSta, custNo*)
Order line (<u>ordNo*</u>, <u>ordLneNo</u>, ordLneQty, prodCode*)

Note that each of the entities becomes a database relationship and all the ER-diagram relationships are represented by either a foreign key or a key that forms part of a multiple entity key. For instance, the order has the foreign key of custNo* that *links* it to the owning customer. A more complex example would be if we needed to find all the details of a given order (where we have the order number) – the access paths via the keys would be:

- Read order: Key <u>ordNo</u>
- Read customer: Key <u>custNo</u> using foreignKey custNo* from Order
- For each order line:
  - Reader order line: Key <u>ordNo*</u> + <u>ordLneNo</u>
  - Read product: Key <u>prodCode</u> using foreignKey prodCode* from order line
  - Read product price: Key <u>prodCode*</u> + <u>priceSDate</u> (price with latest start date <= ordData on order).

For a relational database the exact access path is determined by the SQL engine (as opposed to being specified by the programmer) – SQL is explained in the next but one section. The *challenging* parts of this example are retrieving all order lines for a given order and the appropriate product price for a given product (the SQL would not be too difficult but the performance of the query could be less than optimal).

You should also check out all the other relations shown on the ER-diagram.

Explanation

Keys

A key is a unique identifier. As a student your university/college will have allocated you a student number, a unique identifier that identifies you and the data held about you in the university/college Information Systems. The key can seem impersonal, but it avoids problems with other ways of identifying you, such as your name. Problems with using a name as identity are that there may be other people with the same name or there may be different ways of writing the name (e.g. David Smith, dave smith, D. B. Smith).

In data analysis, file systems and databases we need to be able to access the required entity without any ambiguity. To achieve this, each entity will have a primary key – the primary key of our product entity is prodCode – a unique key for each product held in the system.

In some cases the primary key will be made up of more than one attribute. An example of this is the product price where the key is made up of the prodCode and priceSDate – the product can have several prices starting on different dates.

Entities also have associations (relationships) with other entities. In our example the product belongs to a product category – the key of its category is held on the product entity as a foreign key: prodcatCode *.

Entity is the term we use in data analysis and for the ER-diagram. On a file the entity is referred to as a record and on a relational database the record can, alternatively, be referred to as a relationship.

Example database

The workings of the database are probably best illustrated by example – not the easiest thing to do on paper but we will keep it simple (the companion website to this book includes a Microsoft Access version of this database and an SQL file to create the database on an alternative DBMS).

Before we start taking orders we must load some customer and product (product category, product, product price) standing data. A restricted set of standing data is shown in *Figure 8.2*. Note that attributes such as address would be a full address and would be divided into several data items, but, in the example, only the town is given.

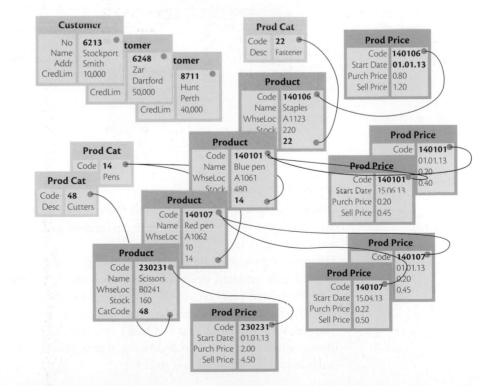

Figure 8.2 Order processing – standing data.

If we then add an order from Zar for 100 blue pens and 50 red pens we get the situation shown in *Figure 8.3* (it would be helpful to add a couple more orders, but the diagram is already too complex).

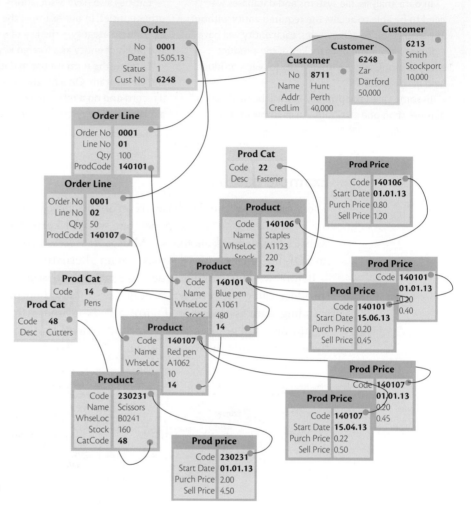

Figure 8.3 Order processing – standing data plus order.

It could be noted that:

- Order line 02 is for 50 red pens but there are only 10 in stock – the system needs to do something about this: an urgent order for new stock would seem appropriate.
- The order's date is 15.05.13. For the blue pens the first price record should be used (the updated price for 15.06.13 is not yet applicable), but for red pens the second price record should be used (the price went up on 15.04.13).
- The order's status indicates the stage the order has reached in its lifecycle. The value '1' indicates that the order has just been input – it can then be incremented when further processing takes place, for example when the order is picked, invoiced and paid for.

SQL

structured query language (SQL): the language used to manipulate and query data on relational databases.

The language used to manipulate and query data on relational databases is SQL; it is based on relational algebra. SQL stands for **structured query language**, but the full form is rarely used.

SQL can be used for all the operations we need to perform on a relational database – setup, updating and queries. We shall look at some simple examples of the use of SQL for the third of these applications.

When used for queries, SQL forms a new relationship that contains the data elements that answer the query. The three principal relational algebra functions are *restrict*, *project* and *join* – these are implemented using the SQL select function and are illustrated below using the order processing data that has been set out in *Figure 8.3*.

restrict SQL: a relational algebra operator that selects a number of rows from an existing relationship to produce a new relationship.

- **Restrict** produces a new relationship consisting of a number of rows selected from an existing relationship. For example, we could select all customers with a credit limit of more than 20,000:

    SELECT Customer.custNo, Customer.custName
        Customer.custAddr, Customer.custCredLim
    FROM Customer
    WHERE Customer.custCredLim >20000;

Using the customer data from Figure 8.3 this SQL would produce the new relationship:

custNo	custName	custAddr	custCredLim
6248	Zar	Dartford	50000
8711	Hunt	Perth	40000

project SQL: a relational algebra operator that selects a number of columns from an existing relationship to produce a new relationship.

- **Project** produces a new relationship consisting of a number of selected columns (attributes) from an existing relationship. For example, we could select just the customer name and credit limit from the customer relationship:

    SELECT Customer.custName, Customer.custCredLim
        FROM Customer;

Again using the data from *Figure 8.3* this SQL would produce the new relationship:

custName	custCredLim
Smith	10000
Zar	50000
Hunt	40000

join SQL: a relational algebra operator produces a new relationship from two existing relationships joined over a common key.

- **Join** produces a new relationship from two existing relationships *joined* over a common domain, that is, a shared key. For example, we could join customer data with the corresponding order data (the example also includes a project so the resultant table includes just customer names and the corresponding order numbers and order dates):

SELECT Customer.custName, Order.ordNo, Order.ordDate
FROM Customer, Order
WHERE Customer.custNo = Order.custNo;

Using the data from our example in *Figure 8.3* this SQL would produce the new relationship:

custName	ordNo	ordDate
Zar	0001	15.06.13

SQL can be used when running the DBMS package or it can be incorporated into the user's program. It is, in effect, a functional language (as opposed to a procedural language): in other words, SQL specifies the requirement as opposed to stating how that requirement is to be executed. SQL also produces a table of results (rather than one line/record at a time); the program will then need to process each data element in turn to produce a report, create totals, or whatever is required.

In principle, SQL should be a standard data manipulation language; it is applicable to any relational database and any relational DBMS. This could be particularly useful in a distributed system where a client could issue SQL to use any database on any server in the system. In practice, while the basic core of SQL is the same across all relational DBMSs, the various database vendors have included their own enhancements and variations in their implementation.

If you, or your college/university, is using Oracle, you are probably taught SQL (and Oracle will license their SQL training packages for educational institutions). Many students are set exercises/assignments using Microsoft Access and will probably use the basic interfaces or wizards – these interfaces generate SQL and the SQL code can be seen using the view SQL option. Microsoft Access can also be programmed using SQL – this approach would be necessary if an Access database were to be accessed from a user program such as a server side script incorporated into a webpage.

Data structures and processing efficiency

The processing time (run time) of an Information System is normally determined by the number of physical file accesses. Commercial systems do not, in general, make intensive use of the processor (and the processor is fast) but they do shift a lot of data to and from secondary storage (and disks, which require the mechanical rotation of the disk and physical movement of the read/write heads are very slow compared with processor speeds).

For systems that batch process large amounts of data or serve a large number of online users, processing time/run time can make the difference between a successful and a failed system. It is the job of the system designer to carry out a **sizing** exercise and make sure that the design, particularly the file/database design, will deliver an acceptable performance. Sizing an online system involves calculating the number of physical disk accesses per transaction,

sizing: calculating the likely run time of an Information System during the design stage.

multiplying that by the expected peak transaction rate and comparing that with the performance of the planned IT system. Similarly, sizing the batch system involves calculating the number of physical disk accesses for each batch run and working out how long that will take. If the predicted performance is not acceptable then the file/database design needs to be optimized (or an IT system that will better cope with the expected workload can be installed – but optimization of the database design should be the first step). There are also further factors, such as which processes can be multitasked against one another and whether performance can be improved by placing parts of the database on separate disk drives – but we will leave these complicating factors out of this introductory level discussion.

For a modern system, sizing and database optimization is difficult. The system typically has a large number of online transactions that require direct access to a small number of records. The system will also have a number of batch processes that require serial access to a large number of records. The issue is that file/database design for random access is incompatible with efficient batch processing. The issue arises from the nature of the disk and the difference between logical and physical disk access:

- Logical access: The user/program requirement is for a single record, for example, a customer from our order processing database. For online processing this would be a specific customer selected by key. For batch processing it may simply be the next customer as we read all the customers in the system.
- Physical access: The disk reads, writes and stores records in blocks. Let us suppose a full block takes 20 customer records. When we read the block it is transferred into memory and the required record is accessible to the program.

So to process customer records. For random access we read the block, unpack the record we need – one physical access (possibly more – we will come to that). For batch processing a single physical access could give us 20 customer records – for a file or 20,000 customers that could reduce the number of physical accesses to 1000, but that is dependent on the file design.

For an online transaction the number of physical accesses can be significant. If, for example, we create Zar's order on our very simple database (see *Figure 8.3*) we need to:

	physical accesses
● Read customer: Key 6248	1
● Write order: Key 0001	2
● Read and update product: Key 140101	2
● Write order line: Key 0001/01	2
● Read and update product: Key 140107	2
● Write order line: Key 0001/02	2

Note to write a record requires the target block to be read, hence 2 accesses.

This is a total of 11 physical disk accesses for this one simple transaction, from a single online user, on a simple database. The numbers could be increased if we used constructs such as indexes. We would probably require our system to log transactions and database updates for recovery purposes, and that would be more physical disk transfers.

Data structures: The number of physical disk transfers is dependent on the requirements of the system and the design of the file or database. To design a file we use a data structure that meets our processing requirements. Adopting a database we make use of the data structures incorporated in that DBMS (and on large DBMSs such as Oracle we can influence the data structures that are applied to optimize the system). The basic data structures are:

serial access: reading data from the start of a file a block and hence a record at a time.

- **Serial:** The simplest way of organizing data is the serial file. For this type of file the records are just stored one after another in whatever sequence the system designer chooses. For the customer data exampled above, the customers could be stored in custNo sequence and packed at 20 per block. There is no updating of the file in situ – to update the file anew, an updated version has to be created.

  Databases update data in situ and do not provide for a serial file structure (in its simple form). It is, however, possible for an area of the database to be read serially if that is applicable to the processing requirements.

hash random: a method of achieving direct access to data held on files or a database. The block of a record is calculated using the key in a hashing algorithm.

- **Hash random:** This is the simplest way of organizing data for random access. This approach uses an algorithm (a hashing algorithm) on the key to calculate the block where the record is to be stored. The basic requirement of the algorithm is that the answer is within the range of the blocks in the file/file area. It is advantageous if the algorithm produces a random distribution, as it should cut down on any problems caused by clustering in the set of keys.

  For our requirement to store customer data and assuming we have 100 blocks for customer data, the algorithm could be:

  block = remainder of (key/100) + 1

So for Customer Zar, with a key of 6248, we get a remainder of 48 and hence store the record in block 49. When the record needs to be read the same algorithm produces the same block address. Once read, the record can be amended or deleted if that is the requirement. The example algorithm is very simple but it would do the job (and, importantly, sequences of keys would be split up across separate blocks). It is also important that a fair amount of spare space should be left in the file area to cope with any clustering of records and to allow space for further updates.

However good the hashing algorithm and however much vacant space is left, there is still the chance of overflow. Overflow occurs when the block calculated for a new record becomes full and the new record has to be placed in an alternative block where there is space. There is then an issue – when we come to read the record the hashing algorithm will point to the original block. Hence we place a small tag record in the original record that contains the record key and a pointer to the overflow block where the record has been placed. Note that access times will be doubled for records in overflow, since once we have used the key to calculate the block and read the tag record we have to then read the overflow block to get the required record.

Databases will normally use hash random to place records (typically within a file area allocated for the relationship).

- **Index:** An alternative way of achieving direct access is to create an index. We continue with the example of Customer Zar, with a key of 6248. This record was placed in block 49 using the hashing algorithm. If we also wished to be able to locate our customers by name we could add an index with the entry:

Name: Zar | Block 49

An index could be good, but it of course comes at a price. To read the record via the index requires two physical accesses (one for the index and one for the record). To write a new customer now requires four physical accesses (to read, update and rewrite the index plus, using the hashing algorithm, to read the block, place the record and rewrite).

A record could be entered in more than one index. For our customer example it could also be useful to index the customer on postcode (zipcode), but that would of course add further processing updates. Also note that we could have more than one customer with the same name and/or the same postcode, so the index structure needs to cope with that eventuality.

Further issues with indexes are that, for big files, they could take up several blocks and they then need their own data structure so that the index entry can be found (or updated) reasonably efficiently.

Databases make extensive use of indexes: as indicated above, they can be very useful by providing alternative access paths but they do come at a price. Indexes on databases can also be used to meet a requirement for serial access to a set of records – the keys can be read off in turn from the index and the records looked up (but presumably each record read would require a separate physical access, so it will not be quick).

An alternative index structure is the **index sequential** file (see the *Index sequential explanation box* overleaf). Given that the data is in sequence we can cut down on the number of index entries. Index sequential is not an obvious data structure for use in a DBMS (but it could be a way of organizing a large index).

- **Linked lists:** This data structure uses pointers to locate related records (pointers to the physical block location as opposed to a foreign key where the physical location has to be calculated or looked up). Linked lists are the base data structure of the network database paradigm (see the *Other Database Paradigms* section of this chapter).

The system/database designer needs to be aware of the structures being used in the database – some of the structures will be inherent in the DBMS and some can be influenced or determined by the system designer. In particular, the designer needs to be aware of the performance implications of adding indexes and must balance their advantages to data retrieval against the overheads they create when data is inserted.

The system/database designer then needs to size their system as outlined at the start of this section and determine whether the system will give the required performance to online users and still complete its batch processing

Explanation
Index sequential The index sequential data structure starts with the records, in our example Customers, stored in key sequence (with some room left in the blocks for later update). The index is created when the data is first loaded; the index entry is for the highest key in each block.

The index sequential structure is illustrated in *Figure 8.4*. To keep things simple in this chapter there are just four data blocks (blocks 1-4), each with space for three records. The initial setup of the file placed two records in each block and the highest key from each block was used to set up the index (block 0). Note that there was a Customer 6314 in block 3 which, in the diagram, has been deleted.

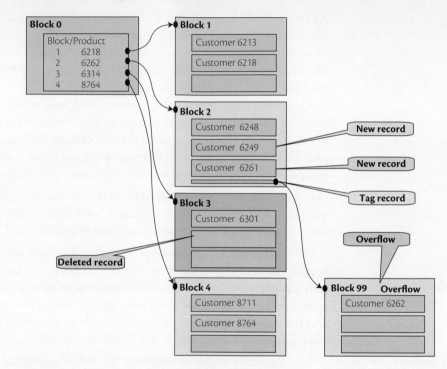

Figure 8.4 Index sequential file.

To understand how this data structure works we will go through some worked examples.

First assume we wished to read Customer 6301. The steps that would be taken are:

- Read the index block – block 0
- Examine first entry in index   – is 6218 >= 6301 – No
- Examine second entry in index   – is 6262 >= 6301 – No
- Examine third entry in index   – is 6314 >= 6301 – Yes
- Read the block 3 as indicated by that index entry
- Unpack the records and process the customer 6301.

For updating we follow the same procedure to read the required record. Assume we wish to change product 6301, which we have just read; we change the relevant data and then write the record back as part of the block it belongs to. Next let us assume we wish to insert a new record with a key of 6249. The steps are:

- Read the block that is to contain the record 6249 (using the procedure for reading a record outlined above – that gives us block 2)
- Unpack the records and check that the record that is to be inserted does not exist (if it is found that is presumably an exception condition)
- Insert the new record into vacant space in the block
- Rewrite the block.

Following this by a second insert, this time a new record with a key of 6261. We follow the same steps as for inserting record 6249, but when we come to insert the record, block 2 is full. The additional steps now are:

- Read an overflow block, insert the new record (or one of the records from the block) in that block and rewrite the block
- Insert a small tag record in the home block and rewrite the block. The tag record contains the key of the additional record and the block where it can be found.

Finally let us assume we want to delete the record with the key of 6314. Again we follow the procedure to read the record – this time it is in block 3. We then remove the record from the block and write block 3 back. Note that key 6314 still exists in the index but the record is no longer on the file.

The state of the index sequential file after these two insertions and one record delete is shown in *Figure 8.4*.

in a workable timeframe. If the sizing gives an inadequate performance, the design needs to be tuned. One obvious area for attention is the use of indexes. Adding indexes could give important advantages for data retrieval, but creates significant overheads when data is inserted. Advanced DBMSs such as Oracle have many facilities that allow database performance to be tuned, but there is always a trade-off between facility and performance.

Other database paradigms

3

The three traditional database paradigms are hierarchical, network and relational. Relational is the newest of the three and has already been discussed.

The hierarchical database structure is, as the name suggests, hierarchical. For our order processing system one hierarchy could be customer, order, and order line and a second hierarchy product category, product and prices plus order line (with order line being duplicated so it is represented in both hierarchies). The hierarchical structure is not necessarily the best way to implement a data structure, but it can be made to work. The most notable implementation of the hierarchical database paradigm was IBM's IMS. As IBM was the predominant supplier of mainframe computers and IMS was its principal database (prior to db2) this ensured that the hierarchical model was widely used.

network database: a database paradigm based on the linked list data structure. Used in the IDMS DBMS.

The **network database** implemented the relationships from the data model as sets. So, for example, the order would have a pointer to the physical location of the first order line and that order line would point to the second, and so on – this is a data structure we call a *linked list*. Pointers in a set could be to the next record, the previous record and/or the owner of the set (the order in the case just outlined). A record might be a member of more than one set – the order line, for instance, would be linked by two sets, to its owning order and product, respectively. The most used implementation of the network database was IDMS which was available on a number of mainframes including IBM (but not supplied by IBM). IDMS included many features that allowed the data model to be implemented efficiently – storing records via their owner so that they were stored on the same page (block) is one example. A network database is documented using a Bachman diagram. The full Bachman diagram for the IDMS implementation of the order processing data model is shown at *Figure 8.5* overleaf.

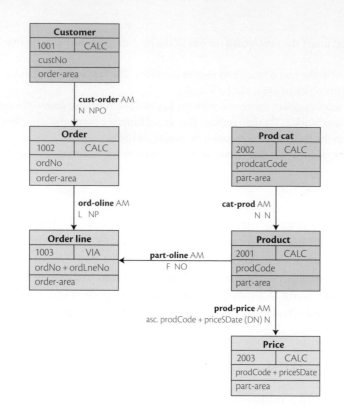

Figure 8.5 Bachman diagram.

The operation of the network database can be illustrated by a brief example. Say we had an order number and we wanted to look up details from the customer, order, order line and product. Using the attribute names already established on *Figure 8.1* and the Bachman diagram shown at *Figure 8.4*, the steps would be:

- Read order
  Key = custNo. Order is CALC, that is, hash random on custNo
- Read customer
  Via the cust-order set using owner pointers
- For each order line:
  - Read order line
    using ord-oline set using next pointers
  - Read Product
    using part-oline set using owner pointers.

There are further notes about the network database, the Bachman diagram and the merits of the network model on the companion website of this book.

The most recently devised database paradigm is the object-oriented database. An object-oriented database can be used for data with complex relationships that is difficult to model and process with a relational database. The object-oriented database can also store multimedia objects and can invoke processing appropriate to the nature of those objects. Mainstream database systems such as Oracle now come with object-oriented features. Note that object-oriented approaches to IS design are further discussed in *Part 4*.

Further reading

Books recommended for further reading are:

Beynon-Davies, P. (2004) *Database Systems*, 3rd ed., Palgrave Macmillan, Basingstoke.
Connolly, T. and Begg, C. (2010) *Database Systems: A Practical Approach to Design, Implementation and Management*, 5th ed., Addison-Wesley, Harlow.
Rob, P., Coronel, C. and Crockett, K. (2008) *Database Systems: Design, Implementation and Management*, Cengage, London.

Comprehension test

This is a short, simple test to enable you to check you have absorbed the material presented in *Chapter 8*.

Q1 The relational approach to database design is accredited to:

a. Bill Gates ☐

b. Thomas Edison ☐

c. Alan Turing ☐

d. Edgar Codd ☐

Q2 On a relational database, the associations between two relationships is established by the:

a. Foreign key ☐

b. Hash key ☐

c. Primary key ☐

d. Linked list ☐

Q3 Which of the following relational algebra functions select columns from an existing table?

a. Restrict ☐

b. Project ☐

c. Join ☐

Q4 The physical unit of data written to and read from a disk is a:

a. File ☐

b. Block ☐

c. Record ☐

d. Byte ☐

Q5 Popular databases such as Microsoft Access and Oracle are based on which of the following paradigms?

a. Hierarchical ☐

b. Network ☐

c. Object-oriented ☐

d. Relational ☐

3

Exercises

The following exercises are designed to aid your understanding of the material presented in this chapter. They can be used for self-study or selected exercises can be used for tutorial discussion.

1 **Comprehension** For the order processing database, used as in an example in this chapter, which relational algebra function would you use to:

   - List all products where the stock (prodStock) is 10 or less.
   - List the product code (prodCode) and warehouse location (whseLocn) of all products.
   - List all products and include the corresponding product category data (prodcatDesc) for each product.

2 **Research** Look up data warehouses on the web. See what more you can find out about how they work, what they are used for and how artificial intelligence (AI) can be used for information retrieval.

3 **Discussion** Databases such as Microsoft Access and Oracle are commercial software products but MySQL is an open source/freeware product. Find out about open source and freeware – how it works and what are the advantages and disadvantages. Assess whether freeware, such as MySQL, is an appropriate choice for organizations that rely on their IS to run their organizations. Discuss the issues raised by this question with the rest of your group.

The companion website of this book contains further database material. There is a Microsoft Access version of the order processing database and a SQL file to create the database on MySQL (or a similar database). Further exercises can then be done using this resource.

ONLINE
RESOURCES
AVAILABLE

9 NETWORKS AND COMPUTER SECURITY

Summary

We live in a networked world. Home computers are linked into the internet, and laptops, tablets and smartphones provide internet access on the move. Personal computing connects people via e-Mail and social networking. Members of the public can also access the vast resources of the World Wide Web, link to commercial computing via e-Business and to public administration in a development called e-Government.

Organizations have their own internal networks used for communications and to access Business Information Systems from the desktop, the shop floor and on the move. Organizations are networked to one another for e-Commerce and e-Government exchanges, and to the outside world by the internet.

The internet, a global web of interconnecting networks, some public and some private, unifies these networks as a global resource – a resource not owned or formally controlled by any corporation or government.

These networks, and the communications that they support, are a complex technical infrastructure. The infrastructure is built with network equipment, a connection and the message protocol – we will look at each of these components.

Networks, apart from their legitimate uses, can provide access to those with illegitimate intents (and that in turn gives rise to questions as to what is legitimate and what is not). In this chapter we look at computer security – in *Part 5* we will take a wider look at the societal implications of (networked) computing.

Learning outcomes

Having read this chapter and completed the exercises, you should:

- Appreciate the range of applications of networking in personal, business and public administration
- Understand, at a conceptual level, the technical components of computer networks
- Appreciate the importance of computer and network security and the range of threats that can affect both personal and business computing.

© Sashkin/Fotolia

Key terms   Network, local area network (LAN), wide area network (WAN), internet, network connection, transmission protocol, TCP/IP, transmission control protocol (TCP), internet protocol (IP), packet-switching, network interface card, computer security, physical security, data security, encryption, access control, network security, malware, cyber warfare.

Networks

network: a connection between computer systems/IT devices allowing the sharing of resources and information.

The PC at home, a tablet computer used in the coffee shop and the office computer at work are (almost) all **networked**. Business computers are linked to one another and to the corporate servers. Personal computers are linked to the internet – as are the smartphones that so many people carry with them. Business and personal computing come together, via the internet, for services such as e-Commerce. The developing world shares in the network revolution with, for example, 90 per cent or the world's population (as of 2010) having coverage from mobile networks. We have a networked world – a mass of interacting, communicating and data transfer that hardly existed 20 years ago:

- In business, almost every desktop and workstation is furnished with a computer. Desktop computers are used for word-processing, spreadsheets and the like. Workstations have specialist terminals such as the electronic point of sale (EPOS) systems in shops. Banks and railway stations have public computer terminals used to withdraw money and buy tickets. All these business computers are networked to corporate servers where they interface with the organization's Information Systems. Corporate servers are again networked with other servers and the outside world. Organizations have formal electronic links to trading partners and public authorities. The organization also has its website, e-Mail service and possibly an intranet, and the internet allows the organization to have less formal, outfacing links to its retail customers and to other stakeholders.
- At college and university, academics can share their research and access specialist facilities such as supercomputers. Students can access e-Learning resources and do part or all their studies using distance learning techniques.
- At home and on the move, our PCs, laptops, tablets and mobile phones are linked to the internet. From our networked personal computers we can e-Mail, tweet, Facebook and connect to all sorts of information and services. High bandwidth services have extended access to services such as video-on-demand. Home computing is also linked to e-Commerce where we can pay bills, book tickets and buy stuff, 24/7.

Networks are used for a number of purposes – often a single network will be used for more than one purpose. These purposes can be put into four categories as follows:

- Online access to Business Information Systems: For many organizations, the primary purpose of the network is to give staff, at their desks and on the shop floor, access to shared Information Systems. These systems could include the order processing system and payroll system, discussed in *Chapter 4*, and the MIS/DSS systems discussed in *Chapter 7*. Access is normally restricted to members of the organization and often staff members will only have access to selected systems and facilities within the overall organizational IS.
- Shared resources: The network can also give access to shared IT resources. Simple examples are a number of desktop systems sharing a single printer

or file space on a departmental server. On a larger scale, cloud computing provides for shared software and data resources that should be accessible anytime/anywhere. The provision of cloud computing resources is often outsourced (see *Chapter 6* for a fuller discussion of cloud computing).

- Communications: The provision of networking has facilitated the use of Information and Communications Technology (ICT) for communications (an alternative to telephone or mail). The main technology for inter-personal communications is e-Mail, while electronic data interchange (EDI) is the technology for IS to IS communications. Both these technologies have had a massive impact on the way business is done. The integration of computer technology, mobile technology and, in some cases, speech recognition is making ICT facilities accessible and available anywhere, on the move, 24/7.

- Information and commercial services: The use of ICT allows access to information, e-Commerce and entertainment services made available by organizations or other members of the public. The internet and the World Wide Web are the main vehicles, and a unifying infrastructure, for accessing information (or disinformation) from any source and across the world.

The nature of the network being installed will, in part, depend on the intended use of the facility. Networks used for business purposes need to be secure and may well be private. Home and academic networking tends to be less constrained and the internet is a more applicable solution. Most networks are used for diverse purposes and the network architecture needs to accommodate this. A simple network is represented in *Figure 9.1*.

local area network (LAN): a network within the premises of an organization. It is owned and controlled by the organization.

wide area network (WAN): a network that reaches out of the building to other branches of the organization or to cooperating organizations. The network has to be provided by a licensed, third-party telecommunications provider.

internet: the worldwide network of networks that uses TCP/IP as its protocol. Most networks are linked into the internet and hence can be considered to be part of the internet.

Figure 9.1 A simple (two computer) network.

Most computers are connected to larger networks, as represented in *Figure 9.2* overleaf. In this diagram the network is represented by a network cloud – showing communication services without being specific about the details of the network architecture. The network may be:

- A **local area network (LAN)**. This is a network within the premises of an organization. It is owned and controlled by the organization and will, usually, be technically heterogeneous.
- A **wide area network (WAN)**. This is a network that reaches out of the building to other branches of the organization or to cooperating organizations. The network has to be provided by a third-party licensed telecommunications provider (such as BT in the UK) and may well use a variety of lines and equipment that are shared with other users.
- The **internet**. This is the worldwide network of networks that uses TCP/IP as its protocol. Most networks are linked into the internet and hence can be considered to be part of the internet.

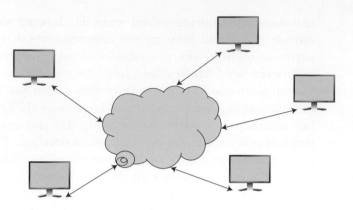

Figure 9.2 A multi-user network.

A network is a communication channel connecting two or more devices. A network must have:

- A connection: At its simplest, this is a wire connecting two computers that allows data to be interchanged. For longer distances and multi-machine networks the connection can involve a range of technologies, but the principle is the same: data is sent from one computer, through the connection and is delivered to a second computer.
- A protocol: The data sent over the connection has to be packaged so that it can be checked and correctly interpreted by the receiving computer; the packaging of the data is specified by the protocol.
- Communications equipment: Each computer connected to the network will need to be equipped with a network card (or equivalent). This equipment allows for signals to be sent and received. Larger networks may also have communications equipment built into the network (in addition to the equipment built into the networked computers).

This chapter gives a brief survey of network architectures although, in general, and as IS practitioners, we rely on technical staff to provide network facilities.

The network connection

The basic technology for telecommunications is copper wire. This is used for all sorts of electronic communications as it has good conductivity, and electrical signals will pass through with relatively little distortion or loss of power. The basic **network connection** is a twisted pair – two thin copper wires, insulated and twisted together. Higher quality connections can be provided using coaxial cable, a thicker wire with better insulation.

The data is transmitted along the wire as an electrical signal. Computer data is digital (with characters coded using a binary code). In digital transmissions, each binary bit is represented by a current level. The basic voice connection is analogue and digital data can be converted to analogue if a voice connection is to be used (that said, a lot of voice communications is digitized and coded as a binary transmission).

A number of alternatives to wire have been developed. These include:

- Fibre optics: This uses glass fibre and light as an alternative to copper and electricity. Fibre optics can transmit more data, at higher speeds and with

network connection: the communications media in a network. Technologies include wire, fibre optics, microwave, satellite and radio.

less distortion than wire – the main disadvantage is that they are more difficult to connect than copper. Most new trunk connections and high speed LANs use fibre optic technology, with wire being used for the local connection (where the data volumes and transmission speeds are lower).

- Microwave: Another alternative to wire for telephone and data transmission is a microwave circuit. The signal is sent, through the air, using microwave radio relay, from one dish to another – there must be a *line of sight* connection between dishes. An advantage of microwave technology is that companies can use private microwave circuits between separate locations (that are no more than a few miles apart) without having to purchase facilities from a licensed telecommunications provider.
- Satellite: These are used for long-distance links across continents or oceans (in the latter case, as an alternative to laying underwater cables). The system requires a geo-stationary satellite and then microwave radio relay transmissions are sent from one ground station, *bounced* off the satellite and received at a second ground station that is hundreds or thousands of miles away.
- Radio: This is not normally used for telecommunication circuits but, with the integration of data communications and mobile telephone technology, the mobile phone networks are increasingly used for data transmission. The mobile phone radio network, in its local connections, uses radio transmission. Bluetooth is also a radio transmission technology.

The transmission capacity of the network is referred to as bandwidth – measured in bits per second.

The choice of network technology depends on a number of factors. When an organization installs a LAN it has a choice – but it is price and performance that really matters, not the technology. When a WAN is used, the customer buys capacity and, very possibly, the data will pass through several different circuit types on its journey to the local exchange, across the trunk network and onwards down local lines to its final destination. A message from a terminal in the UK to another user in (say) the US may well:

- Set off through the office fibre optic LAN
- Travel down a copper, coaxial link to the satellite station
- Satellite link over the Atlantic
- Microwave from the satellite station in the US
- Finally be picked up by the US recipient on a smartphone using a US radio mobile network.

The transmission process could well be more complex still (particularly over the public networks) and, if it is packet-switched (see the subsection on *protocol*), parts of the same message could take different routings.

Protocol

Having established the network, the client and server systems all need to speak the same sort of language and show a bit of courtesy (not speaking until spoken to – or something like that). The way we sort this out on a network is

transmission protocol: specifications for the packaging of data sent over the network so that the data can be checked and correctly interpreted by the receiving computer.

with a set of rules and requirements that are called a network or **transmission protocol**. The requirements of data transmission and the protocol are:

- Data: The data must be in a format that is understandable by both systems. This is the same idea as a record format on a file. There needs to be an agreed way of coding characters and numbers, and each application needs to know what to do with each field in the data.
- Envelope: In addition to the application data the network needs its own data. For each message there will be a header and a trailer (footer) segment that envelop the data. The minimum requirement is for the header to indicate the start of the message and for the trailer to include count/checksum information that allows the network to check that the data has arrived intact. For many protocols the header will also specify the network address of the sending computer and the network address of the destination computer.

Over the years there have been many protocols developed for different network requirements. One of those protocols is **transmission control protocol/ internet protocol (TCP/IP)** which was developed for use on the internet (as an interim measure) and has since become the de facto global standard.

transmission control protocol/internet protocol (TCP/IP): the transmission protocol of the internet. TCP/ IP is a packet-switching protocol.

transmission control protocol (TCP): the transport functions of TCP/IP which ensures that the total amount of bytes sent in each packet is received correctly at the other end.

internet protocol (IP): the protocol that provides the routing mechanism within TCP/IP.

packet-switching: a digital data transmission standard where the message is divided into standard-size packets; each packet is then dynamically routed through the network and finally the message is reassembled at its destination.

TCP/IP is a **packet-switching** standard. Using packet-switching obviates the need to establish a direct and exclusive network connection between sender and receiver (as would be the case when we make a telephone call). For packet-switching a message is divided into packets (datagrams). Each packet is encased in a digital envelope and the header includes the source address, destination address and sequence number within the message. The packets can then be dynamically routed over the network using any available path. Individual packets within a message may follow different paths. The packages are then reassembled into a message in the receiving station using the sequence number to check the order. The receiving station will request the re-transmission of any corrupted or missing package. The format of a TCP/IP packet (datagram) is summarized in *Figure 9.3*; the structure reflects the four levels of the TCP/IP protocol, that is, application, transport, internet and network interface (this is often compared with the seven layer OSI reference model which is widely taught in computer science but not actually implemented – we will not go there).

Datagram				
Frame header	IP header	TCP/UDP header	Data	Frame footer

Notes	
Application:	Data The application (e.g. HTTP/SMP)/data
Transport:	TCP (Transmission control protocol) The packet (including sequence no. in the message)
Internet:	IP (Internet protocol) Addresses of source and destination, etc.
Network:	Frame header and footer Envelope for network, e.g. ethernet

Figure 9.3 TCP/IP datagram.

TCP/IP can be seen as a two-part protocol:

- TCP is the transport function that ensures that the total amount of bytes sent in each packet is received correctly at the other end.
- IP provides the routing mechanism.

Packet-switching allows for an effective use of bandwidth since it means that trunk connections are shared. Packet-switching also gives resilience in that if one network connection is unavailable the network will select another path.

Packet-switching is a WAN technology. LANs have their own ways of sharing capacity, for example, the Ethernet. These LAN topologies can be used in conjunction with TCP/IP.

Note that voice communications can also be sent over the packet-switch network using voice-over IP (VoIP) technology. The voice has to be digitized and then split into packets. The big advantage of VoIP is cost as the call does not require, and is not billed for, a switched connection over a public switched telephone network (PSTN). Skype uses a proprietary VoIP protocol (see *Skype case study*).

Case study
Skype

Skype was founded in 2003 by a Danish and a Swedish entrepreneur – the software was written in Estonia and the development team is still based in that country. Skype was sold to eBay in 2005 and subsequently sold on to Microsoft in 2011.

Skype offers cheap voice telephone calls (particularly for international calls where charges can be quite hefty). Skype calls to other Skype users are free and calls to landline or mobile users are relatively inexpensive. Skype can be used for video, instant messaging and videoconferencing.

Skype is a voice-over internet (VoIP) service. The voice data is digitized, sent as packages over the internet and then reassembled at the receiving end. This obviates the need for a switched-circuit connection and thus avoids the charges associated with a conventional telephone connection.

Network equipment

The wires (or equivalent) have to be interfaced into the computer equipment and the computer needs to be set up to format outgoing signals and receive incoming signals. The basic bit of kit is a **network interface card**. The card works in conjunction with the software to interface the physical network and the application running in the computer. Each network card is identified by a unique address (the MAC address assigned to it by the manufacturer when the card is made). Other network equipment includes:

network interface card: a hardware component that connects the computer to the network and implements the intended network protocol.

- Hubs and switches: Devices in a network that join communication lines together. Desktop PCs are typically connected to a LAN via either a hub or a switch. The hub shares the network capacity between devices whereas the switch can devote the full bandwidth to any devices that are active at the time.

- Bridges and routers: Devices that forward data from one segment of the network to another segment. Bridges are protocol-independent whereas routers have to read the protocol to obtain routing information.
- Multiplexor: A device that combines several low speed transmissions into a single high-speed transmission. The multiplexor can use frequency division multiplexing (where several signals are sent down a single link at different frequencies), time division multiplexing (where the signal is interleaved with other signals on the same frequency) or both.
- Firewall: A network security device that rejects access requests from potentially unsafe sources and accepts data from recognized sources. The firewall is part of computer security, the subject of the next section in this chapter.

The configuration of devices in a network is (diagrammatically) represented in *Figure 9.4*. Computer science books often discuss various LAN topographies (Bus, Star, Ring); the most commonly used standard (network protocol) is Ethernet, which applies to a Bus or Star topography.

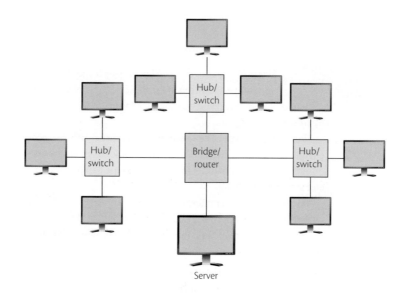

Figure 9.4 LAN with clients, servers and network devices.

Example network

The network of an organization is usually focused on access to business systems, with communications as an important additional element (as opposed to the communications and information services focus of most academic and personal users). To illustrate this usage we will imagine an organization – let's call it Funco plc. This organization has:

- A head office that also houses its central IS/IT facilities
- A number of regional/branch offices, a manufacturing facility and a warehouse/distribution centre
- Mobile staff such as salespeople and teleworkers
- Links to trading partners (including the use of EDI) and to members of the public through its e-Shop.

All the staff of the organization make use of IT. This includes the use of desktop facilities, e-Mail and accessing corporate IS. The general picture is illustrated in *Figure 9.5*, a picture that is typical of many medium and large organizations (with or without manufacturing and warehouse facilities).

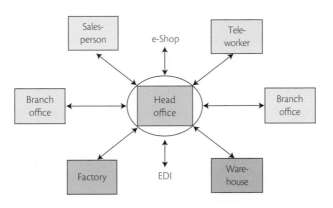

Figure 9.5 Location chart.

Funco needs a network that covers all its locations and its outside links. This will have a number of elements and its design involves some important decisions. The elements are:

- LANs in each location
  The company can have its own network in each of its premises – the network will be a LAN. There are a number of alternative technologies, and the capacity (bandwidth) is largely dependent on how much is spent. The head office will require a high speed network whereas the factory might make less intensive use of IT and a lower capacity network would suffice. The organization needs to be aware of the options but, normally, they will contract out the installation of the network to a specialist organization.

- WAN between locations
  The LANs in the branches, warehouse and factory need linking together and, in this case, the main linkage is to the central IS/IT at head office. There is going to be substantial traffic over the WAN so some sort of open line connection (a circuit that is permanently available) would seem to be required. This can take the form of an open connection rented from a telecommunications provider, or Funco could join a commercial packet-switching service (there are a number of such services available – they are like mini internets but the services are restricted to members and generally they should be faster, more reliable and more secure than the internet).

- Sales persons and teleworkers
  For these people, network traffic is likely to be relatively low and intermittent; these users will use an internet connection – the company could pay for these staff members to have broadband internet services installed. Sales staff will also be out on the road and have laptops/tablets – Funco pays for their mobile phones and provides them with dongles for mobile internet connection.

- EDI

  For EDI Funco will probably join a specialist value added data service (VADS) (see *Chapter 5*). Funco could use the internet to connect to the VADS or have an open line connection, depending on the volume of its EDI transactions.

- e-Shop

  The e-Shop needs to be located on an internet server. The server is connected to other IS/IT facilities on the head office LAN. The internet server will need an open line, high speed connection into the internet; the punters will connect to the e-Shop, over the internet, in the normal way. The e-Shop is separated from other servers by a firewall.

Funco's overall network provision is summed up in *Figure 9.6*.

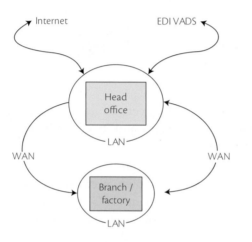

Figure 9.6 The Funco network.

The tendency is for network usage to expand and for technologies to move on. Funco will need to update its network provision at regular intervals if it is to provide an efficient and reliable service to staff and its outside trading partners.

The internet

The network of the organization outlined above is, primarily, a private affair focused on the business IS of the organization. The internet, in contrast, is a public access network open to anybody with a computer and a telecommunications link. The internet is rather a strange phenomenon – we tend to expect facilities to be provided by business or public authorities but this is neither of those things – and it is not entirely clear who owns or controls it (although there are voluntary committees who give it direction).

The origins of the internet are commonly traced back to a US military project, the ARPAnet, commissioned in 1969. The aim of the project was to develop a flexible network that could still function if some of the nodes were knocked out in a nuclear attack – hence the development of packet-switching.

The ARPAnet was followed on by various experimental networks in universities. Significant events in the evolution of the internet include:

- CSNet – the US Computer Science Network was founded in 1981 and split from the ARPAnet in 1984
- TCP/IP was developed in 1982 and put into use on 1 January 1983
- JANET – the UK Joint Academic Network was founded in 1984
- The World Wide Web was developed by the European Laboratory for Particle Physics (CERN) in 1989
- Mosaic, the first web browser (in the way we now understand the term) was developed by the US National Centre for Supercomputing Applications in 1993
- The internet was opened to commercial traffic in 1995 and Amazon.com first opened its virtual doors.

So, at the time of writing, the internet as a public access, information, e-Commerce and communications network is less than 20 years old. It has come from nothing to be the infrastructure of the Information Society and a globalized world. The internet is used by governments, companies, organizations and individuals for a range of activities. These include:

- Personal messaging (e-Mail): For both business and private purposes. The use of e-Mail in the workplace has had a radical effect on the way that business is transacted. e-Mail is asynchronous: the message waits in the recipients mailbox until it is accessed. More immediate interaction, usually for private purposes, is provided using techniques such as instant messaging and chat rooms.
- Social networking: Connects vast numbers of people to Facebook (and other social networking sites). Members provide personal information, list friends and communicate. Businesses are attempting to leverage social network for commercial purposes (anyone want a supermarket as a friend?). Microblogging is sort of a cross between social networking and e-Mail, with Twitter having extensive usage.
- e-Commerce: For both business-to-business (b2b) and business-to-consumer (b2c) exchanges.
- Information retrieval: There is a vast library of information, from all sorts of sources, out there on webpages. Most of these information sources are available free.
- Teleworking: The use of the internet makes home-to-office communications much more available and affordable for those who wish to work from home (on a formal or informal basis).
- Distance education: Online learning is much more immediate than correspondence courses. Teaching material can be delivered in a variety of media to meet the needs of the topic. The internet provides ready access to further research/background material. Interaction with tutors, and fellow students, is facilitated by e-Mail, message boards and video conferencing.
- Entertainment: The internet can also be used for entertainment – surfing to see what one can find or playing one of the many games that are available

3

online (but jogging round the block is a more healthy option). With increased line speeds, video on demand is now a viable option.

While there is the public internet, the internet (or internet technology) can also be used for restricted access networks. These are commonly categorized as:

- Intranets: A network within the organization using web technology for publishing company information and procedures. The intranet may include interactive pages for functions such as booking rooms or registering to attend a meeting.
- Extranet: Similar to the intranet but extending outside the organization (possibly to include commercial customers). This sort of facility is easily implemented on the internet by including a password check before the facilities of the intranet are accessed.

Note that, while organizations do use the internet for commercial purposes, many also use commercial networks for intra- and inter-organizational transactions (see the Funco example above).

Computer security

computer security: a general term encompassing physical security of the equipment, access control, data security, privacy and protection against malware.

The first step in **computer security** is to simply look after the kit. If it is a laptop or a tablet, don't drop it or leave it on the train. If it is a desktop PC then lock the door and don't stand your coffee on top of the processor box. If it is a server, then be even more security-conscious – a lot of people's work (or play) is dependent on it.

The issue of the physical security of the IT equipment is, in most circumstances, less of an issue than the security of the data. For organizations the data on its computer system is vital. Consider the two systems, payroll and order processing, studied in *Chapter 4*. If the payroll data is lost then the staff cannot be paid and the tax calculations are lost. If the order processing data is compromised then the business grinds to a halt: orders cannot be fulfilled, invoices cannot be issued – and that is just the start of the problem. Alongside data security is the issue of privacy. The payroll and order processing systems contain employee and customer data including payment details; the organization cannot afford to have its privacy breached.

So, overall, the issue of computer security is crucial. The importance of IS/IT systems to organizations and the functioning of society is continuously growing. The threat to those systems is increased by the interconnectivity of the systems; networking of computer systems is a powerful tool but it compounds the vulnerability of systems. Threats to computer systems, accidental and deliberate, come from all directions and the organization must make a proportionate response to these threats. For the purpose of this study we consider the issue of computer security under the following headings.

- Physical security
- Data security
- Encryption
- Access control

- Network security
- Process protection
- Malware
- Cyber warfare.

Physical security

Keeping IT kit safe could be seen as common sense but, in an organization, common sense needs a degree of organizing.

The most vulnerable kit is the desktop and laptop PC. Laptops are bought to be used on the move and are therefore most vulnerable to being lost, damaged, stolen or used for unauthorized purposes. The UK Ministry of Defence, for example, has admitted to losing 150 laptops in a recent 18-month period (Say, 2011) – in this case, the issue of what data was on the computer and whether it was safely encrypted is more important than the loss of the kit. Desktop PCs are used in the office and therefore less vulnerable to getting lost or stolen – but that can still happen and they can still be used for unauthorized purposes. Site security, checking who enters and leaves the building, has a role in protecting workplace PCs. An additional **physical security** measure could be to screw the kit to the desk.

physical security: the aspects of computer security that relate to the physical protection of the IT equipment from threats such as accidental damage, deliberate damage, theft and unauthorized usage

More significant to an organization is its server equipment – it is on this kit that the organization's main systems are run and the bulk of the (formal) data is held. Servers will (or should) be stored in a secure area and access should be limited to technical staff only. Control consoles for this kit can also be housed in a controlled area. Consideration should be given to the location of the servers – they should be protected from flooding (not stored in a basement), from intrusion (armoured doors and bricked up windows) and from fire (alarms and a waterless fire suppressant system). Large computer installations, such as banks and server farms, are located in purpose-built, fortress-like computer buildings. Large organizations will also consider what to do in the case of a disaster: for example, what to do in the case of a major earthquake or other natural disaster.

Computer breakdowns can cause the same sorts of damage to the IT equipment as careless or deliberate acts – this is particularly the case should physical damage affect hard disks and the data stored thereon.

Physical security of IT equipment is a first line of defence. Should physical security fail the organization needs a plan to repair/restart its information infrastructure: see *Process protection*, below.

Data security

data security: the aspects of computer security that relate to the protection of that data from loss, damage or unauthorized access. Also the taking of data backup copies and system recovery from backup copies.

The physical security of the IT equipment is important but much more important is the privacy and security of the data (and the software) on that equipment.

Physical security, access control and measures against malware all have an important part to play in **data security**; these topics are looked at in separate subsections.

The backstop on data security is to have data backup so that the data and IS services can be restored should data be lost or corrupted. Organizations need to have a routine for taking data backups – a typical routine would be to copy all the data from the servers to a backup at the end of each working day. The backup itself must be secure – for example, held offsite (not much help if the server room, with the backups, go up in flames). Backup processes can be automated and can be networked to offsite storage. Large, complex and 24/7 operations will need more sophisticated data security procedures – one issue is to secure updates (transactions) that occur between backups (some systems have message and DB update logs). Backup of data held on desktop/laptop machines can also be problematic – there is software available that ensures these files are duplicated on a server (also ensuring all PC data is processed from a server or in the cloud is an option).

Should data be lost, the service must be restored from backups. This can be complex; everyone involved needs to know what has been lost and what has been restored. Data restored from backups can be rolled forward from message and DB update logs (if the systems are in place to do this). Some installations will have *failover* facilities (see the **Process protection** section). Important in all this is that systems should be checked and protected – finding out after a loss of data that the backups cannot be restored is not good, and it does happen.

Finally, there is the question of equipment disposal. Deleting files from hard disks does not erase the data; it just makes it inaccessible by normal means. Disks should be securely erased (and possibly physically destroyed) before disposal.

Encryption

encryption: the process of transforming data, using an algorithm, to make it unreadable by anyone who attempts unauthorized access.

Encryption changes data so that it can only be written or read by a system or user with the required software and correct keys. Data on a system can be encrypted to prevent unauthorized access – this could be particularly appropriate to customer and payment data on (say) an e-Shop where net connectivity is important and hence the data is more vulnerable. Many organizations have a policy that all organizational data on laptops that go off-site should be encrypted. The user/password registry on a system also needs to be encrypted. Secure socket layer (SSL) encryption is used for internet transmissions containing private information.

As with all computer security measures, encryption can be broken – but the hope is that commercially available encryption is good enough to provide adequate protection. The very highest levels of secure encryption are classed, by the US, as munitions and are not available for public use.

Access control

access control: controls to restrict access to permitted users of the computer and/or the network.

Access control is about ensuring that only authorized people can access the system and that their access is limited to the data/facilities they are entitled to use.

Basic access control is provided by a user-id and a password – to gain access to a system the user has to log in. We have to log in to our stand-alone PC when we boot the operating system. At college, university or work we need to type in the correct user-id and password to gain access to the system – and that access will be limited by the permissions that the user-id has been given. Once in the system there may be further password checks to access some of the more secure facilities such as personnel or finance data. Similar login checks can also be applied to an intranet and to specific internet sites.

User-id and password checks can be supplemented by further security checks, such as fingerprint checking or the need to swipe/insert an id-card. Password security can be enhanced by insisting on complex passwords (to stop passwords being guessed or broken by a brute-force attack) and/or frequent changes of passwords (to reduce the risk of unauthorized people getting to know and remember someone's password).

Users may be allowed access to Information Systems but only to selected facilities – this can be achieved by linking the user-id to a limited set of transactions. Access to a database using a query language such as SQL can be limited by linking the user to a specific sub-schema (a restricted view of the data structure of the database).

One problem with password access control is people's ability to remember their passwords   and the more passwords people have, the more complex they are and the more often they are changed, the more people have problems. If the password system is too simple it is insecure – if it is complex then people might well end up writing down their passwords (e.g. on a post-it note attached to their monitor!). There also needs to be a system of resetting passwords for people who have lost their passwords   and that again can be a source of insecurity.

Finally, the user-ids and passwords have to be stored somewhere on the system – the password file needs protection and encryption would seem a good idea.

Network security

network security: protection of a system against unauthorized access/activity originating from a network.

Once computers are networked, and most computers are, they are vulnerable to access from unauthorized locations and **network security** measures should be instigated. User-id and password protection, properly applied, provides a line of security against unauthorized access but not against the determined hacker (and the software/malware that a hacker might use).

A standard line of defence against unauthorized access from a network is a firewall. A firewall is software that permits or denies transmissions based on a set of rules. The firewall might, for example, deny access to telnet messages (telnet allows remote control of a computer system); the rules can be complex and work on a number of levels. The firewall can be software working in the PC, a server or it can be a separate machine used to filter transmissions before they hit the system. System designers can decide to place firewalls between components of their system – for example, in an e-Shop the backoffice system could be separated from the web server by a firewall to give (additional) protection for the e-Shop database.

Large organizations, or organizations with security concerns, may also actively monitor network traffic. At a simple level, a large increase in network traffic could indicate that something inappropriate is happening, such as a denial of service attack.

Data sent over a network can also be encrypted or be protected by a digital signature. The standard procedure to create secure internet transactions is to use SSL encryption (as on https webpages).

Process protection

Keeping the kit safe and the data secure are both vital; but the fundamental aim is to ensure that the Information Systems continue to operate.

At the basic level, we take our backups and then put the system back together should it fail – a process that could take some time.

Further protection and quicker recovery could be provided by including redundancy (spare kit) in the system or having a duplex system. Large organizations, for instance banks, will have a duplex system located at a site geographically remote from their primary data centre. The duplex system can be working on *hot standby* (all transactions are applied on both systems) and can then work on a *failover* basis (if the operational system breaks then standby system switches in automatically without users seeing any service interruption).

Computer equipment is also dependent on its power supply, which may fail. Failure of the power supply gives rise to loss of service and possibly loss of data (or inconsistent data which should be addressed in the software). Organizations can take measures to avoid any power-outs. These can include more than one connection point to the power grid, battery backup (to give kit time to power down) or standby generators. Solutions such as a standby generator that automatically switches on is an expensive option – and an option that might itself fail.

Protecting IS/IT operations from downtime comes at a cost, and any measures taken should be proportionate. IT managers have a problem here – they will have to fight for the money to provide process protection but, if the measures they take prove inadequate, they are likely to be first in line for the blame.

Themes
Outsourcing   Providing a duplex/standby IS/IT infrastructure is an expensive undertaking. One way to address the issue is to outsource the provision to a specialist disaster recovery operator. The provider can possibly share the provision across a number of clients and hence reduce costs.

Malware

Common parlance is to call unwanted, malicious software that might infect a computer system a virus – and we use antivirus software to combat the problem. Technically a virus is a specific type of infection; the proper name to cover

malware: short for malicious software, a general term for any software designed to run on a computer system without the owner's consent.

all malicious software is **malware** (not that the name is too important to the user with a problem). Technical names for various sorts of malware and their deployment include:

Backdoor	A backdoor is a way of bypassing the normal authentication (e.g. login) procedures of a computer system. A backdoor may be created on a compromised system to ease future entry.
Botnet	A number of *zombie* computers controlled from one source.
DoS/DDoS attack	Denial of service/distributed denial of service attack. Commonly effected by generating large numbers of messages that overwhelm the targeted server. If the attack is distributed using a number of attack, possibly *zombie*, computers the volume of attack messages can be dramatically increased.
Malware	Short for malicious software. A general term for any software (or a code script) designed to run on a computer system without consent.
Payload	The payload is the functionality of the malware. The payload might, for example, disrupt computer operation, gather sensitive information (*spyware*) or gain unauthorized access to computer systems.
Spyware	Spyware is *malware* that collects information about the computer user. One form of spyware is key-logging where all the information typed into the system is recorded.
SQL injection attack	Gaining unauthorized access to a website's database. The mechanism is to submit SQL statements through a web form that, if appropriate protection is not coded into the system, are then executed – typically to select and download data.
Trojan Horse	A Trojan Horse (or Trojan) is software that the user downloads or installs for a legitimate purpose without knowing that it includes a malware *payload*.
Virus	A virus is a program that attaches itself to/includes itself in legitimate software. The virus spreads itself when the software is run. The virus may carry a *payload*.
Worm	A worm is a stand-alone *malware* program that replicates itself in order to spread across a network and onto other computer systems. The worm may carry a *payload*.
Zombie computer	A zombie computer is one that is running *malware* on behalf of a third party without the owner being aware of the fact. The typical use of a zombie is to spread spam e-Mail or take part in a *DDoS* attack.

3

Most malware is aimed at PCs (that use Microsoft Windows). This is probably because the PC is the most widely used platform (although it is alleged that the operating system is less secure than its rivals). In principle, any computer system is vulnerable to attack – malware attacks on smartphone platforms have been reported, for instance.

Cyber warfare

cyber warfare: politically motivated hacking to conduct sabotage or espionage.

Cyber warfare is politically motivated hacking to conduct sabotage or espionage. With much of the commercial, civil and military infrastructure of advanced countries reliant on networked computer systems, national and international systems are vulnerable to attack.

It is argued by some that a Cyber Cold War is going on, with the Russians and Chinese allegedly hacking into Western systems to extract secrets and discover vulnerabilities. It is also assumed that Western powers are doing the same in reverse, with the US taking the lead.

One of the allegations is that China has invested heavily in cyber warfare capabilities and that thousands of programmers/hackers are involved in their effort. Secrets that are thought to have been stolen include stealth, nuclear and submarine technology (Hopkins, 2012).

If a cyber attack were to be launched it is possible that infrastructure such as a nation's electricity grid could be attacked and disabled. An attack on the military infrastructure could also redirect a missile from its intended target. It is not suggested that such an attack is likely, but it is possible. A couple of well-publicized cases of cyber warfare, in recent years, have been:

● The denial of service attack on Estonia in 2007 (see the *Estonia case study*)
● The virus attack on the Iranian uranium enrichment facilities in 2009 (see the *Iran nuclear industry case study*).

Case study
Estonia

In 1991, Estonia regained its independence from the USSR (now the Russian Federation). After independence, Estonia laid great emphasis on telecommunications and can claim to be the most wired country in Europe. Electronic transactions are used there, for example, for filing tax returns, voting and paying for the bus (with security based on an ID card that can be slotted into one's computer).

© JohanSwanepoel/Fotolia

In April/May 2007, Estonia suffered a *denial of service attack* that lasted three weeks – it was alleged that Russia orchestrated the attack.

The background to the attack lies in Estonia's history and ethnic mix. The Estonian population is small (1.4m); the majority are ethnic Estonians but there is a large Russian minority. When Estonia was part of the USSR the official language was Russian, but since independence it has been Estonian (an Uralic language, unlike Russian, which is a Slavic language). There has been, and still is, tension between the ethnic Estonian majority and the Russian minority. The Russian minority receive support in their grievances from the Russian Federation. The supposed trigger for the 2007 attack was the removal of a Soviet war memorial from the centre of the capital, Tallinn, to a cemetery on the city outskirts.

The attack began on 27 April 2007 and swamped the websites of many Estonian organizations. The authorities quickly closed down the sites under attack to foreign internet addresses. By isolating their internal services the effect on domestic users was limited, but the country was pretty much cut off internationally for the three-week duration of the attack.

The Estonian cyber attack is regarded as the most intensive and sophisticated instance of cyber warfare to date. It is intensively studied by the military, in many countries, as they plan their own cyber defences.

Sources include Davis (2007) and Kingsley (2012).

Case study
Iran nuclear industry

Iran is developing a nuclear industry. It has a Russian-designed nuclear reactor and is building extensive uranium enrichment facilities (uranium enrichment takes place in large arrays of high speed centrifuges). Iran claims that its program is for peaceful purposes – a number of states, led by the US and Israel, dispute this and say that Iran is developing nuclear weapons (the US and Israel are themselves nuclear armed).

In 2009 a version of the stuxnet worm started infecting computers round the world – the stuxnet worm's payload affects Siemens SCADA process control systems. The version of this worm that is reported to have damaged Iran's uranium enrichment plants is specific to a particular make of frequency converter drive (manufactured in Finland or Iran, with more than 33 devices present and running at high speeds) only likely to be in use in Iranian uranium enrichment plants. The effect of the worm is to affect the speed of the drive and to vary it widely and intermittently. Varying the speed would affect the effectiveness of the enrichment process (which needs to run for a long time at a consistent speed). Moreover, the speed variations might damage the rotors of the centrifuges. Allegedly, a large number of centrifuges suffered serious damage, although the Iranian authorities have sought to play down the extent of the damage.

Some commentators maintain that the development and placement of the malware was a joint US/Israeli operation, although that has never been officially confirmed.

Sources include Zetter (2010).

3

Further reading

Books recommended for further reading are:

Comer, D. E. (2009) *Computer Networks and Internets*, 5th ed., Pearson, Upper Saddle River, NJ.

Kurose, J. F. and Ross, K. W. (2009) *Computer Networking: A Top-Down Approach*, 5th. ed., Pearson, Upper Saddle River, NJ.

Pfleeger, C. P. and Pfleeger, S. L. (2006) *Security in Computing*, 4th ed., Prentice Hall, Upper Saddle River, NJ.

Comprehension test

This is a short, simple test to enable you to check you have absorbed the material presented in *Chapter 9*.

Comprehension test: Networks

Q1 An IT network has three (principal) components. Which of the following is **not** one of those components?

   a. Protocol ☐

   b. Extensible mark-up language ☐

   c. Connection ☐

   d. Communications equipment ☐

Q2 Networks can be classifies as a LAN or a WAN. Which of the following is a WAN?

   a. The network linking PCs in the lab to a server ☐

   b. The network linking lecturers' PCs to the department's e-Mail server ☐

   c. The network that allows academics to access supercomputers at other universities ☐

   d. The network linking lecturers' PCs to the department's colour printer ☐

Q3 Which of the following forwards data from one segment of the network to another segment?

   a. Firewall ☐

   b. Switch ☐

   c. Multiplexor ☐

   d. Bridge ☐

Q4 Which of the following is the network protocol of the internet?

   a. TCP/IP ☐

   b. HTTP ☐

   c. X400 ☐

   d. XML ☐

Q5 Which of the following is the term for a network using internet technology with access restricted to users inside the organization?

   a. ARPAnet ☐

   b. Extranet ☐

   c. Intranet ☐

   d. Mosaic ☐

Comprehension test: Network security

Q6 Data security and system recovery are reliant on:

   a. The internet ☐

   b. Backups ☐

   c. Standby generators ☐

   d. Firewalls ☐

Q7 Security for internet transactions uses which of the following encryption protocols?

   a. Enigma ☐

   b. SSL ☐

   c. Character inversion ☐

   d. SSD ☐

Q8 Network security (to prevent unwanted message types) can be provided by:

   a. Chinese wall ☐

   b. Firewall ☐

   c. Password protection ☐

   d. Message logging ☐

Q9 A distributed denial of service (DDoS) attack can be launched using:

   a. Backdoor ☐

   b. Botnet ☐

   c. Duplex system ☐

   d. Trojan Horse ☐

Q10 Which of the following sub-types of malware spreads itself when infected software is run?

   a. Trojan Horse ☐

   b. Virus ☐

   c. Worm ☐

   d. Spyware ☐

3

Exercises

The following exercises are designed to aid your understanding of the material presented in this chapter. They can be used for self-study or selected exercises can be used for tutorial discussion.

1 Comprehension What is a LAN and what is a WAN?

2 Research Check out the facilities of the computer labs in your university or college. What are the network facilities and what are they used for? Is the software/data you access on the local drive or on one or more networked servers?

3 Discussion Presumably you have your own PC and internet connection. What sort of connection do you have and what are the alternatives? What are the advantages and disadvantages of each of the options you have listed? From the network provider's point of view, which of these options would seem likely to be most profitable?

4 Research Malware attacks are mainly on PC systems (running Microsoft Windows). See if you can find any information on attacks on other platforms.

5 Research Cyber warfare is seen as a growing threat to national security. The book includes two case studies of (alleged) attacks – try to find others and write up a short account of one incident.

6 Discussion Have you ever suffered from a malware incident? If so, what damage did it do (if any) and how did you disinfect your system? A class discussion could be held on this topic.

PART 4 SYSTEM ANALYSIS AND DESIGN

Chapters

Designing, programming and installing an Information System is normally a sizable undertaking. To be successful the activity needs careful planning and the use of appropriate tools and techniques.

The starting point for an IS Project is to determine which system development lifecycle should be applied and which methodology would be appropriate – these issues and options are discussed in *Chapter 10*. Project management has already been discussed in *Chapter 3*.

The analysis and design stages of an Information System project are the responsibility of the system analyst, an IS specialist. The analysis and design process makes extensive use of graphical techniques. In *Chapter 11* we will learn how to draw and how to use the use case diagram, data flow diagram (DFD), entity relationship diagram (ERD), sequence diagram and class diagram.

After analysis and design the system has to be programmed, tested, installed and maintained. These activities are briefly explained in *Chapter 12* (this is not a programming textbook but the IS specialist should have some idea of what is involved).

10 THE SYSTEM DEVELOPMENT LIFECYCLE

Summary

Developing a computer system takes place in stages. The first step is to find out what is required, and this is followed by a design process that maps the requirements onto the IT. The design is implemented by the programming process, which creates the computer code. Finally, the system needs to be tested before it goes live. These stages can be formalized as a system development lifecycle. The lifecycle just outlined is the waterfall lifecycle; an alternative to that is an iterative or evolutionary prototype lifecycle.

Developing a sizable computer system (or implementing a bought-in package) is a lengthy, costly undertaking – and often it does not go to plan. Mapping out the development in terms of a lifecycle and a project plan is a good start to reducing the risks of costly overruns or, worse, failure of the project. The project can be further organized by adopting a methodology that matches up stages with specified activities and techniques. In this chapter we will look at five different methods/methodologies:

- Structured system analysis and design (SSADM) – a complete system analysis and design (SA&D) methodology specifying stages and the techniques to be used at each stage
- DSDM – a methodology that formalizes an evolutionary prototype lifecycle for rapid application development. Techniques are not specified by DSDM
- Object-oriented analysis and design using UML. UML is a modelling language for OO design – UML does not specify a lifecycle but this book suggests how these techniques should be applied
- Agile software development – a *lightweight* (un-bureaucratic) approach to evolutionary system development
- Socio-technical SA&D – an alternative approach that emphasizes the human aspects of the computer system that is to be developed.

Techniques used for SA&D are taught in **Chapter 11** and further aspects of implementing a system are examined in **Chapter 12**.

Learning outcomes

Having read this chapter and completed the exercises, you should:

- Understand the main stages required in the development of an Information System and know how these stages can be sequenced as a lifecycle
- Understand the concept of a methodology and its relevance to Information System development
- Appreciate a range of Information System development philosophies (specifically: structured, object-oriented, agile and socio-technical) that have guided the development of methodologies
- Understand the three underlying principles of object-oriented design/development: encapsulation, generalization and polymorphism.

© Eimantas Buzas/Fotolia

Key terms

System development lifecycle (SDLC), waterfall lifecycle, feasibility study, system analysis and design (SA&D), program and unit test, system and acceptance test, operations, iterative or prototype lifecycle, evolutionary prototype lifecycle, prototype, methodology, computer-aided software engineering (CASE), structured system analysis and design method (SSADM), dynamic system development methodology (DSDM), object, encapsulation, generalization, polymorphism, object-oriented analysis and design (OO-A&D), rapid application development (RAD), agile software development, socio-technical analysis and design, soft systems methodology (SSM).

System development lifecycle

To write a program, or to develop an Information System, requires a number of activities. The developer, or the project team, must:

1. Find out what is needed and design how it is to be implemented – a process we call system analysis and design (SA&D).
2. Create the software – either by writing programs or using some sort of application generator.
3. Test the system to make sure that it works – that we have confidence it will be reliable and produce the correct results.

system development lifecycle (SDLC): the stages that developers must go through to create an Information System.

waterfall lifecycle: a SDLC where the activities/stages are performed in sequence. The stages of the waterfall lifecycle are: feasibility, system analysis and design, program and unit test, system and acceptance test, and operations.

feasibility study: the first stage in a SDLC. A short study to determine that the proposed system is technically feasible, financially worthwhile and ethically justified.

These activities can be expressed in terms of a **system development lifecycle (SDLC)** and it can be further formalized as a methodology – we will look at that in the section on methodologies.

The basic SDLC is the **waterfall lifecycle**. This breaks the project down into a sequence of stages, and the requirement is that one stage is completed and signed off before the next is started. The waterfall analogy refers to a series of pools on a hillside linked by waterfalls. The stages are the pools and we swim around in those pools applying the specified techniques, using tools and producing the required end products before tumbling down the waterfall to start the next stage. Like most analogies it does not bear too close an inspection! The basic waterfall lifecycle structure is shown in *Figure 10.1* overleaf.

The stages of the waterfall lifecycle are:

Feasibility study: The first stage of the waterfall lifecycle is a feasibility study. Developing an IS can represent a sizable investment and it is obviously a good idea for the organization to check out what it is letting itself in for, and what it is likely to achieve, before committing to the development and instillation of a system. The feasibility stage seeks to answer three questions:

- Is the system technically feasible – will it work?

  The question needs to be not just *can it be made to work?* but *is it appropriate to the organization and the task?* Some systems involve new, unproven technologies, and it may well not be appropriate to take the risk of using such techniques.

4

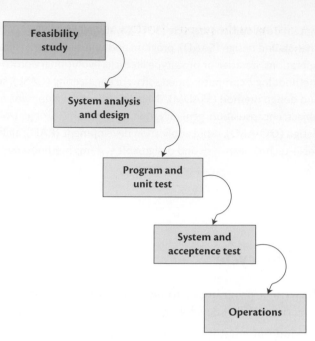

Figure 10.1 Waterfall lifecycle.

- Is the system financially justified – can we afford it?
  The classic approach to cost-justifying a system is a discounted cash flow analysis. An estimate is made of the price of the proposed system and the savings that should be made once the system is installed. Interest charges can then be factored in and a calculation made of the payback that the system will produce over its expected lifespan, if any. This approach is less appropriate when the system is a *must have* (e.g. because the current system is reaching the end of its useful life), or where the system is intended to give competitive advantage but there is no accurate way of estimating the benefit.

- Is the system ethically acceptable?
  Computer professionals are required to act ethically by their professional associations (see *Chapter 14*), and the uses of that system should be within the law (see *Chapter 13*) – the Data Protection Act is one law that could be relevant. The new system also has to be operated by the staff, and a system that threatens jobs or makes people's lives difficult is unlikely to be welcomed by the workforce. These types of issue also need to be evaluated as part of the feasibility study.

To assess the feasibility of the system the business analyst and/or system analyst need to do a mini version of the system investigation that will be conducted in the next stage of the lifecycle. From this study the analysts can draw up a feasibility report that includes:

- An outline of the proposed system. The outline must specify what is included in the system and what functions lie outside the system boundary
- A technical summary of the IT equipment and software that is required, and the way the system should be implemented
- A high-level plan on how the system should, or could, be developed

- A costing of the proposed system and of the benefits that are claimed for the system
- The feasibility assessment: will it work? Can we afford it? And is it appropriate?

The feasibility study should be fairly short and reasonably cheap, but it should also be effective. The intention is to avoid investing a lot of money in a system that will take too long, cost too much, prove ineffective and/or disrupt the organization. To explore these issues is worth some time and effort, but the investment must not be excessive since there is no usable end product.

system analysis and design (SA&D): a stage in a SDLC. The process of determining the requirements of a business system and designing a system that will run on the proposed IT.

System analysis and design (SA&D): If a project is deemed feasible and development is approved, the next stage of the project is system analysis and design. The task is threefold:

- Find out what the business requires: requirements analysis
- Propose a *logical system* that would meet all or most of the requirements: logical design
- Design a computer system that implements the agreed logical system: technical design.

The single lifecycle stage of system analysis and design can be broken down into these three phases, giving the more detailed lifecycle shown in *Figure 10.2*.

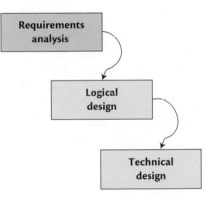

Figure 10.2 SA&D lifecycle.

The first phase, requirements analysis, is concerned with finding out what the users do and how that might be improved. The techniques of requirements analysis are:

- Interviews: Talking to managers and staff to find out what is done and how it might be improved. Interviews are likely to be the main tool in a system investigation.
- Observation: Watch staff using the current system. By observation the analyst can get an idea of what works well and which facilities are inappropriate or difficult to use.
- Questionnaires: These might be used where there are a large number of staff and/or where those staff are dispersed in local offices. Questionnaires can be useful, but the amount of information that is likely to be obtained is limited.
- Current system: The analyst can look at the current system and associated files and documents to see how the job is currently done, the volume of transactions and the data that is used.

From these sources the analyst can document the requirements for the new system. The requirements specification will include diagrams and descriptions that specify the business process and of the objectives for the new system.

The documentation of the requirements leads onto the logical system design. The logical system is a theoretical system that best meets the user's and business's requirements. The logical system is deliberately independent of the IT that might be used. The aim is that, if the design was for a pre-defined technical installation, it may not produce the optimum solution – it is better to first design a theoretical system and then use that to determine the best arrangement and combination of technology for the job. Not all SA&D methodologies include a requirement for a logical system design stage.

The final phase of SA&D is the physical/technical design. It is at this stage we determine what the eventual system will look like, the technology that is needed to implement it and the way it will be used by the organization.

The final end products of the system analysis and design stage will be:

- Diagrams summarizing the processing and data requirements of the system
- Specifications of the IT equipment that is to be bought and the technical procedures that are to be followed
- Details of the organizational structures and procedures that are to be applied when the new system is in use
- Program/process specifications for the software that is to be developed.

The end products of the SA&D stage need to be reviewed and agreed before the project proceeds. It will also be necessary to review the project plan to check that the costings and timescales, put forward in the feasibility study, are still applicable.

program and unit test: a stage in a SDLC. The process of writing program/software code and testing each unit of code in isolation.

Program and unit test: This is the stage where the required system is implemented on the IT equipment. The classic way of doing this is to write computer programs. The system, however, could alternatively be implemented using some sort of application generator or a bought-in package:

- Programming consists of writing sets of instructions in a tightly defined programming language. The program must be logically correct and cover every eventuality that may occur. Programming is further discussed in *Chapter 11*.
- An application generator or fourth-generation language cuts down on the amount of work that the programmer has to do – the overall framework and some of the logic is provided by the system. Those who are familiar with Microsoft Access will understand that the way in which forms and reports can be specified is an example of a simple application generator.
- The adoption of an application package cuts out much, or all, of the programming stage. There might be modifications or additions and the package will still need the system test – the next stage of the lifecycle.

As each program/module is written it needs to be thoroughly tested. There are many paths through most programs and we can only be confident that a program is correct if all paths are tested. Normally, 100 per cent testing is not possible – the amount of testing is, in part, determined by how crucial is the reliability of the system. Thorough testing of a module can take as long, or longer, than it took to write that module.

System and acceptance test: The final stage of developing a system is to put it all together and see if it works. The system test and acceptance test is a two-stage approach to testing the whole system. The requirement is as follows:

- The system test is a technical test by the project team. Given thorough testing of all the components in unit testing, the system test/link test should ensure that all the interfaces work (although it never turns out to be that simple). In carrying out the system test the development team should be ensuring that the system as developed meets the requirements of the specification.
- The acceptance test is a user test. One hopes that the system test has checked out all the bugs and it is the job of the acceptance test to ensure that the system will meet the needs of organization in its everyday operation. There is the possibility that the acceptance test will find significant omissions or misunderstandings – but that is not good news when the system is days or weeks away from going live.

As well as checking the functionality of the system, the system and acceptance testing must also make sure that the system will operate successfully under live conditions. There is a world of difference between one programmer testing a single module and an integrated system working with tens or hundreds of online users accessing a multiplicity of functions in the same timeframe. Multiuser, online systems need to be tested for volume/robustness before they are used in the live environment. Testing is considered in more detail in *Chapter 12*.

Operations: The first event in the operating of a system is going live, or implementation. This may take place as a big bang event (switch off the old system on Friday night and start with the new system on Monday morning) or there may be a phased introduction of the new system (with parallel running of the old system for a period of weeks or months). Switching over to a new system is always a fraught affair – however good the preparation, there are always things that can (and usually do) go wrong.

The preparation for the system going live must include the system and acceptance testing (or equivalent) but also requires some or all of the following activities:

- Installation of new IT equipment and network facilities
- Training of maintenance and support staff (who may be the personnel who developed the system)
- Training of user staff
- Loading of data onto the new system.

These preparations for going live, where there is a large system and/or a substantial number of staff involved, can be major activities in themselves. Often they will run in parallel with the system and acceptance test and they can be planned as part of that stage. Implementation is addressed in more detail in *Chapter 12*.

Once the system has gone live, the true operations stage begins. Initially the maintenance/support team will help the users and deal with bugs that got

system and acceptance test: a stage in a SDLC. System testing is to check that the whole system works on the intended platform and with the expected volumes of data. Acceptance testing is to test that the system meets the user requirements.

operations: a stage in a SDLC. Operations is where the system is released/installed for live use, and the subsequent maintenance and enhancement of the system.

4

through the testing stage. Over time, new requirements will emerge and the system will need to be enhanced by adding new facilities or amending existing facilities. All changes must be made with care and would normally go through their own design, development and testing stages – we don't want to jeopardize the successful running of the system when some minor enhancement is added (see *Chapter 12* for more detail).

Over time, technology and the business will move on. There is only so much that can be done by the maintenance team and eventually it is time to start afresh – back to the feasibility study and start again (but that said, there is some very old software out there in critical business systems – as organizations found out when they had to check out their systems for the millennium bug: see the *Explanation box Millennium bug*).

The millennium bug was the concern that computer systems would not be able to deal correctly with the change of year from 1999 to 2000. The issue arose from the common practice of recording the year as two digits, e.g. 99 or 00. One area where the problem would arise was in comparing dates, e.g. to check when an invoice (or a library book) is overdue or sorting dates to put records in age sequence.

Dates are recorded in computer systems in a number of formats – some of which were millennium-proof and some of which were not. A reasonable way of recording dates could be in reverse order, e.g. 27jan99 would be 990127. The date 990127 was plainly less than 990227 i.e. 27feb99 (although calculating the days difference was a bit more complex, there are software library routines for that). Unfortunately that logic broke down when the new century started and 27jan00 became 000127.

An obvious solution was to include a four-digit year – but many programs had been written years before the turn of the century and at a time when memory and disk space was at a premium. A better solution is to record all dates as days after an arbitrary date (days after 01jan1900 would cover all possibilities) – this solution was adopted by some machines and by the Oracle database management system (in practice the norm is to cater for date and time as a single figure and record the number of seconds (or microseconds) after the selected start date – a big number but it covers all requirements).

So the millennium bug exercise was to check that all systems would cope with the century date

© a_korn/Fotolia

change – some organizations took the option of replacing their systems rather than amending their old systems. In the event most systems coped with the century switch without problem – whether that was good maintenance or the bug was an overhyped scare is another question. One issue publicized at the time was that commercial aeroplanes had several thousand date-sensitive routines in their control software, so it was probably as well that one did not go wrong.

Further date-related problems have occurred since the millennium, with the miscalculation of which year is a leap year catching some systems out, e.g. in 2012, some TomTom Sat Nav systems and Microsoft's Azure cloud computing service (Preimesberger, 2012).

A similar problem is set to occur on 19jan2038. Many versions of UNIX keep time as the number of seconds from the start of 01jan1970 and the count is set to overflow its allotted space on the above mentioned date.

Evaluation: The waterfall lifecycle expects one activity to be finished and signed off before the next activity starts. It allows for clear-cut project management – if a stage that should have been finished four weeks ago is not yet finished then you are a month late and counting. Problems with a waterfall lifecycle are that:

- It is assumed that user requirements are captured early in the process. However, misunderstandings or omissions may well not come to light until the acceptance test stage – a bit late to be making significant changes.
- It is also assumed that no significant changes will take place after the requirements have been signed off. Well, business is not always like that and changes can and do come up which then rather upset the carefully drawn up system design and the development plan.
- Projects developed using the waterfall lifecycle and associate methodologies can be bureaucratic, long-winded and expensive. The problem of long development timescales is partly down to the lifecycle but is also a consequence of the heavyweight methodologies that are traditionally associated with this lifecycle.

These issues have been used to argue against the waterfall lifecycle and for alternative, less formal, approaches that will be discussed in the next section. Yet large systems are complex and expensive. For large systems to have a chance of succeeding they need careful planning, and this is difficult to square with a less formal approach. The waterfall lifecycle should be the starting point for large systems. It is possible, or even probable, that after an overall analysis of the required system, the system can be segmented and detailed design and development can be phased. In the context of a robust overall requirement analysis and system design, less formal methods might be used for each stage.

Iterative lifecycles

iterative or prototype lifecycle: a SDLC where stages are iterated, as opposed to the sequential completion of stages in the waterfall lifecycle.

evolutionary prototype lifecycle: an iterative lifecycle where the requirements are elucidated and the system is incrementally developed, through a series of prototypes.

The main alternative to the waterfall lifecycle is an **iterative or prototype lifecycle**. This approach uses a prototype to elucidate the requirements of the system. The project team knock up a *quick and dirty* version of the main functions of the system and then discuss it with the users. The system can then be modified to incorporate the improvements that the users ask for and to add further functionality. The **evolutionary prototyping lifecycle** is shown in *Figure 10.3* (overleaf).

The stages of the evolutionary prototype lifecycle are:

Feasibility study: As with the waterfall lifecycle, we need to assess the three feasibility questions:

- Is the system technically feasible?
- Is the system financially justified?
- Is the system ethically acceptable?

In the feasibility study we also need to work out what will be in the initial prototype, how we plan the iterations and the timescale for the subsequent stages.

See the waterfall lifecycle for a more detailed description of the feasibility report.

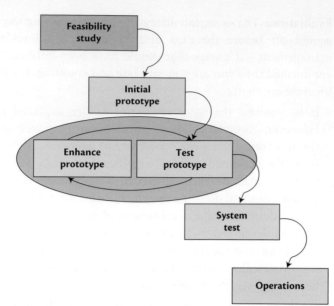

Figure 10.3 Evolutionary prototype lifecycle.

prototype: a model, in this context a computer program, built to test or demonstrate a concept.

Initial Prototype: A prototype is a model or mock-up of the system. The first prototype will concentrate on establishing the user requirements for the main functions of the system – it does not need to bother with the many subsidiary functions and the technical structure that will be required for the final system. For an order processing system, outlined in *Chapter 4*, we would probably concentrate on functions to maintain customer, maintain product, create order and print picking list, while leaving other functions and the setting up of a full-scale database to later. We might also start with a single-user system with software needed for multi-user operation also being left for later.

Prototypes need to be put together quickly and need to be changed quickly. The use of a fourth-generation language/application generator can greatly assist in this process.

Test prototype/enhance prototype: The main two stages of the iterative lifecycle are checking and amending the prototype – this part of the lifecycle is reiterated in *Figure 10.4*.

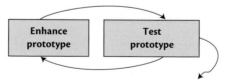

Figure 10.4 Check and amend prototype iteration.

Having created the initial prototype, members of the project team will sit down with the users and test/evaluate the work that has been done. The questions are:

- Does the prototype do what the user requires?
- Is the prototype function well designed?
- What functions and functionality should be added when the prototype is amended/enhanced for the next iteration?

Small details of the prototype may be changed during the testing process but it is normally better to save up substantial changes and additions to the next iteration. One of the problems with prototyping is keeping control of the process, and so planning a limited number of iterations is usually the best way forward. For a medium-size project one would probably plan four or five iterations – the initial iterations establishing the functionality of the major processes and the latter iterations including more facilities but concentrating on adding a fully functional file structure/database and the more technical aspects of the system.

The final iteration of the prototyping loop should produce a fully functional and technically acceptable software system. The system should be accompanied by an agreed level of documentation. Upon completion of these tasks the system can be passed onto system test.

System test: The prototype has been tested as part of its development process but it needs a thorough test before it can be put live. The prototype process has, presumably, covered the requirements of the acceptance test – but the system still needs to be tested for its technical integrity, including any requirement for volume testing.

Operations: Once the system test has been completed the process used to develop it is largely irrelevant. Going live is much the same for a system developed using a waterfall lifecycle or an iterative/prototyping lifecycle.

Evaluation: The iterative approach has a number of advantages, which include:

- It is arguably easier to work out the user requirement, particularly the user interface requirements, using prototypes than using a paper based design process.
- Prototyping approaches are generally quicker than waterfall lifecycle methodologies (in part that is because there is generally less design documentation produced).
- Changes are more readily incorporated into a prototyping approach than a waterfall-based project. That said, changes in the requirements late in the development of a project are always disruptive, whatever approach is used.
- The user is involved throughout the process and there should be less likelihood of producing software that does not meet the user's requirements.

The main drawbacks of a prototype approach to system development are:

- Project management and progress monitoring are not as easy, or as clear-cut, as when using a waterfall lifecycle. On the prototyping stages, the work still to be done is not easily quantified.
- The software that emerges from the prototyping process is unlikely to be well designed. It started as a simple system and has been patched, amended and added to over the period of several iterations – not the best way to produce an elegantly engineered system.
- There is no formal point where the system should be sized – presumably this increases the likelihood of producing a system that does not perform adequately when used in live conditions.
- The prototype approach is probably not appropriate for large-scale projects that are producing monolithic software systems.

4

Nevertheless:

- Many modern software development packages lend themselves to a prototyping approach. The technical architecture of the system can be embedded in the package, and this limits the damage that a somewhat ad hoc approach to development might cause.
- Large-scale monolithic system developments are less common than they once were. Many software developments are relatively small scale, possibly web systems or on client-server systems and linking with other systems to provide the required overall functionality.

The evolutionary prototype lifecycle is an essential element of the rapid application development (RAD) and agile approaches to system development. RAD addresses the notion that systems were taking too long and costing too much to develop. There was also a concern that systems were getting too large as they tried to include provision for every business possibility (the Ninety Percent Rule has it that 90 per cent of the system (program code) deals with only 10 per cent of the cases – this is very possibly true, but there is an imperative that all business cases need to be processed).

Methodologies

methodology: a set of guidelines for the analysis, design and development of an Information System.

A system design and development **methodology** is a package of stages and techniques to help the computer project team develop a computer system. A methodology is defined by Maddison (1983) as:

> a recommended collection of philosophies, phrases, procedures, techniques, tools, documentation, management and training for developers of an information system.

The **philosophy** is somewhat intangible but is, in part at least, reflected in the type of methodology that is adopted. In this section we will look at structured, rapid application development (RAD), object-oriented, agile and socio-technical approaches.

Phases are the stages in the lifecycle. We have looked at the waterfall and evolutionary prototype lifecycles and all methodologies are based on one of these – although they will put their own spin on these underlying approaches. The organization of stages/phases is an essential factor in the management of the project – there needs to be a plan if timetables and budgets are to be adhered to. We have looked at project management in *Chapter 3*.

The **techniques**, for system analysis and design, are diagramming conventions that assist the system analyst in investigating the user requirements, and documenting the proposed design of the system – a selection of these techniques is covered in *Chapter 11*. The diagrams are the basis of the documentation of the system.

computer-aided software engineering (CASE): software designed to assist the analysis, design, development and testing of computer systems.

Finally, the **tools**: the project team can use **computer-aided software engineering (CASE)** software to help in the design and development of their system (see the *CASE explanation box*).

Explanation
Computer-aided software
engineering (CASE)

The analysis and design of a computer system requires the collection of a lot of data and the drawing of design diagrams – CASE is software that helps with this.

The first issue is drawing the diagrams (see ***Chapter 11*** for a selection of SA&D diagrams). Each of these diagrams has its own set of symbols and the drawing of the diagrams can be simplified by having a specialist, CASE, drawing package that includes a pallet of the required symbols.

The diagrams used in SA&D need to cross reference to one another. UML, for example uses the use case, sequence and class diagrams. Each use case can/should have a sequence diagram, the objects referenced on the sequence diagram must be on the class diagram, and so on. The CASE software can assist/enforce these linkages.

System design includes the specification of attributes/data items – these can be held in a repository in the CASE (sometimes referred to as a data dictionary). The data dictionary can be used in database schema generation and also in input/output (screen/report) design. The data dictionary records the usage of each attribute in the various elements of the system design – changes to any attribute can be automatically applied across the whole design.

The use of CASE in SA&D can be referred to as upper CASE. The use of CASE in development can be referred to as lower CASE. Some CASE tools have the facility to generate program shells from the SA&D for the development stage.

Programmers will normally use a program development environment (PDE), which is a CASE tool although the term would not normally be used. The PDE includes the source editor, compiler/interpreter, version control and possibly some testing aids.

A famous CASE tool for UML is Rational Rose (now no longer supported). Microsoft issues Visual Studio for the dot.net environment – this is a CASE tool. Database packages include application generators that link database, screen and report design – Microsoft Access' wizards are a simple example of this.

Source: Stockbyte/Punchstock

4

Structured system analysis and design

structured system analysis and design method (SSADM): a waterfall methodology that structures the process requirement using data flow analysis and the data requirement using entity relationship analysis.

The waterfall lifecycle is most closely associated with structured methods and the leading structured method in the UK is **structured system analysis and design method (SSADM)** – although the idea of *heavyweight* methods such as SSADM is now rather unfashionable (possibly that connects with the failure of some large computing projects over recent years).

SSADM was created and introduced in the 1980s by the UK Government in response to problems that had occurred with a number of large government computing projects. Over the years the method went through a number of iterations and the current (probably final) issue is version 4. The method is public source – that is, it is free for anyone who wants to use it.

SSADM is a waterfall SA&D methodology that tackles only the feasibility study and SA&D parts of the lifecycle. Version 4 has five modules and seven stages, which are shown in ***Figure 10.5*** (see overleaf).

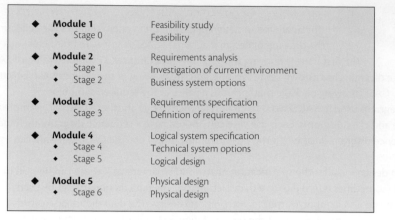

Figure 10.5 SSADM
modules and stages.

Another way of looking at SSADM, which ties up with the detail we looked
at of the waterfall lifecycle, is as three main stages and three smaller transition
stages. This view of SSADM is shown in *Figure 10.6* (with the main stages
represented as the larger boxes and the transition stages as smaller boxes).

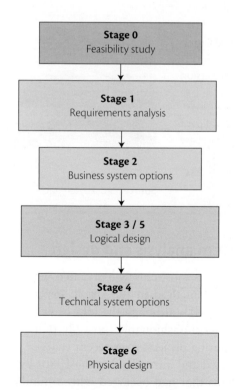

Figure 10.6 The SSADM
lifecycle.

The stages of the SSADM lifecycle are:

● Stage 0: Feasibility – the first of the transition stages. A short sharp study to
decide whether to proceed with the project. The end product is the feasibility
report, which is then assessed by the appropriate managers. If the feasibility
study is accepted we make the transition to the next stage, requirements
analysis.

- Stage 1: Requirements analysis – where the current system is investigated along with the business and user requirements for the proposed system. A feature of the SSADM approach is that it explicitly acknowledges that investigating the user requirement will include looking at the current system. The documentation from the requirements analysis includes:
  - The data flow diagram (DFD) of the current system
  - The logical data structure (LDS) of the current system
  - A problem requirement list.

- Stage 2: Business system options – the second of the transition stages. Stage 1 has investigated the current system and there is a real danger that the project could just re-implement that system on newer technology and miss the opportunity for business system improvement. The job of this stage is to think of alternative business approaches that could be included in the new system and to choose the optimum way forward. The main end product of the stage is the data flow diagram for the proposed logical system.

- Stage 3 and 5: Logical design (definition of requirements plus logical design) where the proposed logical system is specified in some detail. This task is divided into two stages for reasons that will be outlined below (see Stage 4). The documentation for the logical design includes:
  - The data flow diagram of the proposed system
  - The logical data structure of the proposed system
  - Relational data analysis (RDA)
  - Entity life histories (ELH).

- Stage 4: Technical system options – the third and final transition stage. The task here is to choose the hardware, software and communication provision for the proposed system. The stage is scheduled part way through the logical design because that is the earliest point at which there will be sufficient information to make fully informed technical decisions; it is to be hoped that there is still time to set up the technical infrastructure before development starts. The major end product of the stage is a document specifying the technical architecture that is proposed for the system.

- Stage 6: Physical design – where the logical design is mapped onto the intended technical provision. An important part of physical design is to ensure that the system will give an adequate performance with the intended workload. The physical design has to be somewhat iterative as the database and processes designs are tuned to meet performance requirements. The end products for the physical design are:
  - Physical database design
  - Physical process design.

The two main techniques used in SSADM are:

- The data flow diagram, showing the data inputs to the system, the data outputs from the system, the processes and (logical) data stores
- The logical data structure (also known as an ER diagram), showing the data used by the system in terms of entity, attributes and the relationships between the entities.

These techniques feature in *Chapter 11*. Further techniques included in SSADM are:

- Relational data analysis, where the data is analysed to meet the requirements of database design (third normal form)
- Entity life history (ELH) – one diagram for each entity on the LDS showing the processes that affect the entity. Uses Jackson structures
- Effect correspondence diagrams (ECD) – one diagram for each process on the DFD showing entities used in a process. Not widely used (or understood). Uses Jackson structures.

Relational data analysis and Jackson structures are outlined in *Chapter 11*. SSADM also uses Jackson structures for process and dialogue design.

DSDM

dynamic system development methodology (DSDM): an evolutionary prototype lifecycle methodology designed for use in a commercial environment.

Dynamic system development methodology (DSDM) is a methodology that formalizes the prototyping lifecycle and makes it appropriate to a commercial environment. The dynamic part of the name places the methodology into the rapid application development (RAD) camp of methodologies. The method has been updated to embrace the principles of agile software development and is now called DSDM Atern (DSDM, 2012). The consortium is essentially UK-based.

The lifecycle of the DSDM is slightly more complex than the generalized evolutionary prototype lifecycle. It is affectionately known as *three pizzas and a cheese cake* (although in the latest Atern version, the third pizza is no longer pizza-shaped) – it is shown in *Figure 10.7*.

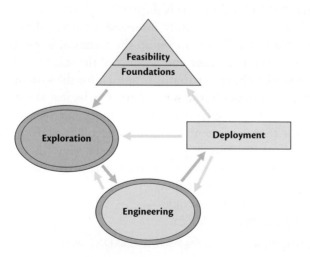

Figure 10.7 The DSDM lifecycle (based on DSDM, 2008).

The stages of the DSDM lifecycle are:

- Feasibility: As with other feasibility studies we need to evaluate what is needed and hence check that the proposed system is technically achievable, affordable and acceptable. For DSDM we also need to check out that a

RAD approach is appropriate. To apply RAD/prototyping techniques the system must not be computationally complex – prototypes model the user interfaces and that is not going to sort out a computationally complex system. RAD also requires commitment and compromise; all stakeholders need to be committed to the approach for it to work.

- Foundations: A short exercise to elucidate the business requirements and determine the technical constraints. The process normally uses facilitated workshops involving all levels and roles of business stakeholders to gain consensus on the requirements and the way the project is to proceed. The end results of the workshops and the stages include:
  - Business area definitions, identifying business processes and the users of the proposed system
  - System architecture definition, specifying the IT requirement including equipment, system software and the development software
  - Outline prototype plan, for the next two stages of the lifecycle.
- Exploration: Where system models (diagrams) and prototypes are used to work out the details of the system requirements. The stage is iterative. The initial prototype will probably be of just the main functions; these will be refined, and further functionality added, in further iterations. The stage concentrates on interfaces and user requirements; the technical infrastructure and performance of the system is more the responsibility of the next stage.
- Engineering: This continues from the previous stage and prepares the system for implementation. This is the stage where we will complete the IT infrastructure and make sure that the system gives adequate performance and is reasonably robust. The engineering stage, like the previous stage, is iterative – the two stages may overlap.
- Deployment: The final stage is to implement the system. This involves the final setup of the IT infrastructure, training of the users and the go live.

With RAD, the emphasis is on early delivery of the system to the users. Getting a computer project delivered on time is not easy; while using a DSDM lifecycle may help, it is also going to raise expectations. DSDM adopts a novel approach to delays in the schedule – if you can't complete the required functionality on time, throw some of it out. One of the principles governing the use of DSDM is:

> Focus on the business need: guarantee the minimum usable subset.

The assumption is that a system can serve a useful business purpose with far less functionality and exception processing than the user may have originally wanted.

DSDM defines a lifecycle and a number of principles designed to keep the project on schedule. The method emphasizes the importance of system documentation but does not define the techniques that are to be used. We might use structured techniques or we might opt for object-oriented design techniques.

DSDM requires commitment of all the stakeholders in the project. It should only be used when that commitment is present, when the project is of an appropriate size and when the functionality is apparent at the interfaces (so that prototyping can be an effective technique).

4

Object-oriented analysis and design

An **object,** in the context of system analysis and design and of programming, is:

> A self contained module of data and its associated processing.

(Freedman, 1999)

The purpose of objects in system development/software engineering is to produce software components that are self-contained and can be used in any system that requires that functionality. There is an analogy with engineering where (say) a standard electric motor or a microchip can be taken and plugged into any product that requires that functionality.

Object-oriented (OO) technology started as a programming technique. The first OO programming language was Smalltalk, which has been followed (and superseded) by further programming languages: C++ and Java are the two most used OO programming languages.

Object orientation claims to be a more natural way of viewing software design (although, for the many of us brought up on structured analysis and procedural programming, that can be less than obvious – apparently we need to make a paradigm shift). As already indicated, a major aim of OO development is to promote and enable software reuse, and this is facilitated by the three major OO concepts of encapsulation, generalization and polymorphism:

- **Encapsulation** – this is the basic concept that the object includes the data and the processing that manipulates the data. This creates a self-sufficient module that can be reused wherever that object is required.
- **Generalization** allows an object to use the characteristics of a more general object (also known as inheritance). This is probably best explained by example: if we have objects for *staff* and *student* they can inherit a lot of their data and processing from a more general object of *person*. The person object includes, and processes, name, address, date of birth and so on. These attributes apply to both staff and students, meaning that the staff and student objects only have to deal with the data and processing that is specific to their particular system requirements.

- **Polymorphism** allows objects to be created whose exact type is not known until run time. In designing our system we might find that different groups of students have different characteristics. We could tackle this by the use of polymorphism with a student object that adapts its behaviour to the requirements of the student type that is currently being processed.

Where object orientation is used as the programming technology the SA&D technique should anticipate that requirement, hence **object-oriented analysis and design (OO-A&D).**

Object-oriented SA&D, as indicated above, grew out of OO programming. The development of OO-A&D techniques has been an area of considerable conflict as theorists (with large egos and/or commercial interests) fought out their various ideological positions. What emerged from this process is:

> UML, the unified modelling language devised by Booch, Jacobson and Rumbaugh.

Surprisingly, UML seems to have gained general acceptance. Possibly this is because it uses a toolbox approach; it sets out a number of techniques but it does not say when you use them – it is a modelling language, not a methodology.

So, we have general agreement on the techniques and everyone can apply them as they see fit (and deviate from the standard if they feel strongly about it). The compilers of UML have their own approach to methodology called rational unified process (RUP); many other organizations and practitioners use OO-A&D in their own different ways.

For the purposes of this book, and as a framework for studying UML techniques, we will have our own sequence/lifecycle as follows:

- Identify user requirements and system boundary
  Technique: use cases
- Identify objects
  Technique: class diagram (conceptual)
- Design use cases
  Technique: sequence diagram
- Design objects
  Technique: class diagram (design).

This simple approach to UML design is shown in *Figure 10.8*. The UML techniques that are being used are explained in *Chapter 11*.

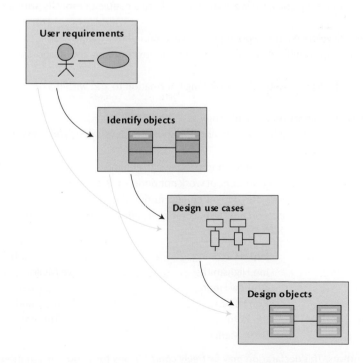

Figure 10.8 Design method using UML.

rapid application development (RAD): an application of the evolutionary prototype lifecycle and techniques such as timeboxing to ensure the rapid development of Information Systems.

Agile development

Agile software development uses iteration and prototyping to evolve a system. It takes a similar (or the same) approach as **rapid application development (RAD)** but is a more modern terminology. Agile development is based on an iterative lifecycle. DSDM started its existence as a RAD methodology but now, in its latest DSDM Atern version, has adopted the agile label. The term was introduced in 2001 by the Agile Manifesto, which is reproduced below.

Explanation
Manifesto for Agile Software Development

Manifesto for Agile Software Development

We are uncovering better ways of developing software by doing it and helping others do it. Through this work we have come to value:

- Individuals and interactions *over processes and tools*
- Working software *over comprehensive documentation*
- Customer collaboration *over contract negotiation*
- Responding to change *over following a plan*

That is, while there is value in the items on the right, we value the items on the left more.

Twelve Principles of Agile Software

We follow these principles:

- Our highest priority is to satisfy the customer through early and continuous delivery of valuable software.
- Welcome changing requirements, even late in development. Agile processes harness change for the customer's competitive advantage.
- Deliver working software frequently, from a couple of weeks to a couple of months, with a preference to the shorter timescale.
- Business people and developers must work together daily throughout the project.
- Build projects around motivated individuals. Give them the environment and support they need, and trust them to get the job done.
- The most efficient and effective method of conveying information to and within a development team is face-to-face conversation.
- Working software is the primary measure of progress.
- Agile processes promote sustainable development. The sponsors, developers, and users should be able to maintain a constant pace indefinitely.
- Continuous attention to technical excellence and good design enhances agility.
- Simplicity – the art of maximizing the amount of work not done – is essential.
- The best architectures, requirements, and designs emerge from self-organizing teams.
- At regular intervals, the team reflects on how to become more effective, then tunes and adjusts its behavior accordingly.

Kent Beck	James Grenning	Robert C. Martin
Mike Beedle	Jim Highsmith	Steve Mellor
Arie van Bennekum	Andrew Hunt	Ken Schwaber
Alistair Cockburn	Ron Jeffries	Jeff Sutherland
Ward Cunningham	Jon Kern	Dave Thomas
Martin Fowler	Brian Marick	

**agile software develop-
ment:** agile software
development uses
incremental and iterative
techniques to design
and develop software. It
uses small empowered
teams to deliver software
components in a short
timeframe.

In practice, agile software development means focusing on small software development tasks that can be delivered quickly, preferably as working software that adds business value. Each task is timeboxed, that is, it has a fixed end date (even if the task has to be simplified to achieve that date – however, quality should not be compromised). The teams are also small to encourage communications – personal face-to-face communication. Teams are cross-functional and self-organizing – a daily meeting is advised (where everyone stays standing to keep it short), and the team must include a customer representative who is empowered to make decisions.

Agile development is not a methodology in the mould of SSADM or a design philosophy such as object-oriented design: it is about team organization (of a fairly minimal kind) and team ethos.

Methods that seek to encapsulate the agile approach include extreme programming (XP), Scrum and DSDM Atern (explained in an earlier subsection). The development method adopted by Facebook fits with the Agile approach (see the *Facebook case study* in the *Preface*).

Agile software development would seem to fit well with an organization like Facebook, which has extremely capable and well-motivated staff who are making (small) incremental changes to an existing system (and web systems provide a flexible development environment). Not all IS/IT staff are as capable and motivated as those employed by high-profile internet companies (although one could argue that conventional IT departments and methods don't provide the same kind of motivation). Not all systems, and system development requirements, are as easily broken down into small, independent software tasks – this would be particularly true of a large, new system requirement where an overall user vision and technical architecture would surely be required. Finally, there should be concern about using an agile approach for requirements such as system software or a safety-critical software development project.

Socio-technical system analysis and design

**socio-technical system
analysis and design:** an
approach to SA&D that
seeks to recognize the
problem situation as a
human activity system.

Socio-technical system analysis and design seeks to analyse the whole problem situation as a human activity system – this approach can also be called holistic or a soft systems approach. A socio-technical system seeks to achieve a joint optimization of the technical aspects of a task and the quality of people's working lives. The structured and object-oriented methods we have looked at thus far can instead be seen as employing a *scientific approach* – they take a problem, that has probably been pre-defined as needing an IT solution, and break it down into its constituent parts (and agile methods have an even more extreme focus on the technology).

The socio-technical approach to SA&D is usually attributed to Checkland and his soft systems methodology (SSM). SSM concentrates on checking out the problem situation and arguably peters out if it is decided that an IT system is the solution, or part of the solution – but then there are plenty of other methodologies available if we need to switch over to (hard) system design.

In this text we will introduce two SSM techniques:

**soft systems
methodology (SSM):** a
socio-technical SA&D
methodology that utilizes
rich pictures and the root
definition.

- Rich picture
- Root definition.

These techniques will be used to examine the problem situation of a university that needs to keep records of its students and their progress through their studies, a requirement that is commonly called the student registration system. These systems have often been a source of frustration to staff. They are *owned* by university management and finance, and seem to disregard the needs of academics and the workload implications on lecturers and departmental/course administrators. Possibly the situation would be better if a socio-technical analysis had taken place – let's see what we can do using a UK university as an example.

The rich picture is an attempt to represent the problem situation. The diagram is very informal (unlike the conventional SA&D techniques covered in *Chapter 11*). To start the diagram we might represent the problem situation as a large circle in the middle of the page. We can then represent:

- The parties involved as stick people (students, academics, administration and finance) – plus UCAS (UK Universities and Colleges Admission Service) who, while outside the circle, provide applications and initial student data
- External interested parties, as eyes (the VC, the vice-chancellor representing management; HEFCE, the Higher Education Funding Council for England covering the government interest)
- Relationships – shown as arrows
- Major concerns – documented as think bubbles
- Conflict areas – represented as cross swords.

The resulting rich picture is shown as *Figure 10.9*.

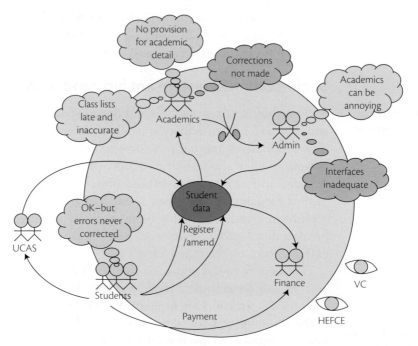

Figure 10.9 Rich picture – student registration.

Following on from the rich picture we attempt to derive a root definition. The root definition is a single sentence (possibly a long one) that attempts to sum up the overall requirement. The definition should encompass six factors represented by the mnemonic CATWOE. The factors are:

- Client: The beneficiary or victim of the activity
- Agent: The actors who operate the system
- Transformation: The changes that take place in the system
- *Weltanschauung*: A German term that means something like worldview or ethos
- Owner: The owner of the system
- Environment: The context in which the activity operates.

So, no pressure – all of that in one sentence (or short paragraph). That said the root definition can be a powerful tool. We could, for example, consider a healthcare provider – whatever may be claimed, it would (or should) be helpful to know whether the *Weltanschauung* is to provide effective healthcare or to make a profit for the partners who control the facility.

For the student registration problem we have been looking at, the current *Weltanschauung* is efficient administration for the finance, higher management (VC) and external funders (HEFCE) – or at least that is the way it appears. A root definition that could encompass the interests of all the stakeholders could be:

> A system for students, academics, administration and management that tracks student progress from application through registration and on to completion (hopefully graduation). The system needs to be accurate, efficient, accessible and timely.

4

Further reading

Books recommended for further reading are:

Avison, D. and Fitzgerald, G. (2006) *Information Systems Development: Methodologies, Techniques and Tools*, 4th ed., McGraw-Hill, Maidenhead.
DSDM (2008) *DSDM Aterm: The Handbook*, DSDM Consortium, Ashford. Available as a free e-Book from: http://www.dsdm.org.

Comprehension test

This is a simple test to enable you to check you have absorbed the material presented in *Chapter 10*.

Q1 For the waterfall lifecycle, which of the following is **not** a component of the system analysis and design stage?

    a. Logical design ☐

    b. Physical design ☐

    c. Discounted cash flow analysis ☐

    d. Requirements analysis ☐

Q2 The evolutionary prototype lifecycle is the basis of which of the following methodologies?

    a. SSADM ☐

    b. DSDM ☐

    c. OO-A&D ☐

    d. Soft systems ☐

Q3 SSADM Stage 4 is:

    a. Business system options ☐

    b. Definition of requirements ☐

    c. Technical system options ☐

    d. Logical design ☐

Q4 Which of the following DSDM stages uses facilitated workshops?

    a. Feasibility/Foundation ☐

    b. Exploration ☐

    c. Engineering ☐

    d. Deployment ☐

Q5 Soft systems methodology (SSM) uses which of the following diagrams?

    a. Use case diagram ☐

    b. Rich picture ☐

    c. Class diagram ☐

    d. Jackson structures ☐

Exercises

The following exercises are designed to aid your understanding of the material presented in this chapter. They can be used for self-study or selected exercises can be used for tutorial discussion.

1 **Comprehension** List five advantages and five disadvantages of the waterfall lifecycle.

2 **Comprehension** List five advantages and five disadvantages of an iterative/prototyping lifecycle.

3 **Comprehension** Your university/college is planning to replace its student record system with a bought-in package and has set up a project to purchase and implement the new system. The university is planning to use a waterfall approach for this project. Outline the main activities to be undertaken at each stage of the waterfall lifecycle and note how this would differ from a project to design and write the system in-house.

4 **Discussion** Socio-technical analysis can be seen as a *touchy-feely* approach concerned with the *quality of people's working lives*, whereas agile methods are typified by some as an excuse for the *nerds* to just *cut code*. Discuss the validity of these characterizations and the merits (or otherwise) of the two system analysis/development philosophies. Are there different types of system where either of these approaches would be more appropriate?

11 SYSTEM ANALYSIS AND DESIGN TOOLBOX

Summary

The process of system analysis and design (SA&D) uses a number of graphical techniques. These diagrams are an essential part of the process of working out the requirements of the system, designing the system and, once the analysis and design process is complete, they become the working documentation for the development of the system. Many SA&D techniques have been developed over the years, but we will be looking at:

- Use case diagram: A technique for capturing user requirements
- Data flow diagram (DFD): A technique for showing the flow of data through the system, including processing and data storage
- Entity relationship diagram (ERD): A technique showing the data requirements of the system in terms of entities and relationships
- Sequence diagram: A technique that shows the usage of classes (objects) by a use case
- Class diagram: Object-oriented design showing classes (objects) and the methods that are required to implement those objects.

SA&D techniques are a vital part of the analysis and design process. It is important that IS students become *literate* in diagramming techniques. There are many cases in business when an issue is best framed as a diagram – possibly one of the above, or possibly a derivative improvised to meet a specific need.

Learning outcomes

Having read this chapter and completed the exercises, you should:

- Be competent at drawing a use case diagram using system information from a case study
- Be competent at drawing a data flow diagram, including a context diagram, using system information from a case study
- Be competent at drawing an entity relationship diagram using system information from a case study
- Be competent at drawing a sequence diagram using system information from a case study
- Be competent at drawing a class diagram using system information from a case study
- Understand the relationships between the system diagrams learnt in this chapter and the lifecycles/methodologies in *Chapter 10*.

Note, tutors may wish to select the diagrams that are to be taught. Structured diagrams are context, data flow and entity relationship diagrams. Object-oriented diagrams are use case, sequence and class diagrams (the first stages of the class diagram are covered in the section on the entity relationship diagram).

4

Key terms   Use case diagram, use case, use case description, data flow diagram (DFD), context diagram, DFD external, DFD process, DFD datastore, entity relationship diagram (ERD), ERD entity, ERD relationship, primary key, foreign key, generalization, aggregation, composition, sequence diagram, class diagram, polymorphism, generalization, encapsulation, state diagram, relational data analysis (RDA), Jackson structures.

Systems analysis and design

Systems analysis and design (SA&D) uses graphical techniques to research requirements and document a design. We will introduce the following design techniques:

- Use case diagram
- Data flow diagram (DFD)
- Entity relationship diagram (ERD)
- Sequence diagram
- Class diagram.

Each of these techniques is demonstrated using the *High Peak Bicycles case study*. Further case studies are used as necessary; there are also exercises at the end of the chapter.

Students should aim to become *literate* in drawing diagrams. Diagrams are widely used in business and are an essential part of SA&D. A diagram is often the best way to examine or explain an issue. The diagrams included in this chapter are designed for SA&D but it may well be that one of the diagrams in this chapter can be applied (or be adapted) to meet other requirements.

Case study
High Peak Bicycles   Derbyshire County Council in the UK has taken over a number of disused railway lines in the Peak District, an upland National Park area, and turned them into cycle paths/hiking trails. There is, at the junction of the High Peak and Tissington Trails, a busy cycle hire shop letting out a wide variety of bicycles, tandems and trailers to people who wish to cycle on the trail but do not bring their own machines.

The shop keeps upwards of 200 machines in stock and on a busy day it is quite a job keeping track of all the rentals. The shop has taken a Business IS placement student and has asked her to computerize the system. The student has completed her fact-finding, and these are the notes she has taken:

1   The hire shop stocks some 200 bicycles. Policy is to offer modern machines. Most bicycles are kept for two years and then sold. A register is kept of all machines; details include a registration number, class (all-terrain, mountain, tandem, etc.), make,

model, frame size, frame number, date of purchase, purchase price. The register is kept in a looseleaf folder. On purchase, each machine is given a registration number and assigned to a class; the details are recorded on a form that is then added into the folder.

2   There is rarely a need to update the forms, but occasionally corrections have to be made to the original details. The form is, however, updated with the selling date and price when the machine is sold. The intention is to keep records for five years so that the depreciation rates of the various models can be analysed. In practice, record-keeping is inconsistent and analysis of depreciation is not available.

3   Rentals are made by the day or half-day; in the summer there is a special rate for *late rentals* that runs from 16.00 to 19.00. Each class of machine has a rental rate for each of these periods, for instance:

	Day	Half-Day	Late Rental
Mountain bicycle (MB)	£18	£10	£6
All-terrain bicycle (AT)	£20	£12	£8

(effective 1 June 2013 until further notice)

The rental rates are displayed on the noticeboard in the shop where staff can see them. When rates are changed the notice is replaced. Superseded rental rates should be retained for use when the accounts are prepared (the tendency is for the old notices to be left lying about and sometimes they become lost).

4   Each rental is recorded on a two-part rental agreement form; general details include customer name, telephone number, date, time out, expected time back, expected period, deposit type (cash/credit card) and total prepaid amount. The rental can be for one or more machines (up to a maximum of four); the details for each machine are class, registration number, model and prepaid amount. When the machine is rented out the customer is given one copy of the agreement and the second copy is retained within the shop. The customer is also asked to pay in advance for the rental and pay a deposit of £20 (or leave a credit card imprint) for each machine. The deposit is kept clipped to the shop copy of the rental agreement pending the customer's return. An example rental agreement is shown below.

5   When the customer gets back the shop copy of the rental agreement is found. The customer should have the top copy with the agreement number on it, otherwise there has to be a search through the pile. Once found, the rental agreement is updated with the time of return, the charges for the actual rental period (the customer is charged for any excess time) and the deposit is returned.

6   Occasionally a machine is not returned. Sometimes bicycles will be found abandoned and be returned (typically by a park warden); sometimes the bicycle will never be recovered. In these circumstances the deposit is retained and the rental slip is updated with details of the circumstances. Where the deposit is a credit card imprint, the customer will be charged £20 for each abandoned machine or the value of the bicycle for any non-recovered machine. Non-recovered machines are written off after ten days – this is recorded on the appropriate sheet of the register. (Attempts will also be made to contact the hirer and/or the matter will be reported to the police – these procedures are outside the scope of any proposed system.)

7   At the end of the day, all rental slips are counted up. Detailed statistics would be useful (e.g. to give a formal basis for deciding what types and quantities of machine to buy) but currently statistics are limited to the number of rentals and the total value.

4

High Peak Bicycles		Bicycle Rental Agreement	
Tel: 01166 434343		Rental No: *008647*	
		Date	*01 Sep 13*
Customer:		**Time Out**	*09:00*
Name: *Sam Higginbottom*		**Expected Time Back**	*12:00*
Tel No: *0181 643 0101*		**Expected Period**	*Half-day*
		Actual Time Back	*13:16*
		Actual Period	*Day*
		Deposit:	~~Cash~~/Credit Card

Machine Class:		Machine:		Payment:	
Code	**Desc.**	**Reg.No**	**Model**	**Pre-paid**	**Actual**
MB	*Mountain Bike*	*001341*	*Raleigh Max*	*10.00*	*18.00*
MB	*Mountain Bike*	*001826*	*Raleigh Max*	*10.00*	*18.00*
TAN	*Tandem*	*000841*	*Falcon 2x2*	*20.00*	*30.00*
TRA	*Trailer*	*000623*	*Baby Bug*	*4.00*	*6.00*
			Totals:	*44.00*	*72.00*

Example Rental Agreement Form
(This is an example of a completed form. Pre-printed elements are in bold and
variable entries are in italics)
*(Note: this case study is based on observation of a number of bike hire operations and is not an exact
representation of any specific bicycle hire operation in the Peak District National Park.)*

User requirements and use cases

use case diagram:
used to capture user
requirements – users are
represented as actors
and requirements as use
cases.

Before we start making a system it is a good idea to find out what the users
want (or what the users need). Finding out the *real* user requirement can be
a bit of a detective job but, in this section, our main concern is to document
the requirement. The technique we will use is the UML diagram, the **use case
diagram**.

The task is to identify the use cases in the requirement and then to represent those use cases as a diagram. A **use case** is:

use case: a UML concept. The user requirement is broken down into use cases, defined as: *a bit of business*, identified within the user requirement.

> a bit of business done with the system.

An example of a *bit of business* from the **High Peak Bicycles case study** would be to transact the rental of one or more bicycles: **rent out**. The use case diagram for this consists of:

- The actor: the person doing the interaction – shown as a stick person
- The use case: the task that is being done – shown as an ellipse containing a couple of words/a phrase summarizing the task
- An association: a line connecting the actor to the use case.

The use case diagram for **rent out** is shown in *Figure 11.1*.

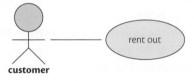

Figure 11.1 Example of a use case diagram.

So, to complete a use case diagram, we should identify all the *bits of business* that need to occur in our system. How do we do that? Well, to a certain extent it is: *I know a use case when I see one* – which is not very helpful to someone new to SA&D. To be rather more helpful, let us first go through the requirement (for us this is the case study) and identify the people who use the system. This will give us a preliminary list of actors. For the **High Peak case study** we have:

- Staff: Mentioned in the paragraph numbered 3 and implicit in all the functions of the system
- Customer: Mentioned in the paragraphs numbered 4, 5 and 6 (where the term *hirer* is used)
- Park warden and police: Mentioned in the paragraph numbered 6.

So having identified (potential) actors we can then go through the case study again, this time looking for *bits of business*. Doing that (and trying to distinguish the task from the detail) we get:

- Para 1: *A register is kept of all machines*
- Para 2: *Occasionally corrections have to be made* and *updated when selling*, both relating to the register of machines
- Para 3: (Rental) *rates are changed*
- Para 4: *Each rental is recorded* (there is a lot of detail here but *the bit of business* is the rental transaction)
- Para 5: *The rental agreement is updated with … return*
- Para 6: *In these circumstances* (non-return) *the rental slip is updated*
- Para 7: *All rental slips are summed up. Detailed statistics would be useful.*

Bringing the two lists together, and using our common sense, we get the following actors, use cases and associations:

- **Staff,** as an actor, who will:
  - ▪ Maintain the bike register: this includes registering new bikes, (occasional) amendments and recording bike sales: **maintain bike register** – how much of that detail we should show is something we have to think about
  - ▪ Maintain rental rates: **maintain rent rates**
  - ▪ Derive management information – the case study does not give much detail and further discussion with the user would seem to be needed: **do management information.**

- **Customer,** as an actor, who will:
  - ▪ Rent out one or more bikes: **rent out**
  - ▪ Return the bikes they have rented: **rent return**
  - ▪ Fail to return the bikes they have rented: **fail to return.**

  (These are joint activities between the customer and the staff – which actor we use is a matter of choice. It is helpful to show the customer; there is a further note on this issue below.)

Using this list, we create the use case diagram shown as *Figure 11.2*. It is a good, simple representation of *what* the system will do (not *how* it will do it – we will come to that in other diagrams). The use case diagram establishes boundaries – it makes it clear what is in the system (anything not on the diagram is not included). It is a diagram that could be presented to management to tell them what the eventual system is to include.

Note that we have not used the park wardens or police as actors – they are people the staff talk to, but they do not directly interface with the system.

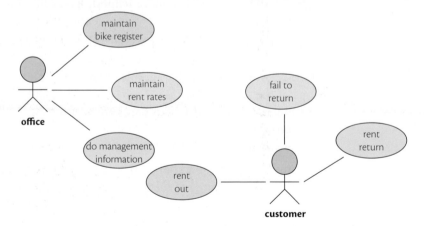

Figure 11.2 Use case – High Peak Bicycles – first cut.

This is the basic use case diagram. We can add to it using a further component of the technique: these are extensions to the use cases adopted to identify common processing and/or to clarify the diagram. There are three types of extensions identified in UML:

- **Include:** A chunk of behaviour that is similar across several use cases – the *include* is associated to the use cases by dotted arrows.

  There is not a need for an *include* in the High Peak Bicycles use case diagram. If, however, we extended the system to include booking of bikes over the internet we could say that both **rent out** and **book online** would need to **allocate bike** and we could show this common piece of behaviour as an *include* (see *Figure 11.3*).

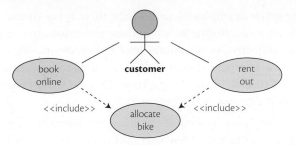

Figure 11.3 Use case – example of include.

- **Extend:** A variation on normal behaviour to include additional, optional behaviour – associated with the extended use case by a dotted arrow.

  As with the *include*, there is not a need for an *extend* in the **High Peak Bicycles case study**. However, let us suppose that we intend to get clever and attach a credit card reader to the system, so that we can process credit card sales. We could then show **process credit card** as an *extend* to the **rent return** use case (see *Figure 11.4*).

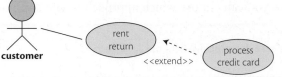

Figure 11.4 Use case – example of extend.

- **Generalization** or *child use case*: Each of the child use cases represents a variation on normal behaviour and any one of them might be invoked – the *generalization* is associated with the parent use case using an arrow.

  The *generalization* is the one use case extension that we will incorporate into the High Peak Bicycles use case diagram. The **maintain bike register** use case covers **register new bike** and **record bike sale**. It could aid clarity if these were to be shown, and a *generalization* seems to be the appropriate format. These *generalizations* are added to the first cut use case diagram to give us the design stage use case diagram in *Figure 11.5*.

4

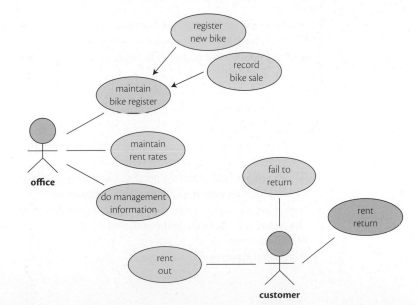

Figure 11.5 Use case – High Peak Bicycles user requirements.

Having given examples of each of the three types of use case extension, it can be difficult to determine which of these extensions to use and when. Remember that our objective is to capture user requirements. We need simplicity. We do not need a complex diagram that captures the minutiae of processing – we will come to that in the design stages. So, only use *include*, *extend* and *generalization* if they are really necessary.

Thus far we have looked at the use case diagram. The use case is actually a description of the *bit of business* (although the usual focus is on the diagram). The use case description is required to cover the basic (usual) course of action for the use case and any alternative courses that may occur. Rosenberg and Scott (1999) write their use cases as narrative whereas Fowler (2004) sets them out as a series of steps. The approach you adopt is up to you (unless your team leader or tutor exercises the option for you!). The narrative approach might work better for a business system (such as our example) and the step approach might be more appropriate for the design of a piece of system software. The use case description for **rent out** is shown in *Figure 11.6* – with both formats to hand you can choose which approach would suit you best.

Use case description: Rent out (as a narrative)

Basic course: The member of staff asks the customer for their customer number (if a registered customer) or their personal details (if a new customer) – these are then used to look up an existing customer record or to create a new customer record. The member of staff must also determine details of the required rental: the period of rental and the number, size and types of bikes he/she requires – these details are also recorded on the system along with the date and time of the transaction. The system allocates specific machines that fit the customer's specification and calculates the (expected) rental cost and deposit requirement. The customer pays and the transaction is completed by the printing of a rental agreement (two copies).

Alternative course: The required machines are not available and alternative models are allocated;
Alternative course: The required machines are not available and no acceptable alternative is available – the transaction is aborted;
Alternative course: The customer finds the charges unacceptable and the transaction is aborted.

- -

Use case description: Rent out (as a series of steps)

Basic course:
1   Check customer details: for an existing customer, check the customer record; for a new customer, set up a customer record
2   Record period of rental and the number, size and types of bikes the customer requires
3   Generate and record date and time of the transaction
4   The system allocates specific machines that fit the customer's specification
5   The system calculates the (expected) rental cost and deposit requirement
6   Record payment
7   Print rental agreement (two copies).

Alternative course (1): At step 4 some/all of the required machines are unavailable:
1   Return to step 2 and specify alternatives.
Alternative course (2): At step 4 some/all of the required machines are unavailable and no acceptable alternatives are available:
1   Abort.
Alternative course (3): At step 5 the customer finds the charges unacceptable:
1   Abort.

Figure 11.6 Use case descriptions for rent out.

Use cases really are as simple as this. There are, however, a couple of qualifications to be added:

- Actors are not always people – they can be other systems. Thus if the High Peak Bicycles system passed financial details of all rental transactions to a separate accounting system, that system would be shown as an actor on the use case diagram.
- Sometimes there is more than one actor involved in a use case and it is not clear which should be shown. In our **rent out** example we have the customer who is hiring the bikes – but we also have the hire shop staff who enter the transaction into the system. Which of the two actors we show does not matter greatly. Fowler (2004) says he likes *to show the actor who gets value from the use case* – which, in this instance, is (presumably) the customer. If you think it makes things clearer you can show both actors: the customer actor associated with the staff actor which is in turn associated with the use case.

For a second example of a use case diagram we will use the *Department of Computing Library case study*.

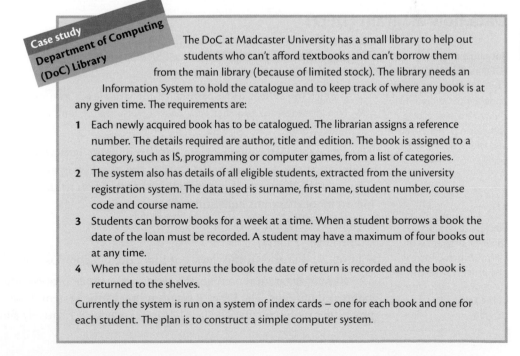

Case study
Department of Computing (DoC) Library

The DoC at Madcaster University has a small library to help out students who can't afford textbooks and can't borrow them from the main library (because of limited stock). The library needs an Information System to hold the catalogue and to keep track of where any book is at any given time. The requirements are:

1   Each newly acquired book has to be catalogued. The librarian assigns a reference number. The details required are author, title and edition. The book is assigned to a category, such as IS, programming or computer games, from a list of categories.
2   The system also has details of all eligible students, extracted from the university registration system. The data used is surname, first name, student number, course code and course name.
3   Students can borrow books for a week at a time. When a student borrows a book the date of the loan must be recorded. A student may have a maximum of four books out at any time.
4   When the student returns the book the date of return is recorded and the book is returned to the shelves.

Currently the system is run on a system of index cards – one for each book and one for each student. The plan is to construct a simple computer system.

4

The requirements are set out in the four numbered paragraphs (life and other exercises are not always that easy!). To represent the requirement as a use case diagram we need:

- Use case: **catalogue book** – actor: **librarian**
- Use case: **register student** – actor: **librarian**. Alternatively we could have the **uni. reg. system** as the actor
- Use case: **borrow book** – actor: **student**. Alternatively we could use the **librarian** as the actor
- Use case: **return book** – actor: **student**. Or alternatively the **librarian**.

The use case diagram for the DoC Library is shown in *Figure 11.7*.

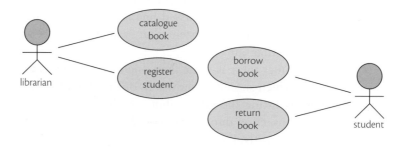

Figure 11.7 Use case – DoC Library user requirements.

And before you go on to the next stage, it would be a good idea to practise what you have learnt: do exercises 1 and 2 shown at the end of the chapter.

Data flow diagram (DFD)

data flow diagram (DFD): a SSADM diagram. The DFD maps the flow of data into (and out of) the system, the change (processing) of the data and where data is stored.

The **data flow diagram (DFD)** is a SSADM diagram. In the words of Avison and Fitzgerald (2006) it:

> enables the system to be partitioned (or structured) into independent units of a desirable size so that they, and thereby the system, can be more easily understood.

The DFD shows the flows of the data from users (externals) into the system, the flows of the data within the system, the processing and the storage of that data, and the flows of information out of the system to the users. The DFD is a hierarchy of diagrams consisting of:

- Context diagram (conceptually level zero)
- The Level-1 DFD
- Level-2 DFD and further levels of functional decomposition, if required.

context diagram: the top level diagram is the DFD hierarchy. There is one process which is then functionally decomposed in the Level-1 DFD diagram.

The **context diagram** represents the system as a single process and includes only external dataflows. The Level-1 diagram breaks the system down into the main processing requirements. The Level-1 diagram is kept relatively simple, showing, perhaps, five or six (and a maximum of, say, ten) processes. Keeping the diagram simple aids comprehension of the system requirements and ensures the diagram can be presented on a single page (or screen). If processes on the Level-1 diagram require breaking down further they can be functionally decomposed as Level-2 diagrams, and so on. Each Level-2 diagram consists of the detail of a single Level-1 process and obeys the same rules on the degree of complexity.

Let us now look at the symbols we have for externals, processes, datastores and **dataflows** – see *Figure 11.8* – and we will use them to draw a DFD.

dataflow: a flow of data into (and out of) the system from externals and between processes and datastores.

DFD external: an entity outside the system, typically a user, which inputs data to the system and/or receives data from the system.

DFD process: a task (transformation) performed on a dataflow.

DFD datastore: a stationary dataflow, such as a file.

External: An entity outside the system, typically a person, which inputs data into the system and / or receives data output by the system. The oval symbol contains the name of the entity, e.g. customer.

Process: A task performed on the dataflow. The processing requirement is represented as an imperative statement, e.g. process order. The top line of the box contains the process number, e.g. 3 (or 3.2 on a level-2 DFD) and the location where the process takes place, e.g warehouse.

Datastore: A stationary dataflow. This could be standing data, e.g. customer data or it could be transactions awaiting further processing, e.g. allocated orders. The symbol contains a label, e.g. D3, and the name of the datastore.

Dataflow: An arrowed line showing the flow of data from externals, to processes, datastores and eventually back out to externals. Properly it is labelled with the attributes (data items) but this is normally too complex and we settle for a description, e.g. order.

Figure 11.8 DFD symbols.

The system we will use to demonstrate the drawing of a DFD is the ***High Peak Bicycles case study*** included at the start of this chapter. We will start with the context diagram and we need to find any external entities in the case study. The way to do this is to go through the requirement and identify the people who put data into the system or who receive data from the system. For the ***High Peak Bicycles case study*** we have:

- Staff: Mentioned in the paragraph numbered 3 and implicit in all the functions of the system
- Customers: Mentioned in the paragraphs numbered 4, 5 and 6 (where the term *hirer* is used)
- Park warden and police: Mentioned in the paragraph numbered 6.

So, having identified (potential) externals, we can go through the case study looking for inputs to the system and outputs from the system. Doing that we get:

- Para 1: *A register is kept of all machines*
- Para 2: *Occasionally corrections have to be made* and *updated when selling*, both relating to the register of machines
- Para 3: (rental) *rates are changed*
- Para 4: *Each rental is recorded*

- Para 5: *The rental agreement is updated with ... return*
- Para 6: *In these circumstances* (non-return) *the rental slip is updated*
- Para 7: *All rental slips are summed up. Detailed statistics would be useful.*

Bringing the two lists together and using some common sense, we get:

- **Staff,** as an external, who will:
  - Input data to maintain the bike register – this includes registering new bikes, (occasional) amendments and recording bike sales
  - Input data to maintain rental rates
  - Extract data in the form of management information – exactly what would be useful here is not made clear and further discussion with the user would seem to be needed.

- **Customer,** as an external, who will:
  - Supply the data required to rent out one or more bikes
  - Supply the data needed when they return the bikes they have rented
  - Fail to return the bikes they have rented.

(These are joint activities between the customer and the staff – which external we use is a matter of choice. It is helpful to show the customer in preference to the member of staff.)

Using this list, we get the context diagram shown at *Figure 11.9*. Note that we have not used the park wardens or police as externals – they are people who the staff talk to, but they do not directly interface with the system. Also note that the context diagram serves much the same purpose as the use case diagram – it represents the user requirements (compare *Figure 11.9* with *Figure 11.2/11.5*). Arguably, the use case diagram is preferable, but the context diagram is a step towards building the DFD so it is included here.

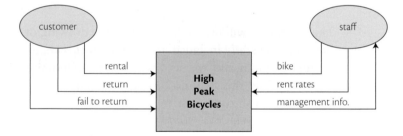

Figure 11.9 Context diagram – High Peak Bicycles.

Moving on from this we can start drawing the Level-1 DFD. Checking through the case study we seem to have all the processing requirements (in this case they correspond to the inputs and outputs). A further check through would then seem to suggest a requirement for the following datastores:

- Para 1: *A register is kept of all machines* – a **bike** datastore
- Para 3: *Rental rates are changed* – a **rent rate** datastore
- Para 4: *Each rental is recorded* – a **rental agreement** datastore and a separate customer datastore.

Taking, for example, the rental transaction we have:

- The **customer** as an external
- A dataflow of **rental** details into the system

- A process to execute that rental: **process rental**. The process would need to:
  - Look up details of existing customers
  - Store details of new customers
  - Find the required machines by reading bike data
  - Cost the rental by reading rent rate data
  - Store the rental agreement.

This portion of the Level-1 DFD is shown in *Figure 11.10* and, following similar logic, we can construct the complete diagram as shown in *Figure 11.11*.

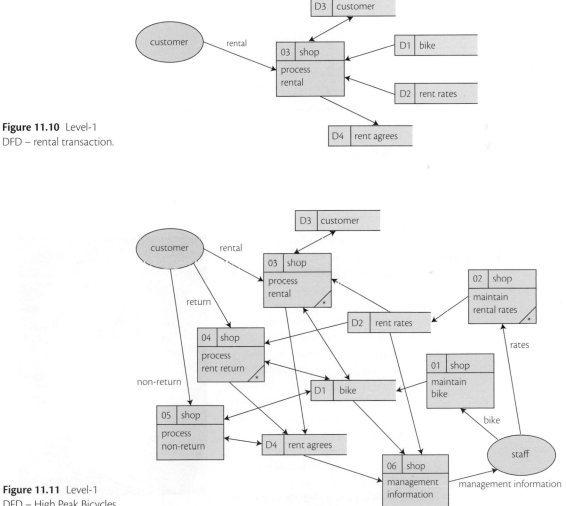

Figure 11.10 Level-1 DFD – rental transaction.

Figure 11.11 Level-1 DFD – High Peak Bicycles.

Processes that are fully functionally decomposed (no further detailed breakdown is required) are shown with an asterisk in the bottom right-hand corner. The first process, maintain bikes, is one where some further details would be useful and a Level-2 diagram is shown as *Figure 11.12* overleaf.

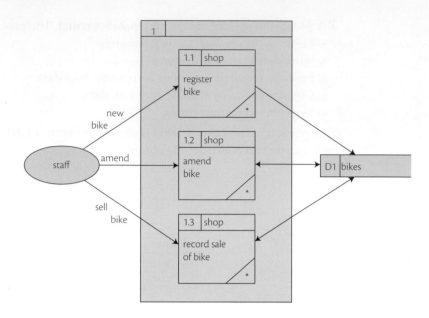

Figure 11.12 Level-2
DFD – maintain bike.

For a second example of a data flow diagram we will use the *Pizza IT case study*.

Case study
Pizza IT

The plan is to open a pizza restaurant with an IT twist – each table will have a touchscreen computer terminal.

The basic plan is that customers can order their meal without the need for a waiter/waitress. On the screen there is detail of pizzas, starters, deserts and drinks – with all the extra toppings and the like – all with pictures, animations and Italian jokes.

So you can take your time to order, change your mind and check the total cost before you press the order button. The order then goes through to displays in the kitchen and the bar, which means there should be no lost orders. The staff – yes, we do have staff – can confirm each item as it goes out to the table. Finally, when you want to pay, you press the

Source: Brand X Pictures

button – the bill is printed out and a member of our staff comes to take your money. And one more thing, we do update the menu so the manager can get into the system and change things about a bit.

The system also includes computer games, internet access and messaging to other tables (but only between consenting adults) – but this software is bought in, so don't include it in your analysis.

Working through the case study we can identify the main processing requirements as:

- The customer inputs their food order (the menu is read from a datastore and the order needs to be stored on the system).
- Kitchen/bar staff see the orders and confirm when the item goes out (hence updating the stored order).
- Customers ask for the bill which is printed out for the staff (using the menu for prices and the stored order data – the order is then marked as paid). Note that this process could be shown as two processes or broken down as a Level-2 diagram.
- The manager can update the menu (held in a datastore).

These requirements can be represented as a DFD (see *Figure 11.13*). Note that we could have first drawn the context diagram before moving onto the full DFD – if you find it easier to use this two-stage process, then please do it that way.

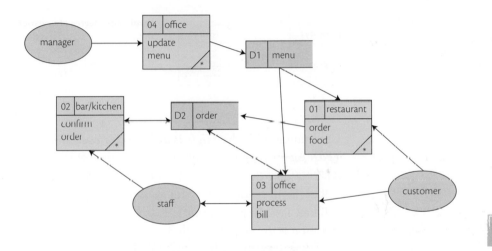

Figure 11.13 Level-1 DFD – Pizza IT.

You should now understand a DFD. Now practise using exercises 3 and 4 at the end of the chapter, before we look at the next technique.

Entity relationship diagram (ERD)

The use case diagram and data flow diagram outline (at differing levels) the processing requirements; now we need to supplement this with an analysis of the data. This is particularly true if we are going to use a database management system (DBMS) to hold the data.

entity relationship diagram (ERD): a SSADM/UML diagram. The ERD documents the entities (data) used in the system and the relationship between those entities.

The process of analysing the data is generally called data modelling. The diagram we produce is called an entity relationship diagram (ERD) – SSADM calls it a logical data structure (LDS). There are a number of conventions for drawing ERD – we will use the UML class diagram conventions.

The symbols we need for an ERD are entities and relationships: see *Figure 11.14*.

ERD entity: a thing of interest to the system about which data is held.

ERD relationship: an association between two entities that is of importance to the system. The **cardinality** of the relationship is documented, e.g. one (1..1) to many (0..*) or (1..*).

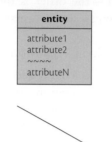

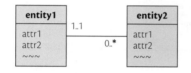

Entity: An entity is: *a thing of interest to the system about which data is held*. We have to look at the underlying data requirement, e.g. the customer whose details are given on an order. Attributes are data elements belonging to the entity, e.g. for customer the custNo and custName.

Relationship: A relationship is: *an association between two entities that is of importance to the system*, e.g. the association between the customer and an order.

Cardinality (degree of a relationship): entity1 is associated with zero, one or many (0..*) occurrences of entity2 – entity2 is associated with one and only one (1..1) occurrence of entity1.

Figure 11.14 ERD – symbols.

Continuing with the ***High Peak Bicycles case study*** we can start to draw an ERD. Again we go through the case study – this time looking for entities, that is, *things of interest to the system*. For the case study we have:

- Bicycle: In paragraph 1 and used throughout the case study
- Bike Class: In paragraph 1
- Rental Rate: In paragraph 3
- Rental Agreement: In paragraph 4
- Customer: In paragraph 4 (presented as an attribute of the rental but could be an entity).

Note that the example (paper) Rental Agreement, in the case study, includes attributes belonging to the Customer (name and telephone number) and the Bicycle (registration number, class and model), as well as the attributes belonging to the Rental Agreement; hence the requirement to *look at the underlying data requirement*. Another way of looking at it is that the Customer and Bicycle data on the Rental Agreement is the same across all the Rental Agreements on which that data might appear – attributes (with the exception of foreign keys, that is, the keys of related entities) should appear only once on our ER diagram.

These are our possible entities and we can also use the case study to look for relationships – *an association between two entities*. Looking through we get:

- Bicycle: Assigned to a Bike Class and associated with all the Rental Agreements it has been hired out on (we need to keep old rentals for the management information)

- Bike Class: See Bicycle
- Rental Rate: For each Bike Class
- Rental Agreement: For up to four Bicycles
- Customer: One for each Rental Agreement.

From this initial list of entities we can construct a first cut ERD (we will look at the attributes later) (see *Figure 11.15*).

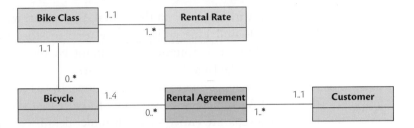

Figure 11.15 ERD – first cut

Let us run through the diagram and see what we have got:

- **Bike Class**, e.g. mountain bike, has many **Bicycles** (0..*) – the zero is to allow for a **Bike Class** without **Bicycles**. The **Bicycle** belongs to one and only one **Bike Class** (1..1)
- **Bike Class** has many **Rental Rates** (1..*) – we have to keep the old ones when a new one is created. A **Rental Rate** belongs to one and only one **Bike Class** (1..1)
- **Bicycle** is related to many **Rental Agreements** (0..*) – zero when first bought – it may or may not be out on hire but we also have to keep details of all the completed **Rental Agreements**. The **Rental Agreement** has many (one to four) **Bicycles** assigned to it (1..4)
- The **Rental Agreement** has one **Customer** (1..1). The case study does not say we reuse the customer details. However, if the same person returns to take out some bikes on another day it would be helpful to reuse the customer details so we will assume that the **Customer** has many **Rental Agreements** (1..*). (*many* may be zero, one or more (0..*) or, one or more (1..*) – you need to work out which is applicable).

OK, but there are some further *rules* that we need to take account of:

- Resolve any many-to-many associations. The **Bicycle** to **Rental Agreement** relationship is many-to-many. The **Rental Agreement** is for up to four **Bicycles** and the **Bicycle** is on many **Rental Agreements** (as we keep details of any current and all completed **Agreements**). Now we could show a many-to-many on the ERD but we cannot readily implement it on a database. For this reason we normally resolve a many-to-many by introducing a link entity: see *Figure 11.16* overleaf (link entities can be shown as *weak entities* but that is a complication we will avoid).

  Using this structure there will be an instance of the link for each valid instance of the relationship. If **entity1** is the **Bicycle** then there is an instance of the **link** for every **Rental Agreement** that bike is used by. Following on from that, if **entity2** is the **Rental Agreement** there will be an instance of the **link** records for each **Bicycle** used by that **Agreement**. The link elements

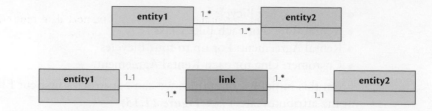

Figure 11.16 ERD –
many-to-many
relationships.

correspond with the lines on the **Rental Agreement**: we can call them **Rental Lines**. The **Rental Line** entity will be used to store the charges made for each **Bicycle** that is rented out (it cannot be shown on either the **Rental Agreement** or the **Bicycle** – think about it).

- Consider removing one-to-one associations. If, for example, a **Customer** for the Rental Agreement was not going to be reused there would be no point in having a separate entity – the **Customer** details could simply be added as attributes of the **Rental Agreement** and the **Customer** entity omitted.

Resolving the many-to-many gives us a second version of the ERD: see *Figure 11.17*.

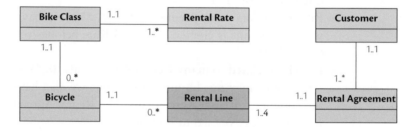

Figure 11.17 ERD –
second cut.

Having identified the entities we must now add the attributes – so we go back to the case study (and the example form) to see what we can find. First, on the **Bicycle** (standing data) side, there are a number of attributes for the **Bicycle** but also for the **Bike Class** and **Rental Rates**:

- **Bicycle**   registration number, class code, make, model, frame size, frame number, date of purchase, purchase price, date of sale, selling price, write-off.
- **Bike Class**   class code, class description.
- **Rental Rate**   class code, start date, day rate, half-day rate, late rate.

Each entity needs a key. The **Bicycle** is identified by its registration number and has the further attributes listed above. One attribute of the **Bicycle** is its class code, for instance 'MB'. The **Bicycle**'s class code can then link to further details applicable to all **Bicycles** of that **Bike Class**, that is, the class description: 'Mountain Bike' for 'MB'. The **Bike Class** also determines the **Rental Rates**. There is a need to keep each version of the **Rental Rates**; so we add a start date so the system can determine which **Rental Rates** are applicable.

Transactions are recorded as the **Rental Agreement**, and as we have already determined, the **Customer** and **Rental Line** data will be held as separate entities.

- **Rental Agreement** rental number, customer number, date, time out, expected time back, expected period, actual time back, actual period, deposit type, total prepaid, total paid.
- **Rental Line** rental number, (bike) registration number, pre-paid amount, actual payment (payments for the one bike).
- **Customer** customer number, customer name, customer telephone number.

Again, each of these entities needs a key. The key for the **Rental Agreement** is the rental number. We add a customer number to identify the **Customer** and this is also included in the **Rental Agreement** to make the association. The **Rental Line** needs the rental number to identify its **Rental Agreement** and the bike registration number to identify the **Bicycle**.

So let's add these to the ERD we have devised thus far (see *Figure 11.18*).

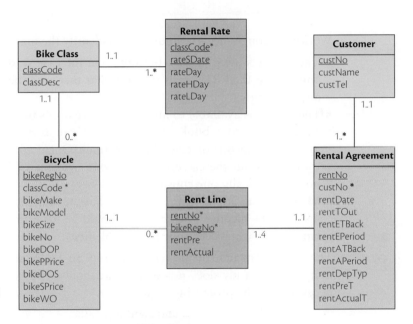

Figure 11.18 ERD – High Peak Bicycles.

primary key: an attribute of an entity that uniquely identifies that entity.

foreign key: an attribute of an entity that identifies a related entity.

For the ERD it is useful to identify the key that uniquely identifies each entity, the **primary key**, and also the key that implements the association (relationship) to another entity, the **foreign key**. These are identified by underlining the primary key and annotating any foreign keys with an *. Thus we have:

- **Bicycle**   Primary Key: **bikeRegNo**
                      Foreign Key: **classCode** *
- **Bike Class**   Primary Key: **classCode**
- **Rental Rate**   Primary Key: **classCode** + **rateSDate** (start date)
                      Foreign Key: **classCode** *
- **Rental Agreement**   Primary Key: **rentNo**
                      Foreign Key: **custNo** *
- **Rental Line**   Primary Key: **rentNo** + **bikeRegNo**
                      Foreign Key: **rentNo** * and **bikeRegNo** *
- **Customer**   Primary Key: **custNo**

4

Note: attribute names have been abbreviated to make them fit reasonably on the diagram.

For a second example of an ERD we will use the *Ancient History Library case study*, see below.

**Case study
Ancient History Library
(data analysis)**

A small, private library specializing in ancient history has a collection of titles available for loan by members. Each member can have a loan of a maximum of eight books at any one time. The library often has several copies of a particular book. If no copies are available for immediate loan, a member can reserve the required book. When a copy of the requested book is returned, the library notifies the reserving member that the book is available, and puts the copy to one side, ready for collection.

Working through the case study we can identify the main data requirements as:

● The library stocks books – but note that the case study uses the terms *titles* and *copies*: the ERD needs to show that there will be one or more **copy** of any given **title**
● The library is available to members – there needs to be a **member** entity
● **Members** borrow books – the member can borrow up to eight books, presumably as one or several transactions. One could record the borrowing transaction but the essential data is one **member** taking out a **loan** of one book: specifically one **copy** of a **title**
● **Members** can also reserve a book. This is similar to a **loan** but in this instance the **member**'s reservation should be for a title (the **member** will be happy with whichever **copy** is available first).

These requirements can be represented as an ERD (see *Figure 11.19*). Note that the case study does not suggest attributes – I have added the attributes necessary for the processing requirement.

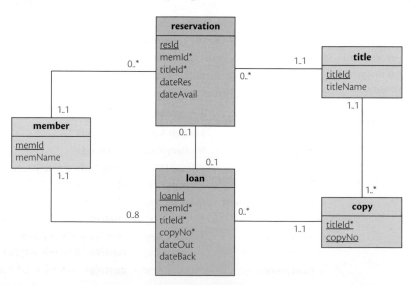

Figure 11.19 ERD – Ancient History Library.

Note that the association between **reservation** and **loan** is one-to-one; we have already noted that a one-to-one suggests the two entities could be merged but for this case we should note:

- There can be a **reservation** without a **loan** (because the **loan** has not yet taken place) – in this case the **copyNo, dateOut** and **dateBack** are null
- There can be a **loan** without a **reservation** – in this case the **dateRes** and **dateAvail** are null
- The **reservation** is associated with a **title** and the **loan** with a **copy** – this distinction can be met by adjusting the cardinality on the associations.

An alternative version of the Ancient History Library ERD is shown at *Figure 11.20*.

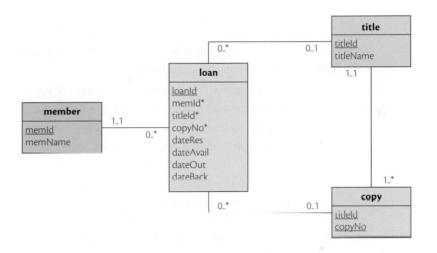

Figure 11.20 ERD – Ancient History Library (alternative version).

This should give you an understanding of an ERD. Now practise using exercises 5 and 6 at the end of the chapter before we look at the next technique. Note the additional features explained below – you might want to include them in your solution.

ERD additional features

Thus far we have restricted ourselves to the features available in traditional ERD diagrams, but we used UML conventions. The UML class diagram provides a number of additional features, and we will now introduce two of these:

- Generalization
- Aggregation and composition.

generalization: an object-oriented concept that allows an entity to use the characteristics of a more general entity.

Generalization is the class diagram convention for documenting the object-oriented concept of inheritance. An example could be that we have identified a requirement for a staff and a student entity. These entities are likely to have quite a lot in common – for example, they are all people with a name, address and date of birth. On the ERD we can document this as a generalization. The common attributes and associations of these entities can be assigned to a supertype of **person**, while the characteristics (attributes and associations) that are different are assigned to the subtypes of **student** and **staff**. The **person** attributes, in effect, belong to the specific occurrence of **student** or **staff** that is being accessed at any specific time. The documentation of this generalization construct is shown at *Figure 11.21*.

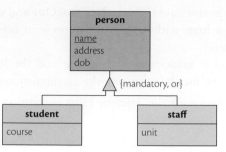

Figure 11.21 ERD – generalization.

The triangle in the association is the symbol for generalization. The generalization can be further documented as:

● Mandatory/optional – indicating whether there has to be a subtype
● Or/and – indicating whether the subtypes are mutually exclusive.

In the example we have {mandatory, or} which indicates that the **person** must have a subtype and that must be **staff** or **student** (not both). Note that the subtypes can have their own attributes and can have their own associations.

Aggregation and composition: The aggregation construct is a special case of association between two classes. Fowler (2004) describes aggregation as *the part of relationship* and says it is *like saying that a car has an engine and wheels as its parts*. The analogy with components of a machine is probably a good one.

　UML provides for two forms of aggregation: **aggregation** and **composition**. Composition is a stronger form of aggregation where the part object can belong to only one whole and its lifespan, creation and deletion are the same as the entity which it is part of. The construct for aggregation is a hollow diamond and for composition a solid diamond; in both cases on the *owning* end of the association. These are shown by the example in *Figure 11.22*. Note that you should be sparing in your use of this construct – use it only on associations where it adds to the clarity of the diagram.

aggregation: a strong association between two entities – a *part-of* relationship.

composition: a strong aggregation (*part-of* relationship) where the part entity can belong to only one whole and its lifespan is the same as that whole.

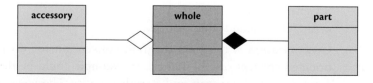

Figure 11.22 ERD – aggregation and composition.

These constructs can now be applied to the *Ancient History Library case study*. If we go back to the version shown in *Figure 11.19* we can:

● Use generalization for the **reservation/loan** aspects of a **transaction**
● Document that a **copy** requires an owning **title** using composition.

This gives a further version of the ERD (see *Figure 11.23*).

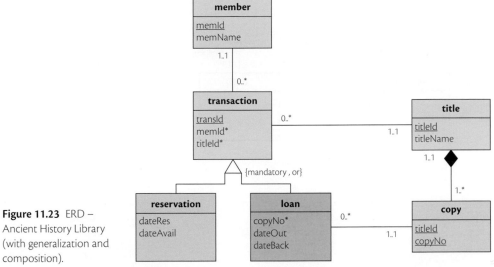

Figure 11.23 ERD – Ancient History Library (with generalization and composition).

It could also be helpful to mention a couple of special cases of relationships:

- Part-of relationship
- Pig's-ear relationship.

The *part-of* covers the situation of a kit or **assembly** which is made up of a number of components or **parts**. This is simple enough, but the **parts** could also be used in other **assemblies** – that is, a **part** can belong to a number of **assemblies**. This is solved by having two relationships between the entities (see *Figure 11.24*). To make the situation clearer we will name the relationships (we can name any relationship on the ERD but normally it does not add much to the clarity of the diagram).

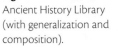

Figure 11.24 ERD – part-of relationship.

The *pig's-ear* is a self-call relationship. If we were to draw an ERD of a software system we would probably have a **module** entity. Software modules can themselves call further modules: this is represented in *Figure 11.25* overleaf. Note, however, that if any (sub)modules were used by more than one (supra)module this could need the part-of structure – and it could get more complex than that!

A second example could be a personnel file with a **staff** entity. In most organizations each member of staff has a manager who is also a member of staff with a manager. We could have a separate entity type for each level of manager but often staff structures are too diverse to make that practical. A simple alternative is to have a single **staff** entity which, using the *pig's ear* structure, own its subordinate **staff** entities (0..*) and is owned by its manager **staff** entity (0..1): this is represented in *Figure 11.25*.

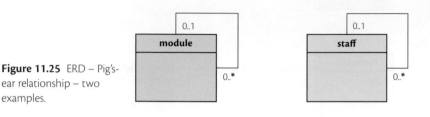

Figure 11.25 ERD – Pig's-ear relationship – two examples.

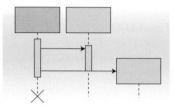

Sequence diagram

sequence diagram: a UML diagram that, for a given use case, documents its interaction with classes in terms of messages that can be added back onto the class diagram as methods.

The **sequence diagram** comes from UML and is part of object-oriented (OO) system analysis and design (SA&D). As explained in *Chapter 10* we can use the sequence diagram to explore the connection between the use case diagram and the class diagram. Taking this approach the steps are:

- Draw the use case diagram – for High Peak Bicycles we have done this at *Figure 11.5*
- Draw an initial class diagram identifying classes (objects) – now classes in OO A&D are much the same as entities and we will use the High Peak Bicycles' ERD at *Figure 11.18*
- Draw a sequence diagram for each use case, showing the use case's interaction with the classes on the initial class diagram
- Use the sequence diagrams to add processing (methods) to the class diagram – hence completing the class diagram. We look at the class diagram in the next subsection.

The sequence diagram is best explained by example – we will start with the simple use case: **maintain rental rates** (see *Figure 11.26*).

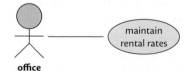

Figure 11.26 Use case – maintain rental rates.

> **Use case description:** Maintain rental rates
>
> **Basic course:** The user selects the bike class for which rental rates are to be created and inputs the appropriate start date and rates. Note that start dates cannot be retrospective.
>
> **Alternative course:** The selected bike class does not exist on the system and the user is invited to correct the selection.

The use case's processing requirement, in terms of entities/classes is:

- Read the **Bike Class** entity/class
- If the **Bike Class** is found:
  - Create a new **Rental Rate** entity/class.

This is represented in the sequence diagram shown at *Figure 11.27*.

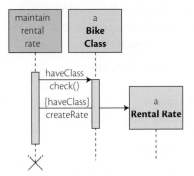

Figure 11.27 Sequence diagram – maintain rental rates.

The meaning of the sequence diagram and its notation is:

- Classes (entities):
  - Each column represents a class
  - We are processing one object from that class and we indicate that by the use of the indefinite article – e.g. a **Bike Class**
  - The lifeline of the object is indicated by the dotted line. If the object pre-exists the use case, then the dotted line starts from the top of the diagram; if the object remains available after the use case the dotted line continues to the bottom of the diagram. The deletion of an object is shown by a cross that terminates its lifeline
  - The use of the object in the use case is shown by the vertical rectangle on the lifeline
- Interface object:
  - The first column is the interface object. It comes into existence when the process is invoked and it is deleted at the end of the process – hence the X at the end of its lifeline.
- Messages:
  - Objects interact by sending messages to each other. The messages are represented by the horizontal arrowed lines on the diagram
  - The first message we have is invoked from the interface object. It uses a method **haveClass** to read the **Bike Class** object (second column) that the user requires; it returns a result in its argument **check()**

■ The second message is also invoked from the interface object. It has a guard [**haveClass**] and it will only be invoked if the **Bike Class** was previously found. If it is invoked, it then creates a **Rent Rate** object (third column) using the method **createRate**.

Let us now look at a more complex use case: **rent out** (see *Figure 11.28*, and *Figure 11.6* for the use case description).

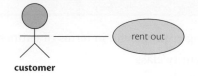

Figure 11.28 use case – rent out

The processing of the objects to be included in the sequence diagram is as set out below. Note that we start by looking up the **bicycles** (as opposed to processing the **customer** and **rental** data) – this is to avoid creating (unwanted) **customer/rental** objects, should the transaction be aborted because of issues with the availability or cost of the **bicycles**.

● For each machine on the rental request:
  ■ Read **Bike Class**
  ■ If **Bike Class** found, then:
    ▲ Until current **Rent Rate** (latest **rateSDate** <= today)[1] found:
     – Read **Rent Rate**
    ▲ Until available bike found:
     – **Read Bike** (if no available bike found – display n/a).
  (details of bike availability and cost can now be displayed).
  [1] assumes **Rent Rates** are read in descending date order.

● If accept, then:
  ■ If existing customer, then:
    ▲ Read **Customer**
  ■ If new customer, then:
    ▲ Create **Customer**
  ■ Create **Rental**
  ■ For each machine on rental request:
    ▲ Read **Bike**
    ▲ Create **Rental Line**.
  (Print rental agreement and transaction complete.)

And from these notes we can draw the sequence diagram (see *Figure 11.29*).

Let us first go through the additional constructs and notation we have used:

● Iterations: An iteration is indicated by an * on the message line. For example, the first message on the diagram is an iteration – we need to process each of the machines that the user has selected
● Control objects: We may have to introduce additional control objects (as opposed to interface and entity objects) onto the sequence diagram. This example has one such object: control (it could have an alternative name if appropriate). The use of the control object (hopefully) simplifies the diagram. In this example: the first use of the control object collects together

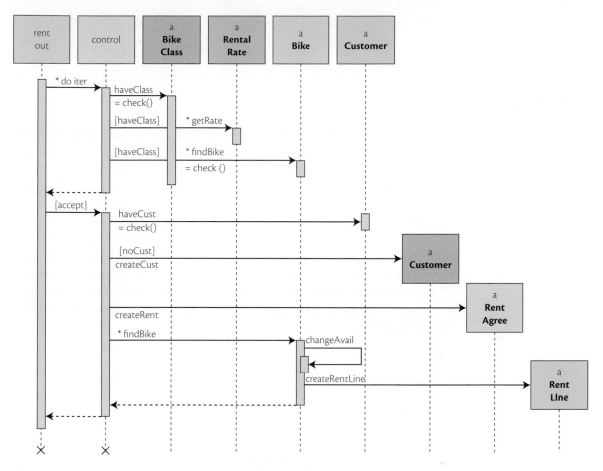

Figure 11.29 Sequence diagram – rent out.

three message lines all governed by the same iteration; the second use collects together several messages governed by the same guard

- Returns: We can add a return message as a dotted line showing that an action (or series of actions) has been completed. These are most helpful for indicating the end of an iteration
- Self call: This is where an object sends a message to itself. I have used this on the **Bike** object to show when the availability entity is updated, indicating that the bike is on hire.

So, while you are suitably confused, let us do some practice – do exercises 7 and 8 shown at the end of the chapter.

Also note that sequence diagrams are being used (or misused?) outside the context of strict object-oriented design to represent other interactions. In *Figure 5.14*, I have used a sequence diagram to show the interactions between the components of an e-Shop system.

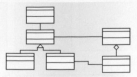

Class diagram

class diagram: a UML diagram. The class diagram represents all classes (of objects) and their associations with the other classes in the proposed system. Each class includes a list of attributes and methods.

The **class diagram** is the essential tool of OO-A&D. As explained in *Chapter 10*, the aim of OO is to first identify the objects used in the system and then encapsulate the processing and data for those objects as a series of reusable modules.

The first step is to identify the objects and, as already discussed, the objects are essentially the same as entities. Hence we will take the entities identified for High Peak Bicycles, in the ERD at *Figure 11.18*, as the starting point for our class diagram. Note that an object is the term for a single occurrence; each object type is represented as a class on the class diagram – hence its name. To illustrate that point, for High Peak Bicycles one of the classes is **Customer** – all the **Customers** are the class – and an individual **Customer** is an object. A summary version of the ERD (without attributes) is reproduced here as *Figure 11.30*.

Figure 11.30 ERD – summary.

The second step is to add the processing. On the class diagram the processing, derived from the use cases, is broken down into components that affect each class by the sequence diagrams – see *Figure 11.27* and *Figure 11.29* for the two we have done thus far. The processing requirement is identified by the messages on the sequence diagram; these are called *methods* when applied to the class diagram. The methods identified thus far are:

- From Maintain Rental Rates (*Figure 11.27*):
  - Class: **Bike Class**: method:
    - **haveClass**
      read **Bike Class** by key and check() if present.
  - Class: **Rental Rate**: method:
    - **createRate**
      create **Rental Rate** object.
- From Rent Out (*Figure 11.29*):
  - Class: **Bike Class**: method:
    - **haveClass**
      read **Bike Class** by key and check() if present.

- Class: **Rental Rate**: method:
  - ▲ **getRate**
    read **Rental Rate** – the next **Rental Rate** for a given **Bike Class**.
- Class: **Bicycle**: method:
  - ▲ **findBike**
    read **Bicycle** – the next **Bicycle** for a given **Bike Class** and check() if available (available and not sold and not written off).
  - ▲ **changeAvail**
    amend **Bicycle** to indicate it is on rental.
- Class: **Customer**: method:
  - ▲ **haveCust**
    read **Customer** by key and check() if present.
  - ▲ **createCust**
    create **Customer** object.
- Class: **Rent Agree**: method:
  - ▲ **createRent**
    create **Rent Agree** object.
- Class: **Rent Line**: method:
  - ▲ **createRentLine**
    create **Rent Line** object.

We should now check the list of methods for any commonality. In the above list the method **haveClass** is used in both the use cases – so that is a bit of commonality and some saving on the programming effort. In checking for commonality, one should be looking for:

polymorphism: the object-oriented concept that allows objects to be created whose exact type is not known until run time.

generalization: the object-oriented concept that allows an object to use the characteristics of a more general object (also known as inheritance).

encapsulation: the object-oriented concept that an object includes both data and the processing that manipulates the data.

- Messages/methods which have the same function but where we have made up different names when designing the sequence diagram.
- **Polymorphism**: similar requirements that could be met by a single method – e.g. **haveCust** is intended to check for the presence of a particular customer (by custNo), but could also serve to retrieve customer details or, possibly search for customer by custName.
- **Generalization**: we have already dealt with this as an additional ERD feature, but we should consider if additional generalization could create more commonality in the processing requirements.
  Note that the OO principles of encapsulation, generalization and polymorphism have already been discussed in more detail in *Chapter 10*.

The methods identified above can now be added to the class diagram (first drawn as an ERD, *Figure 11.18*), giving the updated class diagram shown at *Figure 11.31* overleaf. Note the bikeWO (write-off) attribute is changed to bikeAvail; this is intended as an indicator – values could be: 0 = available, 1 = out on rental and 9 = written off (with scope for other indicators, for example, on maintenance, if ever required in an enhanced system).

4

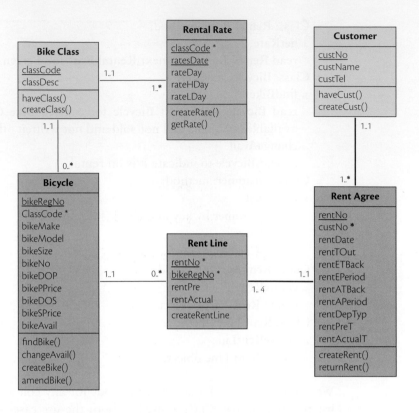

Figure 11.31 Class diagram – High Peak Bicycles.

Included in the class diagram are a number of additional methods (shown in grey). These are:

- Class: **Bike Class**: method:
  - ▲ **createClass**
    create **Bike Class** object.
    Not in case study but would seem to be a sensible addition.
- Class: **Bicycle**: method:
  - ▲ **createBike**
    create **Bicycle** object.
  - ▲ **amendBike**
    amend **Bicycle** object.
    This can deal with general amends and also selling (polymorphism) – it could also cover **changeAvail**, but that has been kept as a separate method.
- Class: **Rental Agree**: method:
  - ▲ **returnBike**
    update **Rent Agree** object with details of the end of the rental.

These methods should cover all the use case for the *High Peak Bicycles case study* (sequence diagrams for each use case could have been included but it would have taken a lot of space).

For a second example of a class diagram we will use the *Ancient History Library case study* (used for the ERD but now expanded to include processing requirements).

A small, private library specializing in ancient history has a collection of titles available for loan by members. Each member can have a loan of a maximum of eight books at any one time. The library often has several copies of a particular book. If no copies are available for immediate loan, a member can reserve the required book. When a copy of the requested book is returned, the library notifies the reserving member that the book is available, and puts the copy to one side, ready for collection. Processing requirements are:

- Create a new member
- Cancel member
- Catalogue new copy (and new title if required)
- Mark copy unavailable (if lost or withdrawn)
- Make loan – with options of:
  - Creating a reservation if copy not available
  - Converting a reservation into a loan
- Return loan
- Notify members with reservations when a copy is available.

Note that all data is to be retained (i.e. when membership is cancelled, copy made unavailable and loan returned).

As our starting point, we will use the ERD shown at *Figure 11.23* as a representation of the data required for the system – we will add attributes memStop to **member** (for cancel member requirement) and copyAvail to **copy** (to indicate: available, on-loan or withdrawn). How to deal with the reservation issue is more complex (where the reservation is for a **title** but it results in the resultant loan of a **copy**). Possibly the simplest approach is to mark the **title** with a titleRes indicator – these would be checked in a daily run and no loan would be allowed on a reserved **title** (a bit crude, but anything else gets rather complex – it could help to set this to the transId of the reservation, but that would set a limit of one reservation per title).

Now we should draw a use case diagram for the requirement and a sequence diagram for each use case but to save space we will just summarize the processing that is to be added to the class diagram:

- Create a new member:
  - Class: **member**: method:
    - ▲ **createMem**
- Cancel an existing member:
  - Class: **member**: methods:
    - ▲ **checkMem** – includes check if exists and memStop
    - ▲ **cancelMem** – set memStop
- Catalogue new copy (and new Title if required):
  - Class: **title**: method:
    - ▲ **getTitle** – includes check if exists
    - ▲ **createTitle**

- Class: **copy**: method:
  - ▲ **getCopy** – to check copyNo or any existing copies
  - ▲ **createCopy**
- Mark copy unavailable:
  - Class: **copy**: method:
    - ▲ **getCopy** – includes check if exists and copyAvail = on loan
    - ▲ **availCopy** – set copyAvail to unavailable
- Create a loan:
  - Class: **member**: method:
    - ▲ **checkMem** – includes check if exists and not memStop
  - Class: **title**: method:
    - ▲ **getTitle** – includes check if exists and reserved status
    - ▲ **resTitle** – to make a reservation/convert reservation to a loan
  - Class: **copy**: method:
    - ▲ **getCopy** – includes check if exists and copyAvail ≠ available
    - ▲ **availCopy** – set copyAvail to unavailable
  - Class: **transaction**: method:
    - ▲ **getTrans** – if following up on a reservation
    - ▲ **createTrans** – if making a loan (or reservation)
    - ▲ **createRes**   ) mutually exclusive
    - ▲ **createLoan**) a loan supersedes a reservation, if there is one
- Return loan:
  - Class: **transaction (loan)**: method:
    - ▲ **getTrans**
    - ▲ **getLoan**
    - ▲ **rtnLoan** – complete dateBack
  - Class: **copy**: method:
    - ▲ **getCopy**
    - ▲ **availCopy** – set copyAvail to available
- Notify available reservation:
  - Class: **title**: method:
    - ▲ **getTitle** – includes check if titleRes = reserved
  - Class: **copy**: method:
    - ▲ **getCopy** – includes check if copyAvail = available
  - Class: **transaction (reservation)**: method:
    - ▲ **getTrans**
    - ▲ **getRes** – to check if transaction is a reservation
    - ▲ **availRes** – to set dateAvail
  - Class: **member**: method:
    - ▲ **checkMem** – includes check if memStop

These methods can now be added to our initial ERD/class diagram to give the completed class diagram (see *Figure 11.32*).

There is an additional case study for you to practise at the end of the chapter – do exercises 9 and 10.

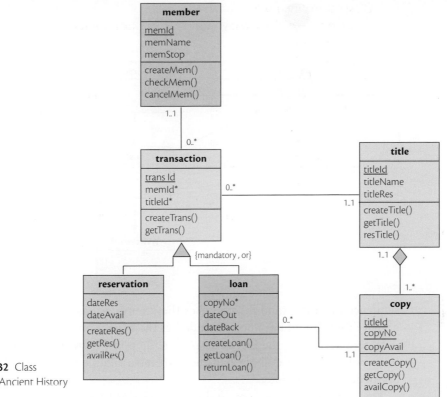

Figure 11.32 Class diagram – Ancient History Library.

Other SA&D documentation

In this chapter we have covered five separate diagramming conventions taken from SSADM and UML – and that is probably enough to be getting on with! However, it should be pointed out that this is only a subset of the diagramming techniques that have been devised; moreover, these examples have been taken from just two of the many methodologies that are out there (although many of the methodologies that have been devised are no longer in use). In this section we will take a brief overview of a small number of the other diagramming techniques and approaches that have been developed over the years but that have not been selected for (full) inclusion in this chapter.

State diagram

state diagram: a UML diagram. The state diagram takes an individual class/object and shows the activities that can affect it during its lifecycle.

If one more technique were to be included in the list of techniques to be examined and explained, it would be the UML **state diagram** (also referred to as a state transition diagram).

The state diagram takes an individual class/object and shows the activities that can affect it during its lifecycle. It is in many ways the inverse of the sequence diagram in that the activities are all the methods that have been planned for that object. Drawing the state diagrams is a cross-check of all the

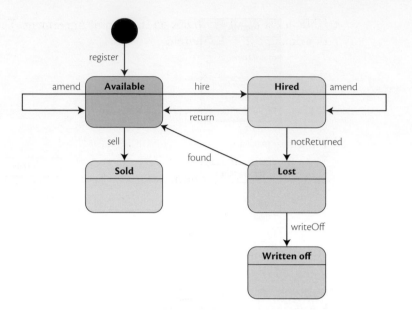

Figure 11.33 State diagram – bicycle.

sequence diagrams (and the use cases they represent) as it should identify any activity that should have been included in the system but has been overlooked. A state diagram for the Bicycle Class is shown in *Figure 11.33*. Note that we have only had to use about half the features available for a state diagram to construct this example.

The state diagram is comparable with SSADM's entity life history (ELH), which uses Jackson structures, outlined later in this section.

Relational data analysis

relational data analysis (RDA): a bottom-up analysis and rationalization of data requirements into entities and attributes.

A bottom-up approach to data normalization is **relational data analysis (RDA)**. The outcome of a RDA exercise can be used to cross-check the ERD (the outcome of a top-down analysis of the data requirements).

For RDA we take each input/output form for the current/proposed system and analyse the attributes into successive normal forms:

- UNF: Un-normalized form – a list of all attributes on the form plus the identification of an overall key for the data on the form
- 1NF: First normal form – identify any repeating groups of attributes, separate them and identify their key. The key for a repeating group will be the overall key (from UNF) plus a key for the group
- 2NF: Second normal form – identify any *partial-key dependencies*, separate them and identify them with their key. These are attributes in the 1NF repeating groups that are identified by only part of the key of that group
- 3NF: Third normal form – identify any *non-key dependencies*, separate them and identify them with their key. These attributes can be in any of the groups identified in the previous stages.

Now, possibly, that does not make a lot of sense without an example, so let's illustrate it using the Bicycle Rental Agreement from the *High Peak Bicycles case study*. The RDA is shown in tabular form in *Figure 11.34* and each stage is explained below.

- UNF: a list of all attributes on the Rental Agreement. The key that identifies this document is the **rentNo**
- 1NF: the *repeating group* is fairly obvious – there are four bikes included on the Rental Agreement. The key is the overall key (from UNF), **rentNo,** plus a key for the group – **bikeRegNo** gives a unique identifier for each Rental Line
- 2NF: the Bicycle attributes are *partial-key dependencies* – the bicycle data is identified by the **bikeRegNo** and is the same whatever Rental Agreement the Bicycle is included on
- 3NF: looking through the 2NF we can identify two *non-key dependencies*:
  - On the Rental Agreement we have **custName** and **custTel** – from this we can create a Customer entity with **custName** as the key/foreign key
  - On the Bicycle we have **classCode** and **classDesc** – from this we can create a Bike Class entity with **classCode** as the key/foreign key.

Note:

- Attribute names can be abbreviated to fit the table format
- Primary keys are <u>underlined</u>
- Foreign keys are marked with an *.

These are the same conventions as we used on the ERD.

Un -Normalized	First Normal	Second Normal	Third Normal
<u>rentalNo</u>	<u>rentalNo</u>	<u>rentalNo</u>	<u>rentalNo</u>
custName	custName	custName	custName *
custTel	custTel	custTel	rentDate
rentDate	rentDate	rentDate	rentTOut
rentTOut	rentTOut	rentTOut	rentETBack
rentETBack	rentETBack	rentETBack	rentEPeriod
rentEPeriod	rentEPeriod	rentEPeriod	rentATBack
rentATBack	rentATBack	rentATBack	rentAPeriod
renrAPeriod	rentAPeriod	rentAPeriod	rentDepTyp
rentDepTyp	rentDepTyp	rentDepTyp	rentPreTot
classCode	rentPreTot	rentPreTot	rentActualT
classDesc	rentActualT	rentActualT	
bikeRegNo			<u>rentalNo</u>
bikeModel	<u>rentalNo</u>	<u>rentalNo</u>	<u>bikeRegNo</u>
rentPre	<u>bikeRegNo</u>	<u>bikeRegNo</u>	rentPre
rentPreTot	classCode	rentPre	rentActual
rentActual	classDesc	rentActual	
rentActualT	bikeModel		<u>bikeRegNo</u>
	rentPre	<u>bikeRegNo</u>	classCode *
	rentActual	classCode	bikeModel
		classDesc	
		bikeModel	<u>custName</u>
			custTel
			<u>classCode</u>
			classDesc

Figure 11.34 RDA – bicycle rental agreement.

In the 3NF column we have identified five entities:

- Rent Agree   Key: **rentalNo**
- Rent Line   Key: **rentalNo + bikeRegNo**
- Bicycle   Key: **bikeRegNo**

- Customer   Key: **custName**
- Bike Class   Key: **classCode**

Multiple part keys are *owned* by single part keys (e.g. Rent Agree, key: **rentalNo** owns Rent Line, key: **rentalNo** + **bikeRegNo**) and foreign keys are *owned* by entities with the corresponding primary key (e.g. Bicycle, foreign key: **classCode*** is owned by Bike Class, key: **classCode**). Thus we have:

- Customer 1..1 – 1..* Rent Agree
- Rent Agree 1..1 – 1..4 Rent Line (the limit of four is in the case study)
- Bike Class 1..1 – 0..* Bicycle
- Bicycle 1..1 – 0..* Rent Line.

This corresponds to our ERD in *Figure 11.18*. The data in the RDA is only a subset of the ERD as the RDA is only an analysis of one form – if we were to analyse all the data/forms for the system we would complete the picture and validate the ERD.

Note that there are no exercises on this technique, but the *Project management* and *Computer help desk* case studies, set as assignments at the end of this chapter, include forms and can be used as practice, if required.

Jackson structures

Michael A. Jackson put forward methods for system analysis and program design based on data analysis. **Jackson structures** were adopted by the UK Government as its mandated method for program design and were also incorporated into later versions of SSADM.

Jackson's methods are no longer in use but the basic principles and the diagramming technique can still be helpful (for instance, in drawing a structure chart for a website design). Jackson's thesis was that there are three, and only three, basic constructs in a data structure and in a program:

- Sequence: A is followed by B
- Selection: a choice of A or B – indicated by ° in the top right of the box
- Iteration: A is repeated zero, one or many times – indicated by * in the top right of the box.

  And there is a bit of a cheat: quit (from one part of the structure) to admit (at a later part of the structure) – in effect a *go to* that jumps over the intervening part of the structure.

To illustrate these constructs, *Figure 11.35* is the bicycle state diagram (*Figure 11.33*) redrawn as a Jackson structure – which is also a SSADM ELH. Let's give that a quick run-through:

- The basic life/states of a **bicycle** are: **register** > **use** > **end** – a *sequence*
- The **usage** consists of an *iteration* of **events**
- The **events** are a *sequence*: starting with the bike being **available** followed by been **hired**, and repeat (the **events** *iteration*)
- The **end** is either the bike is **sold** or a **write-off**, a *selection*.

Omitted from the diagram is the **amend** event (which is not likely to happen) – this would have to be shown as iterations beneath **available** and **hired** – but it would distract from the basic state transition/life history.

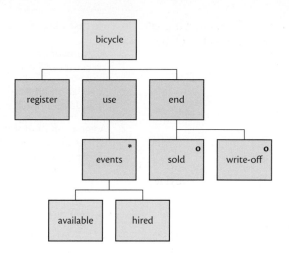

Figure 11.35 Jackson structure – bicycle.

Further reading

Books recommended for further reading are:

Avison, D. and Fitzgerald, G. (2006) *Information Systems Development: Methodologies, Techniques and Tools*, 4th ed., McGraw-Hill, Maidenhead.

Fowler, M. (2004) *UML Distilled: A Brief Guide to the Standard Object Modelling Language*, 3rd ed., Addison-Wesley, Boston, MA.

Lejk, M. and Deeks, D. (2002) *An Introduction to System Analysis Techniques*, 2nd ed., Pearson, Harlow.

Rumbaugh, J., Jacobson, I. and Booch, G. (2010) *The Unified Modeling Language Reference Manual*, 2nd ed., Addison-Wesley, Reading, MA.

Comprehension test

This is a simple test to enable you to check you have absorbed the material presented in *Chapter 11* (five questions for each of the five techniques included in the chapter).

Comprehension test: Use case diagram

Q1 A use case diagram is used to represent:

   a. Processes required to implement a system ☐

   b. The methods required to implement a system ☐

   c. The data requirements of a system ☐

   d. User requirements for a system ☐

   e. The objects that interact with a use case ☐

Q2 A use case diagram includes a symbol for:

   a. Entities ☐

   b. Processes ☐

   c. Methods ☐

   d. Actors ☐

   e. Messages ☐

4

Q3   A use case is defined as:

a.   A data item used by the system ☐

b.   An object used in object-oriented design ☐

c.   A bit of business done with the system ☐

Q4   In a use case diagram, an extend is:

a.   A chunk of behaviour that is similar across several use cases ☐

b.   A variation on normal behaviour to include additional, optional behaviour ☐

c.   A variation on normal behaviour where any one of the child use cases might be invoked ☐

Q5   In a use case diagram, generalization is:

a.   A chunk of behaviour that is similar across several use cases ☐

b.   A variation on normal behaviour to include additional, optional behaviour ☐

c.   A variation on normal behaviour where any one of the child use cases might be invoked ☐

Comprehension test: Data flow diagram (DFD)

Q6   A DFD is used to represent:

a.   Processes required to implement a system ☐

b.   The methods required to implement a system ☐

c.   The data requirements of a system ☐

d.   User requirements for a system ☐

e.   The objects that interact with a use case ☐

Q7   A DFD includes a symbol for:

a.   Entities ☐

b.   Processes ☐

c.   Methods ☐

d.   Actors ☐

e.   Messages ☐

Q8   A DFD:

a.   Represents the data required by the system ☐

b.   Enables a system to be partitioned into independent units ☐

c.   Shows user requirements without the detail of the system ☐

d.   Examines: encapsulation, generalization and polymorphism ☐

Q9   For a DFD, the context diagram is:

a.   An organization chart showing the company context of the system ☐

b.   A diagram showing the other systems that will interface with the system being designed ☐

c.   Conceptually a level zero DFD ☐

Q10 In a DFD, which of the following is *not* permissible:

- a. A dataflow from an external to a process ☐
- b. A dataflow from an external to a datastore ☐
- c. A dataflow from a process to a datastore ☐

Comprehension test: Entity relationship diagram (ERD)

Q11 An ERD is used to represent:

- a. Processes required to implement a system ☐
- b. The methods required to implement a system ☐
- c. The data requirements of a system ☐
- d. User requirements for a system ☐
- e. The objects that interact with a use case ☐

Q12 An ERD includes a symbol for:

- a. Entities ☐
- b. Processes ☐
- c. Methods ☐
- d. Actors ☐
- e. Messages ☐

Q13 An ERD is part of the process of:

- a. Object-oriented system analysis and design ☐
- b. Specifying user requirements ☐
- c. Relational data analysis ☐
- d. Data modelling ☐

Q14 In an ERD, which of the following relationship types needs to be resolved (replaced by an alternative structure)?

- a. A many-to-many relationship ☐
- b. A part-of relationship ☐
- c. A pig's ear relationship ☐

Q15 In an ERD, composition is:

- a. Guidance on the layout of the ERD ☐
- b. A special case of a strong association between two entities (classes) ☐
- c. The way that the degree/cardinality of the relationship is documented ☐

4

Comprehension test: Sequence diagram

Q16 A sequence diagram is used to represent:

a. Processes required to implement a system ☐

b. The methods required to implement a system ☐

c. The data requirements of a system ☐

d. User requirements for a system ☐

e. The objects that interact with a use case ☐

Q17 A sequence diagram includes a symbol for:

a. Entities ☐

b. Processes ☐

c. Methods ☐

d. Actors ☐

e. Messages ☐

Q18 A sequence diagram is used to:

a. Show the order of processes within the system ☐

b. Record the levels of functional decomposition in a DFD ☐

c. Explore the connection between the use case diagram and the class diagram ☐

d. Record one way associations on a class diagram ☐

Q19 The first column of a sequence diagram should normally be:

a. A control object ☐

b. The interface object ☐

c. A message object ☐

Q20 In a sequence diagram, a guard is:

a. An indication of the end of an object's lifeline ☐

b. A conditional ☐

c. A self-call ☐

Comprehension test: Class diagram

Q21 A class diagram is used to represent:

a. Processes required to implement a system ☐

b. The methods required to implement a system ☐

c. The data requirements of a system ☐

d. User requirements for a system ☐

e. The objects that interact with a use case ☐

Q22 A class diagram includes a symbol for:

a. Entities ☐

b. Processes ☐

c. Methods ☐

d. Actors ☐

e. Messages ☐

Q23 A class diagram:

a. Documents the encapsulation of data and processing in an object ☐

b. Classifies entities as standing and transaction data ☐

c. Shows the state transitions of an object ☐

d. Differentiates classes of processing requirements ☐

Q24 The methods shown on the class diagram are:

a. Use cases from the use case diagram ☐

b. Messages from the sequence diagram ☐

c. Instance of aggregation and composition from the ERD ☐

Q25 The object-oriented concept of polymorphism is:

a. The concept that allows related data requirement to be represented by a common supertype and a number of subtypes ☐

b. The process of translating use cases into object-oriented methods on a class diagram ☐

c. A single method that can be used to fulfil two or more related requirements ☐

Exercises

The following exercises are designed to aid your understanding of the material presented in this chapter. Each exercise uses a case study – additional case studies are *Betsy and the band* and *Five-a-side football*, included after exercise 10, and *Project management* and *Computer help desk*, included after exercise 12. The exercises can be used for self-study, set as a tutorial exercise and exercises 11 and 12 are designed to be set as assignments.

1   **Comprehension**   Draw a use case diagram for the *Betsy and the band case study*, see below.

2   **Comprehension**   Draw a use case diagram for the *Five-a-side football case study*, see below.

3   **Comprehension**   Draw a data flow diagram for the *Betsy and the band case study*, see below.

4   **Comprehension**   Draw a data flow diagram for the *Five-a-side football case study*, see below.

5   **Comprehension**   Draw an entity relationship diagram for the *Betsy and the band case study*, see below.

6   **Comprehension**   Draw an entity relationship diagram for the *Five-a-side football case study*, see below.

7   **Comprehension**   Using the *High Peak Bicycles case study* (given at the start of this chapter) draw a sequence diagram for the Maintain Bike Register use case – see

Figure 11.5 for the use case diagram and *Figure 11.18* for the ERD.

8   **Comprehension**   Using the *High Peak Bicycles case study* (given at the start of this chapter) draw a sequence diagram for the Rent Return use case – see *Figure 11.5* for the use case diagram and *Figure 11.18* for the ERD.

9   **Comprehension**   Draw a class diagram for the *Betsy and the band case study*, see below. You have already drawn the use case diagram in *exercise 1* and an ERD in *exercise 5*. You will need to draw a sequence diagram for each use case to identify the required messages/methods.

10   **Comprehension**   Draw a class diagram for the *Five-a-side football case study*, see below. You have already drawn the use case diagram in *exercise 2* and an ERD in *exercise 6*. You will need to draw a sequence diagram for each use case to identify the required messages/methods.

4

Betsy and her band, the Ghost Town Mice, are planning a UK tour. Rightly or wrongly, Betsy has told the record company and the promoters to *get lost* (well, she did express herself rather more strongly than that but the meaning was the same) – so it is going to be a bit of a do-it-yourself job.

The tour has four gigs: 10 June Sheffield, 13 June Glasgow, 17 June Liverpool and 20 June Birmingham (they were coming to Manchester but Betsy fell out with the venue management).

The requirement is to have a computer system that will be used to register customers and sell tickets. The system will require facilities to:

● Register the gig. This is done by the tour manager. The data required is a four-digit event code, the date, start time and location

● Specify a seating plan for each of the venues – again done by the tour manager. Seats are identified by a single letter for the row and a two-digit number for the seat, e.g. seat B10. Prices are set for the row, e.g. row B is £25. Each seat is initially recorded as unbooked

● Register fans of the band. Fans must give their name, address and mobile phone number. The system allocates them a customer number. These details are used to print labels used to mailshot the fans. Registered fans get priority for bookings for the first week after tickets go on sale

● Sell tickets. Registered fans will give their customer number, choose a gig and purchase up to four seats. Payment is by credit card requiring card number and date. Unregistered fans (once tickets go on general release) will also have to give their name, address and mobile number and will be allocated a customer number as part of the booking process. Each transaction is allocated a unique confirmation code that can be used for queries and, where appropriate, to pick up tickets from the venue box-office.

Once customers have bought their seats they will receive a text confirmation (on their mobile phone) including their customer number and confirmation code and, provided they have bought their tickets at least two weeks in advance, their tickets through the post. Tickets for posting are printed once a day and the system is updated to show that the tickets have been despatched. Late tickets will be picked up at the venue and the box-office staff will have an interface that allows them to look up the customer/booking, print the tickets and mark the tickets as collected.

The Madcaster University Foundation Year (FY) students have decided to set up a five-a-side football league (FY5S). Matches will take place on Wednesday afternoon during term time and each team is required to play each other team once. League positions are calculated in the normal way (3 points for a win and 1 point for a draw). The league is completed by the end of the spring term and the VC's Cup is awarded to the top team.

FY5S now requires a computer system to keep track of teams, games and league position. The requirements are:

● Students must form their own teams, give it an identity (short name, full name plus contact e-Mail) and register the team plus the players (minimum of five and maximum of eight – each with student number and name)

- Students are required to contact the other teams and arrange their own matches. Once the match is arranged, it has to be recorded in the system (short name of each team and date)
- Once the match is played, the match details are updated with the score of each team
- At any time, students can request a display of the league (the system calculates this each time the display is requested). Students can also click on their own team to see details of the matches they have played, the matches that have been arranged and the matches that have yet to be agreed.

11 Assignment Undertake structured SA&D for the ***Project management case study***. For your structured design you should complete the following diagrams:

- Context diagram
- Data flow diagram
- Entity relationship diagram.

When you have completed these diagrams, cross-check the detail – for example, you should not have an entity on the ERD that does not correspond to a datastore on the DFD (a datastore may correspond to more than one related entity).

12 Assignment Undertake OO-A&D for the ***Computer help desk case study***. For your object-oriented design you should complete the following diagrams:

- Use case diagram
- Preliminary class (entity relationship) diagram (working document)
- Sequence diagram (for each use case)
- Class diagram.

Case study
Project management

Madcaster University (MU) is implementing the Vice-Chancellor's Agenda for Change. Part of the process is to update the University's IS and IT systems to support new methods of teaching, record keeping and the integration of these systems into a comprehensive, and seamless, service support and delivery package. To facilitate the delivery of these new systems, to an exacting timetable, the MU IS Department is implementing a new Project Planning and Management System (MUitPlan) to track the various IS projects contributing to the Agenda for Change.

The MUitPlan will be implemented using an Oracle database system. Two basic sets of data that must be loaded are:

- Projects: Each project is recorded with its project code, title, start date, delivery date and the staff number of its project manager. The project is further broken down into Activities, each with an (unique) activity code, description, delivery date, estimated hours effort and a skill code (e.g. D=design and P=programming).
- Staff: All the staff working for the MU IS Department are recorded. Each staff member has a staff number, name, skill code, start date, end date (if they are leaving) and the staff number of their manager. Staff records can be amended.

Staff are required to fill in a weekly time sheet, see attached. Each week the time sheet is handed to the MU IS administrator who inputs the details (staff hours on each activity by week number) into MUitPlan. Hence the system has a record of the work hours recorded against each project activity.

On a weekly basis, a report is produced showing progress on each project/activity. The report highlights any activity that is running late or over its hours budget and management then need to determine how the situation is to be resolved.

Weekly Time Sheet

MU IT: Weekly Time Sheet					
		Manager:			
Staff No:	64007	**Staff No:**	32016	**Week No**	
Staff Name:	John Smith	**Staff Name:**	Mary Bell	27	
Project:		**Activity:**			
Code	**Title**	**Code**	**Description**	**Hours**	
G104	Stu Reg Sys	A23	Use cases	4.5	
		A24	Class diagram	7.5	
D073	Moodle VLE	A16	Install V7.3	7.5	
		A17	Test V7.3	7.5	
		A18	Release V7.3	3.0	
D074	Student Portal	A03	Storyboard	7.5	

Case study
Computer help desk

The Department of Computing at Madcaster University (MU) has a large number of computers in student labs and in staff rooms – all looked after by the departmental technicians. It has been decided to create a computer system to keep an inventory of the IT kit and to keep track of the maintenance tasks undertaken by the technicians.

The starting point for the system is the inventory. Each item of IT kit is given a MU serial number. Further data for each piece of kit is a classification (code and description: PC, server, printers, etc.), manufacturer, date installed and location (room number and staff id, where applicable). There is also a disposal date added when the item is disposed of (and the record is then retained for a further five years).

Maintenance tasks can be raised by the user of the kit (typically a fault) or by the technicians (normally an upgrade) and are recorded by the technicians. Each task is given a job id and recorded. Details include MU serial number, date and a description of the problem/task.

The first step is for the tasks to be reviewed by the chief technician (or, in her absence, by her deputy). The task is classified using a standard set of job codes (std job code, std job title and std hours) and allocated to a member of the technical staff (using the staff id).

The technician, once the problem is fixed, signs off the task by inputting the date completed and a description of the action taken.

The system keeps summary details of all members of staff (academic and technical), keyed on staff id; the data is name, job grade and room number. There is a single dummy staff record for students (staff id 9999 and name 'student'), used for all student lab machines. The staff details are maintained by the senior technician.

Equipment Record

MU DoC **IT Equipment Record**	Serial Number:	0600614
Classification:	Maintenance:	

> Code	PC(St)	
> Description	Desktop PC - Staff	
Manufacturer:	Dell	
Room No:	JD E115	
Date Installed	16 May 06	
Disposal Date:	10 May 09	

Maintenance:

Job Id:	070023
Std Job Code:	SWu
Std Job Title:	Software Update
Date Completed:	15 Jan 07

Job Id:	080732
Std Job Code:	HWr
Std Job Title:	Hardware Repair
Date Completed:	29 Nov 08

Job Id:
Std Job Code:
Std Job Title:
Date Completed:

4

12 IMPLEMENTING THE INFORMATION SYSTEMS

Summary

Developing a computer system takes place in stages – the system development lifecycle (SDLC) was discussed in **Chapter 10**. The main role of the Information System (IS) specialist is system analysis and design (SA&D), and a number of SA&D techniques were explained in **Chapter 11**. The key remaining activities/stages that have to be undertaken by the project team are:

- Project planning: The project manager (see **Chapter 3**) must plan the project. The techniques of PERT and Gantt charts can be used for planning and progress monitoring.
- Production (or procurement) of software: This may be achieved by a bought-in system, using an application generator, or by programming.
- Testing: The project team must make sure that the software works, is robust and fulfils the user requirements. Testing cannot guarantee these qualities but it can at least provide some assurance that the software is fit for purpose.
- Implementation: Once the system is ready (or we think it is ready) it has to *go live*. This requires careful preparation – a failed implementation of a *mission-critical* IS can have serious consequences for the organization.
- Maintenance: Once live, the IS will have to be maintained and enhanced. Maintenance is vital but time-consuming and costly.

Eventually, the IS reaches the end of its useful life and we start the SDLC again on a replacement system.

© Photo_Ma/Fotolia

Learning outcomes

Having read this chapter and completed the exercises, you should:

- Understand the project planning function, PERT and Gantt charts and be able to construct a (simple) PERT network
- Understand the purpose of the programming stage of the SDLC and the main options for creating or obtaining software
- Understand the purpose of the testing stage of the SDLC and the types of testing that might be deployed
- Understand the purpose of the implementation activity in the SDLC and the tasks that need to be completed
- Understand the purpose of the maintenance stage of the SDLC and how support functions might be organized.

Key terms

PERT (program evaluation and review technique), critical path, programming, Gantt chart, testing, implementation, maintenance.

Implementing the Information Systems

Part 4 of the book concentrates on the design stages of the system development lifecycle, which is the role of the IS specialist. However, the process of system analysis and design (SA&D) is only one part of the process of developing an Information System. Other tasks to be performed in the development and deployment of an IS project include:

- Project planning
- Production or procurement of the software (programming)
- Testing within the project team and with the users
- Implementation
- Maintenance.

The creation (or enhancement) of an Information System is normally organized as a project. The size of the project team and the duration of the project will obviously depend on the size of the task that is to be undertaken.

Project planning

New Information System requirements will normally be organized as a project. The project structure provides focus. The objectives of the project team must be clear – to deliver the required system on time, on budget and with an acceptable quality standard. The project management function has been discussed in *Chapter 3*. The project manager must plan the project (create the project plan) and check progress (progress monitoring and reporting). Two tools/techniques that can be used for this are:

- PERT: program evaluation and review technique
- Gantt chart.

These two techniques are reviewed below.

4

PERT

A standard approach to project planning is to draw up a critical path analysis/ **PERT (program evaluation and review technique)** network. This technique charts each activity in relation to other activities, taking into account the dependencies between them. This approach can be illustrated using a simple example project that requires the following activities:

PERT (program evaluation and review technique): a project-planning technique that charts each activity in relation to other activities, taking into account the dependencies between them.

- a1   Install IT for development: 1 person for 8 weeks
  start anytime
- a2   System analysis: 3 people for 12 weeks
  start anytime
- a3   Database design: 1 person for 6 weeks
  start anytime
- a4   Install IT for live running: 2 people for 6 weeks
  start after a1, a2 and a3 have been completed

- a5   Programming: 4 people for 12 weeks
start after a1, a2 and a3 have been completed
- a6   Test and implement: 2 person for 8 weeks
start after a4 and a5 have been completed.

The PERT technique requires that these activities are plotted on a chart showing dependencies, that is, that activities a4 and a5 cannot start until a1, a2 and a3 are finished and that activity a6 cannot start until a4 and a5 are complete (see *Figure 12.1*).

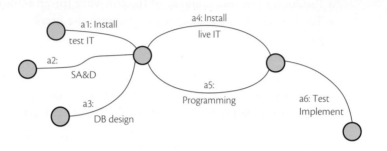

Figure 12.1 PERT chart showing dependencies.

This chart can be developed to show a start and end event for each activity. These events then have:

- Event label – 'a' in the example
(each event is given a unique identifier)
- Earliest time for the event (et)
- Latest time for the event (lt)
- Slack/float time (st), i.e. lt minus et

The network has been redrawn to include this detail in *Figure 12.2*.

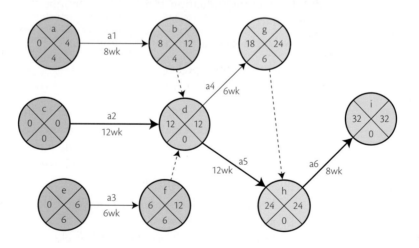

Figure 12.2 PERT chart showing critical path.

critical path: the sequence of activities in a project plan that have no float time and hence determine the overall elapse time for the project.

This enhanced diagram allows us to identify the critical path and the minimum overall elapse time. The **critical path** is the sequence of activities where the slack times are zero – marked in bold on *Figure 12.2* (there may be more than one critical path). The minimum overall elapse time is 32 weeks – the sum total of the elapse times on the critical path. Dotted lines can be used to show dependencies between activities. The PERT chart does not show resource (staff) requirements.

Gantt chart

Gantt chart: a type of bar chart that plots project activity against timescale and is used to document project plans.

The **Gantt chart** (or bar chart) is an alternative representation of a project plan. It plots tasks, their duration and (if required) the number of people involved against a calendar. Using the same example as used for the PERT chart we can construct a Gantt chart (see *Figure 12.3*); a PERT analysis can be a useful precursor, particularly in complex cases.

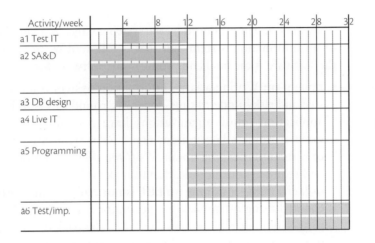

Figure 12.3 Gantt chart.

Having done the planning the project manager then needs to plot progress. Using the Gantt chart in *Figure 12.3* the project manager has recorded the progress of each activity, up to week 10, in orange. The updated chart makes it clear that, while the DB design activity is complete and the SA&D is a little behind schedule (one person a week ahead, one on schedule and one two weeks behind), there is a real problem with activity a1 (installing the test IT equipment) – this activity is four weeks behind and has only two weeks to run.

The Gantt chart can also be used to plan out the activities for each team member. This plots the team member against the calendar with the bar(s) labelled with the activity it (or they) represents (see *Figure 12.4*).

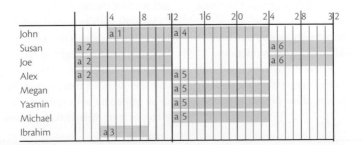

Figure 12.4 Gantt chart (staff).

4

Taking account of skills but adjusting the plan a little (e.g. activity a4, install live IT, is now the task of one person for 12 weeks as opposed to two persons for 6 weeks, and assuming Alex is both a good analyst and a good programmer) we get a plan for the size of the project team and for work allocation (if Susan, Joe and Ibrahim were all good programmers we could reduce the project team size to five – unfortunately that is not the case).

PERT analysis and project planning using Gantt charts can be carried out using software. Microsoft Project is the best known package available for this purpose.

Programming

programming: writing, testing and maintaining the source code for a computer program.

The paper design produced by the system analyst is a vital step in the production of an Information System, but that is followed by the **programming** stage and the software is the final end product. The software for the system can be:

- Bought-in: Writing a large Information System is a time-consuming, expensive and risky undertaking – one way round this is to buy in a ready-written application (most organizations have a number of competitors with the same, or similar, IS requirements). ERP systems are one example of the type of system that can be obtained *off the shelf*. Quite often a bought-in system will require some modification to make it fit the requirements of a particular organization – installing an ERP is normally a major project.
- Created using an application generator: This is a package that allows users to specify their requirements and then the package will generate the application – complex parts of the requirement may need to be separately coded and slotted in. Application generators tend to be associated with database packages, of which Oracle is a good example. A more familiar example will be Microsoft Access where the user sets up the database and then generates forms and reports with little or no recourse to program coding. Large systems created using an application generator will still require the employment of specialist IT staff.

Themes
Competitive advantage

A bought-in Information System, such as an ERP system, sets a pattern of operations for the organizations that use it; the ERP vendors claim to incorporate *best of breed* business practice.

An organization with old systems and outdated business practices could improve its competitive position by changing to a new ERP system; it will only gain the full advantage of its new system if it updates its business practices as part of the project to install the new system.

That said, installing a new ERP system is unlikely to produce a competitive advantage. The new system is the same system as that used in a number of competitor organizations – therefore the new system cannot differentiate the organization from its competitors.

Systems such as payroll and accounting are utility functions, so there is no competitive advantage to be gained, and a bought-in system should serve very well. For strategic functions, the organization should consider whether there is competitive advantage to be gained by writing its own bespoke system incorporating differentiated business practices.

- Programmed: The requirement is interpreted as a set of detailed instructions in an appropriate programming language and those instructions are then used to generate the executable software. A large Information System will require the writing of many programs/modules.

We have already taken a brief look at machine code instructions, the code the computer operates with, in *Chapter 6*. It is unusual for modern systems to be written in machine code – these are normally written in a high-level language that is then translated (compiled or interpreted) into machine code for use on the computer system.

Many programming languages have been developed over the years, for differing purposes, and many of these still have to be used when the original software is maintained. One of these programming languages is Cobol, used for commercial systems on mainframes – there is still a lot of it about. Programming languages that are used for the writing of new software include:

- C, C++ and C#: C is the language of the UNIX operating system and available across a wide range of systems. C is a detailed (low-level) language that tends to be used for system software and real-time applications. C++ is an object-oriented (OO) language derived from C. C# (spoken C-sharp) is the Microsoft, OO, dot.net version of C.
- Java: A language derived from C and generally associated with internet applications (although it can be used for almost any programming job). Applications written in Java are portable across a wide range of platforms without the need to recompile the programs (they are interpreted from an intermediate language at run time). Java also provides for OO.
- Visual Basic (VB): A visual programming language that gives the user facility to paint the user interface and then generates code shells for those interfaces (a code shell being an outline module where the programmer can fill in additional program functionality). VB is a bit of a cross between a programming language and an application generator. VB is a PC language from Microsoft and can be used to add functionality in many of their desktop products.

An example of Java code is shown in *Figure 12.5* overleaf. It is assumed in this book that many students studying this introduction to IS topics will not be studying programming, so the example is intended to give you some idea of what a program can look like. The function of this code is to calculate how long it takes to pay back a loan. You put in the value of the loan, the annual interest rate and the monthly repayments – the program then tells you how long the loan takes to repay, the final month's payment and the total amount repaid (including interest). The program assumes that interest is charged on a monthly basis. If you want to cheer yourself up, type it into a Java development environment and see how much damage your debts could cause you.

4

```
import java.io.*;
public class Payments {

public static void main(String [] args) {
double cap=0.0, capo=0.0, capt=0.0, interest=0.0, rpay=0.0, fpay=0.0;
int mths=0, i;
char ch;
String instring = "    ";
BufferedReader in
  = new BufferedReader(new InputStreamReader(System.in));
System.out.print("Value of loan? : ");
i =0;
try{
  instring = in.readLine();
  cap = Float.parseFloat(instring);
  }
catch (Exception e){System.out.println(e);};

System.out.print("Annual interest? : ");
try{
  instring = in.readLine();
  interest = Float.parseFloat(instring);
  }
catch (Exception e){System.out.println(e);};

System.out.print("Monthly repayments? : ");
try{
  instring = in.readLine();
  rpay = Float.parseFloat(instring);
  }
catch (Exception e){System.out.println(e);};

mths = 0;
capo = cap;

while ((capo > 0.0) && (capo <= cap)) {
  capo = capo + (capo * interest/100.0/12.0) - rpay;
  mths++;
  }
if (capo <= 0.0) {
  fpay = rpay + capo;
```

```
   capt = rpay * mths + capo;
   System.out.println("Repayment period " + mths + " months");
   System.out.println("Final month's payment " + fpay);
   System.out.println("Total amount paid " + capt);
   }
 else {
   System.out.println("Interest exceeds monthly payments");
   }
   }
   }
```

Figure 12.5 An Example of Java code.

When you run the program it will ask you to type in:

- Value of loan: e.g. 2000
- Annual interest: e.g. 10 (i.e. 10%)
- Monthly repayments: e.g. 100

The program then does the calculations and, using the above example figures, gives the answers (we could cut the excessive decimal places but it would require extra coding):

- Repayment period 22 months
- Final month's payment 96.97435707392518
- Total amount paid 2196.974357073925

This example is no more than a snippet. To be useful in an Information System it would need, among other things, to take data from a formatted screen, validate that data, update a database and then present the user with another formatted screen for the next stage in the processing. All of that would require a lot more programming than the example given here.

A system may be a free-standing package on a PC, software on the client within a client-server system or part of a multi-user server system. For the latter two cases, the modules will have to fit within an overall architecture that includes network handling and multi-user provision. Most Information Systems consist of many modules and very often many thousands of lines of code. All of this software should be carefully planned, designed and tested.

It is not the purpose of this book to teach programming – you may be undertaking a separate, introductory, programming module, and there will be a separate recommended text for that unit.

Testing

testing: checking that the software works by submitting test data and checking that the results achieved meet expectations.

Once the software has been written, generated or bought it must be tested, and some of that **testing** is likely to be the province of the IS specialist. Testing can take a number of forms but a basic classification would be:

- Module test: This is where the basic unit of programming, the module, is tested to check that it does the task expected of it. The test is normally the responsibility of the programmer who wrote the code. Once the module is thoroughly tested we should be able to assume it to be internally correct when we use it in later stages of testing. Module-testing can be referred to as a white box test – the test is designed with knowledge of the internal logic of the module.

- Link test: Having checked all the separate modules we can put them together as a program (or subsystem) and check that they work together. This test is likely to be done within the programming team. Given that the modules have already been tested, the focus of this stage is the interfaces between the modules – the modules can be considered as black boxes.
- System test: This requires that the whole system be put together and tested in a live environment. At one level this is a scaled-up link test, but it is also required to test that the data meets the requirements of all subsystems and that the system will cope with the volumes (of data and users) that will occur in live operations.
- Acceptance test: The first three stages of testing are within the project team. The final stage of testing is for the users of the system; it is a final check that the system is an effective business tool. With general-purpose software, such as a Microsoft product, the acceptance test is carried out by pre-release of the package to selected users; this is commonly referred to as the *beta test* (with the internal testing being called the *alpha test*).

The stages in testing a system can be matched to the stages of the design process; this is called the V model and is shown in *Figure 12.6*.

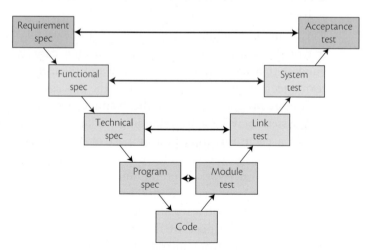

Figure 12.6 Specification and testing – the V model.

Testing, done properly, is a time-consuming business. Programs are (generally) complex pieces of logic and to test most/every path requires careful planning and extensive preparation. It is only by thorough testing of software that we can be confident that it is fit for purpose. The extent of the testing is dependent on the complexity of the system and the degree of importance placed on reliability. The requirement for reliability of (say) a student registration system is rather less than a banking system and a lot less than for an operating system or the software control systems in an aircraft. The amount of project time spent testing can range from (say) 20 per cent up to as much as 60 per cent where reliability is of crucial importance (which is several orders of magnitude greater than the time spent by most students testing any programming assignment that they might undertake).

It is to be noted that while testing needs to be rigorous it does not prove that the software is correct. In the words of Dijkstra (1972), one of the early programming gurus:

> Testing proves the presence of bugs, not their absence.

Implementation

implementation: the act of taking a new Information System from its development stages and installing it for operational use.

Once the system is tested it is time to start reaping the benefit from all the time, money and effort that has been put into developing the system – the system has to be made live.

Implementation of a system will often be a mini project in itself. Tasks that are involved in putting the system live (some of which will have been started during earlier stages of the project) include:

- Installation of new IT equipment: The new system will need the appropriate IT infrastructure. It may be that the new system will run on the existing infrastructure with no alteration or with some minor enhancements. For some large new systems the existing infrastructure may have to be enhanced or replaced, which can become a sub-project in its own right.
- Data capture and data cutover: The data from the existing system (manual or IT) has to be typed into, or converted over to, the new system. For a large organization this can involve many thousands of records and special software may have to be written to make the conversion. It may also have to be a last-minute job as existing data will be changing in the current system up to the time of the switch-over to the new system.
- Training: The users and technical staff, who will be operating and supporting the new system, need to be trained for that system. The training needs to be thorough if the new system is to operate efficiently but the training also needs to be fitted in with minimum disruption to existing operations. Training needs to be supplemented with appropriate documentation and/or help facilities that are built into the software.

The way the system is to be put live also needs to be considered. There are a number of approaches, which can be summarized as follows:

- Big bang: This is where the organization switches off the old system on (say) Friday night and the new system starts on Monday morning. The weekend is spent doing the data conversions, setting up the system and some final confidence tests. For a large system this can be a very full weekend, since the smooth operation of all aspects of the process is crucial.
- Staged roll-out: Sometimes it is possible to implement a new system in stages. This may involve implementing it in one department or branch at a time or it can involve implementing one subsystem at a time. Such an approach is obviously less risky than the big bang approach but it may not suit the nature of the system and/or the operation. The staged approach would, for

4

example, require that the standing data (customers, products or whatever) to be maintained on both the old and new system, which may not be practical.

- Parallel running: This is the safest option but, in most cases, it is not a practical option. Parallel running involves running both the old system and the new system for a few weeks. Data has to be updated and transactions processed through both systems. The outputs from both systems can be compared, and, when the new system is demonstrated to be functioning correctly and reliably, it takes over the operation and the old system is switched off.

As well as an implementation strategy there is normally a fall-back strategy. If things go disastrously wrong, and there is no way to fix the problems quickly, then the organization needs to go back to the existing system to keep the business running. Some implementations are so complex that there is no way back (keep your fingers crossed!).

Whatever approach (or combination of approaches) is used for the implementation of a system it is likely to be a somewhat fraught process. Careful planning and appropriate rehearsals will minimize the risks involved.

Project failures

Many, or even most, new Information Systems do not meet expectations. It is almost accepted as normal that new IS will be delivered late and over budget. Many new IS also fail to achieve their objectives in cost savings and improved business processes. The reasons for these problems are many and various; the roots of the failure will almost inevitably be back in the earlier stages of the system development lifecycle. Problems that can arise include:

- Poor estimating of the time and expense of developing the new IS. Estimating is a very inexact science, and on top of how long an IT job should take is the problem of how long it will take when things go wrong or changes are required. Often there is pressure to come in with a low estimate so that the project can meet the planned budget/cost-benefit analysis, only for the project plan to unravel over time.
- Inadequate sizing. A project of any size or complexity should be sized (how many transactions are there and how long will each one take). Each online transaction has to access and update the database, and all those disk accesses take time. If you factor in the number of concurrent transactions and the database overheads of indexes and the like it is very easy to hit contention, delay and, ultimately, system failure. Each batch transaction accesses a large number of database records, and optimizing the database for online access will have made the data design (very) inefficient for batch work. The system needs to be properly sized – so you should do the sums, and if the sums do not work the design needs to be optimized and/or more, faster kit must be bought.
- User requirements not adequately researched. There is a tendency to listen too much to the management and/or to think that the IS/IT people know best. The people who know how the system works (and what works well and what does not) are actually the people who operate the current system and who will have to work with the new system – listen to them. Also listen to their *war stories* about how they have to bend the current system to get

the job done. Obviously, one must also listen to management, who set the strategic direction (and pay the bills), but they frequently underestimate the complexity of the work their staff do and the difficulties of the environment they have to operate in.

- Changes. As soon as the project team think they know what they are doing changes come along – and changes are disruptive and costly (whatever the agile development people may say). Changes are particularly problematic if they affect the underlying data model, so you need to create a firm foundation by getting that right.

Another area of failure is bought-in software such as ERP systems. ERP systems tend to be large and ERP projects are expensive. Problems arise because:

- Software sales representatives make over-inflated claims for their software. Sometimes they will sell a software package, or features, that are still in design (while presenting them as fully available facilities).
- The ERP not only replaces existing systems but will normally impose changes on the business processes. Many organizations find it difficult to accept (or even recognize) these changes, or are slow to adapt to the change, and so lose competitive features of current business practice that are not supported by the ERP system.
- Installing a new ERP system is a major project and it should be undertaken by experienced (and hence expensive) staff; some organizations try to save money by not employing experienced consultants and as a result get into difficulty. Intuitively, installing ready written, off-the-shelf software should not be too difficult, but apparently the opposite is the case.

The extent of failure with new Information Systems is difficult to determine. Many companies keep quiet about their difficulties (and there is also the question of how one might define failure). Some systems are simply not completed or implemented: the UK Government has recently abandoned its National Health Service (NHS) Electronic Patient Record Project after over ten years and in excess of £10 billion expenditure (although some parts of the system did get to be implemented). Some systems end up in court, with the client suing the software provider or the outsourced project team company. Some systems that do go live subsequently undergo a lengthy and expensive upgrade program before they are fit for purpose.

Arguably, over the years, it has become more difficult to produce and implement a new Information System successfully. In the early days of computerization a new IS would replace a manual system and the operation would be relatively simple (although the IT could be more challenging than today's kit) – today the new IS will very possibly be replacing a fourth or fifth generation of the application and the users (stakeholders) will expect a very capable and sophisticated provision. An alternative scenario is that the organization will be trying to apply IS/IT to a process that is not readily computable (computers are great for calculation and record-keeping but not so good for more unstructured decision-making – an example could be social work where the application of IS seems simply to create bureaucracy without contributing anything to the real purpose of social work, which is case work with clients).

An example of a system that got into trouble is the UK courts' Libra system (see the *Libra case study*). It is noted that a large number of system failures seem to occur in the public sector but note that the public sector can't hush up their failures in the way the private sector can and do. It is also worth noting that the public sector will often let a system run for a number of years before seeking a complete replacement whereas a private organization may well make incremental changes to their systems and hence avoid the need for so many dramatic, big bang, changes.

Case study
Libra

The Libra system is a UK court service's system for case management in the Magistrates' courts. The process of replacing the courts' IS/IT started in 1992. There were many problems and several suppliers were involved. A central issue was whether the system should be used to standardize business practice across all the magistrates' courts or whether it should accommodate the differing practice and procedures that were applied in different courts. By 2008 the costs had risen from £146 million to £447 million and the system was live in only 83 out of 370 magistrate courts; at that time, the problems seemed to be largely solved. However, in 2011 the system was back in the news with the National Audit Office rejecting the court service's accounts because of inadequacies in the financial information available from the Libra system.

Meanwhile the Crown courts were, in 2009, running the 20-year-old Crest system (on computers where the operating system is no longer supported by the manufacturer). One problem was the lack of facility to transfer electronic data, which led to duplication and the risk of errors as staff had to rekey data. It is planned to *replatform* Crest, that is, to re-implement the old existing system onto a new IT infrastructure.

Note that the Crown court tries major crimes whereas the Magistrates' court deals with more minor offences.

Such problems are not unique to the UK. In 2010 the California courts installed a new system reportedly costing $1billion. It is claimed that the system gives vastly improved functionality – that is the management story. The view from the shop floor seems to be rather different. For example, they report that it takes eight times longer than the old system to do routine tasks, when it works at all. The issue is set to go to court (is there an irony there?).

Sources include: ComputerWeekly (2008), Collins (2011), BBC (2009), 10News (2010).

Maintenance

maintenance: for live Information Systems, maintenance involves error correction, enhancement and installing new releases.

Implementing the system is not the end of the story. Once the system is in use it requires maintenance: the system has to be corrected, enhanced and users will need support. Many medium to large organizations have a help desk system where users can raise problems. The help desk answers simple queries and passes on those it cannot handle:

- First-level support sorts out problems with the desktop environment and queries about the IS.
- Second-level support takes over where the problem is more complex – all problems that require changes to the application software are the province of second-level support. Large application systems have their own dedicated maintenance teams.

- Third-level support becomes involved if the problem is more technical involving the system software of the IT installation.

Maintenance also includes enhancements to the system. Business requirements are not set in concrete and the Information Systems need to evolve with changing business requirements and business expectations. Enhancements normally involve a request for change procedure where each proposal is costed, evaluated and prioritized. Where possible, enhancements are batched and included in a new release of the system.

In most organizations some systems are crucial to the day-to-day operation of the organization. Examples of this are the EPOS systems in supermarkets and the ATMs at the banks – these are generally reliable but, should they fail – and they do – the inconvenience and damage to business reputation is considerable. Robust maintenance procedures are essential. Systems normally have maintenance environments that match the live environment where bug-fixes and enhancements can be thoroughly tested before they are put live. Part of the maintenance procedures can be a regression test – this is a comprehensive set of tests that are run before any revised version of the system can be put live.

Even given robust maintenance procedures it is not unknown for changes to live systems to cause serious system failure (see the **_BlackBerry service failure case study_**).

Case study
BlackBerry service failure

The BlackBerry, made by the Canadian firm Research In Motion (RIM), has been the smartphone of choice for businesses and their employees. That lead in the business market has been built on a reputation for reliability and the provision of the BlackBerry secure messaging service. RIM's lead in this market has been challenged by the Apple iPhone, with some large corporate customers switching or giving their executives a choice of handset.

© Peterfactors/Fotolia

On Monday 10 October 2011 the BlackBerry messaging and e-Mail services in Europe started to fail. The problem was reportedly caused by a planned upgrade to the UK data centre. The problem was compounded by the failure of the backup system to take over from the failed system; the switch to the backup system should have been automatic. It is claimed that the problem was quickly fixed but all the time the system was out there were new messages building up. The message build-up then slowed, or stopped, the BlackBerry service to customers in other continents.

Full service was restored on the Thursday, three full days after the problem started. In those three days many business people had been deprived of their messages. No doubt some of these messages were time-critical and real problems were caused. Overall there was considerable damage to RIM's reputation as it battles with Apple for the business smartphone market. The problem was widely reported in the media, which compounded RIM's reputational problems.

Sources include the Guardian (Associated Press, 2011) and Computerworld UK (Savvas, 2011).

4

Further reading

Books recommended for further reading are:

Cadle, J., and Yates, D. (2008) *Project Management for Information Systems*, 5th ed., Pearson, Harlow.
Charatan, Q. and Kans, A. (2009) *Java in Two Semesters*, 3rd ed., McGraw-Hill, Maidenhead.

Comprehension test

This is a simple test to enable you to check you have absorbed the material presented in *Chapter 12*.

Q1 Which of the following programming languages is notable for being portable across differing platforms (without the need to recompile)?

    a. Cobol ☐

    b. C, C++, C# ☐

    c. Java ☐

    d. Visual Basic ☐

Q2 A new business system should be tested by the users to check that it is an effective business tool – which of the following is the user's test?

    a. Module test ☐

    b. Link test ☐

    c. System test ☐

    d. Acceptance test ☐

Q3 One approach to implementing a system is to simply switch off the old system at the end of one day and start the new system at the start of the next (working) day – this approach is called:

    a. Hot transfer ☐

    b. Big bang ☐

    c. Cliff-edge implementation ☐

    d. Kamikaze ☐

Q4 A comprehensive system test used in maintenance before a new version of a system can be released for live running is:

    a. Alpha test ☐

    b. Beta test ☐

    c. Regression test ☐

    d. Black box test ☐

Q5 The acronym PERT stands for:

    a. Project economics and resources target ☐

    b. Project evaluation and review technique ☐

    c. Proceed evaluate review terminate ☐

    d. Program evaluation and review technique ☐

Exercises

The following exercises are designed to aid your understanding of the material presented in this chapter. They can be used for self-study or selected exercises can be used for tutorial discussion.

1 **Comprehension** This chapter includes a sample Java program. If you have access to a Java development environment (and you are not a Java programmer) – type in the example program, try to understand the logic and try it out with some fresh data. You could keep the principle borrowed but vary the interest rate and/or repayments to see the effect. What would the effect be on the total amount paid if the interest remained at 10 per cent but the monthly payments were set at £50?

2 **Comprehension** A university department is intending to build a new computer lab. The following tasks have been identified:

- a1 Build stud walls to form the new lab – 10 days
- a2 Decorate – 5 days
- a3 Install power supply and network cables (after the walls but before the room is decorated) – 5 days
- a4 Order/delivery period for computer equipment – 20 days
- a5 Order/delivery period for power and network materials – 15 days
- a6 Install and test computer equipment – 10 days.

Work out the dependencies (they should be fairly obvious) and draw a PERT chart. Identify the critical path and the minimum elapse time (people only do a five-day working week).

We have six weeks before the start of term – can we do it?

The power and network material (a5) is 10 days late – what is the effect on the critical path and the minimum elapse time (if any)?

3 **Comprehension** Draw a Gantt chart for the project in q2. Task a1 requires three people, a2 is two people, a3 is two people and a6 is five people (tasks a4 and a5 do not require any people).

4 **Discussion** This chapter instances a very problematic implementation of IS/IT in the court services. Look online for examples of other IS projects that got into difficulty and initiate a class discussion to see what lessons might be learnt. Note that a number of failed IS systems involve bought-in software (e.g. ERP systems), outsourcing and off-shoring – consider whether (or not) there were contributing factors.

4

PART 5 INFORMATION SYSTEMS AND SOCIETY

The rapid development of Information Technology and the widespread use of Information Systems are affecting all aspects of our lives. IS/IT are part of our lives whether we are working, studying, shopping or dealing with officialdom – very often even when we relax or entertain ourselves. The cumulative result of all these changes in and applications of technology gives us what has been called the Information Society.

One necessary response to issues raised by the Information Society is to provide a legal framework for it to operate in. In the case of IT, many areas of its application are covered by existing law. Two areas where new law has been required are computer misuse (commonly summed up as hacking) and the privacy of personal data/data protection (not a new issue but one that has been brought to the fore by the extensive use of IS). The issue of computing and the law is addressed in *Chapter 13*.

The extensive application of IS and IT also has an environmental impact. Negative effects of the use of IT include increased power consumption and the problem of disposing of unwanted IT kit. Benefits include using computers to create energy efficiency and computer applications in the study of environmental science. Green Computing is the topic of the second part of *Chapter 13*.

Living in the Information Society can be seen as beneficial but it produces its own challenges and threats. As with all technologies, there is a need for responsibility. The nature of the Information Society is examined in *Chapter 14*.

IS/IT professionals have a vital role in the creation of the Information Society. To help us perform that role, computing is recognized as a profession and there are professional associations in many countries that exist to help develop and regulate the profession. The principal professional association for IS/IT in the UK is the BCS, the Chartered Institute for IT; we look at the BCS in the second part of *Chapter 14*.

Finally, as Business or Computing students you will, presumably, be aiming to get a job at the end of your studies. A brief overview of the computing/IS job market is provided at the end of *Chapter 14*.

13 COMPUTING, THE LAW AND THE ENVIRONMENT

Summary

Computer systems are used for both personal and business purposes. The users of computers require that the systems, and the data they contain, are secure. A deliberate attempt to compromise the operating of a computer system, to access private data without authorization or to use a computer system for fraudulent purposes may well be an illegal act.

For most purposes, illegal actions performed on or using a computer system can be prosecuted under general legalization – this would include theft perpetrated using a computer system and breaches of the copyright of electronic media. One area where specific computing law has been drawn up is the area of computer misuse: in the UK this is addressed by the Computer Misuse Act (1990). A second area of concern, that has been brought to the fore by the widespread use of Information Systems, is that of personal privacy; this issue is addressed by an EU directive and, in the UK, that directive is implemented in the Data Protection Act (1998). The application of the law in the field of computing is reviewed in this chapter.

Computer systems have an environmental impact. The environmental impact of IT concerns how we build and distribute the kit, the energy used in operating the equipment and the disposal of the IT when it is no longer required. The environmental impact of an individual PC is small. The impact of all our computers: personal, business and the many servers in data centres is significant. Manufacturers and users of IT should take account of their impact – it makes sense for the environment and it makes sense economically.

The issue of computers and the environment – green computing – is also reviewed in this chapter.

© Elenathewise/Fotolia

Learning outcomes

Having read this chapter and completed the exercises, you should:

- Be aware of how computer systems can be involved in, and used for, illegal activity
- Appreciate the issue of computer misuse and the application of the law in this area
- Appreciate the issue of data privacy and data protection and the application of the law in this area
- Understand the environmental impact of computing and measures that can, and should, be taken by manufacturers and users to minimize negative effects.

Key terms

Contract, intellectual property, copyright, patent, identity theft, Computer Misuse Act (CMA), hacking, Data Protection Act (DPA), information commissioner, data controller, data subject, green computing, global warming, recycle.

Computing and the law

The use of IS and IT is extensive in administration, commerce and in people's private lives. As with all other areas of human activity the law can be invoked when things go wrong and it can be appropriate to take legal precautions before things get to that stage. Much of the law that applies to the provision of IT services and the use of Information Systems is the same law that applies where IT is not explicitly involved. Examples of areas where the law has had to be interpreted and/or applied for an electronic age include:

contract: an agreement between two parties. A legally enforceable contract requires an offer, acceptance and consideration (exchange of value).

- Electronic **contracts**: The traditional way of making a contract is on paper; in some cases the written agreement will be signed by the contracting parties. However, with electronic data interchange (EDI) and internet e-Commerce the transaction, and hence the contract, is electronic. The question then arises as to whether the contract is legally enforceable and at what stage in the exchanges the contract came into force. The answer is complex. It depends, in part, on what the contract was for and hence which pieces of legislation apply. Many types of trade transaction can be carried out electronically but some exchanges specify paper documentation.

  The general form of an exchange of contract has three steps:

  - An invitation to treat: John wants to sell his second-hand Bob Dylan CD for £2. This is, in effect, an advert. It has no legal status and John can put the price up, sell the CD to anyone or withdraw it from sale.
  - An offer: Susan says 'OK John, sounds cool. I will give you £2 for your Bob Dylan CD'.
  - Acceptance (of the offer unmodified): John says 'Done – you Susan can have my Bob Dylan CD for £2'.

  These three stages are neatly demonstrated in an e-Shop. The invitation is the goods displayed on the screen; the offer is the order form (for retail transactions that is accompanied by payment) and the acceptance is the confirmation screen. Other forms of electronic ordering, such as EDI, seem to (often) miss out the acceptance stage, but these transactions are usually covered by an interchange agreement. Generally, standard electronic trade exchanges, such as these, will not result in disputes (although there have been cases of goods offered online at mistakenly low prices and customers rushing to take advantage of the mistake). Electronic exchanges (e-Mails and electronic document transfers) can also be used for more complex transactions; in these exchanges, errors and delays in sending and receiving the documents could cause problems.

5

- Contracts for computer equipment and computer services: Contracts are also applicable to the purchase of computer hardware, software and the employment of IT staff. This can be an area of difficulty since IT and IS systems are complex and the outcomes of computer projects frequently fail to meet the expectations of the parties involved. Arguably, the best way to avoid disputes is for the parties involved to draw up a comprehensive and explicit contract before work is started or goods are delivered; however, it is difficult to be explicit and cover every possibility in a software development or outsourcing deal. That said, IT contracts are similar to other commercial transactions and the same laws apply. In the UK, the sale of computer hardware is subject to the Sale of Goods Act 1979 and the writing of bespoke software to the Supply of Goods and Services Act 1982. The legal position of contracts for *off-the-shelf* software is far from clear (Bainbridge, 2000). However contracts for goods and services work within the legal framework – that can mean that conditions within the contract are invalid or that conditions that are not stated apply. The Sale of Goods Act, for example, requires that goods must be of satisfactory quality; a piece of IT equipment that failed to operate effectively or continually broke down would seem to fail that test.

intellectual property: inventions protected by patent and original written material protected by copyright. Protection is provided against the unauthorized use, copying or sale of the protected material.

copyright: the right of an author to protect their creative, intangible work from copying and exploitation by others.

patent: the right of an inventor to protect their tangible work from copying and exploitation by others.

- **Intellectual property** (IT equipment and software): Intellectual property rights (IPRs) include **copyright** and **patent** laws. The purpose of these laws is that an inventor of a new device or the author of a document can benefit from their work without others making unauthorized use of the ideas and material. Legal protection has existed in these areas for many years, but the use of computers raises the questions of how to apply patents and copyright laws to something as essentially intangible as software and to material that exists, or is to be reproduced, in electronic form. The answer seems to be that patents apply to hardware while software, and other forms of original work that are electronically recorded, are subject to copyright protection. The applicability of copyright law to software has been made explicit in the Copyright, Designs and Patents Act 1988.

- Intellectual property (electronic material): Intellectual property rights (IPRs), in the form of copyright, also apply to electronic material such as digital versions of music, films and books. A common channel for the sale of artistic creations is the internet. Where this material is for sale, the publisher charges for a copy of the material and the creator is recompensed by a royalty payable on each copy sold. The sale of copyright material gives circumscribed rights to the purchaser that generally exclude the reproduction of the material. The sale of illegal copies was difficult to control when these products were distributed on tangible media – it is even more difficult to control when the material can be downloaded from the internet, and as a result there is a widespread trade in the download of unauthorized copies. The law of copyright still applies but is difficult to enforce. The source of the material is a website that may be owned or operated in any country – another legal jurisdiction – and hence be difficult to prosecute. Owners of copyright or their representatives, most notably the Motion Picture Association of America, have sought to protect their copyright by pursuing intermediaries such as ISPs and search engines which are channels through which the illegal downloading of copyright material can take place. These channels are resisting attempts to blame them for copyright piracy or to require them to introduce measures to prevent illegal downloading. It is an ongoing battle.

Case study
Copyright wars

Do you want to have a copy of an album track or a film that is readily available online? You may find that it is just as easy to find a pirate copy as a legitimate, paid for, copy.

The owners of the copyright, typically corporate record labels and film companies, want to stop the pirates – they are losing a lot of revenue (and the artists can be missing out on royalties as well). The problem is that the pirates are difficult to stop (and chasing the downloader, often a young person, is not a great option either). So an alternative approach is to go after the *channel* – the internet service provider (ISP) and/or the search engine, which are big cooperates and *we know where they live*. The ISPs and the search engines reply that, while they do not condone piracy, it is not their job to censor the content they find and transmit – and it would not work even if they tried.

Copyright wars have been going on for at least 30 years (initially with the copying of physical media and latterly with pirate downloads). There have been attempts to legislate in a number of countries, particularly in the US; the problem is that it is difficult to come up with a measure that is both proportionate and effective.

In 2012 the US considered legalization sponsored by the Motion Picture Association of America (MPAA) and the Recording Industry Association of America (RIAA). The Senate was looking at SOPA (Stop Online Piracy Act), the Congress a parallel measure called PIPA (Protect Intellectual Property Act) and there was an international treaty sponsored by the US called ACTA (Anti-Counterfeiting Trade Agreement). Campaigning against the acts and the treaty were a wide range of internet and free speech activists, backed (or incited) by many big name internet companies. One notable action, in the widespread opposition campaign, was that Wikipedia was taken offline for the day as a form of protest. In the end PIPA and SOPA were stopped and ACTA has only made limited progress in gaining international ratification.

The issues at stake are not just piracy but the freedom of the internet and the nature of copyright. As Jimmy Wales (of Wikipedia) said:

> The internet has changed the world so much that current legislation is not adequate. What are the legitimate limits to copyright? What's the ethical norm for copying? None of that is clear yet. It's going to take time to work that out.

This is an issue that is of concern to this author. There is copyright material that would helpfully have been included in this book but had to be left out because of copyright restrictions, yet that material might be readily available (legally or not) on the internet for free.

The expectation is that MPAA, RIAA and other copyright owners will be back again and that their proposals will not just target the pirates (because, to be fair, that is too difficult). The chance of any settlement on how copyright material can be incorporated in rational discourse, in the internet age, does not seem likely to be resolved any time soon.

Sources include Rushe (2012a).

5

- Theft and forgery (from organizations): Computers are used for many financial transactions; arguably, the smart way to rob a bank is electronically (rather than with a pick-axe handle and a stocking mask). Many computer crimes are inside jobs – perpetrated by an employee of the company or the bank. An example is an employee of Lloyds TSB who stole more than GB£2 million from 38 accounts – he used the money to set up house and maintain the country's biggest collection of exotic birds (Allison, 2003). A more subtle way of using the computer for theft is a technique known as *salami-slicing* where small amounts are taken from many accounts using procedures written into the banking or accounting software. One such fraud rounded all calculations down to the nearest penny and then transferred the fractions of a penny to the perpetrator's own account – in the course of thousands of transactions a tidy sum was accumulated. The vehicle for the crime can be a computer, but the crime is still theft or forgery – the issue is detection, not which law is to be used for prosecution.

identity theft: the stealing of an individual's personal details – usually with the intent of using the details for a fraudulent purpose.

- Theft and forgery (from individuals): A growing problem is **identity theft** and credit/debit card fraud. This is not specifically a computing issue but personal information can sometimes be gathered online and credit/debit card details can be fraudulently used in e-Commerce transactions. The issue of preventing online fraud is looked at in *Chapter 5*. Identity theft is an offence that can be prosecuted under the Fraud Act and/or the Identity Document Act, although the likelihood of the fraudsters being caught appears to be slim. Some offences can also be prosecuted under the Computer Misuse Act, but this is not often used. The individual victim of identity theft is likely to be seriously inconvenienced – they may not lose their money but they will need to spend a lot of time seeking refunds, changing passwords and accounts and getting their credit rating corrected.

In the UK, two areas where legal provision has been made that is specific to the application and use of computers are:

- Computer misuse with the Computer Misuse Act of 1990
- Data protection with the Data Protection Acts of 1984 and 1998.

The Data Protection Act 1998 implements the EU Data Protection Directive, and there are similar provisions in all EU countries. These two IS/IT specific provisions are discussed below.

Computer Misuse Act

Computer Misuse Act (CMA): an Act dealing with inappropriate use of computers (hacking). It is an offence to obtain unauthorized access to a computer system and a more serious offence if content is changed or a crime is intended.

The UK **Computer Misuse Act (CMA)** 1990 was designed to deal with a number of *inappropriate* uses of computers that could not be effectively dealt with under existing law. The Computer Misuse Act is quite limited in its scope; it makes it an offence to:

hacking: finding security weaknesses in a computer or computer network and using them to gain unauthorized access.

- Obtain unauthorized access to computer material (section 1). The intention here is to deter **hacking**. It is the unauthorized access that is the offence and there does not need to be any damage done. Unauthorized access is only an offence if there was intent involved – if you are working on the university computer or on a website and stumble across something by accident then there is no offence.

- Obtain unauthorized access to a computer with the intent to commit or facilitate a serious crime (section 2). This is an extension of the first offence; Bainbridge (2000) suggests it can be summed up as *aggravated hacking*. The offence still applies whether or not the crime is committed (and even if it would not have been possible for the crime to have been committed). The example most often quoted is that of blackmail. It is an offence for someone to hack into another person's computer with the intent of finding material that could be used for blackmail, even if the blackmail is not committed; it is also an offence if the expected blackmail material did not exist or could not be found. Of course if the blackmail did take place, this could (also) be tried under the relevant statute.

- Deliberately make unauthorized changes to the content of a computer (section 3). This offence could include deliberately deleting files or creating and distributing malware that causes damage. The provision requires intent and knowledge – accidentally deleting a file or leaving bugs in a program are not offences.

  Bainbridge (2000) gives, as an example, the case of a nurse who was successfully prosecuted under section 3. The nurse hacked into the hospital computer and changed a patient's prescription in a way that was potential lethal – fortunately no harm was done to the patient and prosecution was limited to an offence under the Computer Misuse Act.

One problem that arises with computer crime is the question of where the offence was committed. I could (in theory at least) from my office in the university, hack into a computer in America and transfer funds to an account in Switzerland. The Computer Misuse Act tries to cover this by making its provisions applicable to acts that originate from the country or are directed at a computer within the country – that is, my actions could be prosecuted as they originated in the UK. It is also possible that the US or the Swiss authorities would wish to bring charges (although any prosecution in the UK, for a specific offence, would take precedence).

It is noted that the Computer Misuse Act does not seem to be much used – Turner (2012), for example, lists three cases in 2011 and five in 2010. Malware is a serious issue for computer users and the authors/publishers of malware could presumably be prosecuted under the Computer Misuse Act, if caught and if operating within the jurisdiction of the UK courts – this does not seem to happen (or it happens infrequently). The main defence against malware is the use of firewalls and antivirus software (see **Chapter 9**). It is also noted that the Computer Misuse Act is not applicable to physical acts against computer/IT systems where the Theft Act or the offence of criminal damage might apply.

For an example of a case brought under the Computer Misuse Act (CMA), see the **CMA *case study***.

Sources used for the section on the Computer Misuse Act include Bainbridge (2000) and Bott et al. (2000). Note that the intention here has been to give an outline of the Computer Misuse Act; this summary should not be seen as constituting legal advice.

5

On 13 May 11, a Salford University student, Paul McLoughlin, was given a suspended sentence of eight months for an offence under the Computer Misuse Act.

The student used malware to break into the personal and webmail accounts of about 100 victims. The malware was made available on a file-sharing network and was claimed to be a gaming utility; it incorporated a password stealing utility.

The case was brought to light by a victim in the US who complained to Salford University that her accounts had been compromised. The university reported the issue to the police. The police investigation was assisted by the antivirus software company McAfee.

The motivation for the scam seems to have been to gain access to free gaming facilities and to enable the originator to boost his online gaming scores.

Sources for this case study include Leyden (2011).

Data Protection Act

Computers allow the creation of large databanks of information. We have discussed how they can be created using an Information System and then used for management information. It is not necessary to have a computer to create and access information, but the use of IT increases the ease with which the data can be stored, searched, correlated and distributed.

The availability of information can be of great advantage in the administration of businesses and services. Yet where it is personal information that is involved, there is a risk that this availability will be seen as an infringement of personal privacy; further, it can cause the individual inconvenience or distress; ultimately, if misused, it is a threat to civil liberties.

Data Protection Act (DPA): an Act that sets out the rules governing the collection, storage and use of personal data by organizations.

In order to regulate the collection and use of personal data by organizations we have data protection legislation. The first UK **Data Protection Act (DPA)** was passed in 1984, and this was superseded by a second act in 1998. The 1998 act was passed to harmonize UK data protection legislation with the provision in other member states of the European Union. Data protection legislation applies only to personal data on living individuals. The Act has the underlying objective of protecting the individual from three potential dangers (Bott, et al., 2001):

- The use of personal information that is inaccurate, incomplete or irrelevant
- The possibility of personal information being accessed by unauthorized persons
- The use of personal information in a context, or for a purpose, other than that for which the information was collected.

The problems of incorrect information and the misuse of information have been illustrated by a number of cases – many of them more of an issue of people messing up than of intentional damage. Bainbridge (2000) quotes the case of a man who was charged with driving while disqualified because of convictions wrongly recorded on the police national computer. Another problem area is credit reference agencies that hold incorrect data or use data inappropriately – the result is that people are denied access to the credit, loans or mortgages for which they would otherwise qualify. A new area of concern relates to the increasing availability of genetic information and the possibility that this data could be used to deny people jobs and facilities such as insurance.

It should be noted that English law, including the Data Protection Act, does not give a general right to privacy. However, the Human Rights Act (1998), incorporating the European Convention on Human Rights into UK law, includes, in Article 8, a provision that everyone has the right to respect for their private family life, home and correspondence. The Human Rights Act is not specific to data protection and still requires interpretation by the courts. However, it seems likely that it will reinforce and extend a right to privacy.

The Data Protection Act (1998) is presided over by the **information commissioner**. The act provides a number of definitions, which include:

- **Data controller**: A person within the organization that holds the data, who determines the purpose and processing of the data. Organizations must designate a person (which can be the organization itself) as being responsible for personal data when they register with the office of the information commissioner.
- **Data subject**: A person who is the subject of personal data.

Under the Act, the data controller is required to notify the information commissioner of the purpose for which they will hold personal data and the processing they intend will take place on that data (there are exemptions to the requirement for notification). The Act also provides the information commissioner with powers to investigate the use of personal data by organizations. The investigation may be triggered by a request received from a data subject. The information commissioner can make rulings that may include, for example, a requirement to rectify or destroy inaccurate data. The information commissioner can issue enforcement notices, set a civil monetary penalty (fine) or bring a prosecution.

The Data Protection Act requires that anyone processing personal data must comply with eight principles of good practice. The principles require:

- Personal data shall be processed fairly and lawfully. The Act specifies the conditions under which it is lawful to process personal data. For *ordinary personal data*, such as names, addresses and telephone numbers, at least one of the conditions set out in Schedule 2 must be met. There is then a more stringent additional test for the processing of *sensitive personal data* where at least one of the conditions set out in Schedule 3 must be met. Sensitive personal data includes information relating to racial or ethnic origin, political opinions, religious beliefs, trade union membership, health, sex life and criminal convictions. One of the conditions set out in Schedule 2 is consent – the corresponding requirement in Schedule 3 is explicit consent. Schedule 2 includes several alternative conditions such as that the data is being used

information commissioner: the commissioner who is responsible for the implementation of the Data Protection Act and the Freedom of Information Act.

data controller: under the DPA, the person in an organization who determines the purposes for which and the manner in which any personal data are to be processed.

data subject: under the DPA, an individual who is the subject of personal data held by an organization.

5

to perform a contract between the parties or data that is necessary in order to comply with a legal obligation. For sensitive personal data, Schedule 3 alternative conditions include the meeting of legal requirements, medical reasons or to ensure/promote equal treatment of racial/ethnic groups.

- Personal data shall be processed for limited purposes. The requirement of the Act is that: *personal data shall be obtained only for one or more specified and lawful purpose, and shall not be further processed in any manner incompatible with that purpose or those purposes.* The purpose for which the data is collected must have been specified to the information commissioner and the data cannot then be used for other purposes.

- Personal data shall be adequate, relevant and not excessive. Put simply, this means that you shouldn't collect more data than you need for the purpose specified. Before you start asking people for their date of birth, religion or even their gender – think whether it is necessary for the declared purpose.

- Personal data shall be accurate and up to date. This requires that the data collection process is conducted with care and that, where necessary, it is updated. A common practice with, for example, staff records is to send out prints of the data on the system and to ask staff to sign as confirmation that it is correct or to update it if necessary.

- Personal data shall not be kept longer than necessary. This requirement is a difficult one (and one that many sources avoid commenting on). If we take as an example your university student record, how long should the university keep those details? Arguably, once the student has left the details can be erased – but what if the student asks for a reference a year later or a duplicate degree certificate ten years after graduation?

- Personal data shall be processed in accordance with the rights of the data subject. There are notices in the Act that prohibit processing that is likely to cause damage or distress, that limit the circumstances where personal data can be used for direct marketing and that relate to automatic decision-making.

  This principle also requires that the data subject is given access, on request, to their data, and details of why it is held and to whom it may be disclosed. This provision is subject to a reasonable administrative charge. A problem with this provision is it is only useful if you know that an organization is holding your personal data.

- Personal data must be kept secure. The requirements of the Act are that: *appropriate technical and organizational measures shall be taken against unauthorized or unlawful processing of personal data and against accidental loss or destruction of, or damage to, personal data.* This requirement is met by making the type of privacy and security provision that would be expected in IS/IT systems. These typically include appropriate virus checking, password-protected access (with access to systems and functions restricted to those staff who have a proper need to use the data) and regular backups of the data (and the backups also need to be subject to an appropriate privacy, security and disposal regime). These provisions are sensible precautions for all business systems – under the Data Protection

Act they become a statutory requirement for systems that store and process personal data.

- Personal data must not be transferred to countries without adequate data protection. The Data Protection Act derives from the Data Protection Directive of the European Community (now the European Union (EU)) and ensures that all EU countries have a similar level of protection for personal data. There are, however, many other countries in the world that have less stringent (or minimal) data protection requirements and so there is an obvious loophole if personal data can be transferred to a jurisdiction where it will not be protected – hence this final principle. This principle is particularly important where personal data is held by a multinational organization. It is to be noted that the US is one country with fairly minimal data protection provisions, which can cause problems since many multinationals are US-based. The use of e-Commerce and the internet add a further complication because it is not necessarily clear as to which countries' laws apply to a multinational online operation. Note that there are exceptions to this principle that include consent to transfer and data used in the performance of a contract.

The operation of two of these principles was illustrated by cases that came up in connection with the poll tax (introduced by the UK Government in 1989). The poll tax changed the basis of local taxation from a tax on property to a tax on the individual, with every adult person required to pay the tax to fund their local authority. The tax met with substantial opposition, including riots, and was subsequently replaced by the council tax (a local tax that is mainly based on property). The legislation in effect at that time was the 1984 Act, but the data protection principles were similar to the current act. The cases that came up stopped councils from:

- Cross-checking the poll tax register with the election register. Obviously there was a disincentive to fill in the forms to register to pay poll tax; it was thought that a cross-check with the list of voters might flush out some of the people who had failed to register. The ruling was that the purpose of the election register was to provide a list of voters and using it for the poll tax was outside that specified purpose.
- Collecting extensive details on the poll tax register. Councils were left to devise their own poll tax registers and many of them asked for extensive personal details on the registration form. The ruling was that the personal details that could be collected were to be limited to those details that were strictly necessary for the administration of the poll tax.

There are exemptions to the requirements of the Data Protection Act and its eight principles. These exemptions include national security and crime prevention. Exemptions can carry with them various qualifications, and usages of data and refusal to disclose data can be the subject of appeal.

Breaches of the Data Protection Act are investigated by the information commissioner who (as of 6 April 2010) has the power to issue civil monetary penalties (CMP), that is, fines of up to £500,000 for serious breaches of the Act. See, as an example, the **DPA case study** overleaf.

5

On 28 May 2012, the Brighton and Sussex University Hospitals NHS Trust were served with a civil monetary penalty (CMP) of £325,000 following a serious breach of the Data Protection Act.

The issue was the discovery of highly personal data belonging to tens of thousands of patients and staff on hard drives sold on an internet auction site.

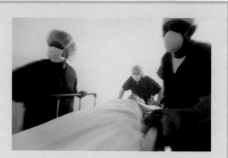

Source: Image 100

The Trust's IT is run by an outsourced service provider. The service provider had engaged an individual to destroy approximately 1000 hard drives that were no longer required. The individual removed at least 252 of the drives (as opposed to destroying them) including the four known to have been sold through the auction site and subsequently shown to contain confidential data.

The ICO Director of Data Protection is quoted as having said:

> The amount of the CMP issued in this case reflects the gravity and scale of the data breach. It sets an example for all organizations – both public and private – of the importance of keeping personal information secure. That said, patients of the NHS in particular rely on the service to keep their sensitive personal details secure. In this case, the Trust failed significantly in its duty to its patients, and also to its staff.

As a result of the case, the Trust committed to improving its security and systems. The commitment included an undertaking to vet IT suppliers and to use only ISO-accredited waste disposal companies.

Information for this case study is taken from the ICO's office ICOnews release, 1 June (ICO, 2012).

Sources used for the section on the Data Protection Act include Bainbridge (2000) and Bott et al. (2000). Note that the intention here has been to give an outline of the Data Protection Act; this summary should not be seen as constituting legal advice.

Green computing

green computing: programs aimed at reducing the resources used in constructing IT equipment, the energy consumption of that equipment and/or the effective and safe recycling of redundant equipment.

The environment, the growth of the world population and **global warming** are, or should be, of concern to us all. Computing is part of the problem:

- The manufacture and distribution of computers and IT equipment consumes resources and energy
- Computers, when operating, consume power and generate heat
- Redundant computers have to be disposed of – and as complex bits of kit, they are not easily recycled.

An individual PC may not, in itself, use a lot of power, but with many thousands of PCs and servers in use the consumption adds up. Estimates suggest that the energy bill for computing (and the associated cooling for data centres)

global warming: the expectation and concern that human activity such as deforestation and the burning of fossil fuels will change the composition of the atmosphere and hence cause climate change, global warming and widespread environmental damage.

could add up to 2 per cent of world energy consumption. The US Department of Energy estimates, quoted by Krishnan (2010), that US data centres represented 1.5 per cent of national energy usage, a figure that is rising at 12 per cent a year.

On the other side of the equation, computing and IT can be part of the solution to environmental issues:

- Computing can be used for electronic communications that are more environmentally friendly than some alternatives – for example, a teleconference as opposed to people travelling long distances to a meeting
- Computers can improve the efficiency of transport and machinery – the electronic fuel injection systems in cars being an everyday example
- Supercomputers are used to model the earth's resources and patterns of global warming to inform decision-making and environmental protection policy.

Environmental issues

Dell summarize their environmental policy as a lifecycle: design, build, ship, use and recycle (see *Figure 13.1*).

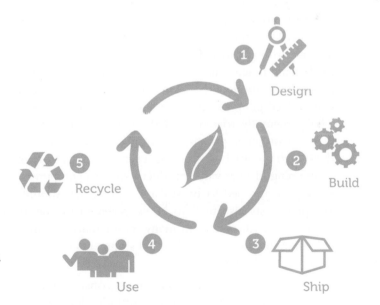

Figure 13.1 Computer Equipment Lifecycle (Dell, 2012) © 2012 Dell Inc. All Rights Reserved.

We can use this model to look at computers, IT manufacturers, IT users and their effect on the environment.

Design: making a complex product environmentally friendly starts at the design stage. Factors that affect the environmental impact of an IT product include:

- Avoidance of materials that are environmentally harmful
- Use of recycled materials where possible
- Designing the product to be as energy efficient as possible

5

- Designing the product for a long life, including the possibility of upgrades to extend the useful life of the product
- Designing the product for effective recycling when it is no longer required.

Manufacturers are designing their computer systems to meet industry, national and international standards; one such example is the US Environment Protection Agency's Energy Star that signifies an energy efficient system.

Build: Manufacturing processes need to be efficient in their use of materials and energy. Efficiency is both beneficial to the environment and (usually) good for the manufacturer – in effect, any waste of materials and energy is also a waste of money.

Computer/IT manufacture is a component assembly industry; hence, to be truly environmentally friendly, the same principles have to be applied by component manufacturers and the transport of components through the supply chain (although since components are generally small and light, transporting them can be less of an issue than it would be in many other industries).

Ship: New computers tend to arrive in large, substantial, cardboard containers and the shipping documentation often indicates that airfreight has played a part in the delivery process. Such packaging and shipping costs (in environmental and financial terms) may be inevitable, but they do deserve inspection.

Efforts are being made to produce packaging that is more environmentally friendly. Manufacturers are dispensing with the use of foam and making more use of cardboard (inside the box as well as for the box itself). Cardboard is made from renewable resources and can be recycled. Dell is using bamboo to make the *cushioning* that is included inside its packaging for product made in China. Dell point out that the bamboo is local, their production facilities are environmentally friendly and the material, once used, is compostable (Dell, 2012). Computer packaging can also be unofficially recycled with some of these high quality boxes getting a second life as storage containers.

Shipping of high value products, such as computers, tends to be by air and road – as opposed to by sea and rail, which should be more fuel efficient. Shipping costs also tend to be exacerbated by the move of manufacture to the Far East (distant from many major markets) and the practice of just-in-time manufacture (with individual shipments to customers as opposed to bulk deliveries to distributors).

Use: Computers, to state the obvious, consume electrical power and produce heat. The power consumption of an individual PC is not large (with desktop machines being more power hungry than laptops and mobile devices that are optimized for longer battery life). Newer PCs require less power than older PCs and flat screens are considerably more power efficient than the cathode ray tube monitors that we used to have. The energy usage of our PCs is reduced when it switches to standby mode and we can save even more power if we switch the PC off when it is not in use.

The power consumption and the heat generated by servers can be considerable – particularly where there are a number of servers collected together in a data centre or server farm. An example of a server farm is Facebook's new European server farm that is being built in Luleå, Sweden. The server farm will cover 30,000 sq metres and will be packed with IT equipment. The location in Sweden has the advantages of a cooler climate and the availability of renewable energy (Gersmann, 2011). One way to reduce the power consumption of data centres is to reduce the number of servers. There is a tendency to install a new server for each application/requirement, but this can be avoided by using existing machines that have spare capacity or by installing fewer, more powerful servers – the sharing of physical servers can be facilitated by creating a number of virtual servers on one machine.

recycle: the processing of used materials into new products. In green computing, the aim is to reuse redundant IT equipment or dispose of it in an environmentally friendly manner.

Recycle: The final stage in the lifecycle is to dispose of unwanted machines when they are replaced or no longer required. Some organizations have a policy of only using modern equipment and will have a replacement cycle of (say) three years – so there is a lot of relatively new IT kit being disposed of. Options for disposal include:

● Pass the old computer onto someone who will make good use of it – there are a number of charities who specialize in passing on unwanted IT kit to deserving/worthwhile causes. Computer Aid International is an example of such a charity – donors include Buckingham Palace.
● Use a recognized recycling contractor who will dismantle the equipment and ensure each part is recycled or properly disposed of.

Under the EU Waste Electrical and Electronic Equipment (WEEE) Directive, redundant computer equipment has to be disposed of responsibly and manufacturers have a responsibility to provide a disposal service. Despite this, many computers are inappropriately disposed of, with a considerable number being exported to third world countries to avoid local environmental regulations. Old IT kit contains valuable metals such as gold and copper but also contains dangerous substances such as mercury. Newer IT equipment should be easier to recycle: some of the dangerous substances have been eliminated in the design process.

One problem with the disposal of unwanted kit is that it will contain data, possibly sensitive data, on its hard drive (and just deleting the file does not remove that data). To be safe, operable hard drives must be overwritten (at the physical, as opposed to the file, level) and inoperable drives must be shredded.

Environmental solutions

The positive side of green computing is the use of computers and IT to save energy or to study climate change and help formulate environment policy.

Saving energy can come from not doing things or doing things more efficiently. Not doing things can include using ICTs for applications such as teleconferencing to avoid unnecessary travel. Doing things more efficiently includes developments such as:

● Embedded IT systems that make energy use more efficient. In a car this includes electronic fuel injection systems and technology that switches the engine off when the car is idling.
● Smart metering that has the potential to switch off unnecessary electricity consumption when the load on the electricity grid is high – postponing the cooling cycle of a refrigerator is the most quoted example.

5

An example of the use of computers in climate change science is the Community Earth System Model (CESM) that runs on a supercomputer. The word *community* in the Community Earth System Model reflects the fact that the model is a collective effort of climate researchers and computer scientists in numerous centres in the US. The supercomputer is used to simulate changes, on land, in the ocean and in the atmosphere using historic data and projecting forward to predict the effects of climate change.

One of the projects related to CESM is the work of Kate Evans at the US Oak Ridge National Laboratory (ORNL). Kate's specific project is working on modelling the thermomechanical properties of ice sheets such as those in Greenland and Antarctica; the results will be used to enhance the overall CESM model.

The supercomputer in use is Jaguar, a Cray XT5, with a calculation speed of 2.3 petaflops (ORNL, 2012) (see also the notes on supercomputing in *Chapter 6*). Despite the fact that the project uses one of the world's most powerful supercomputers, the scientists would still like more power to improve the resolution of their model and the granularity of their projections.

Further reading

Books recommended for further reading are:

Bainbridge, D. (2008), *Introduction to Information Technology Law*, 6th ed., Pearson, Harlow.
Bott, F. (2005) *Professional Issues in Information Technology*, BCS, Swindon.

See also websites:
Information commissioner: http://www.ico.gov.uk.

Comprehension test

This is a simple test to enable you to check you have absorbed the material presented in *Chapter 13*.

Q1 If you hack into a computer system, note some internal data/system details and then inform the owner of the website that their system has inadequate security you are, on the face of it, committing an offence under:

a. The Theft Act ☐

b. The Computer Misuse Act ☐

c. The Data Protection Act ☐

d. No offence has been committed. ☐

Q2 Organizations that hold personal data must register with:

a. The Home Office ☐

b. The information commissioner ☐

c. The data controller ☐

d. The data subject ☐

Q3 The Data Protection Act requires that the data subject:

- a. Agrees how long data is retained ☐
- b. Has a right to access the data that is held about them ☐
- c. Can require the deletion of data that is held about them ☐
- d. Provides information about their gender and ethnicity ☐

Q4 Which of the following are exempt from the provisions of the Data Protection Act?

- a. Educational establishments ☐
- b. Health service and crime prevention ☐
- c. National security and crime prevention ☐
- d. National security and health service ☐

Q5 Which of the following, under EU environmental law, must provide a disposal service for redundant IT equipment?

- a. The manufacturer ☐
- b. The local authority ☐
- c. The European Union (EU) ☐
- d. The Environment Agency ☐

Exercises

The following exercises are designed to aid your understanding of the material presented in this chapter. They can be used for self-study or selected exercises can be used for tutorial discussion.

1 **Discussion** Investigate the topic of hacking. What is the difference between a *white hat* and a *black hat* hacker? Some hackers group together to carry out hacking campaigns often with a political/protest motivation – look up *hackivism* and groups such as Anonymous (and any new groupings that might have emerged). Discuss the methods, motivations and ethics of hacking in a tutorial session.

2 **Discussion** When you applied and registered for your college or university you supplied personal details, further details about you were obtained via UCAS and that data was added to as you progressed through your course. Check:

- That your university is properly registered with the information commissioner – you can do this on the website of the ICO;
- That your university has a data protection policy – this should be available on the university website.

Check, for example, how long the university intends to retain your personal data. If the Data Protection Act is the subject of a tutorial discussion, check with your tutor the implications of the Act and university policy for his/her work.

3 **Discussion** As illustrated by the *Copyright wars case study*, there are many issues surrounding how copyright can and should be interpreted in an internet age. Issues include what should be protected and what should be shared; the responsibility of ISPs and search engines and how copyright can and should be enforced (should users of pirated material be subject to sanction). Investigate and discuss.

4 **Research** Find a computer energy consumption calculator online and work out the power consumption of your computer – compare with your colleagues. Note that you will need to know quite a lot of technical detail about your computer.

5

Summary

Computers and IT are part of our daily lives. We use them at home and work. We use them for entertainment and communications. They are an integral part of our social and commercial infrastructure. They are an essential part of modern life.

The importance of IS/IT, and its rapid development and expansion into most facets of our lives, has been labelled the Information Revolution. That revolution gives rise to notions of the post-industrial society, or more positively, the Information Society.

While the use of IS/IT is vital to the functioning of a modern society, it can also turn into a threat. It can facilitate the democratic process but it also has the potential to enable authoritarianism. Computers are at the heart of an efficient, modern economy and society – but what happens if and when the machine stops?

In this chapter we examine the Information Society and its implications. One group with a special responsibility for the development of the Information Society are the IT professionals. One forum that considers this responsibility and participates in policy formulation is the professional body for computing, in the UK the Chartered Institute for IT (BCS). The chapter considers the role of professional associations and the BCS.

Finally, if you have studied Information Systems as part of a business or computing qualification, your next step could be to find a job. This chapter gives a short overview of the job market for computing and IT specialists.

Learning outcomes

Having read this chapter and completed the exercises, you should:

- Understand and critically appraise the concept of the Information Society
- Understand the effects of the Information Society, positive and negative, on work, social interaction and automated systems
- Understand the potential effects of the Information Society on civil liberties
- Have knowledge of professional associations, specifically the Chartered Institute for IT (BCS). Understand the role of such organizations in their professional field and in society.

Source: Image Source

Key terms   Information Society, globalization, knowledge workers, social networking systems, safety-critical systems, e-Government, government-to-citizen (g2c), citizen-to-government (c2g), digital exclusion, civil liberties, professional society, Chartered Institute for IT (BCS), code of conduct.

The Information Society

Throughout the world, and in particular in the developed world, computers and IT have a part to play in almost every task or activity.

At home we use our computers to communicate and, more recently, computer technology has merged with television technology to facilitate services such as TV on demand. An emerging technology is the *smart home* with inbuilt computer control. The smart home has computers to control lighting, heating, security and entertainment systems – controlled by pre-set programs, a hand-held controller, or remotely using a smartphone or other internet-enabled devices.

When travelling we might buy our ticket online, check our train or bus on the computer-controlled display and read an e-Book or use WiFi services on the journey. Alternatively, we might be entertained by music on a personal MP3 player, with music downloaded from the internet. If travelling by car we might use a Sat Nav system (and the car has a fair number of embedded IT systems in it in any case – possibly one day the IT will drive the car for you).

On arriving at work, most of us login to check our e-Mails and students have to check their Facebook pages before any studying can possibly start (these tasks may have already been started, using a smartphone on the journey). Real work also usually involves a computer; this could be a desktop application, access to an IS on a server, use of an EPOS system in a shop or a computer-controlled production process on the factory floor. For many, work is location-independent – information and IS are accessible (almost) anywhere using online facilities, or cloud computing. At the college or university, lectures are delivered with the help (or hindrance) of computer-controlled teaching aids; students may take notes on their own laptops and they can also access material on the virtual learning environment (VLE).

Information Society: a society where the creation, distribution and manipulation of information is the most significant economic and cultural activity.

Because of this integration of computing, electronic media and electronic communications into so many aspects of life, our society has been described as the **Information Society**. This is a relatively recent phenomenon. The term was initially popularized by Tofler (1980) in his book *The Third Wave*. Yet perhaps the beginning of the Information Society can more accurately be dated to the general availability of the internet in the mid-1990s (when the commercial use of the internet was first allowed). The Information Society is evolving at a rapid rate and where it will lead us all has yet to be seen.

5

The Information Society, or Information Revolution, can be seen as one of several epoch changes that have occurred during the course of human history. Delineating these changes can be problematic (and is disputed), but the following three epoch-defining changes are suggested:

- The Agricultural Revolution
- The Industrial Revolution
- The Information Revolution.

The Information Revolution leads to the post-industrial society in which the factory system loses its relevance as workers do not need to congregate in factories or offices to complete their information-related tasks. Knowledge becomes the new capital and knowledge work is (at least potentially) location-independent.

Arguably, this view of societal change ignores the continuing need for production (mineral extraction, agriculture, manufacture and transport). The factory system remains the predominant model of production – albeit with ever increasing IT integration. The ability to efficiently process information and control supply chains has enabled production processes to be outsourced and offshored – with more and more manufacture being located in countries such as China, India and Brazil. These shifts in economic activity are referred to as **globalization**; IT is the technology of the Information Revolution that enables the processes of globalization.

globalization: the process of international integration, particularly in the fields of trade and financial transfers.

The concept of the Information Society is also criticized academically, for example by Webster (2005). Critics contend that a quantitative increase in information does not necessarily imply a qualitative social change. The concept, however, remains useful to us in examining the effect of IS and IT on society (which all would agree is significant). We will further examine the Information Society under the following aspects:

- Work in the Information Society
- Social interaction in the Information Society
- Automated systems
- e-Government
- Civil liberties.

The profound effect that the application of IS/IT is having on society means that some thought and care should be exercised in the way that IT is applied – we hope to create a better world, not the opposite. This requires a responsible attitude from government, business leaders and the IT profession as a whole. We look at professionalism in the second section of this chapter.

Work in the Information Society

If we were to look at an old factory, there would be a large area of workshop space with a small office building tacked on at the front. In contrast, a modern factory, if it looked like a factory at all, might have a large office block with a small workshop tacked on out the back. These changes reflect many things – they are the result of modern production methods, outsourcing of component manufacture and off-shoring of production, but they also reflect

knowledge workers:
a worker whose tasks involve the application of knowledge (as opposed to manual workers who manipulate tangible objects).

the move from manual work to knowledge work. Similar changes have also taken place in traditional industries such as mining, agriculture and transport: vast numbers of manual workers have been displaced by economic changes and automation, while **knowledge workers** form a growing proportion of the employed workforce.

In addition to the changes in the industrial sectors there has been a steady growth in the service industries. Service industries do require shop floor workers but many of the jobs are in administration, taken by knowledge workers. Some services, for instance the financial services (the UK's largest industry) do not deal in tangible goods and are (effectively) solely concerned with knowledge work. In addition to the private service sector there is public administration which is inherently concerned with administration and hence information processing.

Some knowledge workers have abandoned the office altogether and become teleworkers. A teleworker may be a professional working part time from home and combining (say) accountancy work with caring responsibilities. In other cases the teleworker can be making a lifestyle choice – there are examples of people who live on a Scottish island while maintaining IT systems in the southeast of England. Telework can be formal or informal. Informal teleworkers will be office-based but will occasionally work at home, for example, to finish a task or to avoid travel disruption.

The application of IT to administration has also changed (or has been part of a change in) the way that office work is done. There are two (very different) tendencies that can be detected:

- Empowerment: In some offices staff are being given more responsibility for individual cases (as opposed to a task being routed through a number of departments and being referred to supervisors for sign-off). The use of computing plays an important part in this process. Staff members can readily access the system for the information they need, update the system with the details of the cases in hand and then record the decisions that are made.
- Taylorism: The opposite tendency is to break down a job into component parts that can be processed simply and without much knowledge or skill being required – a process known as Taylorism (after the American engineer Fredrick W. Taylor) when applied to manufacturing processes. This tendency is exhibited in the increasing adoption of call centres where the expectation is that all transactions can be dealt with in accordance with a predefined script and with limited knowledge and access to information.

The use of IT in call centres facilitates a regimented approach to work. The IT records every task that each operator does and the performance of the operator can be assessed at the end of each shift. Some call centres have very regimented employment and supervision practices, which is often coupled with fairly low levels of pay. These types of employment practice, facilitated by IT, are likely to result in low levels of job satisfaction and high levels of staff turnover.

The use of IT has also created an industry supplying the IT equipment, developing the systems and supporting the users of the systems. The manufacture of IT equipment is, in many ways, like other manufacture, but technology

5

changes rapidly and suppliers have had to be quick to adopt technological advances and incorporate them into their products. Employment on the software side has also changed, with many of the skilled jobs moving to software companies and consultancies – some of them offshored. Jobs in user departments are now more concerned with end user support. In the IS service industry we have the help desk – the IT industry's own version of the call centre.

Knowledge of IS/IT is now a pre-requisite for many jobs. This is obviously the case in IT jobs but also for many other jobs where a degree of *IT literacy* is an advantage, if not a necessity.

Themes
The IS Business Model

The IS Business Model emphasized that the operations processes of organizations are backed up by, and work with, support functions and management. Also emphasized is that IS and IT are extensively applied within and across these areas. The organization also works within its environment, including transactions with that environment, and in the context of the technology that is pervasive in that environment. Information flows within the organization, at each level, and to and from the environment are crucial to the success of an organization in the Information Society. The IS Business Model is reproduced here.

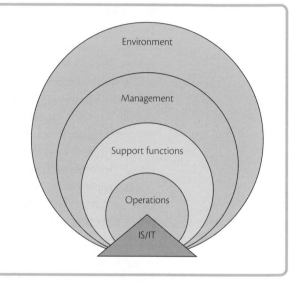

Social interaction in the Information Society

social networking systems: websites that give users the ability to record details about themselves and link to other people with whom they share interests.

In the Information Society we are starting to live much of our lives online using social networking systems (as most students will know better than the author of this book).

The largest social network at the time of writing is Facebook (see also the *Facebook case study* in the *Preface*). Facebook claimed 901 million active monthly users as at the end of March 2012. On Facebook members load all sorts of written and pictorial information about themselves and share it with their *friends*. Facebook is used to communicate with friends collectively or individually. It is just one of several social networking sites, but the others seem to be in decline (why join a site when none of your friends are on it?). Facebook is in constant development – part of the aim is to develop commercial revenue streams, but ordinary members do not always take well to such developments. New social network systems are attempting to enter the market, such as Google+, but whether they can create enough of a *network effect* to make inroads into Facebook's user base remains to be seen.

An alternative social network site for business people is LinkedIn which claims 150 million members. As the site states: *professionals use LinkedIn*

safety-critical system: a system where failure or malfunction may result in death or serious injury to people, loss or severe damage to equipment or environmental harm.

These systems are (or should be) protected by security and resilience measures, such as standby generators, duplex systems and strict malware protection (see *Chapter 9*). A safety-critical system should be written to relevant software engineering standards and be programmed to fail-safe (see the *Safety-critical systems explanation box*). Nevertheless, a complex, technological society is ultimately a vulnerable society.

Explanation Safety-critical systems

A safety-critical system is a system where failure or malfunction may result in death or serious injury to people, loss or severe damage to equipment, or environmental harm. Examples of such systems already quoted in the text include air traffic control, signalling and train control systems, and control systems in complex plants, such as a nuclear power station.

Safety-critical systems must conform to a reliability regime; examples of this are:

- Fail-safe: In the event of a failure the system should shut down (e.g. in railway signalling, if the system fails then all signals should be set to red)
- Fault-tolerant systems: Systems are duplicated; in the event of a fault in one system a second system, which has been running on hot standby, will take over (e.g. the control systems in a nuclear power station).

Software for safety-critical systems must be engineered to exacting software engineering

Source: Superstock

standards. There are standards for safety-critical software specified by relevant industry organizations, such as the aviation regulatory authorities. Formal methods, mathematical methods for specification, development and verification of software, are one of the techniques used in developing safety-critical systems.

e-Government

The government, both central and local government, has made extensive use of computing for many years. Not infrequently we hear about large government computing projects that go wrong (and there are examples of those in this book) but there are many more that are working well (possibly after initial problems) and administering programs such as income tax, state pensions, council tax and so on.

electronic government (e-Government): the use of IS/IT and internet access in the process of government.

Many of these systems are now getting an end user interface using internet e-commerce technology. The process is called electronic government (e-Government), the end user is us – the citizen – and so the model has been dubbed government-to-citizen (g2c). (Note that in the UK we are subjects, not citizens, but we will leave that one aside.) My favourite bit of UK e-Government is renewing my car tax (vehicle excise duty) – it is just so simple and hassle free. The process is summed up as follows:

government-to-citizen (g2c): e-Government transactions between the government and the citizen.

The DVLA (Driver and Vehicle Licensing Agency) post out a reminder about three weeks before the car tax is due. The form contains a reference number

5

and you type it in. The system checks with other data that you have current car insurance and a valid MOT (annual vehicle roadworthiness test) certificate. Pass those tests, you type in your payment details and a few days later the tax certificate arrives in the post. OK, the DVLA website is not too pretty and there is a lot of verbiage about special cases (important if they apply to you), but it beats digging out all that car paperwork and traipsing out to, and queuing up in, the post office.

The system is actually quite impressive. It links up with the insurance industry where all those companies who provide car insurance provide data on the car insurance policies they have issued. Similarly, it links up with systems that keep details of all MOT certificates (from small, often backstreet, MOT testing stations all over the country). It is a public agency working in close coordination with private sector partners, and it works. The same data and linkages also work for the police checking which cars are legal and which are not – including cars detected using automatic number plate recognition technology on gantries on the motorways.

The DVLA system is part of a program we call e-Government which the UK Government brands *Directgov: Public services all in one place*, with its own web domain .gov.uk. The Directgov website has a long list of topics that can be addressed online (and no doubt many more at lower levels of the indexing system) – picking a few examples, we can start the process of applying for a passport, research student finance or apply for a job. Some of these topics are just advice, for some there is an online form to download and in a few cases, as in the car tax example above, the job can be done online.

In a similar way to central government, local government – the county councils, district councils (boroughs in London) and unitary authorities (that in some areas combine the role of county and district council) – are rolling out e-Government. Hantsweb is the e-Government site of Hampshire County Council, giving local news and access to local facilities. Hampshire is a county council – there are 11 district councils within the county and again each has its own e-Government webpage, Winchester City Council being one example. Hampshire County Council and its chief information officer (CIO) is the subject of one of our **Managing Information Systems in the 21st Century** videos.

It is to be noted that the number of transactions that can be done entirely online is limited. Part of the issue is that governments are putting online service transactions that were designed to be conducted on paper and over the counter. There is also the issue that the e-Government provision has to follow legislation that can seem to make simple transactions overly complex (there can be a lot of exemptions and special cases provided for and, whatever their merits, they do not make for simple transactions). However, there are also the crucial issues of privacy and security. To take but one example, obtaining a passport must be a secure transaction – the government needs to know that the person applying is the person they say they are, and that sort of information can be much more secure (but not guaranteed) if the application is carried out in person.

Managing Information Systems in the 21st Century: Jos Creese

Jos Creese is the Chief Information Officer (CIO) for Hampshire County Council. In addition to running the IT group of technology and business professionals, Jos supports a variety of business change programmes enabled by IT for the Council. Hampshire IT also provides services to several hundred other public sector organizations, and demands for shared services are growing.

Jos has over 25 years of IT management experience, and has worked for central government, district and unitary councils. He is the founder and chair of the Local Public Service CIO Council, a member of the National Government CIO Council and was president of Socitm (the membership association for all ICT professionals working in Local Authorities and the Public and Third Sectors) in 2010/11. In 2011 he was voted the most innovative and influential UK CIO in the Silicon CIO50 survey.

Visit www.palgrave.com/business/whiteley to watch Jos talking about Information Systems and careers as an IS professional, and then think about the following questions:

- In your view, are IT and IS mission-critical for a public sector organization?
- What are the advantages and risks of using electronic identities with public institutions? Discuss.

citizen-to-government (c2g): e-Government transactions between the citizen and the government.

As well as g2c transactions there is the concept of **citizen-to-government (c2g)** transactions. One could argue that it is difficult to distinguish between what is g2c and what is c2g, but for this discussion we will take c2g to indicate citizen participation: we, the governed, telling our governments what we want and what we think – not just an odd letter to our member of parliament and an election every few years but what we think, now.

One manifestation of c2g e-Government in the UK is the government's e-Petition website, which allows people to set up a petition. Current examples include animal welfare, a recent rail passenger franchise decision, benefit cuts affecting the disabled and roadworthiness requirements for historic vehicles – the range of topics is wide. A petition with 100,000 signatures secures a debate in parliament (but there is no guarantee it will go any further).

The technology could be applied more widely. Online voting would make it possible to have frequent referenda on topics of the public's choosing and online petitions to recall our elected representatives. Online voting is of course a problem area – making sure the voter is the person they say they are is not an easy problem to solve (there is an exercise on this in *Chapter 7*).

Whether g2c e-Government would improve the process of government is another question. There would probably be more votes in online referenda for cutting taxes and raising expenditure than the other way round. There would also be a problem for a government trying to implement a specific programme if parts of it could be overturned by instant referenda – any coherence the programme had would soon be lost. Government in democracies is generally *representative government*: we elect our representatives, who then make decisions on our behalf – not a perfect system but, as Churchill said: *democracy is the worst form of government except all the others that have been tried.*

5

digital exclusion: the exclusion of sections of the population from e-Commerce and e-Government services because they don't have, or can't effectively use, internet services.

In all this discussion of e-Government there is, or should be, the question of **digital exclusion** or the *digital divide*. Not everyone has a computer, smartphone or internet connection, and not all those who do are too good at using them.

Excluding people from government services because they cannot make use of the technology is not, or should not be, acceptable. The use of IS, IT and e-Government can make the provision of government services cheaper and more efficient, and, naturally, the government properly wants to avail itself (and us) of these advantages. The use of e-Government can and does make information and access to services easier for the many in the population who can readily use these services. Yet it is often the disadvantaged, the poor, old and disabled who perhaps most need government services, who are most likely to be unable to access e-Government services (they might also be the least likely to vote, which can push them down the priority ranking for politicians).

To include people in online, participatory, c2g e-Government can also be problematic. Greater communication gives a louder voice to those who already have a voice – the special interest groups. There is an issue if e-Government empowers the vocal minority over the silent majority. The use of c2g e-Government could reignite interest and participation in government, politics and public affairs (where participation has been in decline for many years), but there is no guarantee that that will be the outcome.

Civil liberties

civil liberties: the rights of the citizen in a free and democratic society. The right to *life, liberty and the pursuit of happiness.*

George Orwell, in his book *1984*, painted a picture of a dystopian society where Big Brother was always watching you – and now we have the technology.

Big Brother watches us on CCTV when we walk down the high street and go into shops. Big Sister knows where we are, within a few metres, if we move about with a mobile phone switched on. Uncle Google retains all the search terms we use (apparently that helps us). Aunty government could well be intercepting our phone calls and our e-Mails. And very possibly, quite soon, all cars will have electronic equipment that allows their location to be monitored and recorded.

Big Brother is on our side. IT can help prevent traffic congestion, fight crime and can even give us directions to the nearest McDonald's. As with all technologies, IT can have wider effects than intended. It could:

● Catch out a person who has told their partner they are working late but is out with a colleague doing something other than work – possibly they deserved to be caught?
● Record the identities of all the students taking part in an anti-tuition fees demonstration. Possibly there is no harm done, but the authorities have a rather ambivalent attitude to the right to protest and to those who take part in demonstrations.

Big Brother did not just watch, he remembered – and computers are good at remembering. The university will keep data on us – it needs a list of its students, what courses they are doing, where they live, whether or not they have paid and how they are progressing. There will also be data on us:

- At the bank: Each bank account, building society account and credit card company keeps personal details of each of its customers.
- With the insurance company: The system needs details of each policy holder. The insurance industry also pools information between insurance companies to help track down fraudulent claims.
- At the doctor's: The GP wants a record of past problems and previous treatments because these can affect the current diagnosis.
- With our employers: They need details on who they employ and what to pay us. The personnel file can also include reports from our supervisor and details of our sick record – which may not be complimentary.
- At the supermarket: A loyalty card can look up everything we bought each time we went shopping, supposedly to help us with our shopping experience (or to help them sell us more).
- With government: In the United Kingdom, for example, there are records at the tax office and with the Department of Social Security. If we have a car we are with the Driving Vehicle Licensing Authority (DVLA). If we commit an offence (as a third of young males in the UK do) we will be on the police computer, and the internal intelligence services (MI5) keep some sort of record on millions of law-abiding citizens. When we fill in a census form that data goes onto a computer as well – they are not supposed to use the data to identify individuals, but they could do so.

All (or at least most) of this data is there for good reason. Organizations need data to conduct business on behalf of their clients and the government needs to administer its social and public order programmes. This plethora of information can be a problem, however:

- When it is wrong: People have been refused credit, turned down for jobs or, in a few cases, arrested on the basis of wrong information held on a computer. To make it worse, these mistakes can be very hard to correct: organizations seem to be more likely to believe their computer records than clients who claim they have acted on the basis of misinformation.
- When the information gets into the wrong hands: It may be that there is information held by organizations, on individuals that the individuals concerned are entitled to keep private (e.g. an offence that has expired or a medical test that revealed a genetic vulnerability to a disease). If this information is revealed to an employer or an insurance company the individuals could be severely disadvantaged.

The question of how the availability of information affects civil liberties is difficult to assess. At a first look it would seem that the more information that is available the better. Yet we all have aspects of our past that we would not be happy to publicize, and other aspects that we would rather downplay – when we fill in a job application we emphasize the positive, and it might act to our disadvantage if all aspects of our past, however trivial, were available to the potential employer. Across the European Union, and in many other countries, there is data protection legislation (in the UK, the Data Protection Act) that

5

attempts to keep a balance between the use of personal information and our right to privacy. This is further discussed in *Chapter 13*.

Finally, it is noted that this discussion of personal data and civil liberties has been in the context of a democratically governed liberal democracy. Out of that context, the availability of information is a powerful tool in the hands of an authoritarian government or in a society that chooses to discriminate against some minority groups.

Interestingly, in the so-called Arab Spring of 2011, it was the internet and social networks that gave the protesters some advantage. However, governments can intercept and block messaging systems, as happened in Iran with the suppression of the Green Movement following the disputed 2009 presidential election. China also has extensive systems for monitoring online activity and blocking access to websites that contradict the party line (or the interests of party officials). Monitoring online activity also takes place in Western democracies. For instance, in 2012 the UK Government is planning to introduce a new Communications Bill that will allow police and intelligence agencies *to access vital communications data under strict safeguards to protect the public* (Williams, 2012). Critics of the bill doubt the veracity of the strict safeguards and have branded the measure a *snooper's charter* – whatever the current intentions, once the mechanisms are in place there is always the potential for abuse by individuals or by authorities that feel in some way threatened.

The IT profession

The way IT and IS are applied in society is a responsibility of government and the organizations who use IT, but it is also a responsibility of the professionals who plan, create and operate computer systems.

It is a responsibility of professionals to adhere to appropriate standards, and their responsibility to society is enshrined in the codes of conduct of professional societies. The best-known example are medical doctors with their Hippocratic Oath – a doctor who behaves in an inappropriate way can be suspended or *struck off* by the General Medical Council (and there are similar organizations for the medical profession in other countries). The activities of professional societies include:

professional society: an association of members of a learned profession that seeks to set standards and to promote the interests of its profession and its members.

- Controlling entry to the profession: To become a member of a professional society a candidate has to demonstrate a certain level of knowledge – typically there are a number of levels of membership determined by qualification and experience. Entry normally requires that the candidate passes the society's exams, is nominated by an existing member and that a satisfactory level of experience can be demonstrated. Exemption from (some of) the exams can be achieved by passing an accredited course, typically a degree.
- Enforcing standards: Professional societies have codes of conduct which their members are expected to adhere to. A breach of the standards is a disciplinary offence and the member can be suspended or struck off. Where membership is a condition of practice (as is the case for doctors), being suspended or struck off means that the person can no longer practise his or her profession.

● Statutory duty: Professional societies, in the UK, are set up by Royal Charter or statute (Act of Parliament). In some cases the process imposes a number of duties and responsibilities on the society.

Chartered Institute for IT (BCS): the professional association for computing in the UK.

For computing in the UK the professional association is the British Computer Society (BCS) – now rebranded as the **Chartered Institute for IT** (although the **BCS** acronym is retained). The Institute of Engineering and Technology (IET) also represents some of the more technical areas of computing. Other countries have their own professional societies for computing. Examples are the Association for Computing Machinery (ACM, US), the Australian Computer Society (ACS), the Institute of Electrical and Electronics Engineers (IEEE, US) and the Institute of IT Professionals (NZCS, New Zealand) – these associations also actively recruit membership outside their home countries.

The BCS was formed in 1957 and was granted a Royal Charter in 1984. Computing is recognized by the Engineering Council as an *engineering profession* and the BCS as a chartered engineering institution. Members of the BCS need to demonstrate appropriate levels of relevant education and/or experience. Membership starts with student membership and associate membership (AMBCS) and there are two professional levels, member (MBCS) and fellow (FBCS). Computing practitioners with appropriate academic qualifications can also achieve chartered engineering status: grades include chartered IT professional (CITP) and chartered engineer (CEng) – the CEng status requires a master's level qualification.

The BCS accredits courses appropriate to the requirements of the IT profession and as qualifications for chartered status. Your course might have accreditation – ask your tutor if you are interested in joining the BCS. As of May 2012 the BCS claim a membership of 70,000 (BCS, 2012). It is not necessary to be a member of the BCS to practise computing – the fact of membership does, however, imply a high level of competence; moreover, membership can be helpful to the individual in gaining employment (this may be most relevant overseas).

The BCS provides a number of services to IT professionals including local branches (an opportunity to network and hear speakers on topics of interest), access to professional development training and the job shop on the BCS website.

code of conduct: a set of rules governing the behaviour expected from members of a club or association – in this case a computing professional society.

The BCS also has its own **code of conduct**. This code sets out the responsibility of members in the areas of:

● The public interest
● Professional competence and integrity
● Duty to relevant authority
● Duty to the profession.

The effect of the code is somewhat limited compared with, for example, the codes of conduct in the medical and legal professions where membership of the society is a condition of practice, or compared with other engineering professions where some tasks are reserved to chartered engineers. There is also a problem of how an employee should apply professional standards when applying them would go against the instructions given by the employer. Bott

5

et al. (2000) give a number of examples of possible ethical conflicts. Examples include where an organization is contracted to provide IT systems for a totalitarian regime or where a safety-critical system is behind schedule and staff are urged to cut corners to ensure on-time delivery.

Careers in IS

According to the Chartered Institute for IT (BCS) there are more than a million people working directly in IT in the UK (BCS, 2012). Traditional roles in computing include business analyst, system analyst and programmer, but it is a very diverse field with a bewildering array of job titles (many of them being alternative names for the same role – for example, a software developer is, in essence, a programmer). With the spread of end user computing the biggest growth area in IT jobs has been end user support.

Employment in IS/IT can be with a provider of computer services or a consumer of computer services. Providers of computer services can be writing software, running outsourced computing services or providing consultancy to their clients. The consumer of computer services will have their own IT department, might be developing new applications and supporting existing applications, and will provide support to their end users (some or all of these functions may be outsourced).

Taking a snapshot of jobs on offer through the BCS (in the Newcastle area in the UK, for one week in May 2012) there are 43 jobs on offer. These include:

- Project manager: Runs a project and a project team. The project could be to write a new IS or to implement an ERP system.
  Two vacancies for permanent positions; salaries up to £50k.
- System administrator: Manages the system software (operating systems, etc.) on the organization's servers. Responsible for software upgrades and the efficiency and reliability of the service.
  Eight vacancies for permanent positions; for UNIX, Linux and Windows systems; salaries up to £47k.
- Database administrator: Manages the databases and DBMSs on the organization's servers. Responsible for the data model, the software and security of the data.
  Four vacancies for permanent positions; salaries up to £44k.
- Network administrator: Manages the network and services such as e-Mail and intranet/internet. Responsible for hardware and software upgrades on the network.
  Two vacancies for permanent positions; salaries up to £45k.
- Programmer/developer: Writing and testing programs.
  Six vacancies, five for permanent positions; for C#, PHP and Java (mainly C#); salaries up to £48k.
- Tester: The organization is planning to install a substantial new IS and needs staff to thoroughly test the system before it is made live.
  Ten vacancies, nine for contract positions on a daily rate of up to £420.

- Help desk management: The organization has an extensive network of desktop PCs. The help desk is first-line support for any user queries and fault reports. Two vacancies for permanent positions; salaries up to £26k.

There were no end user support positions listed – this sort of position might well be advertised locally. End user support deals with desktop machines: installation, upgrades and user queries (see also help desk management above). End user support can be an entry level position, with staff moving onto more specialist or managerial roles if they do well.

A further look at the BCS job listing for London revealed 2773 job vacancies. The majority of the jobs were technically oriented; business-oriented jobs included: e-Commerce business analyst (£45k), business analyst (£60k), SAP functional analyst (£65k), project manager (£75k), global service desk manager (£65k).

Salaries for IT jobs cover quite a wide range but tend to be higher than the national average. At the time of writing, the UK median wage for full-time employment is £26,244 per annum.

In IS/IT jobs there is much emphasis on experience (which is not good news for students …). IT functions are crucial to the operations of the organization and it is easy for them to be disrupted – employers are looking for experience and a proven track record since they see this as the safest option. Training/apprentice posts in IT are limited.

Temporary or contract employment is also quite common in IS/IT. Organizations usually have a core of permanent employees, but technical expertise required for project work will often be hired in on a temporary basis. These temporary workers can come from a consultancy or can be contractors. Contractors are individuals who work through their own limited companies – placement can be through an agency. Contractors will work for an organization for a period of months and then look for their next contract – they do not have employment rights because the organization is hiring the services of their company. A contractor with in-demand expertise and a good track record can command substantial fees (that will be paid to their company).

Further reading

Books recommended for further reading are:

Bott, F. (2005) *Professional Issues in Information Technology*, BCS, Swindon.
Orwell, G. (1949) *1984*, Penguin, London.

See also websites:
Association for Computing Machinery (ACM, US) http://www.acm.org
Australian Computer Society (ACS): http://www.acs.org.au
Institute of Electrical and Electronics Engineers (IEEE, US) http://www.ieee.org
Institute of IT Professionals (NZCS, New Zealand): http://www.iitp.org.nz
The Chartered Institute for IT (BCS): http://www.bcs.org

5

Comprehension test

This is a simple test to enable you to check you have absorbed the material presented in *Chapter 14.*

Q1 The Information Society is a concept that seeks to encapsulate:

   a. The extensive use of computer systems in business and government ☐

   b. The importance of education to a modern economy ☐

   c. The integration of computing, electronic media and electronic communications into most aspects of life ☐

   d. A professional association for computing personnel ☐

Q2 Formal methods are an approach used in:

   a. The design or structured work practices known as Taylorism ☐

   b. Work practices that empower staff ☐

   c. Safety-critical systems ☐

   d. Recording and codifying data by security and law enforcement agencies ☐

Q3 The UK professional association for computing is the:

   a. British Computer Society ☐

   b. Chartered Institute for IT ☐

   c. Information Systems Association ☐

   d. Society of Computing and Telecommunications Workers ☐

Q4 The UK professional association for computing is a:

   a. Friendly society ☐

   b. Trade union ☐

   c. Chartered engineering institution ☐

   d. Educational institution ☐

Q5 The UK professional association for computing offers a number of types of memberships – which of the following acronyms represents the chartered membership status?

   a. AMBCS ☐

   b. MBCS ☐

   c. FBCS ☐

   d. CITP ☐

Exercises

The following exercises are designed to aid your understanding of the material presented in this chapter. They can be used for self-study or selected exercises can be used for tutorial discussion.

1 **Comprehension** Think about the systems that (probably) hold your personal details. Are there any systems you can think of in addition to those indicated in this chapter? (Draw a mind map.) Use a tutorial session to compare notes and find out if any of your colleagues have been inconvenienced by personal data held on computers.

2 **Discussion** The police use fingerprints in their detective work and make increasing use of DNA analysis. Fingerprints and DNA details are kept on a computer system that can be used for matching when fresh evidence is found. Currently DNA data is held for people who have been arrested and retained, whether or not they are eventually convicted. There have been proposals to reduce the scope of DNA data retention but, equally, it is suggested that it could be appropriate to collect and retain the DNA data of the whole population. Discuss what is appropriate.

3 **Discussion** Computer systems are used for a wide variety of applications and in countries with differing degrees of democracy, corruption and/or repression. Are there any computer applications you would not be prepared to work on? Are there any applications or types of data that should not be computerized? These questions could also be discussed in a tutorial.

4 **Discussion** The professional association for computing is the Chartered Institute for IT (BCS). Should membership of a professional association be compulsory for all IS/IT professionals (as would be the case, for example, for lawyers and medical doctors)? Discuss.

5

GLOSSARY

Acceptance test Once software is written it must be tested for errors in the programming and flaws in the design. Acceptance testing is carried out by the users (with the assistance of the project team). The purpose of the acceptance test is to check that the system does what the users require of it – that it is fit for purpose. System and acceptance tests are stages in the *system development lifecycle*.

Access MS Access is Microsoft's *relational database management system*. It is essentially a desktop package but it can be used on a server and it can be accessed using *SQL*.

Access control Controls to restrict access to permitted users of the computer and/or the network. Access control for a computer is typically by *password* and to a network by *user-id* and *password* – access control can also require a physical token such as a swipe card.

Accumulator A small unit of memory in the CPU, holding a word or small number of bytes. Data is retrieved from main memory to the accumulator before a maths/logic operation and returned to main memory once the operation(s) are complete. See also *register*.

Actor A symbol, drawn as a stick person, on a *UML use case diagram* – representing an external user of the *use case*/system.

Ad hoc report A *management information* report which is constructed to meet a specific information requirement (as opposed to scheduled reports that might be produced every week or month).

After-sales The final stage of the *trade cycle* (used in the discussion of *e-Business*). After-sales involve dealing with returns, warrantee and/or maintenance, depending on the requirements of the goods or services being provided.

Aggregation A symbol qualifying an *association* on a *UML class diagram* – an aggregation indicates a strong association, a *part-of* relationship. Drawn as a hollow diamond on the association, see also *composition*.

Agile Manifesto A list of principles or intentions, published in 2001, that served to crystallize the underlying approach to lightweight/rapid system/software development methods – and to re-label them as agile methods.

Agile software development Agile software development uses incremental and iterative techniques to design and develop software. It uses small empowered teams to deliver software components (which may well be part of a larger system) in a short timeframe. See also the *agile manifesto*.

AI See *artificial intelligence*.

Algorithm A step-by-step procedure for calculation. For a *hash random* file, and hashed record location on a *database*, an algorithm is used for the calculation of the *block* address, and hence the *record* location, for a given record key.

Alpha test Alpha and *beta test* is a testing scheme usually used on *system software*, such as an *operating system* where the user will be a third party. The alpha test is carried out by the software developer and the beta test on pre-release versions of the software issued to a limited number of selected users.

ALU See *arithmetic logic unit*.

Amazon An *internet e-Commerce* bookshop that opened for business in 1995. Generally accepted to be the first retail organization to operate on the internet. Amazon has expanded greatly and covers many more categories of merchandise than just books.

ANA See *Article Numbering Association*.

Analogue In the field of computing, analogue represents information using a continuous function. Analogue transmission uses a modulated signal as opposed to transmitting a *digital* signal.

Analysis report A style of *management information* report where totals are set out in a two-dimensional grid, e.g. sales by region for each month.

AND gate A *logic gate* which produces an output of one when all inputs are one – the output is zero for all other input combinations.

ANSI-X12 An *electronic data interchange* format developed and used in the USA (also known as ASC-X12).

Anthony's triangle A business model representing the levels of decision-making in an organization. The model is used in the discussion of *management information*.

App Short for *application*. Common usage is for a *program* that can be downloaded and used on a *smartphone* – a *smartphone app*.

Apple Apple is an electronics company. Apple Computers was formed in 1976 and was one of the first makers of micro computers (personal computers), initially in kit form. Apple continues to make PCs and it has a dedicated following in the PC market. The Apple PCs are stylish and particularly suitable for graphical applications. The Apple has its own distinct architecture/operating system while most (all) other PCs are IBM PC clones. Apple makes a number of other products such as the iPod, the iPhone and the iPad and achieves a good degree of integration across this range of products.

Application An *Information System*, e.g. *payroll* or *order processing*.

Application generator *Software* used to generate an *application* (as opposed to writing *programs*). *Database management systems* such as *Access* and *Oracle* include application generators – in Access the application is generated using the wizards. Complex processing can require that program code is included in the generated application.

Application service provider (ASP) An organization that provides a computer-based service over the internet. The service would normally include the use of *application software* on a pay-for-use basis.

Application software Programs used for a business purpose – an *Information System*.

Archive Data that is no longer required for every day usage can be copied from *secondary storage* and stored offline on a medium such as CD, DVD or magnetic tape.

Ariba A supplier of *electronic business* software and services. Noted for its *internet* based *e-Market* services.

Arithmetic logic unit (ALU) The *logic circuits* used for arithmetical and logical (program) instructions in the computer *central processor*.

ARPAnet A US military project, commissioned in 1969. The aim of the project was to develop a flexible *network* that could still function if some of the nodes were knocked out in a nuclear attack – hence the use of *packet-switching*. The *internet* evolved out of the ARPAnet project.

Array processor This is a *supercomputer* model that uses an array of *processors* applied to a single problem. This model contrasts with the *vector processors* – although supercomputers are likely to use both these techniques to achieve their performance.

Article Numbering Association (ANA) The Article Numbering Association is the body that administers ANA codes, as represented in *EAN* product codes and *barcodes*.

Artificial intelligence (AI) The discipline devoted to producing computer systems that perform tasks that would require intelligence if done by a human being.

ASP See *application service provider*. Also a microsoft .net *server side scripting* (*programming*) language.

Association Used in *UML*. In the *use case diagram*, used to associate an *actor* with a *use case*. In the *class diagram* used to associate two *classes*; where the class diagram is used as an *entity relationship diagram*, the association is a *relationship*.

ATM See *automatic teller machine*.

Attribute A term used in the context of the *entity relationship diagram*, *class diagram* and *databases* (in the design process). An attribute is a data-item belonging to an *entity* or *object*, e.g. a student entity or object would have: studentNo, studentName, etc. as Attributes.

Audit trail A chronological record of transactions used for security or audit purposes. For *EDI* a *trusted third party* would need to keep an audit trail of EDI messages so it could adjudicate in any dispute between trading parties.

Automated system A system operating without human intervention. Systems such as automatic train control are automated systems and they need to be developed as *safety-critical systems* because of the dangers inherent in any malfunction.

Automated teller machine (ATM) A public-access, automated banking machine, often in a public place. Bank customers can use their bankcard/credit card, together with a pin code, to gain access and then service their account, e.g. check their balance or withdraw cash. The automated teller machine (ATM) is *computer*-controlled and linked to banking systems via a *network*.

Automatic recording device Sensors or measuring devices that operate without human intervention and, if joined to a *network*, submit data to an *Information System*, e.g. sensors in aeroplane jet engines that report operating data to engineers in a central control room.

Baby Officially known as Small Scale Experimental Machine, was produced at Manchester University with its first run in 1948. It was a *valve machine* but hardly small at 5.2 metres long (though considerably smaller than the *ENIAC*). It was the first of the early computers to implement the **Von Neumann** stored program principle. Other early computers mentioned in this text are **Colossus**, **ENIAC** and **Zuse**.

Bachman diagram Diagram used to define the schema of a **network database** – based on the **entity relationship diagram**.

Backdoor In **computer security**, a backdoor is a way of bypassing the normal authentication (e.g. login) procedures of a computer system. A backdoor may be created, by a **hacker**, on a compromised system to ease future entry.

Backoffice As opposed to the front office where the public is served – the backoffice is where the *paperwork* is done. In terms of **e-Commerce**, the backoffice is where orders are processed and payments cleared using appropriate backoffice **Information Systems**.

Backup A copy of computer files taken as a security (in case the original copy becomes corrupted or unavailable). Backups should be taken at frequent intervals and stored in a separate location.

BACS A UK organization for the clearing and settlement of automated payments (**electronic funds transfers**). Founded in 1968 and originally known as the Bankers Automated Clearing Service. Other electronic payments services are SWIFT and CHAPS – typically used for larger or more urgent money transfers – one use of BACS is to transfer wages into employee bank accounts.

Bandwidth The transmission capacity of the **network** – measured in bits per second.

Barcode A barcode represents a small amount of data in machine readable form. The traditional barcode is a series of vertical stripes that represent a number, typically an **EAN** product code of 13 characters. Barcodes have a wide variety of other applications, e.g. to identify packages being handled by parcel delivery services. A further development is the two dimensional (2D) barcode – the **QR Code** (that is a square with a pattern of smaller squares inside it – no bars!). These 2D barcodes contain more data and are used in applications such as airline boarding passes.

Base two The **binary** system is base two, as opposed to the decimal system which is base 10. The digits available in the binary system are 0 (zero) and 1. In binary arithmetic 1 + 1 =10, c.f. decimal where 9 + 1 = 10.

Basket A temporary datastore on an **internet e-Commerce** system where the user accumulates their intended purchases prior to checkout – the system allocates a datastore using **session variables** (or a

similar system feature) to each user. Also referred to as a (shopping) **trolley** or **cart**.

BCS See **Chartered Institute for IT** (renamed from British Computer Society).

Benchmarking The process of an organization comparing its performance with other (leading) organizations in its market sector – in order to establish and adopt **best practice**.

Best practice Business term for a way of operating that is considered superior to other models. **ERP** systems claim to implement best practice.

Beta test **Alpha test** and beta test are testing schemes usually used on **system software**, such as an **operating system** where the users will be a third party. The alpha test is carried out by the software developer and the beta test on pre-release versions of the software issued to a limited number of selected users.

Bezos Jeff Bezos is founder and chief executive of Amazon, the first (or first notable) **internet e-Commerce**, **e-Shop**.

Big bang implementation A big bang implementation is where the old **Information System** is taken out, say at the end of work on Friday, and the new system installed (as a complete replacement) for use on Monday morning. Alternative approaches would be to implement in stages or to **parallel run** the two systems, but this is not always practical.

Big Brother A fictional character in George Orwell's novel *1984*. In the novel, everyone in the totalitarian state of Oceania is under complete surveillance, mainly through the telescreens. The term Big Brother, from Orwell's novel, has entered the lexicon as a synonym for abusive government power and intrusive surveillance.

Binary The binary system is **base two**, as opposed to the decimal system which is base 10. The digits available in the binary system are 0 (zero) and 1. In binary arithmetic 1 + 1 =10, c.f. decimal where 9 + 1 = 10.

Biometric The identification of a specific person by their characteristics or traits. In computing, biometrics can be used to identify a person in applications such as **access control**. Biometrics that can be recognized by **Information Technology** include fingerprints, voice and retina scans.

Black box test Black box testing assumes that the logic of the module is correct (previously tested) and concentrates on testing linkages/interfaces between modules. See also **link test** and **white box test**.

Block The physical unit of data transfer from a **secondary storage** device such as a **hard disk**. A block will typically contain a number of records (the logical unit of data) and the *records* are unpacked by the file-handling software.

Bluetooth A *radio* transmission technology and *protocol* used for transmissions over short distances (of no more than a few metres) creating a personal area network (PAN).

Bot Short for robot. Used to refer to programs that search the *web*, for instance, to create the indexes for a *search engine* or to make price comparisons, a *shopbot* (although many price comparison sites work by arrangement with selected suppliers and hence the term bot is inaccurate).

Botnet In *computer security*, a number of *zombie computers* controlled from one source.

Bottom-up Analysis from the detail and abstract to the more general. In *system analysis and design*, *relational data analysis* is a bottom-up technique (as opposed to *top-down*).

BPR See *business process re-engineering*.

Bricks-and-clicks This refers to a retail organization that sells through a conventional store (bricks) and an *e-Shop* (clicks). An example of bricks-and-clicks could be Tesco as opposed to *Amazon* which is online only and can be referred to as *pure-play*.

Bricks-and-mortar This refers to the conventional (as opposed to *internet e-Commerce*) operation of a retail store.

Bridge A bridge is a *network* device that forwards data from one segment of the network to another segment. Bridges are protocol independent, c.f. *router*.

Brought forward An accountancy term for a value copied from a previous set of accounts. In an *Information System* a brought forward file is a data set from the previous run, e.g. last month's payroll file. See also *carry forward*.

Browser A web browser is client software that interacts with a web server over the *internet*. The browser receives the website in *HTML* and renders it on the user's screen. Data can be input and sent to the server using the HTML form facility.

Bureau An organization that hosts/runs *Information Systems* for third parties. Many *server farms* offer bureau services.

Business A business is an *organization* that makes things or provides a service with the aim of making a profit. Businesses range in size from international companies to sole traders (businesses run by an individual). Examples of large businesses are the Ford Motor Company and amazon.com. Businesses are distinguished from other organizations by the

purpose of making a profit. In most other ways there is little to distinguish a business from a non-business organization of the same sort of size, e.g. a government department or a university – both types of organization employ staff, require management and use IS/IT. University courses in business studies could more properly be called organization studies.

Business analyst A member of the *Information Systems* staff. The business analyst develops the business case for a new Information Systems development/investment.

Business environment See *environment*.

Business process re-engineering (BPR) Restructuring a business process to make it more efficient or effective – the term implies substantial change, as opposed to simply improving the current process.

Business study An analysis of the business requirement and business process.

Business system options A stage in the *SSADM system development lifecycle*. The business system options stage follows the *requirements analysis* stage and suggests a number of alternative business solutions for those requirements.

Business-to-business (b2b) Transactions between businesses/organizations. The term business-to-business is used in *e-Commerce* to differentiate between business-to-business and *business-to-consumer* transactions.

Business-to-consumer (b2c) Transactions between businesses/organizations and their customers (retail consumers). The term business-to-consumer is used in *e-Commerce* to differentiate between *business-to-business* and business-to-consumer transactions.

Byte A byte is a unit of digital information, normally consisting of eight bits (in *EBCDIC* characters are represented by an eight bit code). For byte machines, such as the IBM 360 mainframe and the 8085 micro *processor*, a byte is the basic addressable element (the 8086 used a 16 bit word length). See also *word*.

b2b See *business-to-business*.

b2c See *business-to-consumer*.

C A general-purpose *programming language*. The design of C provides constructs that map efficiently onto *machine code* and therefore it is widely used for writing *system software*, e.g. the *UNIX operating system*.

CAD See *computer-aided design*.

Call centre A centralized office where a number of staff are employed making telephone calls (to potential customers) or answering telephone calls from customers/users. Many call centres make extensive use of *Information Systems* with operators often required to follow on-screen scripts. Call centres can be operated in-house but many organizations *outsource* or *off-shore* to specialist providers.

CAM See *computer-aided manufacture*.

Cardinality The degree of a *relationship* on an *entity relationship diagram* e.g. a relationship between the customer and order would have: the customer has zero, one or many orders (0..*) and the order has one and only one customer (1..1).

Carry forward An accountancy term for a value to be copied into a future set of accounts. In an *Information System* a carry forward file is a data set to be used in a future run, e.g. a payroll file to be used in next month's run. See also *brought forward*.

Cart US term for a conceptually large electronic (shopping) *basket* used on an *e-Shop*.

CASE See *computer-aided software engineering*.

CATWOE Refers to the *root definition* in *soft systems methodology*. The root definition should sum up, in a sentence, the overall requirement of the system, covering: client, agent, transformation, *Weltanschauung*, owner and environment, i.e. CATWOE.

Central Processor Unit (CPU) The computer part of the computer – disregarding the keyboard, display, disk, etc. In *Von Neumann Architecture* the *main memory*, *control unit* and *arithmetic logic unit*.

Chartered Institute for IT (BCS) The professional association for computing in the UK. The acronym that is used is BCS, which is derived from its previous title, the British Computer Society.

Chartered IT Professional (CITP) The chartered professional membership of the *Chartered Institute for IT*. Further membership grades are Associate Member (AMBCS), Member (MBCS) and Fellow (FBCS). Chartered Engineers (CEng) may also be members.

Checkland The originator of the *sociotechnical* methodology – *soft systems methodology*.

Checksum A digit at the end of a code, or a number at the end of a record/data segment. Used in data entry to check that a code has been properly entered or in data transmission to check that the message has been received without corruption. The checksum is calculated, using all the data in the code/message, in accordance with a predetermined formula.

Chief information officer (CIO) A senior management role; typically responsible for all *Information Systems*

and *Information Technology* in an *organization*. The CIO would be expected to take a strategic view of the use of information in the organization.

Chip Short for *silicon chip*. Used in *data capture*, a chip can be embedded in a plastic (credit/debit) card or in a document such as a passport. Contains more data and is more secure than alternatives such as a *magnetic strip*.

CICS IBM's *TP monitor* – used on *mainframe* computer systems.

CIO See *chief information officer*.

Citizen-to-government (c2g) *Electronic government* transactions between citizen and the government, especially electronic participation in the process of government decision-making. See also *government-to-citizen*.

CITP See *Chartered IT Professional*.

Civil liberties The rights of the citizen in a free and democratic society, such as the *right to life, liberty and the pursuit of happiness* (to borrow from the US Declaration of Independence). The use of *Information Technologies* can give *authority* considerable power in monitoring the citizen, and the use of this power has the potential to threaten civil liberties.

Class For *object-oriented* design and development, a class is a set of *objects* with the same characteristics.

Class diagram An *object-oriented system analysis and design* technique; included in *UML*. The class diagram represents all *classes* of *objects* and their *associations* with the other classes in the proposed system. Each class includes a list of *attributes* and *methods*.

Click-and-collect A mode of *internet e-Commerce* where the customer shops online and then goes to a conventional retail outlet of the business to collect their purchases.

Clickthrough A web advertisement that hyperlinks to the webpage of its sponsor when clicked.

Client The user *computer*, typically a *PC*, used to access a *client-server system*.

Client-server system This is a distributed model of computing – the system is wholly (or partly) located on a *server* and is accessed by the users through their *client* computers, typically a PC. See also *thin client* and *thick client*.

Client side script *Web* technology where program code is included in the code of the webpage, downloaded to the *client* system and then executed on the client machine. Used for functions such as client side validation.

Cloud computing Processing or data storage that is carried out on *Information Technology* provided by a third party. Cloud computing is similar to *outsourcing* but the relationship with the provider is less formal and the facilities are more generic (or at least that is the implication).

Cobol Cobol stands for common business-oriented language. It is a second-generation *programming language* aimed at commercial application *programming*. Mainly used on *mainframe* systems, and whilst some of these systems are still in use, the language is no longer commonly taught or used.

Codd Edgar Edgar Codd worked in the IBM laboratories in the late 1960s. He is credited with developing the *relational* approach to *database* design.

Code of conduct A set of rules governing the behaviour expected from members of a club or society. The code of conduct referenced in this book is that of the *Chartered Institute for IT*.

Colossus Was made at Bletchley Park as part of the British code-breaking effort in the Second World War. It was demonstrated in late 1943 and became operational in early 1944 – by the end of the war there were ten of these machines in operation. It was a *valve machine* and designed for a specific purpose in the wartime code-breaking effort – *programming* was by means of plugging patch panels and setting switches (as opposed to the stored program principle of *Von Neumann architecture*). Other early computers mentioned in this text are *Baby*, *ENIAC* and *Zuse*.

Competitive advantage An attribute of business (or organization), its products or services that persuades customers to do business with it, as opposed to one of its competitors. *Porter* identified three generic competitive advantages: price, differentiation and focus.

Compiler *Software* that translates source code (the language the programmer writes) into object code (the *machine code* of the target *computer*). See also *interpreter*.

Composition A symbol qualifying an *association* on a *UML class diagram* – a composition indicates a strong association, a *part-of* relationship where the part object can belong to only one whole and its lifespan, creation and deletion is the same as the *entity* which it is part of. Drawn as a diamond on the association. See also *aggregation*.

Computer A computer is an electronic data processing machine where the *program* and data are held in the same memory space and the program can be varied (not hard coded). Computers range from *PC*, through

servers and *mainframes* to *supercomputers*. Using this definition a *smartphone* is also a computer.

Computer-aided design (CAD) *Software* used for design – technical drawings. CAD is used in engineering, electronic circuits and architectural design. CAD software can check the design, for instance for stress. CAD designs can be fed into *computer-aided manufacture* systems.

Computer-aided manufacture (CAM) The use of *computer software* in production machinery – particularly machine tools. The numerical control for the CAM process is normally derived from a *computer-aided design* process.

Computer-aided software engineering (CASE) Software designed to assist the analysis, design, development and testing of computer systems. An important feature of CASE software is facilities to assist with the drawing of *system analysis and design* diagrams. CASE will also form linkages between diagrams and can include facilities linking design to development.

Computer Misuse Act The Computer Misuse Act (1990) deals with inappropriate use of computers (*hacking*). It is an offence, under the act, to obtain unauthorized access to a computer system and a more serious offence if content is changed or a crime is intended.

Computer security A general term covering privacy (preventing unauthorized access) and security (ensuring the data and equipment is protected from loss, damage or breakdown). Protection against *malware* is another aspect of computer security.

Context diagram The top-level diagram in a hierarchy of *SSADM data flow diagrams*. The context diagram shows all the external *dataflows* with the system represented as a single box.

Contract An agreement between two parties. A legally enforceable contract requires an offer, acceptance and consideration (exchange of value).

Control unit The logic in a *CPU* that interprets the *machine code* instruction (in the *program*) and switches in the appropriate circuits in the *arithmetic logic unit*. With integrated circuits, the control unit and the arithmetic logic unit are both part of the *processor* chip.

Conventional file A free-standing file on *secondary storage*, i.e. not part of a *database management system*.

Conventional machine A data processing machine from the era before the commercial use of computers.

Generally known as *Hollerith* card machines (although the most common card format was the IBM card). The most common machines were the card punch, sorter, collator and *tabulator*. Programmed using wiring boards.

Cookie In web technology, data storage placed on the client's systems. Cookies can be persistent, enabling the website to access retained information about the user, when that user re-accesses the website. Cookies can be used in connection with *malware*.

Copper wire Widely used for electronic communications as it has good conductivity and electrical signals will pass through with relatively little distortion or loss of power.

Copyright The right of an author to protect their creative, intangible work from copying and exploitation by others (and hence benefit from any revenues accruing from the use or sale of the work). Copyright is applicable to *program* code. It is one form of *intellectual property right*. See also *patent*.

Corporate database A single, unified *database* for all (or most) of the *Information Systems* of an organization (as opposed to each Information System having its own database and some data being replicated and possibly becoming inconsistent).

CPU See *central processing unit*.

Critical path The sequence of activities in a *project plan* that have no float time and hence determine the overall elapse time for the *project*. The critical path can be identified using the *program evaluation and review technique* (PERT).

CRM See *customer relationship management system*.

CSNet The US computer science network – founded in 1981 and split from the *ARPAnet* in 1984. A predecessor *network* to the *internet*.

Customer not present (CNP) A protocol that allows credit cards to be used on the internet or over the phone. In the case of customer not present the signature/pin checks cannot be applied.

Customer relationship management system (CRM) An application for managing the organization's interactions with customers/clients. At the heart of the system is a *database* of clients (and potential clients). Sales activity with the client is recorded and the system can also be used to record orders. One advantage of such a system is that a second sales person can pick up client contact if, for any reason, the original sales person is unavailable.

Cyber warfare Politically motivated *hacking* to conduct sabotage or espionage.

c2g See *citizen-to-government*.

C++ An *object-oriented* version of the *C programming language*.

C# Microsoft.net's version of the *C programming language*. Pronounced C-sharp.

Data analysis Examining the data requirements of a system – leading to the production of an *entity relationship diagram*. *Relational data analysis* is a technique that can be used in the process.

Database (DB) A file management system that holds all (or most) of a system's/organization's data within one conceptual file and provides sophisticated methods to access that data. Databases are managed using *database management system* (DBMS) software, e.g. *Microsoft Access*, *My SQL* and *Oracle*.

Database designer An *Information System* specialist with expertise in *data analysis* and the design of *databases*.

Database management system (DBMS) Software used to set up, update, access and maintain a *database*.

Database update log An element of the *data security* and recovery mechanism of a *database*. The *database management system* can include provision to record all database updates on a log file and, in the event of a failure, reapply the updates to a *backup* copy.

Data capture Getting the data from the people who have it and into a form that can be input into an *Information System*.

Data capture technology Technology used for *data capture*. This can be a keyboard and screen but the term is more usually applied to automated data capture, e.g. *barcode scanner* or *optical character recognition*.

Data controller The person in an organization who determines the purposes for which, and the manner in which, any personal data are, or are to be, processed. The data controller must be registered with the *Office of the Information Commissioner* under the provisions of the *Data Protection Act* (1998). Note that the person can be the organization (as organizations legally have a persona).

Data cutover Converting data from the format used in an old *Information System* to the format required by the new Information System – as part of the *implementation* process. Data cutover could involve data cleansing and additional *data capture*.

Data dictionary A *database* of the data requirements of a system – derived from the *data analysis* process – can also be referred to as a *repository*.

Dataflow A symbol on the **SSADM** *data flow diagram*. A dataflow shows the flow of data into (and out of) the system from **externals** and between **processes** and **datastores**.

Data flow diagram (DFD) A **SSADM** technique that maps the flow of data into (and out of) the system from **externals**, the change of the data by **processes** and where a **data flow** is stationary in a **datastore**. The DFD is a hierarchy of models using **functional decomposition** – the top level of the hierarchy is the **context diagram**.

Data-mining Retrieving and analysing data from a **database** or **data warehouse** – with the intention of discovering new patterns in large datasets.

Data modelling Documenting the result of **data analysis** as an **entity relationship diagram**.

Data processing system A computer system that processes data – an early (and possibly more accurate) name for an **Information System**.

Data Protection Act The Data Protection Act (1998) sets out the rules governing the collection, storage and use of personal data by organizations.

Data security The aspects of **computer security** that relate to the protection of the data from loss, damage or unauthorized access. The backstop on data security is to have **backup** copies so services can be restored should the data be lost or damaged.

Datastore A symbol on the **SSADM**, **data flow diagram**. A datastore is a stationary **dataflow**. The datastore is analogous to a **file** in a physical system.

Data structure The organization of data in a **computer program** or on **secondary storage** that enables efficient access. Data structures discussed in this book include **index sequential** and **hash random**.

Data subject An individual who is the subject of personal data held by an organization and hence subject to the provision and protections of the **Data Protection Act** (1998).

Data warehouse A (large) **database** designed specifically for analysis and reporting. The information on the data warehouse is normally uploaded from operational systems and is separate from those systems.

DB See **database**.

DBMS See **database management system**.

db2 IBM's **relational database management system**.

DDoS See **distributed denial of service**.

Decision Support System (DSS) A Decision Support System is an **Information System** that aims to support decision-making. The system will use as its starting point data extracted from other sources, very possibly the organization's own Information Systems. The DSS provides analysis tools that, for instance, aim to detect trends and project them forward or give *what if* capabilities so decision makers can try out different scenarios (e.g. *what if* inflation rates increase/decrease). The system may incorporate **artificial intelligence** tools. The DSS goes beyond a **MIS** that restricts itself to analysing data.

Denial of service (DoS) A hacking attack to close down a **server** or a **network** – most commonly by saturating the target with external communication requests.

Desktop A computer, typically a **PC** on someone's desk for them to work with. Also used to describe a standard configuration of services on a PC.

Despatch note A document, produced by an **order processing system**, listing the details of a consignment of goods and sent with the consignment to the customer. The despatch note can be electronic and be sent by **EDI**.

Development team A team of **Information System** professionals developing an IS. A **project team** but specific to the development stages of the **SDLC**.

DFD See **data flow diagram**.

Digital In the field of computing, digital is using discrete (**binary**) values. Digital data transmission sends data coded into binary values as opposed to transmitting an **analogue** signal.

Digital exclusion The exclusion of sections of the population from **e-Commerce** and **e-Government** services because they do not have, or cannot effectively use, **internet** services.

Digital signature A data segment added to a message that is designed to verify the identity of the sender and to verify that the message has arrived intact and has not been tampered with.

Directgov The UK Government's **e-Government** portal.

Directory List of files held on **secondary storage** – used by the **operating system** to manage physical file placement and file access. Microsoft Windows call their directories folders.

Discounted cash flow analysis A system of assessing the cost benefit of an investment, e.g. a new **Information System**. The analysis starts when an estimate is made of the price of the proposed system and the savings that should be made once the system is installed. Interest charges can then be factored in and a calculation made of the payback that the system will produce over its expected lifespan.

Distance learning Teaching and learning where the student is separated from the tutor by geography (and very possibly time – asynchronous learning). Modern distance learning is likely to be heavily reliant on *ICT*.

Distributed denial of service (DDoS) A *hacking* attack, from a number of *computers*, to close down a *server* or a *network* – most commonly by saturating the target with external communication requests. The attack may be sourced from a *botnet*.

Distributed system An *Information System* that is run across more than one *server*.

Document management system A computer system used to store electronic documents or electronic images of paper documents. The system catalogues the documents and can track the processing of the stored documents. One application could be the processing of insurance claim documents by the claims department of an insurance company.

Dongle A small piece of hardware that plugs into a computer. Used as a key that allows usage of propriety software. The term dongle is also used for a plug-in device that supplies computer access to the mobile phone network.

DoS See *denial of service*.

dot.net Microsoft's suite of *program* development tools, including *Visual Studio* and *C#*.

DP system See *data processing system*.

Drop down menu A list of options displayed when the controlling *icon* or value is selected – once displayed the user can select the required option. Can be used to offer valid alternatives in *data capture*.

DSDM See *dynamic system development methodology*.

DSS See *Decision Support System*.

Duplex An *Information System* can be duplexed – it is run on two separate *servers*/*mainframes* with the second system being available as backup should the first system fail. A duplexed system can provide for updates to be applied to both systems and the system can then *failover* to the second system should the currently live system fail.

Dynamic system development methodology (DSDM) An *agile*/*rapid application development methodology* that formalizes the *evolutionary prototype lifecycle* and makes it appropriate to a commercial environment.

EAN See *European Article Number*.

eBay An *internet e-Commerce* site offering web-auctions – one user places an item for auction and other users place their bids with the final deal being done between the item owner and the winning bidder. eBay also now acts as a host for a large number of (small) online retailers.

EBCDIC EBCDIC stands for extended binary coded decimal interchange code. It is an eight-bit character-encoding system – this gives one character per *byte*.

e-Business See *electronic business*.

e-Cash See *electronic cash*.

ECD See *effect correspondence diagram*.

e-Commerce See *electronic commerce*.

EDI See *electronic data interchange*.

EDIFACT *Electronic data interchange* (EDI) for administration commerce and transport. The agreed international electronic data interchange message coding standard.

EDI interchange agreement An agreement signed by *electronic data interchange* trading partners setting out the terms for their electronic trade exchanges.

EDI standard A standard for coding business documents as *electronic data interchange* messages.

Effect correspondence diagram (ECD) A *SSADM* diagram that documents the use of *entities* (from the *entity relationship diagram*) by a *process* (from the *data flow diagram*).

e-Fulfilment The process of shipping goods from the supplier to the customer in an *internet e-Commerce* business. The term e-Fulfilment can be applied to tangible or intangible (electronic) goods.

e-Government See *electronic government*.

EIS See *executive Information System*.

Electronic business (e-Business) Commercial operations conducted using *e-Commerce*.

Electronic cash (e-Cash) Monetary value that is deposited in an electronic account and can be spent with participating Internet *e-Commerce* vendors. Money held in a *PayPal* account is an example of e-Cash.

Electronic commerce (e-Commerce) Commercial transactions formulated at a location remote from a trading partner and executed using *Information and Communications Technologies*.

Electronic contract Traditionally contracts have been paper documents signed by the contracting parties. Contracts agreed electronically cannot be signed (in the normally accepted sense) but can still be valid contracts (if appropriate provision has been made in the relevant legal systems).

Electronic data interchange (EDI) Electronic data interchange is used for the transfer of structured data, by agreed message standards, from one computer system to another, by electronic means. Examples are orders and invoices used in trade exchanges and coded using an agreed message standard such as *EDIFACT* or an agreed standard within *XML*.

Electronic funds transfer An *electronic data interchange* system for transferring monetary value between bank accounts. *BACS*, SWIFT and CHAPS are electronic funds transfer systems.

Electronic government (e-Government) The use of *IS/IT* and *internet* access in the process of government. e-Government can be used to provide access to government information, interact with services and facilitate public participation in government decision-making – at both national and local levels.

Electronic market (e-Market) An *Inter-Organizational Information System* that allows buyers and sellers to exchange information about price and product offerings.

Electronic point of sale system (EPOS) A computerized shop checkout system that will typically: read a barcode, look up prices, record the sale and total the customer's bill.

ELH See *entity life history*.

e-Mail Electronic mail – messages sent from one computer user to another. e-Mail systems use *post and forward* networks and thus the recipient of the message does not need to be online when the message is sent.

e-Market See *electronic market*.

Empowerment A working practice that delegates responsibility for, and decision-making on, a task from managers to staff.

Encapsulation The *object-oriented* design and *programming* concept that the *object* includes both data and the processing that manipulates the data. This creates a self-sufficient *module* that can be re-used wherever that object is required.

Encryption The process of transforming data, using an *algorithm*, to make it unreadable by anyone who attempts unauthorized access.

Engineering The second iterative stage in the *DSDM* lifecycle. The stage in which the *functional model* prototypes are refined into a working system.

ENIAC A *valve machine* constructed for the US Army by the University of Pennsylvania. It was completed in 1946. It was designed to be general purpose – programming was by means of plugging patch panels and setting switches (as opposed to the stored program principle of *Von Neumann architecture*). Other early computers mentioned in this text are *Baby*, *Colossus* and *Zuse*.

Enterprise resource planning system (ERP) Third-party *application software* that provide *organizations* with system integration across a range of standard business processes.

Enterprise system An *Information System* essential to the functioning of the core *operations* of the *organization*.

Entity A thing of interest to the system about which data is held; e.g. a customer in an *order processing system* or an employee in a *payroll system*.

Entity life history (ELH) A *SSADM* diagram that documents the application of *process* (from the *data flow diagram*) to an *entity* (from the *entity relationship diagram*).

Entity relationship diagram (ERD) A *SSADM/UML* diagram that documents the *entities* (data) used in a system and the *relationships* between those entities.

Envelope In a *transmission protocol*, the envelope is the header and trailer segments that *envelope* the data. The minimum requirement is for the header to indicate the start of the message and for the trailer to include count/checksum information that allows the *network* to check that the data has arrived intact. For many protocols the header will also specify the network address of the sending computer and the network address of the destination computer.

Environment This term can have more than one usage:
1. Business environment. The economic, political, social and technological context in which the *organization* operates.
2. Natural environment. The concern, in the context of this book, is the impact of *computing* (positive and negative) on the environment, see *green computing*.

EPOS See *electronic point of sale*.

ERD See *entity relationship diagram*.

ERP See *enterprise resource planning system*.

e-Shop The website of an *internet e-Commerce* business.

Estimating Working out how long a task will take to do or how much the task will cost. Projects must be estimated as part of the *feasibility study* in the *system development lifecycle*.

Ethernet *Local area network* technology and *transmission protocol*.

European Article Number (EAN) Now used worldwide and referred to as an International Article Number although the EAN acronym is retained. The EAN is a coding system for uniquely identifying products. The most common code is EAN-13 which consists of 13 digits and would normally be printed on the product/product packaging as a *barcode*.

Evolutionary prototype lifecycle A *system development lifecycle* where the system requirements are elucidated and the system is incrementally developed, through a series of *prototypes*. At each *iteration*, the functionality of the prototype is incremented until the final prototype can be *system tested* and then used as the live *Information System*.

Exception report A style of *management information* report where only cases that meet exception criteria are reported, e.g. invoices not paid by the deadline.

Executive Information System (EIS) An *Information System* (or subsystem) specifically designed to produce *management information* for senior management.

Exploration The first iterative stage in the *DSDM* lifecycle. The stage in which *prototyping* is used to develop a *functional model* of the system.

Extend A feature of the *UML use case diagram*. The extend is used to show a variation on normal behaviour to include additional, optional, behaviour.

EXtensible mark-up language (XML) A mark-up language that defines rules for encoding documents using a system of mark-up tags. XML is a meta-language – the tags are user-defined (unlike, for example, *HTML* where the tags are part of the language definition). XML has extensive applications in web-related documentation – including as an alternative to traditional *EDI standards*.

EXtensible stylesheet language transforming (XSLT) *XML* language used for transforming XML documents, e.g. to transform a XML document to *HTML* or plain text.

External A symbol on the *SSADM data flow diagram*. An external is a person or entity outside the system that submits data to the system or receives data from the system.

Extract File A *conventional file* of *records* selected from a larger file or *database*. Records on an extract file can often be processed more quickly than directly from the database.

Extranet A private *internet* facility that extends outside the organization. See also *intranet*.

Extreme programming (XP) An *agile software development* method. A feature of extreme programming is its advocacy of programming in pairs and its extensive use of code reviews.

Facebook A *social networking system*, at the time of writing the market leader.

Failover The process whereby a second system will automatically take over should the currently live system fail. To implement failover the *Information System* must be running on *duplexed servers/mainframes*.

Fallback strategy A term used in planning the *implementation strategy* for a system. The fallback strategy is a contingency plan to revert to the previous system should the implementation of the new system fail.

Feasibility report The end product of the *feasibility study* – used to determine if the project should get the go-ahead.

Feasibility study The first stage in a *system development lifecycle*. A short study to determine if the proposed system is technically feasible, financially worthwhile and ethically justified. The feasibility study produces the *feasibility report* that is used to determine if the project should get the go-ahead. If the project is to proceed the feasibility study will include the terms of reference, a project plan and budget estimates for the future stages of the development.

Ferric oxide A magnetic material used for coating disks – data is then recorded magnetically on the disk.

Fibre optics Fibre optics and light signals are used for *telecommunications* as an alternative to *copper wire* and electrical signals. Fibre optics can transmit more data, at higher speeds and with less distortion than wire.

File A logical area on a *secondary storage* device that is used to store a set of data *records*. Available to a computer *program* via the *operating system*.

File sharing A system that allows more than one user to access a *file* or set of files. Files can be shared on a *server* or in a *cloud* by users with appropriate access permissions. Files can also be shared using peer-to-peer (P2P) technology – these systems have legitimate usages but they are commonly associated with illegal downloads of music and films.

Firewall A *network security* device that rejects access requests from unsafe sources and accepts data from recognized sources.

First-generation computer Early *computers* dating from the 1950s. They were large machines: the logic functions were implemented using valves (*vacuum tubes*), each valve was a *logic gate*.

First mover advantage The advantage that can be gained by the organization that is first to market with a new product or service. The drawback of being the first mover is the high development and marketing costs that might be avoided by later entrants to the market.

First normal form (1NF) In *relational data analysis*, first normal form is derived from the *un-normalized form* by identifying all repeating groups of *attributes*, separating them and allocating each group a compound key.

Foreign key An *attribute*/data item in an *entity*/*record* on a *database*, that identifies a related entity/record. The main way of linking related records on a *relational database*.

Fortran A *programming language* suited to numeric and scientific computing. Dates from the 1950s; currently its main area of use is on *supercomputers* where its *array processing* features can be used to optimize processing speeds.

Fourth-generation language (4GL) A high-level *programming language* designed to reduce the time and effort taken to write *programs*. Also referred to as an *application generator* – can be linked to a *database* package using the schema definition as the basis for generating interface designs and the logic that links the interface and the *database records*.

Functional decomposition Starting from the whole and breaking the requirement down into its constituent parts, e.g. a hierarchy of *data flow diagrams* or breaking down a *programming* requirement into a hierarchy of *modules*.

Functional language A category of *programming language* that is executed by evaluating expressions (as opposed to the more usual *procedural language* which is composed of statements that are executed in turn). *SQL* can be seen as a functional language as it is used to state the data retrieval requirement (as opposed to spelling out in procedural terms how the data is to be accessed).

Gantt chart A type of (horizontal) bar chart that is used to document *project plans*. The Gantt chart plots project activity against timescale; it can also show the allocation of staff and actual progress against the timescale.

GDS See *global distribution system*.

Generalization An *object-oriented* design and *programming* concept that allows an *object* to use the characteristics of a more general object (also known as *inheritance*). Generalization is represented on the following *UML* diagrams:
1. *UML use case diagram*. A generalization is used to show a variation on normal behaviour and any one of the generalizations might be invoked.
2. *UML class diagram*. Object-oriented generalizations that have been identified in the *design* process

are documented on this diagram. Also shown on *entity relationship diagrams* drawn using UML conventions.

General ledger The main accounting record used in double entry bookkeeping – the general ledger includes a record of all purchases and sales. For most organizations, the general ledger will be a computerized *Information System*.

Global distribution system (GDS) Airline booking *electronic market* systems. The GDSs process bookings for all the world's major airlines. The major GDSs are Sabre, Amadeus, Galileo and Worldspan – they can be accessed by *internet e-Commerce* booking sites such as Expedia, Opodo and Travelocity.

Globalization The process of international integration, particularly in the fields of trade and financial transfers. The process of globalization is, in part, facilitated by *electronic commerce* technologies.

Global warming The expectation and concern that human activity such as deforestation and the burning of fossil fuels will change the composition of the atmosphere (by increasing greenhouse gases) and hence cause climate change, global warming and widespread environmental damage. Computing consumes resources when IT equipment is manufactured and operated and hence is a contributor to global warming. *Green computing* is a term for efforts to mitigate these effects.

Go live The process of implementation – the act of turning on and commencing use of a new *Information System*.

Goods-in A warehouse term for the delivery area of the warehouse – from goods-in the product/stock is moved into the storage areas of the warehouse. Where product is required for urgent delivery it may be *cross-docked* to *goods-out* for immediate delivery.

Goods-out A warehouse term for the despatch area of the warehouse – product/stock is moved from the storage areas of the warehouse to goods-out to be made ready for delivery. Many warehouses have a number of *loading bays* where delivery vehicles can be *docked* – in these circumstances, product will be moved to the correct loading bay within the overall goods-out area.

Google An internet *search engine*. The company Google has also diversified into other products such as a smartphone *operating system* and the Chrome *browser*.

Go to A *procedural programming* instruction that changes the sequence of execution of the *program*.

Government-to-Citizen (g2c) *Electronic government* transactions between government and the citizen, see also *citizen-to-government* (c2g).

Green computing Programs to mitigate the effect on the environment of *Information Technology*. Green computing is concerned with reducing the resources used in constructing IT equipment, the energy consumption involved in operating the equipment and the effective and safe recycling of redundant equipment. Note also that computing and IT has a role to play in reducing the environmental impact of other areas such as travel and is extensively used in environmental research projects.

Hacker A *computer programmer* who performs *hacking*. Hackers are motivated by a variety of reasons such as challenge, protest or criminality.

Hacking This term can have more than one usage:
1. Writing complex *software* quickly (and for fun) – making extensive use of the technical features of the *programming language* that is being used.
2. Finding security weaknesses in a computer or computer network and using them to gain unauthorized access.

Hand-held device A hand-held *computer* that can be used for *data capture* on location, e.g. stocktaking around the store or warehouse or meter reading in people's homes.

Hard disk An electromechanical device for storing and retrieving information. Consists of one or more rotating disks (platters), coated with magnetic material, and magnetic heads that are stepped in and out over the disks surfaces to read and write the data.

Hash random A method of achieving direct access to data held on *secondary storage*. Direct access is achieved by calculating the *block* address that contains the target *record* (or where the record is to be written) using the required Key in a hashing *algorithm*. Hash random is also used for *database random access*.

HCI See *human computer interaction*.

Heap A file stored in the sequence that the data becomes available. A storage structure in a *relational database*.

Help desk An information and assistance resource that troubleshoots *Information Technology* and *Information System* problems reported by users of the organization's systems.

Help desk system An *Information System* that records IT problems reported to the *help desk*. The help desk system will normally also record the diagnosis of the problem and the steps taken to resolve it.

Hierarchical database A *database* paradigm based on hierarchies and used by IBM's IMS. No longer widely used (if at all).

High level (programming) language A *programming language* where each statement generates (is compiled into/interpreted as) a number of *machine code* instructions. In general, the higher the level of the language the fewer statements need to be written to solve any given problem.

Hollerith An American statistician who developed an early *tabulator* that used *punched cards*. The term Hollerith gets applied to all *conventional machinery* and the punched cards that they processed.

Hosting Providing *server* (*server farm*) space and facilities for customer applications, e.g. hosting web pages.

HTML See *hyper text mark-up language*.

Hub A hub is a *network* device that joins communication lines together. The hub shares the network capacity between devices. See also *switch*.

Hub and spoke A term used to describe an *electronic data interchange* trading pattern. The hub is a large organization, such as a supermarket, and the spokes are its suppliers.

Human computer interaction (HCI) The science, or art, of designing system interfaces, principally for *data capture* but also for *operating system* interfaces, websites, transaction output and *management information*. The study of HCI involves the disciplines of psychology, sociology, linguistics, graphic design and ergonomics.

Hyper text mark-up language (HTML) A mark-up language used to specify a *web* page.

IBM An American multinational computing and consulting company. IBM are the market leaders in the supply of *mainframes* (although the use of the mainframe is much less widespread than it once was).

IBM PC The first business *PC*. It set the standards for the PC industry. IBM no longer make or market a PC.

ICL A UK computing company that once made and marketed the ICL 1900 and 2900 mainframes. ICL were merged into Fujitsu in 2002.

i-Commerce See *internet e-Commerce*.

Icon In *computing*, a small pictogram on a screen that allows a user to select an option, e.g. a picture of a disk that indicates the save file option. A way of presenting a *menu*.

ICT See *Information and Communications Technology* (also an early name for the company *ICL*).

Identity theft The stealing of an individual's personal details (name, date of birth, bank account, etc.) – usually with the intent of using the details for a fraudulent purpose (opening a bank account, obtaining a passport, etc.) in the name of the targeted individual.

Implementation The act of taking a new *Information System* from its development/testing stages and installing it for operational use. Note the term Implementation can also be used for the activity of *programming*, i.e. implementing the design as program code.

Implementation strategy The strategy to be adopted for *implementing* a new *Information System*. Options include a phased or a *big bang* approach.

Inbound logistics Obtaining supplies of components or merchandise – from *Porter's Generic Value Chain*.

Include A feature of the *UML use case diagram*. The Include is used to document a chunk of behaviour that is similar across several use cases.

Index access The use of an index file (or index records) to look up the *block* location of a *record* with a given value in the specified field. Indexes can be applied to *database* records.

Index sequential file A *secondary storage conventional file* where *random access* is achieved by looking up the *block* that contains the target *record* (or where the record is to be written) in an index. Indexes are also used for *database random access*.

Information and Communications Technology (ICT) The combination of *computing* and communications (*network*) technologies (now the norm as almost all *computers* come with built-in communications facilities).

Information Commissioner The UK Information Commissioner is appointed by the Queen. The Commissioner is the head the *Office of the Information Commissioner* which is an independent and official body. The commissioner is responsible for the implementation of the *Data Protection Act* and the Freedom of Information Act.

Information revolution The change from an Industrial to a post-industrial or *Information Society*, facilitated by the widespread availability and use of *Information and Communications Technologies*.

Information Society A society where the creation, distribution and manipulation of information are the most significant economic and cultural activities.

Information System A business application of a computer. Examples of Information Systems are a *payroll* and *order processing*.

Information System department The department in an organization that is responsible for the provision and maintenance of *Information Systems* and *Information Technology*.

Information Technology Computing equipment (hardware) – the term is now normally understood to also encompass communications technology, see also *Information and Communications Technology*.

Inheritance An *object-oriented* design and *programming* concept that allows an *object* to use the characteristics of a more general object (also known as *generalization*).

Initial prototype The first (and normally very restricted) *prototype* – produced in a development *project* using a *prototype lifecycle* or *evolutionary prototype lifecycle*.

In-source Taking work back into the organization that had previously been *outsourced*.

Integrated circuit An electronic circuit that is created using lithography on a small wafer of silicon – also referred to as an *silicon chip*.

Integration test Once *software* is written it must be *tested* – testing checks for errors in the programming and flaws in the design. Integration testing links *modules* together into complete *programs*/subsystems. Given the modules have been tested in isolation they can be seen as black boxes (see *black box testing*) and the integration test can concentrate on testing the linkages/interfaces between modules. Integration testing is a technical test and would normally be the responsibility of the *programmer*/program team. Integration testing can be followed by *system* and *acceptance testing*.

Intellectual property rights (IPR) Inventions protected by *patent* and original written material protected by *copyright*. Protection is provided against the unauthorized use, copying or sale of the protected material.

Interface design Designing the *human computer interface* to be easy and efficient to use. Applicable to *data capture* but also to interfaces such as websites, touch screen devices and outputs from *Information Systems* in print or on screen.

Interface object An *object* created in a *UML sequence diagram* to represent input from the *actor* in the *use case*.

Internet The worldwide *network* of networks that uses *TCP/IP* as its protocol and is open for public access. Most networks are linked into the internet and hence can be considered to be part of the internet.

Internet e-Commerce (i-Commerce) A business operation processed via an *e-Shop* business operation. The shop front is a website that connects to a *back office* system on a *server.* Used for both *business-to-consumer* and *business-to-business* operations.

Internet protocol (IP) *TCP/IP* is the *transmission protocol* of the *internet*. IP provides the routing mechanism.

Internet service provider (ISP) An organization that provides *internet* access and facilities to third parties.

Inter-Organizational Information System (IOS) *Information Systems* in separate organizations that are closely coupled and effectively work as a single Information System. An example could be organizations in a *supply chain* with the coupling implemented using *electronic data interchange*.

Interpreter *Software* that executes source code (the language the programmer writes), by converting it into the *machine code* of the target *computer*, at run time. See also *compiler*.

Intranet A private *network* within an organization using *web* technology.

IOS See *Inter-Organizational Information System*.

IP See *internet protocol*.

IPR See *intellectual property rights*.

IS See *Information System*.

ISP See *internet service provider*.

IT See *Information Technology*.

Iteration To iterate is to repeat a process with differing inputs or making incremental changes. Specific uses of iterate/iteration in *Information Systems* are:
1. In an *evolutionary prototype lifecycle* where the *prototypes* are iterated until the required functionality and performance are achieved.
2. In the *UML sequence diagram* where messages can be required to iterate.
3. In *Jackson structures* where one of the three basic constructs is the iteration.

Iterative lifecycle A *system development lifecycle* where stages are *iterated*, as opposed to the sequential completion of stages in the *waterfall lifecycle*. Iterative lifecycles are normally associated with *prototyping*, see also the *evolutionary prototype lifecycle.*

Jackson structures A diagramming convention promulgated by Michael A. Jackson. Jackson's thesis was that there are three basic constructs in a data structure and in a *program*; these are sequence, selection and *iteration*.

JANET The UK Joint Academic Network – used by universities and other educational establishments. Founded in 1984. Part of the *internet*, in effect an *extranet*.

Java A *high level*, *object-oriented*, *programming language*. Java achieves machine independence by a two-stage process: Java is *compiled* to a machine independent code which is then executed on a machine dependant Java Virtual Machine at runtime.

Join A *relational algebra* operator that produces a new *relationship* from two existing relationships joined over a common key. The function is implemented in *SQL*

Just-in-time A production (or retail) strategy that seeks to reduce inventory – components/merchandise are delivered at the time they are needed on the production line, in the distribution centre or on the shelves in a retail operation.

Key target report A style of *management information* report where performance data is calculated and set out against pre-defined targets, e.g. on-time arrivals for train services.

Knowledge worker A worker whose tasks involve the application of knowledge (as opposed to manual workers whose tasks are the manipulation of tangible objects).

LAN See *local area network*.

Laptop A *personal computer* with the screen, keyboard *hard disk* (or solid state equivalent) and *processor* built into a single portable unit. Powered by a rechargeable battery.

LDS See *logical data structure*.

Legacy system An *Information System* that has been around for some time – possibly implemented using technologies that would (probably) not be used for a new system. The term has a pejorative tone but very often the legacy systems are the *enterprise systems* of the organization.

Leo 1 The first *computer* to run a routine office job – a *first-generation computer*. The Leo 1, developed by Joe Lyons (a British catering company) in conjunction with Cambridge University. It first operated in 1951.

Lifeline On a *UML sequence diagram* – the lifeline indicates whether the *object* pre-exists the *use case* and whether it is persistent (un-deleted) after the use case.

LinkedIn A *social networking site* for professional people and business contacts.

Link test The testing of a complete *program* (or *Information System*) where the component *modules* have previously been separately *module tested*. The link test proves the interfaces and further testing of the functionality and usability, e.g. *system test* and *acceptance test*, will still be required.

Linux A *UNIX* like *operating system*. Developed using *participatory software development* principals/ techniques. Available as freeware.

Local area network (LAN) A *network* within the premises of an organization. It is owned and controlled by the organization and will, usually, be technically heterogeneous.

Logical data structure (LDS) The *SSADM* term for the *entity relationship diagram*.

Logical design Following the gathering of user requirements the logical design specifies the user system in a technology independent manner. Logical design is followed by *technical design* that specifies how the system will be implemented on the proposed IT. More specifically, logical design is a *SSADM* stage.

Logic circuit In a *digital computer* or an electronic component in another device. An arrangement of *logic gates* to perform a specific logic function, e.g. to add two *binary* numbers together.

Logic gate An element in a *logic circuit*. Logic gates documented in this text are *AND*, *OR* and *NOT* gates – some texts also describe *NAND*, *NOR* and *XOR* gates. Logic gates were originally implemented using valves (*vacuum tubes*) which were superseded by *transistors* and then by *transistor equivalents* on a *silicon chip*.

Login To obtain access to a computer system that has privacy protection – a login normally requires a *user-id* and *password*.

Lower CASE *Computer-aided software engineering* (CASE) applied to the later (*programming* and *testing*) stages of the *system development lifecycle*.

Machine code The native *programming language* of the computer (or *processor* chip) is its machine code. Instructions in the machine code correspond one to one with processor functions.

Magnetic core memory *Main memory* in a *second-generation computer*. Made up of small magnetic rings each threaded with wires to read and write information.

Magnetic disk A *secondary storage device*, see *hard disk*. Also exchangeable disks, floppy disks and diskettes which are in principle much the same but now little used.

Magnetic ink character recognition A form of character recognition used primarily in the banking industry. The technology reads characters recorded in magnetic ink, in a standard position, on documents such as a cheque.

Magnetic strip Used on cards, e.g. credit/debit cards. It can be pre-recorded with up to 60 characters of data and is read by swiping through a reader.

Mailbox In a *post and forward* network, the computer file where outbound messages are stored awaiting download by the intended recipient.

Mainframe A large powerful *computer* used for commercial applications – essentially a *server* but distinguished by its size and resilience.

Main memory The *processor* memory of a computer – directly accessible by the program instructions as they are executed in the processor.

Maintenance Applicable to live *Information Systems* – it involves error correction (bug fixes), enhancement and (for bought-in *software*) installing new releases.

Malware Short for malicious *software*. A general term for any software (or a code script) designed to run on a computer system without the owner's consent.

Management The act of organizing people and resources to achieve desired goals – normally understood to be a function of staff appointed to a managerial role.

Management information Information output from an *Information System* to aid staff in effective decision-making in the *management* of the organization.

Management Information System (MIS) An *Information System* (or subsystem) specifically designed to produce *management information*. In the US, MIS is synonymous with IS.

Mark sensing Mark sensing works by reading marks recorded in pre-set positions on a paper form. The main current application is for lotteries.

Massively parallel Where a large number of *processors* are used to perform elements of a single task – a technique used in *supercomputing*.

Materials and requirement planning (MRP) A system used in manufacture to plan production schedules and to ensure that the necessary components are available (in stock) or on order (and due for *just-in-time* delivery).

m-Commerce See *mobile e-Commerce*.

Menu A list of processes in a system, displayed on a screen, where the user selects the process they wish to use. Also *drop down menu* where the user can select an option – can be used to offer a list of valid data values in *data capture*.

Message This can have more than one usage:
1. A transmission between the user and the server/ *transaction processing system*.
2. In *object-oriented design* and on the *sequence diagram* a message is an action/interaction between the *classes*/*objects* represented on that diagram.

Message log A file where input messages are recorded. Used in *transaction processing/database management systems* for recovery (roll-forward of a restored *database*).

Meta tag An *HTML* tag on a webpage used to provide metadata about that webpage, e.g. keywords intended for indexing by *search engines*.

Method This can have more than one usage:
1. Similar in meaning to *methodology* but generally less complete or prescriptive.
2. The method is the processing requirement specified for an *object*/*class* on an *UML class diagram* – taken from *message* on the *UML sequence diagram*.

Methodology A set of guidelines for the analysis, design and development of an *Information System*. A methodology will normally encapsulate a philosophy and specify the stages (*system development lifecycle*) and techniques that should be used.

Microblog An internet broadcast media for text messages where the allowable character length is strictly limited, e.g. *Twitter*.

Micro chip This can have more than one usage:
1. A *silicon chip*, e.g. a *processor* chip or a memory chip.
2. Micro chips can be embedded in items such as credit/debit cards and used for *data capture* through a card reader device. The chip can be contactless using *RFID* technology. On a passport the chip includes *biometric* data.

Micro computer Originally a computer where the *processor* was on a single chip. Now, if the term is used, it is synonymous with a *personal computer* (PC).

Microsoft Office A suite of desktop productivity programs for use on *PCs*. The Microsoft Office Suite includes a word processor (MS Word), spreadsheet (MS Excel) and desktop *database management system* (MS Access).

Microwave Used for *telecommunications* as an alternative to *copper wire*. The signal is sent, through the air, using microwave radio relay, from one dish to another – there must be a *line of sight* connection between dishes.

Millennium bug This bug was the concern that *computer* systems would not be able to deal correctly with the change of year from 1999 to 2000. The issue arose from the common practice of recording the year as two digits, e.g. 99 or 00. Systems had to be amended to use four digit century dates or to record dates in some other *century proof* format.

Milliondollarhomepage The milliondollarhomepage was created in 2005 by Alex Tew. It contains one million pixels, sold (in blocks of ten) for a dollar each. Users of the site click through to the webpages of the owners of the pixels that are clicked on.

Mini computer A term used in the era of *second-generation computers* for a computer that was smaller than a *mainframe* (and very possibly did not require the temperature controlled environment that was required by mainframes).

Minitel An early (and very successful) French videotext system – started in 1978 and eventually *retired* in 2012. French *telecommunications* users were issued with free Minitel terminals.

MIS See *Management Information System*.

Mission-critical A component in an activity, the failure of which would lead to the failure of the whole activity. In an organization, components of the *Information System*/*Information Technology* infrastructure will be mission-critical as their failure would lead to the close down of the organization and its *operations*.

Mission statement A statement of purpose of an organization. Normally short, a mission encapsulates the organization's aims, stakeholders and value proposition. It can seek to define the ethos of the organization.

Mobile See *mobile telephone*.

Mobile e-Commerce (m-Commerce) *i-Commerce* conducted using a mobile device – a *smartphone*, *laptop* or *tablet computer* – when away from the home or office.

Mobile telephone (Mobile) A portable, wireless telephone that can send and receive voice messages over a radio link. Many mobile telephones also connect to the *internet* and provide a wide range of additional facilities – see also *smartphone*.

Modelling language An artificial language that allows structures to be defined. *Unified modelling*

language (UML) is referred to as a modelling language (as opposed to a *system analysis and design methodology*) when it should, perhaps, be more properly described as a diagramming convention.

Module A component that forms part of a whole. In *software* development, a unit of code that performs a defined purpose and is separately *compiled* and *tested* but is then used as a component in a larger *program*.

Module test The testing of a *module* as a separate unit of code – prior to the module being incorporated into the larger unit of *software* where it can be *link tested* and where it will eventually be used.

Mosaic The first *browser* (in the way we now understand the term). Developed by the US National Centre for Supercomputing Applications in 1993.

MRP See *materials and requirements planning*.

Multiplexor Combines several low speed transmissions into a single high speed transmission. The multiplexor can use frequency division multiplexing (where several signals are sent down a single link at different frequencies), time division multiplexing (where the signal is interleaved with other signals on the same frequency) or both.

Multiprocessing Some computer systems will have two or more *processors* – the *operating system* must support and make optimum use of all the processors.

Multiprogramming Effectively the same as *multitasking*.

Multitasking Many computer systems will run more than one application at a time. The *operating system* must ensure effective *time-sharing* between all these *programs* (the basic trick is that while one program is suspended waiting for a data transfer another program can be making use of *processor* time).

Multithreading *Multitasking* within an application, e.g. a *TP system* with many users logged on at any time.

My SQL A *relational database management system* (DBMS). An open source, freeware product (but commercially owned) extensively used, particularly for online systems.

NAND gate A *logic gate* which produces an output of one when any input is zero – the output is zero when all inputs are one. The effect of a NAND gate is the same as an *AND + NOT gate*.

Needle's Business in Context Model The model represents business/organization in four layers: activity, strategy, organization and environment. Business functions are ascribed to each of these layers. The model makes the important point that an organization does not function in isolation but in an external social and economic context. See Needle (2010).

Network A connection between *computer* systems/IT devices allowing the sharing of resources and information.

Network connection The communications media in a network. Technologies include *copper wire*, *fibre optics*, *microwave*, *satellite* and *radio*. This book uses the term network connection but it is not a generally used term.

Network database A *database* paradigm based on the linked list *data structure*. Used in the IDMS *database management system*.

Network effect The network effect is the scenario that the higher the usage of a product or service then the more valuable that product or service becomes. An example is a *social networking site*: there is not much point in joining a site where there are few members to socialize with.

Network interface card A hardware component that connects the *computer* to the *network*. The logic of the card implements the intended network's *transmission protocol*, e.g. *ethernet* on a *LAN*.

Network security Protection of a system against unauthorized access/activity originating from a *network*. A *firewall* system can be a component in network security.

Non-repudiation Mechanisms to prevent the issuers of transactions, especially financial transactions, subsequently denying responsibilities for those transactions. Applicable mechanisms include the use of *digital signatures* and *trusted third parties*.

NOR gate A *logic gate* which produces an output of one when all inputs are zero – the output is one for all other input combinations. The effect of a NOR gate is the same as an *OR + NOT gate*.

NOT gate A *logic gate* which produces an output of one when the input is zero – the output is zero when the input is one.

Object An object is a self-contained module of data and its associated processing – the aim is that objects are reusable. See also *encapsulation*, *generalization* and *polymorphism*.

Object-oriented (OO) An approach to *SA&D* that aims to design the system in terms of *objects*, represented on a *class diagram*.

Object-oriented database A *database management system* where the data is stored in the form of *objects* (and the *object-oriented* principles *of encapsulation*, *generalization* and *polymorphism* should be implemented). Some *relational databases* incorporate object-oriented principles (or so it is claimed).

Object-oriented system analysis and design (OO SA&D) An approach to *system analysis and design* that aims to design the system in terms of *objects*, represented on a *class diagram*.

OCR See *optical character recognition*.

Odette An *electronic data interchange* message coding standard used by the European automotive industry.

Office of the Information Commissioner See *information commissioner*.

Off-shore *Outsourcing* to an overseas supplier – for this book an overseas supplier of *Information Systems*/*Information Technology* services.

On the fly Web pages where the *HTML* is generated at runtime. Most large *e-Shops* will generate many of their web pages on the fly from data held on a *database* – this enables the information to be up to date with any changes to price, stock figures, etc.

OO See *object-oriented*.

OO SA&D See *object-oriented system analysis and design*.

Operating system *System software* that manages the *computer* hardware (including *secondary storage* and *multiprogramming*) and provides an interface to the *application software*. Examples of PC operating systems are Microsoft Windows and Apple *OS X*.

Operations This term can have more than one usage:

1. The basic function of an *organization* – what it does, its productive function, e.g. making cars or selling groceries; as opposed to the *support functions* that facilitate the operations.
2. The part of the IS/IT department that operate the *Information Technology*.
3. The final stage in the *system development lifecycle*. The stage where the system is released/installed for use: the *go live*. Also the use of that live system and any maintenance and enhancement that is required.

Optical character recognition (OCR) Electronic reading of characters, scanned from paper documents and converted to machine encoded text. Various systems have been deployed using standard forms but this is largely discontinued. OCR can be used to read in typed manuscripts, e.g. to digitize books where an electronic version is not available. Also used to recognize characters written with a stylus on *tablet* devices. See also *magnetic ink character recognition*.

Oracle A *relational database management system* (DBMS). The market leading DBMS for large *Information Systems*.

Order processing system An *Information System* for processing customer orders. The main input transaction is the customer order which is processed, using customer and product data, to output the delivery note and invoice transactions. The order processing system may well be integrated with *e-Commerce* systems such as *EDI* and/or an *e-Shop*.

Organization An organization is an entity that employs people in order to achieve an objective. Some organizations are *businesses* and they also aim to make a profit, e.g. Ford Motor Company and amazon.com. Examples of non-profit-making organizations could be a government department or a university. All organizations employ people, have to be managed and use *Information Systems* and *Information Technology*. The study of business and Information Systems generally relates to all types of organization.

OR gate A *logic gate* which produces an output of one when any input is one – the output is zero when all the inputs are zero.

OS X Apple's PC *operating system* – based on *UNIX*.

Outbound logistics Despatching finished/sold products – from *Porter's Generic Value Chain*.

Outsource Obtaining goods or services from an outside supplier in place of an internal source. Functions of the internal *Information Systems department* that might be outsourced include: desktop (PC) maintenance and support, *software* development (of bespoke applications) and hosting (using *servers* operated by an outside supplier).

Packet-switching A digital data transmission standard where the message is divided into standard size packets; each packet is then dynamically routed through the *network* and finally the message is reassembled at its destination. Packet-switching avoids the need for a switched network between the source and destination (and hence reduces connection costs). Packet-switching can also work round equipment failures and bottlenecks by dynamically selecting alternative routings.

Paperless trading An informal definition of *EDI*, see also *electronic data interchange*.

Parallel running An approach to system *implementation* where the new and the old *Information System* are both operated for a period of time until the new system is proved to be satisfactory. This is a very safe approach, since the old system can be reinstated if any problems occur, but it is often impractical, since all transactions have to be applied to both systems (and there has to be the *Information Technology* capacity to run both systems).

Participatory software development *Software* development by an informal grouping of individuals who contribute code, amend other peoples code and share the testing of a software product. Commonly associated with the Free Software Movement. Notable software products developed in this way include *Linux*.

Password A code used to gain access to a computer system, *Information System* or website. The password is personal to the user and should be kept secret – it is often used in conjunction with a *user-id*.

Patent The right of an inventor to protect their tangible work from copying and exploitation by others (and hence benefit from any revenues accruing from the use or sale of the work). One form of *intellectual property right*. See also *copyright*.

Payload The payload is the functionality of *malware*. The payload might for example, disrupt computer operation, gather sensitive information or gain unauthorized access to *computer* systems.

PayPal An *e-Commerce* organization that facilitates payments and money transfers made via the *internet*. PayPal can be used for one-off payments by credit or debit card but also acts as an *e-Cash* service where users can maintain an account balance to accept and make online payments.

Payroll system An *Information System* for processing a payroll. This system starts with details of employees and their rates of pay and processes this data to produce bank transfers, payslips, etc. The payroll was one of the earliest systems to be computerized. Many organizations *outsource* their payroll process – there is no *competitive advantage* to be gained from running such a basic system in-house.

PC See *personal computer*.

Personal computer (PC) A small, general-purpose *computer*, used by one person. The computer can be used stand-alone or to access systems or data over a *network*. The term PC is taken to include *desktop*, *laptop* and *tablet* machines – *Apple* computers are included in the concept.

PERT See *program evaluation and review technique*.

Phishing Attempting to obtain information (and possibly money) by masquerading as someone who the user might trust, e.g. the e-Mail purporting to be from the bank that asks for your *login* and security details.

Physical design An alternative term for *technical design*.

Physical security The aspects of *computer security* that relate to the physical protection of the *Information Technology* equipment from threats such as accidental damage, deliberate damage, theft and unauthorized usage.

Picking list A list, produced from an *order processing system* of stock items that are to be collected from the warehouse and despatched to the customer. A picking list can be on paper or electronic (say on a *hand-held device*). The picking list can be sorted to optimize the time taken to pick the required items.

Pipeline An approach to speeding up computer processing by overlapping the processing of *machine code* instructions or data items in a vector (one dimensional array).

Plan (machine code) The *machine code* of the *ICL* 1900 series computers.

Polymorphism An *object-oriented* design and *programming* concept that allows *objects* to be created whose exact type is not known until run time.

Porter Michael E. Porter is a leading academic authority on business competitiveness and business strategy. Responsible for: Porter's Model of Competitive Advantage (The Five Forces Model), *Porter's Generic Value Chain* and Porter's Generic Competitive Advantages.

Porter's Generic Value Chain This model shows all activities that a business must undertake (although the way they are organized and the emphasis on each activity will differ between industry sectors and between businesses). The model divides activities between primary (productive) and secondary (overhead) activities. The difference between the cost of the activities and value of the output is the margin (profit). See (Porter, 1985).

Postbox In a *post and forward* network, the computer file where inbound messages are (temporarily) stored before being moved to the *mailbox* of the intended recipient.

Post and forward A network provision where an intermediary system receives messages (into the user's *postbox*) and sorts them (into the *mailboxes* of the intended recipients) for later collection at the recipient's convenience. An essential feature of a *VADS*.

Primary key An *attribute*/data item in an *entity*/*record* that uniquely identifies that entity/record.

Primary supplies Supplies used in the business *operations*, e.g. components required for a manufacturing process or merchandise required for a retail operation (as opposed to *secondary supplies* used in internal processes).

Primary validation The checking of data against pre-set rules (for format, range, etc.) during *data capture*, see also *secondary validation*.

Problem requirement list A *SSADM* technique – a list of the problems the user has with the current system and the features they would like to add in the new (replacement) system.

Problem situation The term used for the area of investigation is *sociotechnical systems* – summarized as a *rich picture* in the *soft systems methodology*.

Procedural language A category of *programming language* composed of statements that are executed in turn (as opposed to *functional languages* that are executed by evaluating expressions). Languages such as *C* and *Fortran* are procedural languages.

Process A general term for an application, or part of an application, run on a *computer*, e.g. an *order processing system*. Also, and more specifically:
1. A symbol on the *SSADM data flow diagram*. A process transforms one or more input *data flows* to produce one or more output dataflows. The process is analogous to a *program* in a physical system.

Processor The central processing unit of a computer – essentially the decode unit, the *arithmetic logic unit* and the *control unit*. The processor *silicone chip*.

Prodigy An early *videotext*, online information service provider in the US.

Professional society An association of members of a learned profession. The professional society seeks to set standards for the profession and to promote the interests of its profession and its members. For *computing* in the UK the main professional society is the *Chartered Institute for IT* (BCS).

Program A unit of *machine code* that is executed on a computer to perform a specific function. The program will normally have been compiled or interpreted from source code, written by a *programmer* in a *programming language*, e.g. *Java*.

Program and unit test The process of writing program/software code and testing each unit of code in isolation. Program and unit test is a stage of the *system development lifecycle*.

Program evaluation and review technique (PERT) A *project planning* technique that charts each activity in relationship to other activities taking into account the dependencies between them. The technique facilitates the determination of the minimum overall elapse time and the *critical path* for a *project*.

Program team leader The leader of a team of *programmers* – normally an experienced programmer will take this role.

Programmer An *Information Technology* specialist who writes and tests *programs*. Derogatory term: *Code Monkey* – people use it when they get annoyed by programmers!

Programming Writing, testing and maintaining the source code for a *computer program*. The source code must be written in strict conformance with the specification of the *programming language* and must be a complete logic solution for the *application*.

Programming language An artificial language used for communicating instructions to a computer. The language of the computer is its *machine code*. *Programmers* typically use *high-level languages* which are *compiled* or *interpreted* into *machine code* for execution.

Progress monitoring Checking the work completed against the expectations of the *project plan*. A *project management* function.

Project This term can have more than one usage:
1. A task, such as the development of an *Information System*, which is assigned to a *project team*.
2. A *relational algebra* operator that selects a number of columns from an existing *relationship* to produce a new relationship. The function is implemented in *SQL*.

Project management Management of the *project team* to ensure that the *project* is delivered on time and on budget.

Project manager The manager of a *project team*. The role of the project manager is to plan the project, run the project team and ensure that the project is delivered on time and on budget.

Project plan A plan developed by the *project manager* to ensure that the *project* is delivered on time and on budget. Project planning involves *estimating*, planning (using techniques such as *PERT* and *Gantt charts*), work allocation and *progress monitoring*.

Project team Any significant *Information System* development will normally have a project team set up to do the work involved. The job of the project team is to deliver the *project* on time and on budget.

Protocol See *transmission protocol*.

Prototype A model built to test or demonstrate a concept. In *Information Systems*, a prototype is a simple program, quickly constructed, to demonstrate or elucidate the requirements of a *process* or system.

Prototype lifecycle A *system development lifecycle* that uses *prototypes* to elucidate and demonstrate the requirements of the proposed *Information System*. Once the requirements are established the Information System can be developed using a conventional (*waterfall lifecycle*) approach or the prototypes can be enhanced in a series of iterations to produce the required Information System, see also *evolutionary prototype lifecycle*.

Public private key A cryptology system used, for example, in *secure socket layer* (SSL) internet *encryption*. In brief, when the browser requests a secure webpage, SSL works as follows:

1. The server sends a public key (k1 – the key is not made public but could be intercepted).
2. The browser generates a random key (k2) and encrypts it with the public key (k1).
3. The server decrypts the encrypted k2 with its private key (k3).

The rest of the encrypted session can now proceed using k2 as the encryption key.

Punched card A data capture system where characters are coded as combinations of holes in columns on standard size sheets of card. The cards are then fed through a card reader and the data is transferred into the computer system.

Punched card system A system that uses *punched cards* processed on *conventional machines*.

Pure-play This refers to a retail organization that sells through an *e-Shop* (clicks) and does not have any conventional retail outlet. An example of pure-play is *Amazon*, whereas Tesco (a large UK supermarket chain) has conventional stores plus an *e-Shop* and can be referred to as *bricks-and-clicks*.

QR code A two-dimensional (2d) *barcode* (QR stands for quick response). The QR code is a square with a pattern of smaller squares inside it – no bars. The QR code contains more data than a standard barcode. Applications include airline boarding passes and encoding website URLs (these can be read by devices such as a *smartphone* and, with the right *app*, can then link to the website).

Quality assurance In general, quality assurance is the systematic monitoring of a production process or service delivery to ensure that (minimum) standards are being achieved. For an *Information Systems project* the role of quality assurance is to ensure that appropriate standards are applied and the end product is fit for purpose – it needs to meet business

objectives. An *Information Systems* project should be delivered on time and on budget – arguably these are also quality objectives.

Quick and dirty A *program* written very quickly without attention to structure and possibly excluding peripheral functionality such as *validation* and exception processing. A quick and dirty program might be produced as a first *prototype* in an *iterative lifecycle*.

Quick response A retail version of *just-in-time*. Quick response seeks to reduce inventory – merchandise is delivered at the time it is needed in the distribution centre or on the shelves in a retail operation.

RAD See *rapid application development*.

Radio Used for the local connection in mobile telephony (and *mobile*/*smartphones* are increasingly used for data communications/*internet* access).

Radio button A limited set of options on a *data capture* screen where the user can select only one of the offered options, e.g. for specifying gender.

Radio frequency identification device (RFID) A cheap *chip* that can be attached to an object. When the object (and hence the chip) comes within range (limited to a few metres) of an interrogator (reader) it is activated and transmits its identification data.

RAID A *secondary storage* technology using an array of disk drives and incorporating resilience features. RAID stands for redundant array of independent disks.

Random access On *secondary storage*, reading a required *record* by direct access. The file-handling software uses an *index* or a *hashing* algorithm to determine the *block* and hence a record that is to be read. See also *serial access*.

Rapid application development (RAD) Rapid application development uses the *evolutionary prototype lifecycle* and techniques such as timeboxing to ensure the rapid development of *Information Systems* (or components of *Information Systems*). The term predates *agile*, but the philosophies have much in common.

Rational rose A *CASE* tool designed to document and implement *unified modelling language* (UML).

Rational unified process (RUP) A *methodology* designed to complement the *unified modelling language* (UML) techniques.

RDA See *relational data analysis*.

Record On a *conventional file* or *database*, a logical unit of data, e.g. all the data held on a single customer. Records are packed into *blocks*, the physical unit of access/transfer on *secondary storage*. On a

relational database the record can be referred to as a **relationship**.

Recycle The processing of used materials into new products. In **green computing** the concern is that redundant **Information Technology** equipment should be reused or disposed of in an **environmentally** friendly manner – this can include upgrading to prolong the useful life of the kit, passing it on for use by someone else (possibly a good cause) and dismantling so parts might be reused or processed into recycled materials.

Register This term can have more than one usage:
1. To join an online service – often involving the creation/allocation of a **user-id** and **password**.
2. A small unit of memory in the **CPU**, holding a word or small number of bytes. Data is retrieved from main memory to the register prior to a maths/logic operation and returned to main memory once the operation(s) are complete. See also **accumulator**.

Registration The process of joining an online service – often involving the creation/allocation of a **user-id** and **password**.

Relational algebra The mathematical approach of **relations** and sets underlying the design of a **relational database**.

Relational data analysis (RDA) An analysis and rationalization of data requirements into **entities** and **attributes** – each entity has a unique key attribute (or a unique compound key formed by more than one attributes). RDA is a four-stage, bottom-up process progressing from **un-normalized form**, through **first normal form**, **second normal form** to **third normal form**.

Relational database A **database** organized in accordance with relational principles. The relational approach to **database** design is credited to Edgar **Codd** who worked in the **IBM** laboratories in the late 1960s. The relational approach is based on the mathematical concepts of **relations** and sets. **Database management systems** such as **Access**, **MySQL** and **Oracle** are based on the relational approach.

Relationship This term can have more than one usage:
1. A symbol used in an entity **relationship diagram**. The relationship is an **association** between two **entities** e.g. a relationship between the customer and order entity. The relationship will normally show the **cardinality** of the relationship.
2. The term used for a **record** on a **relational database** – also referred to as a **tuple** in **relational algebra**.

Replenishment The process of ordering new (replacement) stock (replenishment works in conjunction with **stock control**).

Replenishment order An order sent to a supplier by the **replenishment system**.

Replenishment system An **Information System** for ordering new (replacement) stock. The system produces a **replenishment order** and also processes **goods-in** and payments. The replenishment system may well be integrated with **EDI**, **e-Commerce** systems.

Repository In a **CASE** tool – a **database** of the **attributes** (and possibly other artefacts) required in the system.

Request for change A procedure for requesting changes to an **Information System** (that is live or under development). Requests for change are evaluated, costed and prioritized – they can then be scheduled with appropriate resources allocated to the work.

Requirement analysis An activity in the **system analysis and design** stage of the **system development lifecycle**. Also a named stage in the **SSADM** lifecycle. The stage is where the **system analyst** studies the business activity and business requirement for a proposed **Information System**.

Requirement specification A document that records the user requirements (functional and non-functional) of the proposed **Information System**.

Resilience The ability of a system to withstand stress or to recover quickly should a failure occur. Resilience provision can include: ensuring data **backups** are taken regularly, installing a **standby generator** and **duplexing** the system.

Restrict A **relational algebra** operator that selects a number of rows from an existing **relationship** to produce a new relationship. The function is implemented in **SQL**.

RFID See **radio frequency identification device**.

Rich picture A technique in the **soft systems methodology**. The rich picture is intended to represent the **problem situation** from the points of view of all the stakeholders in the system.

Roll-over An **icon** or button on a webpage that changes colour or design (implemented by a replacement image) when the mouse cursor is passed over it.

Root definition A technique in the **soft systems methodology**. The root definition is a single sentence that attempts to sum up the overall requirement of the system. The definition should encompass six factors represented by the mnemonic **CATWOE**.

Rotational delay On a **secondary storage** disk, the delay incurred in waiting for the disk to rotate until the required **block** is under the read-write heads. The delay is a very small time but adds up if a large number of **blocks**/**records** are to be processed.

Router A **network** device that forwards data from one segment of the network to another segment. Routers read the **protocol** to obtain routing information. See also **bridge**.

RUP See **rational unified process**.

SaaS See **Software as a Service**.

Safety-critical system A system where failure or malfunction may result in: death or serious injury to people, loss or severe damage to equipment or environmental harm, e.g. air traffic control, railway signalling and control systems in complex plants, such as a nuclear power station.

SAP A major supplier of **enterprise resource planning** (ERP) systems.

Satellite Used for long-distance **telecommunications** links across continents or oceans (in the latter case, as an alternative to laying under-water cables). The system requires a geo-stationary satellite and then **microwave radio** relay transmissions are sent from one ground station, *bounced* off the satellite and received at a second ground station.

SA&D See **system analysis and design**.

Scanner In computing, a device that optically scans and records a digital image. Scanners can include **optical character recognition** capability.

Scrum An **agile software development** method. The basic unit of development is a timeboxed task called a *sprint*. A **project** is divided into a number of sprints. As each sprint is completed it is implemented and hence the functionality of the delivered system grows incrementally.

SDLC See **system development lifecycle**. Sometimes assumed to have a more restrictive meaning of referring specifically to the **waterfall lifecycle**.

Search engine Software designed to search for information on the **World Wide Web**. Search engines set up a complex index to the web using web crawlers (software that searches the web). The index also contains sponsored entries and historically involved manual indexing. The search engine then responds to user requests by searching its own index.

Search engine optimization (SEO) The process of improving a webpage's ranking in **search engine** results. Possible tactics include adjusting the page content to reflect expected search terms and creating links from other webpages. The search engines try to

detect *cheating* and will downgrade pages that seem to be manipulating their rankings.

Second-generation computer Computers that came into commercial use in the 1960s; they used **transistors**, in place of the valves (**vacuum tubes**), for their logic circuits.

Second normal form (2NF) In **relational data analysis**, second normal form is derived from the **first normal form** by identifying any partial-key dependencies, separating them and identifying them with their key.

Secondary storage Any medium to which the computer can write data in machine readable format. The essential secondary storage device is the **hard disk** but other secondary storage devices include the solid-state drives, the optical disk (CD/DVD) and various sizes and shapes of magnetic tapes.

Secondary supplies Supplies used in internal processes, e.g. stationery and computer consumables (as opposed to **primary supplies** used in the business **operations**).

Secondary validation The checking of data against other data already held in the system during **data capture** (for instance to check that a key for an item of **standing data** already exists in the system), see also **primary validation**.

Secure socket layer (SSL) A cryptographic protocol used to encrypt messages sent over the web – implemented using a **public private key** system.

Sequence diagram A **UML** diagram that, for a given **use case**, documents its interaction with **classes** – in terms of **messages** that can be added back onto the **class diagram** as **methods**. Also used more generally as an interaction diagram showing how **processes** interact with one another and in what order.

Serial access On **secondary storage**, reading data from the start of a **file** a **block** and hence a **record** at a time. See also **random access**.

Serial file A **secondary storage conventional file** or **database** area that is written and read sequentially from the start of a **file** a **block** and hence a **record** at a time.

Server A **networked computer** that runs applications and/or stores **software**/data for access by end user computers (**clients**).

Server farm A physical location housing a large number of **servers**. Usages of a server farm include the hosting of a single large application, such as **Google** or **Facebook**, and the provision of a **cloud computing** service to a number of clients.

Server side script *Program* logic embed in (or associated with) a webpage that is executed on the *server* before a response is sent to the user.

Service-oriented architecture (SOA) The *software* architecture of *web services*. SOA describes: service provider, service requestor and service registry functions. The interfaces use protocols described within *XML*.

Session variable A feature of *server side scripting* languages. The session variable holds data about one user and is accessible to all pages in that user's session.

SGML See *standard general mark-up language*.

Shopbot Shopping robot used to access other *internet e-Commerce* businesses, e.g. a price comparison website. Third-party sites can be accessed without agreement using a process known as *web-scraping*. Most price comparison websites act in agreement with third party websites using *web-services* interfaces (and hence are not technically robots).

Silicon chip An electronic circuit that is created using lithography on a small wafer of silicon – also referred to as an *integrated circuit*.

Sizing Calculating the likely run time of an *Information System* during the design stage.

Smart grid An electric power supply grid that has the ability to monitor usage electronically.

Smart meter A meter for power supply, usually electricity supply, which records power usage at frequent intervals and has the ability to communicate readings to the supply company electronically.

Smartphone A *mobile* phone with additional *computing* and *communications* facilities, including *internet* access.

Smartphone app A *program* that can be downloaded and used on a *smartphone* – examples are computer games that operate on a smartphone or an interface to an *internet e-Commerce* site (substituting for the website and the *browser*).

SOA See *service-oriented architecture*.

Social media Web technologies that facilitate social interaction – including *social network systems* and *micro blogs*.

Social networking system A website that gives users the ability to record details about themselves and link to other people with whom they share interest. *Facebook* is the prime example for social relationships and *LinkedIn* for business relationships.

Sociotechnical SA&D An approach to *system analysis and design* that aims to recognize the *problem situation* as a human activity system. Sociotechnical systems seek to achieve joint optimization of the technical aspects of a task and the quality of people's working lives.

Soft system methodology (SSM) A *sociotechnical SA&D methodology* devised by *Checkland* – utilizes *rich pictures* and the *root definition*.

Software Computer *programs*. The term software is more often applied to *system software* than *application software*.

Software as a Service (SaaS) A pay-for-use service to access an *Information System*. The software and users data is located in the *cloud* and the user accesses the service on a pay-for-use basis using their *browser*.

Software developer Analogous to *programmer* – can imply more technical programming such as writing *system software*.

Speech recognition Recognizing what is being said and recording it as text (for *data capture*). Applications include call centre automation. Speech recognition is available for some PC applications, e.g. input to a word processor.

Spyware *Malware* that collects information about the *computer* user and computer usage. One form of Spyware is key-logging, where all the information typed into the system is recorded.

SQL See *structured query language*.

SQL injection attack This is gaining unauthorized access to a website's database. The mechanism is to submit *SQL* statements, through a web form, that are then executed – typically to select and download data.

SSADM See *structured system analysis and design*.

SSL See *secure socket layer*.

SSM See *soft system methodology*.

Standard general mark-up language (SGML) A generalized mark-up language from which both *HTML* and *XML* are derived.

Standby generator An electric power generator, typically diesel powered, which is available for use should the mains electricity power fail. A continuous power supply installation should ensure the automatic switch on of the standby generator and the continuous operation of IT equipment in the event of a power failure.

Standing data Data held in an *Information System* that is relatively constant over time and is used as reference data during the processing of *transactions*. Examples of standing data in an *order processing system* are customer and product data.

State diagram A *UML* diagram. The state diagram takes an individual *class*/*object* and shows the activities that can affect it during its lifecycle.

State transition diagram See *state diagram*.

Stock control The process of keeping a record of stock quantities and ensuring that an appropriate quantity of product is available.

Stock control system An *Information System* that ensures that an appropriate quantity of product is available (in the warehouse or in retail on the shelves in each branch). Works in conjunction with *order processing* and *replenishment* systems.

Strategy The long-term plan, or direction, of the organization.

Structured decision Structured decisions can be made where there are clear rules and the necessary information is available.

Structured query language (SQL) The language used to manipulate and query data on *relational databases*; based on *relational algebra*.

Structured system analysis and design (SSADM) A *waterfall lifecycle methodology* that structures the process requirement using *dataflow* analysis and the data requirement using *entity relationship* analysis.

Subtype An *object-oriented* design and *programming* concept – a subtype class *inherits* properties from the *supertype class*, in a *generalization* structure.

Supercomputer A large powerful *computer* used for scientific applications – optimized for processing large vectors or arrays of floating-point numbers.

Supertype An *object-oriented* design and *programming* concept – a supertype class provides properties, through *inheritance*, to the *subtype class*, in a *generalization* structure.

Supply chain The network of organizations that supply components to a manufacturer or merchandise to a retailer. Each first-tier supplier has their own suppliers and so on, which together make up the total supply chain.

Supply chain logistics The organization of the physical movement of product through *supply chain* – transport, warehousing, etc. Effective supply chain logistics minimizes costs, product handling and storage whilst ensuring optimum availability of product.

Support functions The additional activities of an *organization* that facilitate its *operations*. Support functions include management, finance, accounting and human resources.

Switch A switch is a *network* device that joins communication lines together. The switch can devote the full bandwidth to any devices that are active at the time. See also *hub*.

System analysis and design (SA&D) The process of determining the requirement for a business system and then to design a system that will run on the proposed *Information Technology*. The system analysis and design process includes: a detailed study of the business needs of the organization; the mapping of the requirements into a *logical design* and the translation of the logical design into the *technical design*. System analysis and design is a stage of the *system development lifecycle*.

System analyst A member of the *Information Systems* team who investigates the user requirements for a new system and then designs how that requirement will be realized as an Information System using *Information Technology*. The system analyst is also involved in the analysis and design of amendments/enhancements to existing systems.

System development lifecycle (SDLC) The stages that developers have to go through to create an *Information System*.

System software Generic software that operates and controls the IT and provides an interface for the running of *application software*, e.g. the *operating system*.

System test Once *software* is written it must be tested – testing checks for errors in the *programming* and flaws in the design. Note that testing can never guarantee that no errors remain undiscovered in the software. System testing is to check that the whole system works on the intended platform and with the expected volumes of data (*volume test*). The system test is preceded by *integration testing* – the integration testing (at a system level) can be considered as part of the system test. System testing is the responsibility of the *project team* – it is followed by *acceptance testing*. System and acceptance test is a stage of the *system development lifecycle*.

System tester A member of the *Information System* staff who designs and checks the system test – often this is a function of the *system analyst*.

Tablet A *PC* type device with a *touch screen* and no physical keyboard, e.g. the *Apple* iPad.

Tabulator A *conventional* (*punch card*) *machine* that printed reports from data read in from a deck of *punched cards*. The tabulator was programmed using a wiring board (which was removable – there would be a set of boards, one for each application). The print could be fully formatted with headings, totals, for example.

Tag record A small *record* on a *file* or *database* – inserted into the calculated logical position of a record to point to the physical position of the record. Used to resolve overflow problems (where there are too many records to fit into a specific location).

Taylorism Also called *scientific management* – jobs are analysed and broken down into their component tasks that can be allocated to separate workers. The use of production line techniques as opposed to craft skills.

TCP See *transmission control protocol*.

TCP/IP See *transmission control protocol/internet protocol*.

Technical design Following the gathering of user requirements (and *logical design*) the technical design specifies how the system will be implemented on the proposed *Information Technology*.

Technical system options A stage in the *SSADM system development lifecycle*. The technical system options stage follows the *logical design* stage and suggests a number of alternative technical solutions for the development and implementation of the proposed system.

Telecommunications The transmission of information (sound or digital data) in electronic form over a significant distance. Telecommunications can use land lines (usually copper wire or fibre optics) or radio/microwave linkages.

Teleworker An employee (or contractor) who works from home (or another location remote from the employer's premises) using *Information and Communication Technologies* to perform tasks and to submit completed work.

Testing Checking that the software works by submitting test data and checking that the results achieved meet expectations. For a new *Information System* tests should be thorough and should be planned. Testing schemes include: *white box test* and *black box test*; *module test*, *link test*, *system test* and *acceptance test*; *alpha test* and *beta test*.

Test prototype A *prototype* created to test a concept or technique.

Text file A *conventional serial file* containing only character data.

Thick client Within a *client-server system* a thick client is a *client* with significant application logic in it (and possibly local data storage) – the *application software* and business processing is partly on the client and partly on the *server*. Local processing on the client can speed up the system and cut down on *network* traffic – but it does mean that application logic has to be replicated and maintained on every client. See also *thin client*. Note that a thick client does

not refer to diminished intelligence – in this context it is the exact opposite.

Thin client Within a *client-server system* a thin client is a *client* with little or no application logic on it – all the *application software* and business processing is on the *server*. See also *thick client*.

Third-generation computer Evolved from *second-generation computers* with *integrated circuits* replacing *transistor logic circuits* and *magnetic core memory*.

Third normal form (TNF/3NF) An analysis and rationalization of data requirements into *entities* and *attributes* – each entity has a unique key attribute (or a unique compound key formed by more than one attribute). In TNF, no entity includes any attributes that repeat (occur more than once) for any key value and each attribute is identified by the key of its entity. Analysis of data into TNF is achieved by *relational data analysis*. TNF is derived from the *second normal form* by identifying any non-key dependencies, separating them and identifying them with their key. The analysis of data into TNF is part of the process of drawing (or checking) the *entity relationship diagram* and that, in turn, is an essential step in the design of a *database* schema.

Time-sharing Effectively the same as *multitasking*.

TNF See *third normal form*.

Top-down Analysis of a system by progressively breaking it down into subsystems. In *system analysis and design*, the *data flow diagram* is a top-down technique (as opposed to *bottom-up*).

Touch screen A screen where control/data input is achieved by touching on-screen icons or an on-screen keyboard (an alternative to a keyboard and mouse). Used on *smartphones* and *tablets* but also on *PCs* for example, in retail applications.

TP monitor *Software* that facilitates a *transaction processing system*. The TP monitor accepts incoming user messages and routes them to the application code for the required function. Similarly when the processing is complete the outgoing message is routed back to the appropriate user. The TP monitor is a multi-user system supporting many functions. The system has to process interrupts and deal with any contention when handling input and output messages. The system may have facilities to process more than one request concurrently – a facility known as *multithreading*, it uses *time-sharing* techniques. The system also needs to retain data for each logged-on user and make it available when that user's messages are being processed.

TP system See *transaction processing system*.

Tradacom An early *EDI* message standard used principally in the UK.

Trade cycle The steps/exchanges involved in a commercial transaction, e.g. search, negotiate, order, delivery, invoice, payment and after-sales for a *business-to-business* exchanges.

Trading partner A second organization that the organization buys from or sells to.

Transaction A business document (possibly electronic) that is input to an *Information System* and processed to produce a business result. Transactions will usually be processed with reference to *standing data*. For example, the main transaction in an *order processing system* is the order.

Transaction data The data content of a *transaction*. For an order, the transaction data would include orderNo, orderDate, customerNo, etc.

Transaction processing system This can have more than one meaning:

1. An *Information System* processing business *transactions*, e.g. customer orders.
2. An Information System using a *TP monitor* that processes online transactions from a number of users (*clients*).

Transfer of undertaking protection of employment regulations (TUPE) Regulations that protect employees whose employing organization is being transferred to another organization. TUPE is the UK implementation of the European Union business transfer directive. TUPE provides a measure of protection from changes in terms and conditions of employment and from dismissal.

Transistor An electronic semiconductor component used for amplification or switching current. *Second-generation computers* used transistors for their *logic circuits*.

Transistor equivalent A *logic gate*, serving the same purpose as a *transistor*, on a *silicon chip*.

Transmission control protocol (TCP) TCP is the transport function which ensures that the total amount of bytes sent in each packet is received correctly at the other end.

Transmission control protocol/Internet protocol (TCP/IP) TCP/IP is the *transmission protocol* of the *internet*. TCP/IP is a *packet-switching* protocol.

Transmission protocol The data sent over the communications *network* has to be packaged so that it can be checked and correctly interpreted by the receiving *computer*; the format of the packaging of the data is specified by the transmission protocol.

Trojan horse (Trojan) Software that the user downloads or installs for a legitimate purpose that, without their knowledge, includes a *malware payload*.

Trolley Conceptually large electronic (shopping) basket used on an *e-Shop* – see *basket*.

Trusted third party An organization empowered to arbitrate. For instance, in an *EDI interchange agreement* a trade body or the *VADS* could be designated as a trusted third party. The trusted third party could keep an *audit trail* of transactions.

Truth table A mathematical table used to specify a logic function. In logic design the truth table shows all possible combinations of inputs and the output for each of those combinations. Used in specifying *logic circuits*.

Tuple A term used in *relational algebra* for a *record* on a *relational database* – also referred to as a *relationship*.

Twitter A *micro-blogging* site. At the time of writing, the market leader (excluding China).

UML See *unified modelling language*.

Unified modelling language (UML) A toolbox of design diagrams used for *object-oriented design* – includes *use case*, *sequence* and *class diagram*.

Unit test Once *software* is written it must be *tested* – testing checks for errors in the *programming* and flaws in the design. Note that testing can never guarantee that no errors remain undiscovered in the software. *Unit testing* is applied by the *programmer* to a single *program* (*module*) in isolation. Unit testing is *white-box testing*, the tester has knowledge of the logic of the module. Unit testing can be followed by *integration*, *system* and *acceptance testing*.

Universal product code (UPC) A coding system for uniquely identifying products. The most common code is UPC-A which consists of 12 digits and would normally be printed on the product/product packaging as a *barcode*. The UPC is mainly a US system. See also *European article number* (EAN).

UNIX A multitasking *operating system* that conforms to the UNIX specification.

Un-normalized form (UNF) In *relational data analysis*, un-normal form is a list of all *attributes* from the document being analysed – plus the identification of an overall key.

Unstructured decision A decisions that has to be made without clear rules and where the necessary information is incomplete or unavailable.

UPC See *universal product code*.

Upper CASE *CASE* applied to the early (*system analysis and design*) stages of the *system development lifecycle*. For CASE, see *computer-aided software engineering*.

Use case A *UML* concept. The user requirement is broken down into use cases – the use case is: *a bit of business* identified within the user requirement.

Use case description A written description setting out the processing requirements for a *use case*.

Use case diagram A *UML* diagram. Used to capture user requirements – users are represented as *actors* (stick people) and requirements as *use cases* (ovals).

User-id Short for user identification – a code assigned to a user that is used as part of *login*/security/privacy processes on a *computer* or *network* system.

User interface The space where the interaction between a human (user) and a machine takes place. The term is applicable to the screen design of the interfaces for an *Information System* or the user interface of an *operating system* on, for example, a PC or *smartphone*.

Utility program *Software* that performs a utility function on a *computer* system, such as copying a file. On Windows systems many utility functions are built into the *operating system*.

Vacuum tubes An electronic component (looks like a small light bulb) used for rectification, amplification or switching current. *First-generation computers* used vacuum tubes (also known as valves) for their *logic circuits*.

VADS See *value added data service*.

Validation The checking of data for format and credibility in *data capture* applications. See also *primary validation* and *secondary validation*.

Value added data service (VADS) A networked intermediary that provides additional services, a *post and forward* service normally being the minimal provision. Used for *EDI* transmissions (although the use of the internet is an alternative).

Value added network (VAN) An alternative term for a *value added data service*.

Valve machine A *first-generation computer*. The logic functions were implemented using valves (*vacuum tubes*), each valve was a *logic gate*.

VAN See *value added network*.

VB See *visual basic*.

Vector processor A computing technology that implements instructions that operate on a one-dimensional array (as opposed to a single data item). Used in early *supercomputers* but subsequently implemented in limited form in other *processor* technologies. See also *array processor*.

Venn diagram A diagram that shows all possible logical combinations in a specific problem domain – typically using a series of intersecting circles or ellipses. The logic of the Venn diagram is related to set theory.

Videotext An early implementation of online information services – often the text information was displayed on television screens. The most successful Videotext service was France's *minitel* service that had its own terminal systems.

Virtual learning environment (VLE) An online environment that provides a range of interactive educational facilities – the VLE can be used as an adjunct to traditional educational delivery or for *distance learning*.

Virtual organization An organization that exists online – the organization operates by combining the skills and outputs of its participants.

Virus A virus is *malware* that attaches itself to/includes itself in legitimate *software*. The virus spreads itself when the software is run. The virus may carry a *payload*.

Visual basic (VB) A programming language and development environment from Microsoft – with facilities for the rapid development of graphical user interface applications.

Visual studio Microsoft's *CASE* tool for the *dot.net* environment.

VLE See *virtual learning environment*.

Voice recognition Recognizing who is speaking as a *biometric* for *access control*.

Volume test *Testing* an *Information System* to prove it can cope with the number of users and/or the volume of data that can be expected in live running.

Von Neumann architecture The computing principle introduced by Von Neumann, back in 1945, is that the program should be stored in the computer memory along with the data – still applicable to all digital *computer* architecture.

WAN See *wide area network*.

Waterfall lifecycle A *system development lifecycle* where the activities/stages are performed in sequence. The stages of the waterfall lifecycle are: *feasibility study*, *system analysis and design*, *programming* and *unit test*, *system test* and *acceptance test*, and *operations*. Note: some authors may sub-divide these stages or apply alternative terminology, but the basic principle is that of performing a number of stages in sequence.

Web Shorthand for the *World Wide Web* but also used (somewhat imprecisely) as a shorthand for the *internet*.

Web-scraping A *software* technique for extracting data from websites. The data presented on the website can be extracted by an analysis of the *HTML* and further data can be obtained by the program completing and submitting online forms automatically.

Web services A flexible way of deploying and accessing applications across the *web*. See also *service-oriented architecture* (SOA).

Web 2.0 *i-Commerce* (or non-commercial *internet*) system that utilizes user-provided content (a relatively ill-defined concept but *social networking systems* fall within this concept). The *participatory web*.

White box test *Testing* carried out with knowledge of the logic of the *module* under test. See also *unit test* and *black box test*.

Wide area network (WAN) A *network* that reaches out of the building to other branches of the organization or to cooperating organizations. The network has to be provided by a licensed, third party, *telecommunications* provider and may well use a variety of lines and equipment that are shared with other users.

Wikipedia The (or a) free encyclopaedia that is collaboratively edited and freely available over the *internet*.

Wikis A website that allows users to modify its content using a *browser*.

Windows This can have more than one meaning:
1. Microsoft Windows – the Microsoft PC *operating system*.
2. A display rectangle used for interacting with a *program* – a computer system may have several windows open at one time.

Wizard A facility in a *software*/application package that guides users through a series of dialogue boxes to complete a task, e.g. setting up a query in Microsoft *Access*.

Word This can have more than one meaning:
1. The word processing software in the *Microsoft Office* package.
2. An addressable unit of data in the *main memory* of a *computer*. Word lengths vary between computer

designs – 16, 24, 32 and 64 bits to a word are (or have been) used. The alternative to a word was the smaller 8-bit *byte* used in early PCs and the IBM 360 mainframe.

Workstation A terminal *computer* system that accesses computing and *Information Systems* facilities over a *network*. The workstation can be a standard PC but the term can also imply a high-end PC used for scientific applications or a specialist computing facility, e.g. a computer system used by bank counter staff.

World Wide Web (WWW) A system of documents connected by hypertext links and accessed over the *internet* using a *browser*. The documents can incorporate different media (text, images, video, and sound), provide for user input using the *form* construct and connect with *program* logic using client and *server side scripts*. The development of the World Wide Web is credited to the CERN scientist Tim Berners-Lee.

World Wide Web consortium (W3C) The governing and standards setting body for the *internet*.

Worm A standalone *malware* program that replicates itself in order to spread across a *network* and onto other *computer* systems. The worm may carry a *payload*.

WWW See *World Wide Web*.

W3C See *World Wide Web consortium*.

XML See *eXtensible mark-up language*.

XOR gate A *logic gate* which produces an output of one when the inputs contain at least one one and at least one zero – the output is zero for all other input combinations (i.e. all zeros or all ones).

XSLT See *eXtensible stylesheet language transformations*.

Year 2000 See *millennium bug*.

Zombie computer A *computer* running *malware* on behalf of a third party without the owner being aware. The typical use of a zombie is to spread spam *e-Mail* or take part in a *DDoS* attack

Zuse The Zuse Z3 was made in Berlin and completed in 1941. It was an electro-mechanical machine – programs were stored on tape. The Zuse Z3 is generally acknowledged to be the world's first programmer computer. Other early computers mentioned in this text are *Colossus*, *Baby* and *ENIAC*.

BIBLIOGRAPHY

agilemanifesto (2001) *Manifesto for Agile Software Development*, http://agilemanifesto.org (accessed 1 August 2012).

Allison, R. (2003) 'Doing bird, the parrot loving conman', *Guardian*, 3 September.

Anthony, R. N. (1965) *Planning and Control Systems: A Framework for Analysis*, Harvard University Press, Cambridge, MA.

Associated Press (2011) 'BlackBerry service restored after three days outage', *Guardian*, 14 October.

Avison, D. and Fitzgerald, G. (2006) *Information Systems Development: Methodologies, Techniques and Tools*, 4th ed., McGraw-Hill, Maidenhead.

Bainbridge, D. (2000) *Introduction to Computer Law*, 4th ed., Longman, Harlow.

Bainbridge, D. (2008) *Introduction to Information Technology Law*, 6th ed., Pearson, Harlow.

Barkham, P. (2011) 'Amazon warehouse gears up for Christmas rush on Cyber Monday', *Guardian*, 1 December.

BBC (2009) 'Watchdog warning on court delays', *BBC News*, 6 March, http://news.bbc.co.uk (accessed 7 August 2012).

BCS (2012) *The Chartered Institute for IT*, http://www.bcs.org (accessed 31 May 2012).

Been, J., Christiaanse, E., O'Callaghan, R. and Van Diepen, T. (1995) 'Electronic markets in the air cargo community', Third European Conference on Information Systems, Athens.

Beynon-Davies, P. (2004) *Database Systems*, 3rd ed., Palgrave Macmillan, Basingstoke.

Bott, F. (2005) *Professional Issues in Information Technology*, BCS, Swindon.

Bott, F., Coleman, A., Eaton, J. and Rowland, D. (2000) *Professional Issues in Software Engineering*, 3rd ed., Taylor and Francis, London.

Brady, J., Monk, E. and Wagner, B. (2012) *Concepts in Enterprise Resource Planning*, 4th ed., Thompson, Boston, MA.

Cadle, J. and Yates, D. (2008) *Project Management for Information Systems*, 5th ed., Pearson, Harlow.

Chaffey, D. (2007) *e-Business and e-Commerce Management: Strategy, Implementation and Management*, 3rd ed., Prentice Hall, Harlow.

Charatan, Q. and Kans, A. (2009) *Java in Two Semesters*, 3rd ed., McGraw-Hill, Maidenhead.

Clark, A. (2002) 'Tail of woe', *Guardian*, 10 September, http://www.guardian.co.uk (accessed 1 December 2012).

Clark, J. (2011) 'Natwest glitch downs phone and internet banking', *ZDNet*, 5 November, http://www.zdnet.co.uk (accessed 12 June 2012).

Clifton, H. D., Ince, D. C. and Sutcliffe, A. G. (2000) *Business Information Systems*, 6th ed., Prentice Hall, Hemel Hempstead.

Collins, T (2011) 'HM Courts service hides "Libra" IT's new shortcomings', *Campaign4Change*, http://ukcampaign4change.com (accessed 7 August 2012).

Comer, D. E. (2009) *Computer Networks and Internets*, 5th ed., Pearson, Upper Saddle River, NJ.

Computer Weekly (2008) 'HM Courts Service turn around troubled Libra magistrates system', *Computer Weekly*, 29 January, http://www.computerweekly.com (accessed 7 August 2012).

Computing (2011) 'PAC tells HMRC to get its PAYE system in order by 2012', *Computing*, 4 March, http://www.computing.co.uk (accessed 12 April 2012).

Connolly, T. and Begg, C. (2010) *Database Systems: A Practical Approach to Design, Implementation and Management*, 5th ed., Addison-Wesley, Harlow.

Davis, G. (2011) 'Online food retail – case studies from Tesco to Migros', *just-food*, http://www.just-food.com (accessed 12 October 2011).

Davis, J. (2007) 'Hackers take down the most wired country in Europe', *Wired*, 15 September, http://www.wired.com/politics/security/magazine/15-09/ff_estonia?currentPage=all (accessed 29 April 2012).

Dell (2012) 'Environment (Dell Earth)', *Dell*, http://content.dell.com/us/en/corp/dell-environment.aspx (accessed 29 May 2012).

Dijkstra E. W. (1972) 'Notes on Structured Programming', in J. Dahl, E. W. Dijkstra and C. A. R. Hore (eds), *Structured Programming*, Academic Press, London.

DSDM (2008) *DSDM Aterm: The Handbook*, DSDM Consortium, Ashford.

DSDM (2012) *DSDM Consortium*, http://www.dsdm.org (accessed 1 August 2012).

Filloux, F. (2012) 'Facebook's $100bn privacy dilemma', *Guardian*, 16 April, http://www.guardian.co.uk (accessed 19 July 2012).

Fowler, M. (2004) *UML Distilled: A Brief Guide to the Standard Object Modelling Language*, 3rd ed., Addison-Wesley, Boston.

Freedman, A. (1999) *The Computer Desktop Encyclopedia*, 2nd ed., Amacon, New York.

Fujitsu (2011) *Fujitsu: What is a Cloud*, http://www.fujitsu.com (accessed 7 August 2012).

Gersmann, H. (2011) 'Facebook builds "green" datacentre in Sweden', *Guardian*, 27 October.

Goldfarb, C. F. (2003) *XML Handbook*, 5th ed., Prentice Hall, Upper Saddle River, NJ.

Hennessy, J. and Patterson, D. (2012) *Computer Organisation and Design: The Hardware/Software Interface*, 4th ed. Morgan Kaufmann, Waltham, MA.

Hitchcock, J. (2012) 'HRMC saves £200m after Aspire outsourcing deal overhaul', *Guardian Professional*, 14 March.

Hopkins, N. (2012) 'Militarisation of cyberspace: how the global power struggle moved online', *Guardian*, 16 April, http://www.guardian.co.uk (accessed 19 July 2012).

IBM (2011) *IBM System Z*, http://www.ibm.com (accessed 7 August 2012).

ICO (2012) Information Commissioner's Office, http://www.ico.gov.uk/ (accessed 7 June 2012).

Jelassi, T. and Enders, A. (2008) *Strategies for e-Business: Creating Value through Electronic and Mobile Commerce*, 2nd ed., Prentice Hall, Harlow.

Johnson, G., Whittington, R. and Scholes, K. (2010) *Exploring Strategy: Text and Cases*, 9th ed., Prentice Hall, Harlow.

Johnson, J. (2010) *Designing with the Mind in Mind: Simple Guide to Understanding User Interface Design Rules*, Morgan Kaufmann, Burlington, MA.

Jones, R., Tims, A. and Osborne, H. (2012) 'NatWest fiasco: the meltdown, the impact, and the aftermath', *Guardian*, 29 June, http://www.guardian.co.uk (accessed 12 July 2012).

Kambil, A. and van Heck, E. (1998) 'Reengineering the Dutch flower auctions: a framework for analyzing exchange organizations', *Information Systems Research*, vol. 9, no. 1, pp. 1–19.

Kessell, C. (2011) 'Real time rail passenger information: jungle or minefield', *Rail.co (The Rail Engineer)*, 6 September, http://www.rail.co/2011/09/06/ (accessed 30 March 2012).

Kingsley, P. (2012) 'Estonia: switched-on nation that became an internet titan', *Guardian*, 16 April.

Koch, C. and Wailgum, T. (2008) 'ERP definition and solutions', *CIO*, http://www.cio.com (accessed 30 July 2012).

Krishnan, R. (2010) 'IT and climate change: computing and the environment', *Environmental Leader*, 8 January, http://www.environmentalleader.com/2010/01/08/it-and-climate-change-computing-for-the-environment/ (accessed 29 May 2012).

Kurose, J. F. and Ross, K. W. (2009) *Computer Networking: A Top-Down Approach*, 5th ed., Pearson, Upper Saddle River, NJ.

Lejk, M. and Deeks, D. (2002) *An Introduction to System Analysis Techniques*, 2nd ed., Pearson, Harlow.

Leyden, J. (2011) 'UK student hacker sentenced over gaming Trojan', *The Register*, http://www.theregister.co.uk/2011/05/18/gaming_trojan_conviction/ (accessed 7 June 12).

McAfee, R. P. and McMillan, J. (1997) 'Electronic Markets', in R. Kalakota and A. Whinston (eds.) *Readings in Electronic Commerce*, Addison-Wesley, Reading, MA.

Maddison, R. N. (1983) *Information System Methodologies*, Wiley, Heyden, Chichester.

Magal, S. and Word, J. (2012) *Integrated Business Processes with ERP Systems*, Wiley, Hoboken, NJ.

Malone, T., Yates, J. and Benjamin, R. (1987) 'Electronic markets and electronic hierarchies', *Communication of the ACM*, vol. 30, no. 6, pp. 484–97.

Marston, R. (2011) 'Tesco's triumphs under Sir Terry', *BBC News Business*, http://www.bbc.co.uk/news (accessed 20 October 2011)

Morrison, J. (2011) *The Global Business Environment: Meeting the Challenges*, 3rd ed., Palgrave Macmillan, Basingstoke.

Needle, D. (2010) *Business in Context: An Introduction to Business and Its Environment*, 5th ed., Cengage, Andover.

Nielsen (2012) *Nielsen BookNet*, www.nielsenbooknet.co.uk (accessed 26 July 2012).

Ocado (2011) *Ocado*, http://www.ocadogroup.com/ (accessed 12 October 2011).

O'Reilly, T. (2005) *What is Web 2.0: Design Patterns and Business Models for the Next Generation of Software*, http://oreilly.com/web2/archive/what-is-web-20.html (accessed 25 January 2012).

ORNL (2012) 'Climate Scientist Compute in Concert', *Oak Ridge National Laboratory*, http://www.olcf. ornl.gov/2012/02/27/climate-scientists-compute-in-concert/ (accessed 29 May 2012).

Orwell, G. (1949) *1984*, Penguin, London.

Osborne, H. (2011) 'HSBC computer failure leaves customers short of cash', *Guardian*, 4 November, http://www.guardian.co.uk (accessed 12 June 2012).

Osborne, H. (2012) 'RBS admits some Ulster bank accounts won't be up and running until 16 July', *Guardian*, 4 July, http://www.guardian.co.uk (accessed 12 July 2012).

Out-Law (2012) 'Disabled access to websites under UK law', *Out-Law.com*, http://www.out-law.com/page-330 (accessed 28 June 2012).

Petzold, C. (2000) *Code: The Hidden Language of Computer Hardware and Software*, Microsoft Press, Redmond, WA.

Pfleeger, C. P. and Pfleeger, S. L. (2006) *Security in Computing*, 4th ed., Prentice Hall, Upper Saddle River, NJ.

Porter, M. (1985) *Competitive Advantage: Creating and Sustaining Superior Performance*, Free Press, New York.

Porter, M. (2001) 'Strategy and the internet', *Harvard Business Review*, March 2001, pp. 62–78.

Pressman, R. (2009) *Software Engineering: A Practitioner's Approach*, 7th ed., McGraw-Hill, Maidenhead.

Preimesberger, C. (2012) 'Microsoft Azure leap year glitch: key lessons learnt', *eWeek*, 1 March, http://www.eweek.com (accessed 3 August 2012).

Rob, P., Coronel, C. and Crockett, K. (2008) *Database Systems: Design, Implementation and Management*, Cengage, London.

Rosenberg, D. and Scott, K. (1999) *Use Case Driven Object Modelling with UML: A Practical Approach*, Addison-Wesley, Reading, MA.

Ritter, T. (2010) 'HMRC benefits as new PAYE system issues wrong tax codes', *Computer Weekly*, 26 January, http://www.computerweekly.com (accessed 12 April 2012).

Rumbaugh, J., Jacobson, I. and Booch, G. (2010) *The Unified Modeling Language Reference Manual*, 2nd ed., Addison-Wesley, Reading, MA.

Rushe, D. (2012a) 'The online copyright war: the day the internet hit back at big media', *Guardian*, 18 April, http://www.guardian.co.uk (accessed 7 September 2012).

Rushe, D. (2012b) 'Five reasons not to buy Facebook shares', *Guardian*, 16 May, http://www.guardian.co.uk (accessed 19 July 2012).

Sabre (2012) *Sabre Holdings*, www.sabre.com (accessed 26 July 2012).

Savvas, A. (2011) 'RIM', *Computerworld UK*, 13 October.

Say, M. (2011) 'MoD acknowledges laptop losses', *Guardian*, 25 November, http://www.guardian.co.uk (accessed 1 May 2012).

Sayid, R. (2010) 'Millions dump online supermarket shopping and going back to filling trollies themselves', *Daily Mirror*, 4 December 2010, http://www.mirror.co.uk (accessed 12 October 2011).

Telegraph (2011) 'Online grocery sales will double within five years', *Telegraph*, 11 March, http://www.telegraph.co.uk (accessed 12 October 2011).

Tesco (2011) *Tesco*, http://www.tescoplc.com (accessed 12 October 2011).

Tofler, A. (1980) *The Third Wave*, Morrow, New York.

Top500 (2012) *Top500 Project*, http://www.top500.org/ (accessed 9 August 2012).

Turban, E., King, D., McKay, J., Marshall, P., Lee, J. and Viehland, D. (2008) *Electronic Commerce 2008: a Managerial Perspective*, Prentice Hall, Upper Saddle River, NJ.

Turner, M. (2012) *Computer Evidence*, http://www.computerevidence.co.uk/Cases/CMA.htm (accessed 7 June 2012).

Vasudevan, V. (2001) *A Web Service Primer*, http://www.xml.com/pub/a/ws/2001/04/04/webservices/index.html (accessed 22 November 2005).

Visa (2006) *Top Three POS System Vulnerabilities Identified to Promote Data Security Awareness*, http://usa.visa.com (accessed 19 October 2011).

Waldman, S. (1999) 'Internet revived the radio star', *Media Guardian*, 31 May.

Wallop, H. (2009) 'Christmas comes early for Amazon', *The Telegraph*, 30 November, www.telegraph.co.uk (accessed 12 September 2012).

Watts, S. (1993) 'Computer virus hits nuclear power site', *Independent*, 11 November, http://www.independent.co.uk (accessed 12 June 2012).

Webster, F. (2005) 'The Information Society revisited', in S. Livingstone and L. Lievrouw (eds), *Handbook of New Media: Social Shaping and Consequences of ICTs*, Sage, London.

Whiteley, D. (2000) *e-Commerce: Strategy, Technology and Applications*, McGraw-Hill, London.

Whiteley, D. (2002) *The Complete e-Shop*, Spiro, London (first published by Chandos, Oxford).

Wild, R. (1985) *The Essentials of Productions and Operations Management*, Holt Rinehart & Winston, London.

Willcocks, L. P., Cullen, S. and Craig, A. (2011) *The Outsourcing Enterprise: From Cost Management to Collaborative Innovation*, Palgrave Macmillan, Basingstoke.

Williams, C. (2012) 'Snooper's charter web spying Bill announced', *Daily Telegraph*, 9 May, http://www.telegraph.co.uk (accessed 14 June 2012).

Wood, Z. (2010) 'Ocado to create 2,000 jobs with second distribution centre', *Guardian*, 12 October.

Wood, Z. and Lyons, T. (2010) 'Clubcard couple head for checkout at Tesco', *Guardian*, 29 October, http://www.guardian.co.uk, (accessed 12 October 2011).

W3c (2012) 'Web content accessibility guidelines', *The World Wide Web Consortium*, www.w3.org (accessed 28 June 2012).

yeeguy (2011) 'How Facebook Ship Code', *Framethink*, http://framethink.wordpress.com/2011/01/17/how-facebook-ships-code/ (accessed 19 July 2012).

Zetter, K. (2010) 'Clues Suggest Stuxnet Virus Was Built for Subtle Nuclear Sabotage', *Wired*, 15 November, http://www.wired.com/threatlevel/2010/11/stuxnet-clues/ (accessed 30 April 2012).

10News (2010) 'Questions raised about SD civil court computer system', *10news*, 18 July, http://www.10news.com (accessed 7 August 2012).

INDEX